2004 – 2005 EDITION

PICTORIAL PRICE GUIDE TO

AMERICAN ANTIQUES

and objects made for the American market

ILLUSTRATED AND PRICED OBJECTS

by

Dorothy Hammond

First published 2004
© Dorothy Hammond
World copyright reserved

ISBN 1 85149 464 2

British Library Cataloguing-in-Publication Data
A catalogue record for this book is available from the British Library

Printed in Italy
Published in England by the Antique Collectors' Club Limited

Contents

In Loving Memory of April Beattie Farrell

April 28, 1977 – August 29, 2003

A dealer, collector and lover of antiques – as well as butterflies

<u>The Butterfly</u>
<u>A Poem</u>
<u>By</u>
<u>April Beattie Farrell</u>

Oh isn't a butterfly so beautiful and graceful
as it flows through the air

I love to see its delicate wings fly across the sky

They fly like a gentle bird looking for
something to eat

Now how sweet is that

If you are very quiet maybe they will talk to you

But you have to be silent or you won't hear a
word

For they speak very softly and can hardly be
heard

Introduction

It has been exciting assembling my first full-color Pictorial Price Guide. Like the title itself, this 2004 edition includes twenty-two categories featuring approximately 4,000 illustrated objects acquired from auction houses from late 2002 to November 2003. Each entry is keyed to the auction house where the item sold, with the state abbreviation, because prices vary in different regions of the country. The year and month the item sold is also included. An introductory essay provides background information to each chapter with the exception of Miscellaneous.

Although we are living in a time when many other areas of investment lack stability, the market for fine art, antiques and collectibles continues to show strength. Early in the year the middle market just plodded along while exceptional pieces were setting records. With the approach of spring, antiques dealers and collectors suddenly discovered it was a good time to be a buyer and auction houses had a healthy buyer response.

Serious collectors look to auctions as the ultimate price determinant because they reflect market trends. When comparing similar pieces within this edition, the reader must always take into consideration that fluctuations in the market, in addition to the quality of the object, its popularity, and the region in which it is sold, determines the hammer price.

Collecting remains a very fascinating enjoyable pastime throughout the country, because of its seemingly endless categories. In our fast-paced society, the material past will always hold its allure. Antiques and collectibles produced during the late nineteenth century, and well into the twentieth, continue to dominate a large segment of the market. Among the major trends are an increase in values of upper end collectibles and fine period furniture, with continued dominance of the formal look. During this period in time, quality and craftsmanship were symbols of pride and achievement. Thankfully, craftsmanship is still very appreciated today by many fine cabinetmakers… producing outstanding custom-made pieces. I am convinced that their creations are the antiques of tomorrow, and certainly worth collecting.

Enthusiasm for fifties objects is heating up and they are readily becoming "hot" collectibles because of their availability. The 1950s was a decade of change in America, and the field is extensive. Many of the younger set, therefore, are opting for contemporary furniture, glass, plastics, textiles, ceramics, stoneware and metalware. Although these items are not technically "antiques", they are finding their way into the marketplace in almost every price range.

I am hopeful that this price guide will enhance the joy of collecting. Good hunting!

6

Acknowledgments

I wish to express my sincere gratitude to my Publisher, Diana Steel, Managing Director of Antique Collectors' Club Ltd., Woodbridge, Suffolk, England, for her assistance in the preparation of this book, and her many constructive suggestions that have all played an important part in its final form. Special thanks are due to all those individuals on her staff – Tom Conway, Primrose Elliott, Sandra Pond and Pam Henderson, for their role in contributing to the final product. And I am particularly indebted to Dan Farrell, Managing Director of Antique Collectors' Club, North America, for his continued commitment and dedication to the book. His insight and guidance have been invaluable. To Jean Israel, my project coordinator, I extend my deep appreciation for her patience and dedication to make this book a reality. Special thanks are due to Jessica and Erin Israel, for their editorial contributions.

Every book has its share of behind-the-scenes players, each of whom plays their part in the final production. I wish to express my sincere gratitude to the following individuals and auction galleries who have so generously provided pictorial and textual material for this 2004 edition:

Cover Image:
Garth's Arts & Antiques
Amelia J. Jeffers

Alderfer's Fine Art & Antiques
501 Fairgrounds Road
Hatfield, PA 19440
215-393-3000
www.alderferauction.com

Noel Barrett Antiques & Auction Ltd.
6183 Carversville Road
Carversville, PA 18913
215-297-5109

Bertoia Auctions
2141 DeMarco Drive
Vineland, NJ 08360
856-692-1881
www.bertoiaauctions.com

Brunk Auction Services, Inc.
P.O. Box 2135
Asheville, NC 28802
828-254-6846
www.brunkauctions.com

Charlton Hall Galleries, Inc.
912 Gervais Street
Columbia, SC 29201
803-779-5678
www.charltonhallauctions.com

Clum Auctions, Inc.
7795 Cincinnati-Zanesville Road, NE Rushville,
OH 43150
740-536-7421
www.clum.com

Conestoga Auction Company, Inc.
768 Graystone Road
Manheim, PA 17545
717-898-7284
www.conestogaauction.com

Craftsman Auctions, Inc.
333 North Main Street
Lambertville, NJ 08530
609-397-9374
www.ragoarts.com

David Rago Auctions
333 North Main Street
Lambertville, NJ 08530
609-397-9374
www.ragoarts.com

Early Auction Company
123 Main Street
Milford, OH 45150
513-831-4833
www.earlyauctionco.com

Robert C. Eldred Company, Inc.
1483 Route 6A
P.O. Box 796
East Dennis, MA 02641
508-385-3116
www.eldreds.com

Fontaines Auction Gallery
1485 West Housatonic Street
Pittsfield, MA 01201
413-448-8922
www.fontaineauction.com

Garth's Arts & Antiques
2690 Stratford Road
P.O. Box 369
Delaware, OH 43015
740-362-4771
www.garths.com

Glass Works Auctions
P.O. Box 180
East Greenville, PA 18041
215-679-5849
www.glswrk-auction.com

Guyette & Schmidt. Inc.
P.O. Box 522
West Farmington, ME 04992
207-778-6256
www.guyetteandschmidt.com

Tom Harris Auction Center, Inc.
203 South 18th Avenue
Marshalltown, IA 50158
641-754-4890
www.tomharrisauctions.com

Horst Auction Center
50 Durlach Road
Ephrata, PA 17522
717-738-3080
www.horstauction.com

Jackson's International Auctioneers, Inc.
2229 Lincoln Street
Cedar Falls, IA 50613
319-277-2256
www.jacksonsauction.com

James D. Julia, Inc.
P.O. Box 830
Fairfield, ME 04937
207-453-7125
www.juliaauctions.com

Northeast Auctions
93 Pleasant Street
Portsmouth, NH 03801
603-433-8400
www.northeastauctions.com

Pook & Pook, Inc.
P.O. Box 268
Downingtown, PA 19335
610-269-0695
www.pookandpook.com

Skinner, Inc.
63 Park Plaza
Boston, MA 02116
617-350-5400
www.skinnerinc.com

Treadway Gallery, Inc.
2029 Madison Road
Cincinnati, OH 45208
513-321-6742
www.treadwaygallery.com

Waasdorp Pottery Auction
P.O. Box 434
Clarence, NY 14031
716-759-2361
waasdorp@antiques-stoneware.com

Willis Henry Auctions, Inc.
22 Main Street
Marshfield, MA 02050
781-834-7774
www.willishenry.com

The above auction galleries charge a buyer's premium (a surcharge on the hammer or final bid price at auction) which will vary. For readers' convenience I have included a complete address and website.

Although most auction houses give detailed catalog descriptions of items sold, others do not. Every effort has been taken in the compilation of this book to include as much information as possible to ensure accuracy. However, neither the author nor the publisher accepts any liability for any financial or other loss for any errors that might have incurred as a result of typographical or other errors.

— Dorothy Hammond

Abbreviations

adv.	advertising	ht.	height	patt.	pattern
Am.	American	illus.	illustrated	pc.	piece
approx.	approximately	imp.	impressed	pr.	pair
attrib.	attributed	imper.	imperfect/imperfections	prof. restor.	professional restoration
C.	century	in.	inches	Q.A.	Queen Anne
ca.	circa	incl.	including	qt.	quart
comp.	composition	incor.	incorporating	qtr.	quarter
cond.	condition	int.	interior	ref.	refinish
const.	construction	L.	left	repl.	replaced/replacement
decor.	decorated/decoration	lb.	pound	repr.	repair, repaired
dia.	diameter	lg.	length	rest.	restored/restoration
dov.	dovetail/dovetailed	litho.	lithograph	sgn.	signed
dp.	depth	mah.	mahogany	sm.	small
D.Q.	diamond quilted	mini	miniature	sq.	square
ea.	each	mkd.	marked	unmkd.	unmarked
emb.	embossed/embossing	MOP	mother-of-pearl	w/	with
Eng.	England/English	mts.	mounts	wd.	width
est.	established	OF	open face	wt.	wrought
ex.	excellent	N. Eng.	New England	yrs.	years
exc.	excluding	n/s	no sale		
Fr.	France	orig.	original	The common and accepted
gal.	gallon	oz.	ounce	abbreviations are used for states.
Ger.	Germany	pat.	patent		

A-PA Feb. 2003   Pook & Pook Inc.

#210 Needlework Picture, Philadelphia Folwell School, silk embroidered & painted, depicting a young couple flanking a basket of fruit, w/ children & farmers harvesting fields in the landscape, 15½in. x 23in. **$4,888**

The word advertising comes from the French word "avertir" meaning to notify. Advertising is actually as old as trade, probably beginning with what present day businessmen call personal selling. In essence, it informs people of the various advantages of a product, an idea, or a service. When manufacturing developed, few persons could read, as universal free education did not exist until the 1800s. Therefore, businessmen used symbols such as a shoemaker used a sign shaped like a shoe over his shop door, or a jeweler displayed a dummy clock. Later, when words were added, the symbols became trade signs.

Today, with new collectors appearing on the scene daily, the serious collecting of early advertising mementos has become widespread throughout the country. Searching out these collectibles is an endless adventure... and values have escalated which forces the serious collector to be more discriminating and build a more meaningful collection.

Nostalgia has created the current craze to acquire early advertising memorabilia because, in our hectic, parlous, plastic world today, the older generation, as well as the young, are fascinated by advertising collectibles in every media.

A-PA Feb. 2003   Glass Works Auctions

Tin Lithographed Serving Trays

#369 Commemorative Serving Tray, "Grand Old Party 1856 to 1908, Standard Bearers", showing William Taft & James Sherman. The rim of tray features preceding presidents & year of their term, dia. 9⅝in. **$350**

#370 "Clysmic King of Table Waters" by The Meek Co., Cochocton, OH, ht. 13¼, wd. 10½in. **$650**

#372 "El Gallo, Roy Lopez CA Key West Cigars", w/ litho cock bird in center & cock fight scenes around edge of tray, one minor dent, dia. 10½in. **$300**

#373 "Standard Distilling & Distributing Co., New York, U.S.A., Victor Cocktails, Absolutely Pure", mkd. H.D. Beach Co., Cochocton, OH, dia. 12¼in. **$400**

#374 "Walter Baker Co., Ltd. Registered in U.S. Patent Office", dia. 10¼in. **$325**

#375 "Red Raven 'Ask The Man' Dear Old Red Raven", mkd. Chas. W. Shonk Co., Litho, Chicago, dia. 12in. **$325**

#376 "Tom Moore Cigar, America's Favorite, Hirschhorn, Mack & Co. Makers, N.Y.", mkd. Standard Adv. Co., Coshocton, OH, w/ edge chips, dia. 13⅛in. **$1,450**

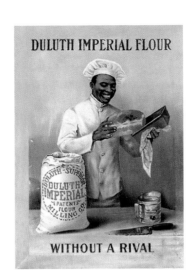

A-PA Feb. 2003   Glass Works Auctions

#389 **Advertising Sign**, "Duluth Imperial Flour Within A Rival", prof. rest., 18 x 25in. **$850**

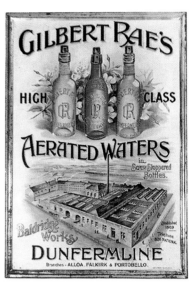

A-PA Feb. 2003   Glass Works Auctions

#390 **Advertising Sign**, "Gilbert Rae's High Class Aerated Waters in Screw Stoppered Bottles", litho on embossed tin, mkd. Hunt & Frenkel, Blackfriars Rd. S.E., w/ some paint loss, 20 x 28¼in. **$600**

A-PA Feb. 2003   Glass Works Auctions

#392 **Advertising Sign**, "Stoneware The Best Food Container", litho on tin w/ cardboard backing, by Am. Art Works, Coshocton, OH, slight paint loss, 13 x 19in. **$850**

A-PA Feb. 2003   Glass Works Auctions

#393 **Coca-Cola Advertising Tray**, "Wherever Ginger Ale, Seltzer of Soda is Good, Coca-Cola is Better – Try It, etc." mkd. Western Coca-Cola Bottling Co., Chicago, IL, dia. 12¼in. **$11,000**

A-PA Feb. 2003   Glass Works Auctions

#399 **Framed Advertising Sign**, "De Laval Cream Separators, etc.", litho on tin, 30 x 41in. **$2,300**

A-PA Feb. 2003   Glass Works Auctions

#397 **Advertising Sign**, "Chew Wrigley's Juicy Fruit Chewing Gum", some litho loss, trimmed, breaks to cardboard, 22 x 16¼in. **$1,300**

A-PA Feb. 2003   Glass Works Auctions

#401 Framed Advertising Sign, "The Diamond Wine Co., etc." litho on paper, mkd. Copyright 1896 by The Gray Lithograph Co., N.Y., 25¾ x 34in. **$850**

A-PA Feb. 2003   Glass Works Auctions

#403 Tin Framed Advertising Sign, "John Gund Brewing Company, LaCrosse, Wis.", showing deer hunt, mkd. The Meek Company, Coshocton, OH, w/ prof. rest., 26½ x 21in. **$950**

A-PA Feb. 2003

Glass Works Auctions

#423 "Hills Bros. Coffee Enameled Thermometer", mkd. Pat. March 16, 1918, Beach, Coshocton, OH, 8¾ x 22in. **$475**

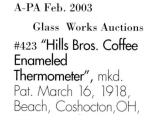

A-PA Feb. 2003   Glass Works Auctions

#409 Self Framed Tin Sign, "In The Shade Of The Old Apple Tree", advertising the Ebbert Co., Owensboro, KY, unused condition, 37½ x 25½in. **$1,900**

A-PA Feb. 2003   Glass Works Auctions

#416 Advertising "Coca-Cola" Hanging Lamp, w/ red/green & white stained glass w/ two minor cracks in one white glass dome panel, dia. 12½ x 17in. **$3,100**

A-PA Feb. 2003   Glass Works Auctions

#430 Towle's Log Cabin Syrup Tin, showing an Express Office on one side, w/ orig. tin screw top, few scratches, ht. 5¾in. **$80**

A-PA Feb. 2003

Glass Works Auctions

#438 Sand Pail, tin, w/ litho depicting Roosevelt's excursion to Africa & safari scene w/ battleship Maine in background, mkd. J. Bros., ht. 4⅛in. **$220**

A-PA Feb. 2003   Glass Works Auctions

#436 Biscuit Tin, "Huntley & Palmers", London, litho on tin in shape of an artist's palette, 7¾ x 9¼in. **$180**

A-PA Feb. 2003

Glass Works Auctions

#483 Bill File, "Ceresota Flour Prize Bread Flour of the World". $150

#484 Old Dutch Cleanser Advertising Can, litho on die-cut cardboard in shape of can, double sided, ht. 5¼in. $60

#487 Blu-J Brooms, advertising die-cut litho in shape of bluejay, ht. 10¼in. $30

431

432

433

434

435

436

437

438

439

440

A-IA Oct. 2002

#431 Old Seneca Stogies Tin of Chief Seneca, some wear. $207

#432 Reichard's Cadet Cigar Tin depicting cadet smoking, wear. $69

#433 Tungsten Cigar Tin w/ embossed paper label. $126

#434 Blue Boar Silvered Humidor & Tobacco Tin, Reed & Barton, w/embossed scenes w/ colorful paper label. lg. 8¼in. $103

#435 Central Union Tobacco Pail, tin w/ litho & hinged lid,

Jackson's International Auctioneers

missing clasp. $2

#436 Tone Bros. Coffee Tin, 2lb. w/ hinged lid, together w/ ½lb. Butternut coffee tin (not illus.). $69

#437 My Favorite Coffee Tin, 3lb. paper label. $80

#438 Ocean Blend Tea, 5lb. tin litho of luxury ocean liner. $92

#439 Licorice Lozenges Tin, 19th C., w/ stencil painted label w/ inset glass front. $28

#440 Korff's Cocoa, tin litho. $80

ADVERTISING

#441 Schepp's Cocoanut, tin litho scene of children, dome top. $195

#442 Large Lard Bucket w/ litho label on tin, ht. 14in. $92

#443 Butternut Coffee Bucket, 10lb. w/ paper label. $46

#444 Cream City Flour Bin/Sifter, wear & oxidation. $46

#445 White House Biscuit Barrel w/ stenciled letters on tin w/ red ground, losses. $28

#446 McLaughlins Coffee Tin, 1lb., some losses. $2

441

442

443

444

445

446

#279 Diamond Dies Cabinet, embossed tin litho w/ two doors & divided interior, ht. 15¼in. $92

#280 Tea Bin, tin w/ polychrome decor., 19th C., w/ scalloped front, losses, ht. 18in. $69

#281 Pine Spice Cabinet w/ nine drawers & titles plates & remnants of mustard print., ht. 18in. $195

#282 Hershey Chocolate Bar Vendor, nickel plate w/ one cent playcard, some oxidation., ht 18in. $92

#283 Parke's Coffee Container w/ 5lb. tin screen label, Alligator finish, ht. 9in. $28

#284 Uneeda Biscuit Bowl, depicting 3 scenes of trademark, wear, ht. 3in. $23

#285 Coffee Container, Montgomery Ward, litho "Java & Arabian Mocha," 5lb. $57

#286 "Ross's Indian Tonic Water" Creamer, mkd. "Campbell Belfast", ht. 3¼in. $80

#287 Sears Roebuck Coffee Container, 5lb. cardboard litho, "Malden Brand", ht. 10in. $46

#288 Black Hawk Coffee Container, 5lb. tin litho "Dinner Party" brand, ht. 9¼in. $115

#289 Nabisco Glass Canister, emb. "National Biscuit Company, Uneeda Bakers", w/ logo, tin lid, ht. 9in. $57

#290 Gumball Vendor, ca.1905, oak w/ glass front "Victor Vending Co.", no key, ht. 12in. $46

#291 Butter Color Container, Hansen Lab., 1gal. tin litho w/ spout, ht. 10in. $34

#292 Coffee Container, Western Grocer Mills, 1lb. oval tin w/ "Scarlet King" paper label, ht. 6¼in. $230

#293 Lipton Tea Container, tin litho w/ scenes of Ceylon natives. lg. 9in. $69

#294 Tobacco Tins, "George Washington" Cut Plug (no handle), & "Four Roses" pocket tin w/ some losses, ht. 4 & 3in. $34

#295 Planters Peanut Canister, pillow form w/ embossed base & figural lid, ht. 13in $69

#296 Cast Iron String Dispenser w/ pedestal foot, embossed cage top, ht. 8in. $69

#297 Baking Powder Container, "Little Chief", w/ paper label of child saluting, ht. 5¼in. $28

#298 Coffee Containers, pair, cardboard, "State House" & "Lady Hellen", ht. 5¼in. $103

#299 Yucatan Gum Container, tin litho w/ hinged lid, losses, lg. 6in. $46

#299A Clarks Tea Berry Gum Pedestal, glass w/ flared foot, lg. 7in. $46

#300 Planters Peanut Canister, pillow form embossed glass w/ tin lid, lg. 9¼in. $92

#301 Union Leader Tobacco Tin, pocket size, tin litho, ht. 4¼in. $28

#302 Bonita Coffee Container, 1lb., tin w/ paper label, ht. 6in. $46

#303 Morrell's Meats Fan, heart shape paper litho w/ adv. in reverse. $28

#304 Superba Coffee Canister, 1lb., painted tin w/ checked finish, ht. 7¼in. $28

#305 Sunshine Biscuit Container, embossed glass, "Loose Wiles Co.", chips on lid, ht. 10in. $34

#306 Heinz Display Pedestal, embossed glass logo on acid finish ground, roughness, sq. $80

#307 Duncan's Coffee Sign depicting package in reverse painted glass, losses. lg. 8in. $23

#308 Bliss Native Herbs Match Holder, tin litho w/ scene of Capitol, ht. 6¼in. $80

#309 Edgeworth Tobacco Humidor, 2lb., tin litho w/ hinged lid, ht. 7in. $28

#310 Oak Tobacco Box, 5lb., "J.T. & H. Clay Registered 1877", displays 5# tobacco stamp on base, lg. 13in. $34

#312 Live Mouse Trap, ca.1900, wood & tin w/ paper label "Catch Me Alive", lg. 5¼in. $57

#311 Salada Coffee Sign, enameled, losses, lg. 12in. $57

#313 Match Holder, ca.1920, wood w/ scene of mother & child, ht. 8in. $46

#314 Briggs Bros. Seed Box, walnut, dov. w/ brass mts. & litho labels, lg. 10in. $138

#315 French Iron Shoe Blacking Display, 19th C., mkd. Pat. 1891, lg. 21in. $138

#316 Mikado Tea Canister, 19th C., tin litho for "Sprague & Warner, Chicago." ht. 7¼in. $34

#317 Schepp's Brewing Tray, ca.1925 w/ tin litho scene of car, losses, lg. 14in. $126

ADVERTISING

A-IA Oct. 2002
Jackson's International Auctioneers

#318 **Myonara Tea Container**, 5lb., sq. tin litho w/ hinged lid, ht. 10¼in. **$34**

#319 **McLaren Cone Dispenser**, glass w/ hinged nickel plate lid & base, ht 16in. **$690**

#320 **Diamond Dyes Sign**, litho tin w/ court scene, losses, ht. 19, wd. 15in. **$46**

#321 **Advertising Calendar**, 1905 for Reliable Steam Laundry, LaCrosse, WI, ht. 11¼in. **$115**

#322 **Happy Boy Confections Tin**, 2lb. litho for Funke's, LaCrosse, WI, ht. 9¼in. **$46**

#323 **Grocery Basket**, ca.1930 checkerboard, printed cardboard w/ bentwood handles, lg. 15in. **$69**

#324 **Blackbell Tobacco String Holder**, tin litho w/ mounted cutter, mkd. "Bayliss Tobacconists," ht. 5in. **$92**

#325 **Mother Hubbard Flour Container**, 12lb. printed cardboard w/ lid, stains, ht. 9in. **$28**

#326 **Tea Canister**, 19th C., embossed w/ Japanese motifs, w/ lid., ht. 8in. **$5**

#327 **Albert Pick Fountain Dispenser**, brass urn shape w/ lighted satin glass globe on marble base, damaged, ht. 23in. **$316**

#328 **Cut Chewing Tobacco Dispenser**, litho tin w/ hinged cover, losses, ht. 10in. **$17**

#329 **Spice Container**, 19th C., stenciled tin, hinged lid, losses, ht. 9¼in. **$172**

#330 **Coffee Canister**, 1lb., tin litho for "Woods' Boston Coffee" w/ scenes of old Boston, threaded lid, ht. 7½in. **$57**

#331 **Hamilton Beach Drink Mixer**, Model #51, chromed finish, tumbler repl., ht. 14in. **$103**

#332 **Berkshire Peanut Butter Can**, 1lb., tin litho, dia. 4in. **$34**

#333 **Tobacco Pails**, pair, tin litho for Central Union & Mayo's cut plug. **$57**

#335 **State House Coffee Container**, paper litho over cardboard w/ Chief Black Hawk on reverse & Iowa capital on reverse. **$103**

#336 **Lager Animated Sign**, ca.1950, reverse w/ rotating color wheel, lg. 24in. **$230**

#337 **Sugar Cleaver**, 19th C., scrolled iron armature w/ wood handle on tray w/ rosemaling, lg. 12in. **$546**

#338 **Grand Union Tea Canister**, 2lb. tin litho w/ round cap, some oxidation, ht. 8¼in. **$34**

#339 **Keen-Maid Door Handle**, embossed zinc plate w/ bronze handle, lg. 18¼in. **$57**

#340 **Wrigley's Countertop Display**, black enameled tin & nickel plate w/ glass dividers, lg. 11in. **$92**

#341 **Gold Flake Peanut Butter Pail**, 1lb. tin litho for Kelly Peanut Co., ht. 3¼in. **$69**

#342 **Wrigley's Countertop Display**, tin w/ green wrinkle finish & red lettering, some oxidation, lg. 17in. **$184**

#343 **Havana Fives Box Display**, tin litho for East Prospect Cigar Co., ht. 3in. **$23**

#345 **McLaughlin Coffee Scoop** w/ embossed name & slogan, lg. 14in. **$74**

#346 **Match Holder**, wood w/ two receptacles for Schroeder & Stone, ht. 8in. **$69**

#347 **Dice Tumbler**, early rotating wire cage on nickel plate stand, ht. 12in. **$57**

#348 **Cracker Jack Die Cut Display**, early stand up version, some losses, ht. 10¼in. **$138**

#349 **Mechanical Call Bell**, ca.1930, spring wound w/ push button on wood frame, lg. 7in. **$23**

#350 **Advertising Calendar Mount**, glazed front w/ pumpkins & children, ht. 8¼in. **$11**

#351 **Black Bass Tobacco Sign** in form of large bass "Chew Black Bass Navy" hanging litho, some oxidation, lg. 19in. **$402**

#352 **Curtiss Baby Ruth** porcelain gummed tape dispensers, lg. 10¼in. **$46**

#353 **The Nut House Peanut Container**, Lynn, MA, lg. 2¼in. **$28**

#354 **Paw-Nee Toy Rolled Oats Whistle**, ca. 1920, ht. 4in. **$46**

#355 **Eagle Lye Match Holder**, tin litho, ht. 5in. **$46**

#356 **Globe Tobacco Display**, tin litho box w/ glass insert in hinged lid, lg. 9in. **$80**

#357 **Dunlap Seed Sales Box**, walnut w/ marquetry bands & orig. 1902 seed labels, lg. 8¼in. **$103**

#358 **Standard Oil Advertising Calendar**, tin litho, dated 1936, lg. 6in. **$86**

447

448

449

450

451

452

453

454

A-IA Oct. 2002
Jackson's International Auctioneers

#447 **Towle's Log Cabin Syrup Tin**, 12oz., repl. cap. **$57**

#448 **Ardenter Mustard Display Case** w/ paper litho labels over wood, lg. 23in. **$92**

#449 **Union Leader Cut Plug Pail**, tin litho picnic basket form, some oxidation. **$5**

#450 **Union Leader Cut Plug Pail**, tin litho w/ orig. paper band. **$57**

#451 **Sweet Cuba Tobacco Pail**, tin litho w/ bail handle & wood grip. **$23**

#452 **H-O Cut Plug Tobacco Pail**, tin litho w/ repl. cap. **$11**

#453 **Tiger Chewing Tobacco Tin** w/ bright finish. **$17**

#454 **Brotherhood Tobacco Container**, tin litho w/ hinged lid. **$80**

455   456   457   458

459   460   461   462

463   464   465   466

467   468   469   470

471   472   473   474

A-IA Oct. 2002   Jackson's International

#455 Anchor Coconut Container, 12lb. tin w/ paper label. **$11**

#456 Daintie Soda Cracker Container, 2lb. tin litho for White House brand. **$40**

#457 Krak-R-Jak Biscuit Container, 3lb. tin for Union Biscuit Co. **$23**

#458 Independent Baking Co. Biscuit Container, 3lb. w/ paper label. **$5**

#459 Fairy Soda Cracker Tin, 6lb. w/ Iten Biscuit Co. paper label. **$17**

#460 Campfire Marshmallow Tin, 5lb. w/ display top. **$161**

#461 Sunshine 2lb. Biscuit Tin, w/ scenic litho depicting 1939 NY World's Fair. **$17**

#462 Sunshine Biscuit Tin, 2lb. w/ scenic litho depicting 9 U.S. warships. **$28**

#463 Sunshine Biscuit Tin, depicting story of Hiawatha. **$126**

#464 Eight Sunshine Biscuit Tins, each depicting a different theme. **$92**

#465 Candy Container Tin, litho for The Candy Men. **$17**

#466 Cremo Cigar Tin, 1lb. w/ adjustable ventilator. **$14**

#467 Dill's Best Sliced Plug Tin, 1lb. w/ minor wear. **$34**

#468 Jockey Harness Dressing Tin, litho w/ hinged lid, depicts a racing sulky. **$126**

#469 McCobb's Plain Chocolate Tin, 19th C., losses. **$15**

#470 Diamond Brand Coffee Case Tin w/ stenciled letter for W. Murphy Co. **$17**

#471 Midgets Soda Cracker Container, 2lb. cardboard litho. **$57**

#472 Mt. Vernon Tea Case, paper litho over wood, zinc lined, "Black Hawk Spice Co." **$80**

#473 Peanut Butter Tins, group of 3, "Peter Pan", "Thrift" & "Table Talk". **$149**

#474 Tobacco Tins, group of 3, "Cinco", "Belfast" & Emilia Garcia". **$92**

BANKS, Still & Mechanical

Small banks for depositing coins became popular in the United States when hard currency was introduced in the 18th century. The adage "a penny saved is a penny earned" has represented an important part of Americana from the time of Benjamin Franklin. It was a time when parents taught their children the art of saving at a very early age, by giving them "penny" banks. Almost every substance has been used to make a still bank, all of which are very collectible. And hundreds of different types have been produced.

Still banks, so called to differentiate them from banks with mechanical parts, have been produced in quantities since the 19th century. They depict a range of buildings, animal and human figures. The most elaborate were made by leading manufacturing companies including Arcade, A.C. Williams, J. & E. Stevens and Kenton.

The most complex banks were mechanical cast-iron models produced from the 1870s. These banks operate on two principles: the weight of the deposited coin will cause the action to begin, or a person, after inserting a coin, presses a lever that activates a spring, setting the bank in motion. There were hundreds of different types of mechanical banks made until the 1930s by J. & E. Stevens and W.J. Shepard Hardware Company.

A-NJ Oct. 2002   Bertoia Auctions

Still Banks
#109 **Santa Claus w/ Tree,** Ives, ca.1890s, cast iron, japanned overall, ht. 7in. **$990**
#110 **Statue of Liberty,** Kenton, cast iron, painted silver w/ gold trim, ht. 6⅜in. **$330**
#111 **Mickey Mouse,** French, slot in back of head, prof. rest., ht. 8in. **$660**
#112 **The Trust Bank,** J. & E. Stevens, missing trap, ht. 7½in. **$5,225**

A-NY Oct. 2002   Bertoia Auctions

Still Banks
#113 **Baby Bird,** Arthur Shaw Co., England, coin slot in mouth, ht. 3in. **$275**
#114 **Walking Pig Bank,** German, lead, slot in back, hinged at neck, missing lock, ht. 5¼in. **$605**
#115 **Pelican w/ Ball,** German, lead w/ coin slot in tin ball, hinged top, trick lock, wd. 4½in. **$330**
#116 **Poised Fox,** German, lead w/ hinged neck & trick lock, lg. 6¼ in. **$1,045**

A-NJ Oct. 2002 Bertoia Auctions

Mechanical Bank
#381 **Uncle Sam,** Shepard Hardware Co., pat. 1886. **$2,200**

A-NY Oct. 2002   Bertoia Auctions

Still Banks
#135 **Yellow Cab,** Arcade w/ rubber tires, slot in hood, lg. 8in. **$3,300**
#136 **Battleship Kentucky,** J. & E. Stevens, repl. mast & flagpole, lg. 9½in. **$3,850**
#137 **Yellow Cab,** Arcade, cast iron, slot on roof, mkd. "Camden 4100" on rear, lg. 7¾ in. **$880**

A-NY Oct. 2002   Bertoia Auctions

Still Banks

#138 **Shell Out,** J. & E. Stevens, ca.1882, cast iron, base 2½ x 4¾ in. **$467**

#139 **Jack-O'-Lantern Bank,** glass, googlie-eyed, ht. 2½ in. **$440**

#140 **Barrel on Stand,** sterling silver w/ key-lock (orig.), lg. 3¼ in. **$220**

#141 **Money Box,** silver w/ embossing, orig. key, ht. 3½in. **$385**

#142 **Sundial,** cast iron, painted gold overall, ht. 4¼in. **$1,540**

#143 **Charlie Chaplin w/ Ash Barrel,** Borgefeldt & Co., clear glass, base mkd. "Charlie Chaplin", ht. 3in. **$137**

A-NH Oct. 2002   Bertoia Auctions

Mechanical Bank

#267 **Eagle & Eaglets,** J. & E. Stevens Co., pat. 1883, w/ orig. bellows. **$1,980**

A-NY Oct. 2002   Bertoia Auctions

Still Banks

#144 **Pillar Box,** "U.R.: England, stenciled "Post Office Savings Bank," ht. 5½in. **$2,750**

#145 **Time is Money Clock,** H.C. Hart, cast iron base & top w/ electroplated tin face w/ paper insert & dial, ht. 4⅞in. **$495**

#146 **Stop Sign,** Dent Mfg., cast iron, ht. 5¾in. **$302**

#147 **Stop Sign,** Dent Mfg., cast iron, ht. 5¾in. **$440**

#148 **Street Clock,** A.C. Williams, cast iron w/ steel back, face painted gold, ht. 6in. **$467**

#149 **Gas Pump,** Arcade w/ gold painted globe on top, ht. 5¾in. **$137**

A-NJ Oct. 2002   Bertoia Auctions

Mechanical Bank

#292 **Hen & Chick,** J. & E. Stevens Co., pat. 1901. **$2,200**

A-NJ Oct. 2002   Bertoia Auctions

Mechanical Bank

#298 **I Always Did Spise A Mule,** J. & E. Stevens Co., pat. 1897. **$1,100**

A-NJ Oct. 2002   Bertoia Auctions

Still Banks

#155 **Hall Clock,** Hubley, w/ paper face, cast iron w/ steel money box container, clock face repl., ht. 5½in. **$192**

#156 **Radio,** Kenton, w/ combination doors & nickel plated dial, ht. 4½in. **$247**

#157 **Singer Electric Sewing Machine,** German, tin & iron, ht. 5⅛in. **$192**

#158 **Crosley Radio,** Kenton, nickel plated w/ gold highlights, ht. 4½in. **$440**

#159 **Crosley Radio,** Kenton, nickel plated w/ gold highlights, ht. 4½in. **$275**

Below left.

A-NJ Oct. 2002   Bertoia Auctions

Still Banks

#160 **Cook Stove,** Kenton, w/ nickel plated top & oven door, ht. 4in. **$550**

#161 **Elephant & Chariot,** Hubley, conversion, cast iron, slot on back, lg. 6⅞in. **$1,210**

#162 **Radio Bank** w/ three dials, Kenton, cast iron w/ nickeled front panel, lg. 4½in. **$110**

#163 **Basket Puzzle Bank,** Nichol Co., w/ orig. label, nickel plated, missing wing nut, ht. 3 in. **$176**

#164 **Radio Bank** w/ three dials, Kenton, cast iron w/ nickel front panel, lg. 4½in. **$165**

A-NJ Oct. 2002 Bertoia Auctions
Still Banks
#180 Chimney Sweep on Cottage Roof, slot in head, key-lock trap at base, ht. 4¼in. **$4,400**
#181 Swan Bank, German, lead w/ hinged trap on back w/ trick lock, lg. 4¾in. **$220**
#182 Clothes Basket, German, tin w/ dove finials, lg. 4¼in. **$88**
#183 Rabbit by Washtub, German, lead & nickeled tin w/ orig. key, lock trap on base, ht. 4in. **$275**

A-NJ Oct. 2002   Bertoia Auctions
Still Banks
#184 Standing Bear in Top Hat, German, lead w/ hinged neck & trick lock, hat embossed "From Burns Cottage," ht. 5¼ in. **$1,430**
#185 West Point Mule, Japan, lead, souvenir bank, slot in saddle, lg. 4½in. **$385**
#186 Seated Teddy Bear, Germany, lead, w/ hinged neck & trick lock, ht. 4½in. **$1,210**
#187 Seated Grey Cat w/ bow, German, lead, hinged neck w/ slot in head, ht. 4¼in. **$770**
#188 Black Cat in Top Hat, German, lead w/ hinged neck & trick lock. Embossed "A Present From Okekampton," ht. 4¾in. **$1,430**

A-NJ Oct. 2002 Bertoia Auctions
Still Banks
#223 Home Savings Bank, cast iron, japanned, front panel reads, "Property of Equitable Loan & Savings Assn., Dayton, Ohio", orig. drawers inside, ht. 10, wd. 6in. **$3,850**
#224 Trader's Bank, Canada, cast iron, nickel plated w/ extensive detail w/ street names embossed on all sides & orig. drawers inside, ht. 8½in. **$2,475**
#225 Church w/ cigar cutter, Gebruder Bing, Nuremberg, Germany, litho hand painted tin w/ trap door in base, ht. 11¾in. **$880**
#226 People Savings Bank, cast iron, embossed "Property of People Savings Bank, Grand Rapid, Mich." ht. 10½in. **$1,980**

A-NJ Oct. 2002   Bertoia Auctions
#304 Initiating First Degree, Mechanical Novelty Works, pat. 1880 w/ paint touch-up. **$3,025**

A-NJ Oct. 2002
                                  Bertoia Auctions
Mechanical Banks
#379 Uncle Remus Bank, Kyser & Rex Co., ca.1890s w/ crack on fence. **$4,400**

A-NJ Oct. 2002   Bertoia Auctions
Mechanical Banks
#252 Calamity w/ box, J. & E. Stevens Co., pat. 1904. **$34,100**

A-NJ Oct. 2002   Bertoia Auctions
Mechanical Banks
#240 **Boy Scout Bank,** J. & E. Stevens

Co., ca.1915, repl. figure & flag w/ touch up. **$1,980**
#241 **Boy Stealing Watermelon,** Kyser &

Rex Co., ca.1894. **$2,750**
#242 **Bread Winners Bank,** J. & E. Stevens Co., ca.1886. **$23,100**

#253 **Calumet Baking Powder Bank,** pat. 1924. **$275**
#254 **Cat & Mouse Bank,** J. & E. Stevens

Co., pat. 1891. **$2,090**
#255 **Chief Big Moon,** J. & E. Stevens Co., pat. 1899. **$1,430**

#256 **Chimpanzee,** Kyser & Rex Co., pat. 1880 w/ repl. rivets. **$5,500**

A-NJ Oct. 2002   Bertoia Auctions
#322 **Milking Cow,** J. & E. Stevens Co., ca.1885, orig. fence repl. **$11,000**

A-NH Oct. 2002   Bertoia Auctions
Mechanical Banks
#261 **Creedmore,** J. & E. Stevens Co., pat. 1877. **$2,750**
#262 **New Creedmore,** J. & E. Stevens Co., pat. 1891. **$4,950**

#263 **Darktown Battery,** J. & E. Stevens Co., pat. 1888. **$4,125**
#264 **Dentist Bank,** J. & E. Stevens Co., ca.1880-1890. **$12,100**

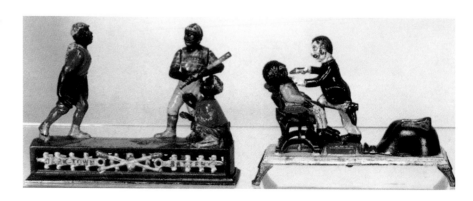

BASKETS

The art of basketry was one of our earliest crafts and is recognized today as yet another interesting form of folk art. Because basketry was common on the Continent, many of the first settlers were experienced basketmakers and quickly adopted new techniques from the Indians, who were excellent basketmakers.

During the decades following the first colonization, the need for containers and storage facilities was immense. Materials were abundant, so the art of basketmaking literally flourished until around the late 1800s when basket factories became established.

Among the most desirable baskets of interest to collectors these days are the Shaker, American Indian, the so-called Nantucket Lightship baskets, and the coiled rye straw baskets that are characteristically Pennsylvania Dutch.

Baskets continue enjoying much popularity among collectors, regardless of vintage. After all, everything collected these days was "new" once. An interesting collection can still be assembled inexpensively, unless one's taste preference includes one of the above types.

A-NY June 2003
Willis Henry Auctions, Inc.
#278 Cheese Basket, Shaker, black ash splint w/ hexagonal base, double wrapped, ht. 10in., dia. 21½in. $400

A NY June 2003   Willis Henry Auctions, Inc.
#219 Feather Basket, Shaker, black ash w/ attached lid & ring pull & tall handle, ht. 15in.; together w/ bread tray, ash w/ double wrapped rim, ht. 3in., lg. 18½in. $700

A-NY June 2003
Willis Henry Auctions, Inc.
#286 Bean Sieve, Shaker, woven ash, oak rim & copper rivets, New Lebanon, NY, ca.1840-50, dia. 19in. $200

A-NY June 2003
Willis Henry Auctions, Inc.
#117 Work Basket, Shaker, black ash w/ double wrapped rim, carved handles & slight inverted bottom, ca.1860, ht. 14½in., dia. 22½in. $600

A-NH Nov. 2002   Northeast Auctions
#519 Nantucket Swing-Handle Baskets, nest of five, each cylindrical, dia. 4⅞in. to 9in. $19,000

BASKETS

A-NJ May 2003   Craftsman Auctions, Inc.
#125 **Mission Basket,** California, of coiled const., ca.1920s w/ minor losses in coil, ht. 4½in. **$550**

A-NJ May 2003   Craftsman Auctions, Inc.
#126 **Mission Basket,** California, of coiled const., ca.1920s w/ minor losses to coil around rim, ht. 4¾in., dia. 13¼in. **$1,500**

A-NJ May 2003   Craftsman Auctions, Inc.
#123 **Pima Basket,** Arizona, olla of coiled const., ca.1900, minor losses, ht. 9½in. **$750**

A-NJ May 2003
Craftsman Auctions, Inc.
#124 **Pima Basket,** Arizona, olla of coiled const., ca.1900, minor breaks & losses, ht. 12in. **$750**

A-NH Aug. 2003   Northeast Auctions
#6 **Nantucket Basket** w/ swing handle, sgn. w/ maker's label who served on the South Shoal lightship from 1854-1905, dia. 12¼in. **$550**
#7 **Nantucket Basket** w/ swing handle, sgn. w/ maker's label who served on the South Shoal Lightship during the 1854-1904 period, dia. 10 ¾in. **$350**

A-NH Aug. 2003   Northeast Auctions
#11 **Nantucket Covered Purse Basket** w/ ivory seagull & swing handle, mkd. "Made in Nantucket" w/ outline of island on bottom & indistinctly dated 195 - -, ht. 6¾in., lg. 8¼in. **$3,300**
#12 **Nantucket-Style Covered Purse** w/ whale mount & a 1985 penny affixed to bottom, ht. 8in. **$1,900**
#13 **Lightship Pocketbook** w/ whaling scene on bone medallion on lid, sgn. by maker, & mkd. "Nantucket, 1963, top 8in. by 6½in. **$200**

A-NH Aug. 2003
Northeast Auctions,
Inc.

#656 Circular Covered Nantucket Basket w/ swing handle & deep patina. The hinged cover w/ turned wooden finial & rim has raised brass tacks, dia. 12in. **$1,200**

A-NY June 2003   Willis Henry Auctions, Inc.
#94 Work Baskets, one, black ash w/ open weave bottom, carved handles, ht. 6¼in., 15 in sq.; together w/ round black ash basket w/ inverted bottom & carved hickory handles, ht. 7½in. to handle. **$1,550**

A-PA Oct. 2002
Conestoga Auction Company, Inc.
#368 Field Basket, white oak w/ rib type const., open work body & doubled rib bottom, minor losses, ht. 14½in. **$550**
#370 White Oak Rib Basket w/ unusual binding to secure handle & rim sections, minor losses, ht. 15½in. **$632**
#372 Arched Back Ribbed Basket, white oak w/ strengthening dowel at rim, minor losses, ht. 12in. **$522**
#374 Oak Rib Basket w/ unusual binding for securing handle w/ brass rivet and wrapped splint binding, ht. 11½in. **$330**
#376 Rye Straw Storage Basket, coiled & lidded w/ leather thong hinges, ht. 12¾in. **$5,500**
#378 White Oak Rib Basket w/ checkerboard plaited handle overlay, losses, ht. 9½in. **$330**
#380 White Oak Rib Basket of oval form, dark patina surface, ht. 7½in. **$660**
#382 Typical White Oak Basket w/ rib type const. & plaited overlay dec. handle, ht. 10in. **$247**

A-NH Aug. 2003   Northeast Auctions
#4 Nesting Nantucket Baskets w/ swing-handles, each mounted w/ brass plaque & mkd. by maker, dia. 5in. & 6½in. **$850**
#5 Swing Handle Basket w/ maker's stenciled inscription, dia. 6in. **$600**

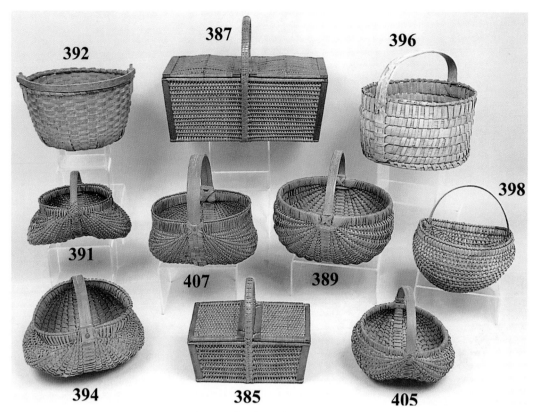

A-PA Oct. 2002
Conestoga Auction Company, Inc.
#392 Swing Handle Basket w/ double base const., white oak, ht. 7in. **$495**
#387 Double Lidded Basket, white oak & walnut w/ dec. bands of red & green dyed splint, minor loss, ht. 13in., wd. 18in. **$715**
#396 White Oak Basket of unusual const., incor. rib basket making to achieve a cylindrical form, losses, ht. 11in. **$192**

#391 White Oak Rib Basket w/ unusual plaited lashing joining handle & rim, losses, ht. 7in. **$93**
#407 Rib Basket, white oak w/ plaited dec. covering lower handle section, losses, ht. 10in. **$247**
#389 White Oak Rib Basket nicely colored from age, ht. 10in. **$440**
#398 Pocket or Key Basket, white oak, ht. 8in. **$302**

#394 Rib Basket, white oak w/ "shot head" nails securing top hoop & copper harness rivets fasten handle to frame, minor loss, ht. 7in. **$495**
#385 Lidded Basket w/ red dyed splint accents, oak & walnut, w/ wrapped handle & brass hinges, ht. 7½in., lg. 10½in. **$577**
#405 White Oak Rib Basket w/ minor breaks, ht. 7½in. **$330**

A-NH July 2003   Northeast Auctions, Inc.
#167 Field Basket w/ push-up base & cutout handles, ht. 13½in. **$100**
#168 Splint Drying Basket w/ loop side handles & peg feet, ht. without handles 14½in. **$175**
#169 Canterbury Splint Basket w/ four loop handles & burlap lining. n/s

#170 Canterbury Shaker Basket w/ fixed handle & inscribed "IY" for infirmary, dia. 15in. **$350**
#171 Rectangular Basket w/ stationary center handle, 19in. by 15in. **$200**
#172 Gathering Basket w/ swing handle & push-up bottom. The double wrapped rim w/ two raised ears secure swing handle w/ looped ends. **$200**

#173 Buttocks Basket w/ striped dec. & fixed handle, lg. 18in. **$100**
#174 New Lebanon Shaker "Cat-Head" Basket w/ stationary handle & #2 in black paint, ht. 8in. **$6,800**
#175 Square Basket w/ double swing handles, 15in. sq.; together w/ lidded (repl.) carrying basket, dia. 13½in. **$80**

A-PA Oct. 2002   Conestoga Auction Company, Inc.
#395 Classic Pennsylvania Rye Straw Basket w/ applied chip carved white oak handles & splint wrapped "foot" at base, losses, ht. 12in. **$3,575**
#400 Coiled & Lidded Rye Straw Basket w/ applied white oak side handles, minor losses, ht. 13in. **$4,400**
#397 Rye Straw Storage Basket, oval & lidded, ht. 13in., lg. 24in. **$3,190**
#402 Coiled Rye Straw Bee Skep Basket, ht. 15½in., dia. 12in. **$660**
#388 Oval & Lidded Rye Straw Basket w/ hinged cover & applied oak handles, ht. 7in., lg. 14in. **$1,245**

A-MA Feb. 2003   Skinner, Inc.

First Row

#851 Potato Stamp Woven Splint, probably by Eastern Woodland tribes, 19th C. & dec. w/ two bands painted salmon & yellow w/ salmon & green flower sprig potato stamp design, minor breaks, ht. 5½in., lg. 19¼in. **$470**
#852 Small Painted Splint Basket w/ cover, Am., 19th C., w/ mustard yellow paint w/ green & black painted bands & design, losses, ht. 8¼in. **$499**
#853 Two Small Splint Baskets, painted red w/ carved handles, ht. 4¼in. & 6¼in. **$1,175**
#854 Small Round Splint Basket, 19th C., w/ carved handles, blue interior & green exterior, minor breaks in lacing, ht. 5in., dia. 6in. **$1,880**

#855 Oval Splint Basket, Am., 19th C., w/ carved handle on light blue painted basket w/ pine base, minor breaks, ht. 17in., lg. 24in. **$764**
#856 Nantucket Basket, ca.1927, w/ contrasting light & dark cane weave, mkd. on base "Made by Chadwick Is. House 1927", ht. 11¼in., dia. 12½in. **$2,468**

Second Row

#857 Nantucket Basket, 19th C., w/ carved wooden swing handle on basket w/ turned base, mkd. w/ minor wear, ht. 8½in., dia. 11¾in. **$2,115**
#858 Painted Splint Basket, Am., 19th C., w/ carved handles, painted salmon w/ hand-stitched brown cotton lining, ht. 3¼in., lg. 5⅜in. **$1,058**
#859 Round Nantucket Basket, late 19th early 20th C., w/ carved swing handle &

turned base, ht. 6⅝in. dia. 8¾in. **$2,585**
#860 Round Nantucket Basket, 19th C., w/ carved swing handle & turned base, w/ minor breaks in caning, ht. 11⅜in., dia. 9⅝in. **$1,645**
#861 Nantucket Utility Basket, early 20th C., w/ two carved handles, turned wooden base & contrasting caning, repairs, ht. 12½in., dia. 18in. **$3,760**
#862 Covered Basket, 19th C., painted deep salmon color exterior, upright handle w/ minor breaks, ht. 5¼in. **$1,998**
#863 Round Splint Basket w/ carved swing handle & minor breaks, ht. 11⅞in. n/s
#864 Nantucket Basket, round form w/ carved swing handle & make-do copper band repair on base, minor cracks on base, ht. 10⅝in., dia. 14½in. **$3,055**

BOTTLES

The "golden era" of bottle collecting escalated during the 1960s and well into the 1980s. It was a time when there was a steady supply of unusual new finds being discovered, either privately or through auctions which fueled collectors' demands. Bottle price guides were published, and eastern and mid-western auction houses began offering more bottles in their auctions. And it was at this time that major auction houses added specialists to their staff, as they moved into this "new" collectible field which became a major hobby for many collectors. The most desirable and pricy bottles are historic flasks, bitters, ink, figural and perfume.

A-PA Oct. 2002

Historical Flasks
#5 **Bust of Washington & Taylor** (reverse), Baltimore Glass Works, ca.1825-1835, yellow olive quart w/ pontil scarred base. **$22,000**
#7 **Bust of Washington & Sailing Ship** (reverse), Albany Glass Works, ca.1825-1835, med. emerald green pint w/ pontil scarred base. **$5,000**
#8 **Bust of Washington & Sailing Ship** (reverse), Albany Glass Works, ca.1825-1835, med. golden amber pint w/ pontil scarred base. **$2,600**

Glass Works Auctions

A-PA Oct. 2002

Glass Works Auctions

#48 **Masonic Arch Flask – Eagle / "J. K. / B.,"** (inside oval), ca.1815-1825, med. yellow green w/ gray amber coloration in the shoulder & neck, w/ pontil scarred base, pint. **$4,000**

A-PA Oct. 2002

Glass Works Auctions

#74 **Scroll Flask,** Louisville Glass Works, amber w/ red iron pontil, ca.1845-1860, pint. **$1,000**

A-PA Oct. 2002

Glass Works Auctions

#62 **Corn For The World Flask,** Monument/Baltimore, ca.1865-1875, med. orange amber, w/ chip on base, quart. **$900**

#64 **Sunburst Flask,** ca.1815-1835, bright grass green w/ pontil scarred base, & tooled mouth, pint. **$1,300**

A-PA Feb. 2003   **Glass Works Auctions**
#822 **Saltbox Cabin Ink,** by George Orr Pottery, Am., ca.1880-1900, w/ dark green glaze, ht. 3⅛in. **$3,750**

792.

793.

794.

795.

796.

797.

798.

799.

801.

A-PA Feb. 2003   Glass Works Auctions
Inkwells
#792 Salt Glaze Stoneware, dark gray w/ cobalt lettering & scalloped rim w/ three quill holes, dia. 3½in. **$1,300**
#793 Stoneware, Am., ca.1850-1870, gray w/ cobalt decor., two quill holes & filler hole on top, ht. 1⅛, dia. 2⅜in. **$900**
#794 Salt Glaze, Am., ca.1840-1870, light gray w/ cobalt slip, three quill holes, vent & filler holes, ht. 2, dia. 5in. **$450**

#795 Wooden, Am., ca.1840-1860 w/ multi-colored paint, three blown clear glass wells, James L. Chappell factory, ht. 2¾, dia. 6¼in. **$475**
#796 Rockingham Type, English, ca.1850-1880 w/ raised grotesque face on each side, dark brown glaze, four quill holes & center filler hole, ht. 2¾in. **$170**
#797 Soapstone, Am., ca.1780-1820, carved w/ concentric rings around pen hole, ht. 1⅝in. **$50**

#798 Carved Soapstone, Am., ca.1780-1830, sq. w/ carved diamond patt., orig. wood sliding cap held by wooden dowel, ht. 1⅝in. **$550**
#799 Carved Soapstone, probably Am., ca.1780-1820, pyramid shape, ht. 2, dia. base 2½in. **$100**
#801 Figural, w/ Rockingham glaze, English or Am., ca.1860-1880, reclining woman w/ hat, ht. 3¾in. **$180**

(reverse)

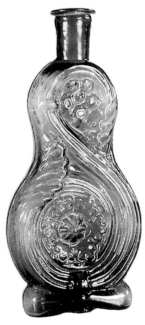

A-PA Feb. 2003   Glass Works Auctions
#721 Spirits Flask, German, ca.1859 w/ yellow & white enamel decor. inscription in German. Translation is "To have love & nothing else is harder than carrying stones," ht. 6¾in. **$900**

#722 Spirits Flask, German, ca.1780-1810, Nailsea type w/ white loopings, orig. pewter neck band w/ screw threads, ht. 7½in. **$900**

#724 Cologne Bottle, Am., ca.1825-1845 w/ pontil scarred base & flared lip, ht. 5⅝in. **$1,900**

BOTTLES

A-PA Feb. 2003   Glass Works Auctions

Inkwells

#219 Teakettle Ink, Am., ca.1875-1895, cobalt blue w/ five point star embossed on base & orig. brass neck ring & hinged lid. lg. ⁵⁄₁₆, wd. ⅛ in. **$220**

#220 Teakettle Ink, ca.1875-1890, opaque lime green w/ smooth base, orig. brass neck ring & hinged lid. Possible Sandwich. **$300**

#221 Teakettle Ink, Am., ca.1875-1890, opalescent yellow green w/ remains of orig. enamel decor., 8-sided, w/ orig. brass neck ring & hinged lid, ht. 2⅜in. **$375**

#222 Teakettle Ink, Am., ca.1875-1890, amethyst, 8-sided w/ orig. brass neck ring w/ tiny qtr. base flake, ht. 2⅛in. **$425**

219.

220.

221.

222.

240.   241.   242.   243.   244.

A-PA Feb. 2003   Glass Works Auctions

Snuff Bottles

#240 "Linton & Woodward," Am., ca.1830-1845, golden yellow amber w/ pontil scarred base, ht. 4½in. **$4,000**

#241 "G.W. Gail/Baltimore," Am., 1830-1850, med. amber w/ pontil scarred base, ht. 5¼in. **$4,500**

#242 "J.J. Mapes, No. 61 Front St., N. York," Am., ca.1830-1850, med. yellow amber, pontil scarred base, w/ air bubbles, ht. 4⅜in. **$2,500**

#243 "J.J. Mapes, No. 61 Front St., N. York," Am., ca.1830-1850, olive amber w/ pontil, ht. 4⅜in. n/s

#244 "E. Roome/Troy/New York," Am., ca.1830-1850, light med. blue green, w/ pontil ht. 4¼in. **$2,000**

A-PA Feb. 2003 Glass Works Auctions
#727 Bunker Hill Monument Cologne, Am., ca.1875 w/ label reading "Cologne Water For The Toilet," ht. 6½in. **$500**

#728 Bunker Hill Monument Cologne, Am., ca. 1875 w/ smooth base & rolled lip, ht. 6½in. **$550**

#733 Sunburst Scent Bottle, Am., ca.1820-1835 w/ scarred base & rolled lip, ht. 2½in. **$400**

#735 Blown Three-Mold Decanter, Am., ca.1815-1835 w/ scarred base & flared lip, glass is bubbly & full of swirled lines, ht. 7⅝in. **$50**

#738 Cologne Bottle, Am., ca.1865-1875, corset waist form, 8 sided w/ smooth base & rolled lip, ht. 4⅝in. **$300**

A-PA Feb. 2003   Glass Works Auctions
Candy Containers
#831 "Amos & Andy" Automobile, by Victory
Glass Co., Jeannetta, PA, lg. 4½in. $425

A-PA Feb. 2003   Glass Works Auctions
#855 Cannon, cobalt blue w/ original metal
screw cap & carriage, chip off edge of cannon
barrel, ht. 5¼in. $450

A-PA Feb. 2003
          Glass Works Auctions
#858 Baby Chick w/ original
yellow & black paint & original
tin sliding closure, ht. 3½in.
$160

A-PA Feb. 2003
Glass Works
Auctions
#860 Chicken
On The Nest
w/ red &
green paint,
mfg. by J.H.
Killstein Co.,
missing
closure, ht.
4⅝in. $50

A-PA Feb. 2003
          Glass Works
          Auctions
#892 Lantern
"Fancy Square,"
w/ orig. tin
fittings, ht. 3⅝in.
$70

A-PA Feb. 2003
          Glass Works Auctions
#861 Crowing Rooster, clear
glass w/ most all black, red &
gold paint, ht. 5in. $375

A-PA Feb. 2003 Glass Works Auctions
#874 Felix The Cat Bank Container,
© 1922/24 by Pat. Sullivan, ht.
3½in. $170

A-PA Feb. 2003
Glass Works
Auctions
#896 Opera
Glasses,
"Souvenir
Wausa Neb,"
milk glass w/
original paint
& metal screw
lids, ht. 3in.
$180

A-PA Feb. 2003
          Glass Works Auctions
#887 Pumpkinhead
Witch w/ 80%
original paint, missing
goggles, w/ original
screw lid, ht. 7⅞in.
$800

A-PA Feb. 2003
          Glass Works Auctions
#948 Telephone, mkd.
Candy Lane Phone,
Omaha, Neb., bell
mkd. Manufactured
by Redlich Manfg.
Co., Chicago, w/
orig. contents, ht.
6⅝in. $750

A-PA Feb. 2003 Glass Works Auctions
#895 Mule Pulling Two Wheeled
Barrel, w/ driver, repaint w/ orig.
lid, mkd. J'Net, PA, U.S.A., ht.
2¾in. $70

A-PA Feb. 2003   Glass Works Auctions
#876 Fire Engine, mkd. V.G. Co., Little
Boiler, U.S.A., closure missing & one
chip on edge of running board, ht.
2¾in. $30

BOXES

BOXES

Boxes are fascinating collectibles. They come in a variety of shapes, sizes and materials, and have been used for various purposes throughout our recorded history. Finding two early examples exactly alike is almost an impossibility, except for those that were made on molds or in wood factories during the 1800s.

Wooden boxes are favorites of the country collector. Wood used for making these containers are generally pine, birch, maple, ash or beech. For assembling the earliest boxes, short wooden pegs were used to fasten the bottom to the side and top to the rim. Later examples were fastened with copper or iron nails. Round boxes were the most common shape. These were used in pantries and in kitchens for storage, and rarely decorated.

Spice boxes – metal or wooden – are especially favored by collectors, in addition to candleboxes with their sliding covers, salt, pipe, sewing, writing, trinket, and interesting Bible boxes, oftentimes embellished with carving.

Bright and delightfully colorful boxes became popular during the late 1800s. These were common in the Pennsylvania German areas. And the interesting band box, oftentimes covered with colorful printed papers depicting well-known sights or historical events, have remained popular. These were used for storage as well as transporting clothing and personal effects.

Many boxes used in American homes were not originally of American manufacture. Before and after the Revolution, many commercially produced items were imported in exchange for domestic goods sent overseas. Among the 18th and early 19th centuries imports were snuffboxes made of china, silver, tortoiseshell, tin, papier-mâché and leather. Decorative Battersea enamel patch boxes were advertised during the 1760s. Elegant mahogany knife boxes became popular in England during the George III period (ca.1765), and are still available but very pricey. From the late 18th and early 19th centuries, a period without equal in the history of tea caddies, many rare and exciting examples were made in a wide range of shapes, sizes and decorative finishes. During the last decade, tea caddies made in England and Germany in the form of fruits and vegetables during the second half of the 18th century have literally set auction records. This may aptly be referred to as "The Golden Age of the Tea Caddy".

A-SC Mar. 2003   Charlton Hall Galleries, Inc.

#001 **Battersea Enamel Patch Boxes,** 18th C., four, one oval yellow case w/ motto; an oval green from York Cathedral; one blue dec. w/ bird & motto; and one oval blue w/ friendship motto, first three w/ crack & chip to interior, lg. 1¾in. **$650**

#002 **Battersea Enamel Boxes,** late 18th C., one w/ love motto; one dec. w/ profile portrait of a gentleman & motto; & center box w/ lid depicting woman seated w/ dog, cracking to top & broken mirror inside. **$650**

#003 **Nutmeg Cases,** three, two Eng. enamel cases, one multicolor w/ damage to interior, one yellow, 19th C., & one millefiori, early 20th C. **$650**

001
002
003

A-SC Mar. 2003   Charlton Hall Galleries, Inc.

#004 **Battersea Enamel Boxes,** late 18th C. w/ portrait of Paul Jones, sm. chips on underside, & one cartouche-form case dec. w/ hunt scene. **$550**

004

A-NE Aug. 2003 Northeast Auctions
#323 **Chip Carved Box,** top covered w/ pinwheels, hearts & starflowers w/ red mustard highlights, base painted green, dia. 8in. **$8,000**

A-PA Feb. 2003   Pook & Pook, Inc.

#222 **Spool Box**, N. Eng., tiger maple & cherry, ca.1830 w/ pin cushion top, ht. 9¾in., wd. 8½in. **$748**

#223 **Dresser Box**, Am., mahogany, ca.1840 w/ mirrored lid & fitted interior, ht. 8½in., wd. 10in. **$3,738**

#224 **Tea Caddy**, Federal, mahogany, ca.1790 w/ three compartments & line inlays, ht. 8in., wd. 11½in. **$690**

A-PA Feb. 2003   Pook & Pook, Inc.

First Row

#258 **Document Box**, ca.1820, rosewood grained panels w/ yellow pinstriping & green borders, 6⅜in. by 13⅞in. **$460**

#259 **Bentwood Oval Brides Box**, early 19th C. w/ overall tulip dec., ht. 6½in., wd. 15¾in. **$1,150**

Second Row

#260 **Slide Lid Candlebox**, PA, pine,

ca.1800 w/ overall orange & amber stippled dec., w/ green borders, ht. 6in., lg. 12¾in. **$633**

#261 **Storage Box** w/ Friesland chip dec., incl. incised stars & sawtooth border, retaining green painted surface, ht. 4¾in., lg. 11in. **$374**

#262 **Tole Document Box**, ca.1830 w/ yellow swag & floral dec., ht. 7¼in., lg. 9¾in. **$1,035**

A-SC June 2003   Charlton Hall Galleries, Inc.

#512 **Knife Urns**, Georgian style, mahogany w/ inlay, each w/ stepped dome-shaped lid raising to fitted interiors over ovoid body w/ bellflower swag inlays, ht. 25in. **$1,600**

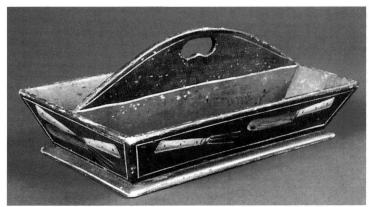

A-NH Aug. 2003   Northeast Auctions

#958 **Cutlery Box**, dec. w/ bone-handled crossed knife & fork on each side, red painted ground w/ yellow stripes, lg.14in. **$3,800**

A-NH Aug. 2003   Northeast Auctions

#218 **Valuables Dome-Top Box**, Am., in old surface w/ yellow ground panels dec. w/ floral sprigs, lg. 10in. **$6,000**

BOXES

#173 **Candlebox,** PA w/ sliding lid, dec. w/ red on green ground, ca.1840, sgn., top 9 ½in. by 5in. **$3,600**
#174 **Candlebox,** PA w/ sliding lid, & mustard dec., top 8in. by 4in. **$5,000**

A-SC Dec. 2002   Charlton Hall Galleries, Inc.
#009 **Tea Caddy,** Regency, rosewood, ca.1823, casket shaped w/ hinged lid, fitted interior w/ two hinged lid boxes & a mixing well, brass lion's head pulls, bun feet, ht. 8½in., wd. 13in. **$700**

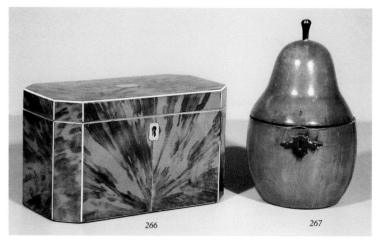

A-SC Dec. 2002   Charlton Hall Galleries, Inc.
#266 **Tea Caddy,** George III, green tortoiseshell, ca.1780 w/ ivory veneer, silver escutcheon, divided interior forming two compartments, each lid w/ tortoiseshell veneer, minor damage, ivory handle, ht. 4¼in., wd. 7¼in. **$10,000**
#267 **Tea Caddy,** George III, pear-form fruitwood, 19th C., restoration to hinge, separation to lid & repair to side, ht. 7in. **$2,100**

A-PA Oct. 2003

Conestoga Auction Company, Inc.

#199 **Candle Box,** Am., w/ paint dec., ca.1830, attrib to Lancaster Co. PA. **$2,600**

A-SC June 2003
Charlton Hall Galleries, Inc.
Tea Caddies
#042 **George III Caddy,** tortoiseshell veneer w/ paneled dome top, silver finial, ivory line inlay & silver mounting,

repair to veneer, ht. 7in., wd. 5in. **$1,400**
#043 **Georgian Double Tea Caddy,** inlaid satinwood, opening to two covered compartments, ht. 4¾in., wd. 7½in. **$6,000**

#044 **Georgian Satinwood Caddy,** ca.18th C., w/ inlaid seams, silver gilt leaf on interior, small loss to veneer, top warped, key missing, ht. 4½in., wd. 5½in. **$2,100**

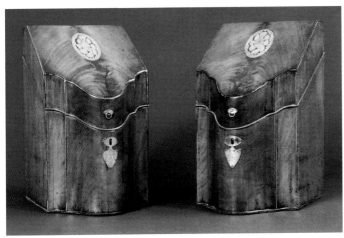

A-NH Aug. 2003   **Northeast Auctions**
#888 **Knife Boxes,** Federal, pr., inlaid mahogany w/ shell inlay, silvered shield escutcheon & fitted interior, ht. 15in. **$4,250**

A-PA Sept. 2002   **Pook & Pook, Inc.**
#210 **Knife Boxes,** pr. of George III, mahogany, ca.1790 w/ line inlaid ovolo shaped front & fitted w/ tray interiors, ht. 15¼in., wd. 9½in. **$2,990**

A-NH May 2003   **Northeast Auctions**
Tea Caddies
#600 **Apple-Form Fruitwood** w/ silvered escutcheon plate & remnants of lining, ht. 5in. **$2,800**
#601 **Pear-Form Fruitwood** w/ silvered escutcheon plate & remnants of lining, ht. 7in. **$2,800**
#602 **Melon-Form** w/ mottled green surface, ht. 7in. **$6,400**

A-NH Aug. 2003   **Northeast Auctions**
#1169 **Tea Caddy,** fruitwood, pear-form w/ escutcheon plate, lock & key & silvered interior, ht. 7in. **$3,800**

A-PA Oct. 2003
Conestoga Auction
Company, Inc.
#204 **Comb Box,** chip carved w/ painted dec. on all sides, back features pyramid shaped chip carved hanger w/ applied heart, ht. 10in., wd. 10in., dp. 4in. **$750**

A-MA Mar. 2003   **Robert C. Eldred Co., Inc.**
#25 **Tea Caddy,** Eng., mahogany in rectangular form late 18th C. w/ string inlay & double compartment interior, lg. 6½in. **$1,254**
#26 **Tea Caddy,** Eng., fruitwood w/ separate painted leaf-form base, ca.1800, ht. 6in. **$13,000**

The earliest clocks came to America with the first settlers. At that point in our history, a clock had more prestige than practical value because time meant very little to the colonist who spent his daylight hours building a homestead or tilling the soil.

Over the years, America has added its fair share of illustrious names to the world's great clockmakers. Some craftsmen were working here as early as the 17th century and, during the 18th century, every colony had a clockmaker. It took months to produce a single clock because each of its innumerable parts was carefully made by hand.

The two main district communities producing clocks during the 18th century were Philadelphia and Boston. The early craftsmen – English, Dutch and German descendants – followed the traditional styles they had learned while apprentices; therefore, at first sight it was oftentimes difficult to distinguish the colonial tall-case clock from its progenitor in Europe. But, with the passage of time, American clockmakers developed their own recognizable styles. They chose for their cases the finest of hardwoods – walnut, mahogany and cherry preferred, with satinwood and other exotic hardwoods used.

Clocks did not become common in American homes until after the 1800s. Their manufacture in quantity began in 1840, fathered by Chauncey Jerome, a Waterbury clockmaker. His new methods of manufacture quickly replaced wooden movements with rugged interchangeable brass-geared works which eventually led to mass production. Surviving examples of the early tall case clocks, wall and shelf in addition to watches, are very collectable these days... and those in fine original condition and in good running order are very much in demand.

A-MA Feb. 2003   Skinner, Inc.

#802A Banjo Clock, Federal-style, w/ mahogany case, by Elmer O. Stennes, Weymouth, MA, w/ cast brass eagle above dial, dec. w/ mah. crossbanding & stringing, ht. 34¼in. **$1,528**

#802 Presentation Banjo Clock, Federal, ca.1828, mkd. "E.

Currier" on tablet w/ scrolled vine designs, framed by gilt moldings w/ flanking brass side pieces, minor imperfections, ht. 40in. **$3,525**

#803 Banjo Alarm Clock, Simon Willard & Son, eight-day movement, old finish, lower tablet replaced, ht. 32½in. **#3,290**

A-IA Sept. 2003
Jackson's International Auctioneers
#938 **Mantel Clock** by E.N. Welch, w/ painted scenic glass door, ht. 26½in. $225

#939 **Figural "Mystery" Clock** of a lady supporting a pendulum weighted clock, ht. 28in. $925

#940 **Kitchen Clock,** Victorian "Ginger Bread" style by Seth Thomas, walnut case, ht. 22in. $780

#941 **Victorian Regulator Wall Clock,** "Vienna" style, in walnut case w/ turned dec., ht. 36in. $225

#942 **Regulator Wall Clock,** Victorian "Vienna" style in walnut case w/ turned dec., ht. 31in. $225

#943 **Oak Wall Regulator Clock,** ca.1920, ht. 31in. $125

A-IA Sept. 2003

Jackson's International Auctioneers

#944 French Figural Table Clock, parian ware w/ gilt bronze, depicting a young girl & a nest of fledgling birds, mid-19th C., w/ incised mark, ht. 10in. **$300**

#949 Two Mantel Clocks, one by Ingraham & New Haven, together w/ a Victorian walnut clock shelf. **$140**

#945 Continental Scroll Case Mantel Clock, ca.1900 w/ green marble front & polished slate columns, ht. 17in. **$250**

#947 Victorian Shelf Clock w/ gilt dec. glazed door, New Haven Clock Co., ht. 22in. **$160**

#948 Walnut Shelf Clock, Victorian w/ gilt dec. scenic glazed door, ht. 18½in. **$100**

A-NH Mar. 2003   Northeast Auctions

#680 Tall Case Clock, Timothy Chandler, Concord NH, mah. w/ enameled dial, ht. 91in. **$10,000**

#946 Italian Carved Alabaster Clock, 19th C., in scrolled case w/ ormolu crest, ht. 10½in. $100

A-PA May 2003
        Pook & Pook, Inc.
#244 Cherry Tall Case Clock, PA, Federal, ca.1815, w/ white painted face, ht. 92in. $4,600

A-NC May 2003   Brunk Auction Services, Inc.

#0570 French Tall Case Clock, 19th C., enameled face mkd. "Godard à Castel Sarazin," w/ large brass pendulum & press brass cornucopia spandrels, scruffs & scratches, ht.91½ in. $3,000

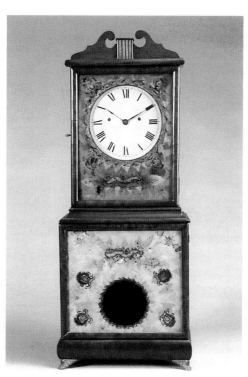

A-PA May 2003   Pook & Pook, Inc.

#370 Cherry Tall Case Clock, Sheraton, ca.1820, w/ white painted face inscribed "Geo Bush, Easton, No 211", ht. 93in. $4,025

A-NH Mar. 2003   Northeast Auctions
#568 Mahogany & Eglomisé Shelf Clock by Joseph Morse, MA, Federal, w/ gilt paw feet, ht. 32in. $8,600

A-PA May 2003   Pook & Pook, Inc.
#415 Cherry Tall Case Clock, PA, ca.1790, sgn. "Daniel Rose Reading", rest., ht. 96¾ in. $5,463

A-IA July 2002　　　　　　　　　　Tom Harris Auctions
#111 **Shelf Clock,** Gilbert "Calliope" w/ walnut case, time & strike. **$770**
#81 **Ansonia Shelf Clock,** walnut, time & strike w/ alarm. **$1,155**
#171 **Ansonia Shelf Clock,** "Monarch", w/ walnut case. **$1,320**

A-IA July 2002　　　　　　　　Tom Harris Auctions
#97 **New Haven Wall Clock,** "Winnipeg" time & strike, walnut case, ht. 32in. **$825**

A-NH Mar. 2003　　　　　　　Northeast Auctions
#567 **Walnut Tall Case Clock,** Am., Chippendale walnut case w/ moon phase dial, calendar & seconds, ht. 91in. **$4,000**

A-IA July 2002　　　　　　　　Tom Harris Auctions
#195 **Shelf Clock,** E. & G. W. Bartholomew, Bristol, CT, ca.1830, hollow columns for weights, whaling scene on bottom glass, gilt paw feet & brass finials, ht. 38in. **$2,750**

A-IA July 2002　　　　　　　　Tom Harris Auctions
#301 **Kitchen Clock,** Seth Thomas, "Reno" walnut case, time & strike. **$187**

A-NH Mar. 2003　　　　　　　Northeast Auctions
#557 **Q.A. Tall Case Clock** by David Blasdel, MA, sgn., w/ pewter dial & a glazed bull's eye on plinth base, ht. 50in. **$5,250**

A-IA July 2003

Tom Harris Auctions

#108 **NYS Watch** w/ rare worm gear & Dueber Silverine case. **$360**

#72 **Swiss Repeater,** ¼ hr. w/ multicolor church scene on dial, sterling silver OF case, Park Watch Co. **$465**

#74 **R.H. Ingersoll** "Columbus" w/ Waterbury Bee movement, brass plated tin case, souvenir Columbian Expo. 1893 w/ opener. **$510**

#80 **Hamilton 926,** made for F. McIntyre, South McAlester I.t. (Indian Territory) OK, OF case w/ rear display crystal. **$305**

#110 **M.J. Tobias Liverpool** w/ engraved silver scenic dial & heavily engraved works & case. **$595**

#120 **Benedict & Burnham Long Wind,** 1880 w/ base metal OF case. **$480**

#124 **Hamilton 968** Masonic dial, pendant set; OF Dueber 10kt. gold case. **$415**

#122 **Elgin Model I Convertible** w/ Ferguson dial & engraved stag on hunting case **$305**

#134 **Swiss Duplex Captain's** observateur watch, 3 dial, 1880, black enamel on silver. **$360**

#98 **New York Standard** w/ multicolored dial w/ engraved dog on back. **$330**

#68 **Sterling silver** w/ Henry Randel movement pinset w/ butterfly, Marion Watch Co. **$330**

A-IA July 2002   Tom Harris Auctions

#279 **Steeple Shelf Clock,** Jerome & Co., ca.1850, time & strike, mah. case. **$165**

A-IA July 2002   Tom Harris Auctions

#299 **New Haven Kitchen Clock,** walnut case, time & alarm only. **$148**

A-PA Feb. 2003

    Pook & Pook, Inc.

#73 **Cherry Tall Case Clock,** PA., Chippendale, ca.1790, w/ painted face bearing the name "Solomon Yeakle" (Hereford Twp.), alterations, ht. 96½ in. **$7,495**

A-PA Nov. 2002

    Pook & Pook, Inc.

#389 **Cherry Tall Case Clock,** PA., Federal, ca.1820, 30 hour works, face sgn. "J. Weifs, Allentown", ht. 96in. **$3,450**

A-PA Nov. 2002

    Pook & Pook, Inc.

#390 **Maple Tall Case Clock,** N. Eng., w/ three brass finials over white painted face, ht. 87in. **$2,990**

A-IA July 2002   Tom Harris Auctions

#126 Calendar Clock, Ingraham, walnut w/ double dial, ht. 22in. **$825**

A-IA July 2002   Tom Harris Auctions

#105 Schoolhouse Clock, Waterbury "Heron", regulator, oak case. **$412**

A-IA July 2002   Tom Harris Auctions

#103 German Vienna Regulator w/ carved top, multicolored porcelain dial w/ seconds, two weights. **$770**

A-MA Feb. 2003   Skinner, Inc.

#141 Tall Case Clock Watch Hutch, Sailor-made, Am., late 18th C., or early 19th, w/ carved inlaid ivory dec., an engraved whalebone dial & whalebone stringing outlining the doors, raised on shaped bracket whalebone feet, a few repairs, ht. 16⅜in., wd. 3⅝in., dp. 3½in. **$3,290**

#142 Tall Case Clock Watch Hutch, Am., late 18th or early 19th C., w/ various wood, ivory & baleen inlays, shaped

bracket feet, imperfections, ht. 13¾in., wd. 3⅜in., dp. 1⅞in. n/s

#143 Watch Hutch, Am. or Eng., late 18th C., carved in the form of a tall clock, w/ tombstone door on base w/ various wood inlays depicting a three-masted ship, & inlaid ebony stringing, minor losses to stringing, ht. 10in. **$940**

#144 Carved Mahogany & Ivory Watch Hutch, Am., w/ ivory dec., on shaped bracket feet, ht. 14⅜in. **$3,290**

#145 Three Mahogany Watch Hutches,

Am. or Eng., 19th C., one in the form of a tall case clock w/ light & dark inlay borders; one w/ three brass acorn finials & arched crest; & one w/ turned urn-form whalebone finials & bun feet, ht. 13in., 10in. & 7½in. **$999**

#146 Funeral Watch Hutch, 18th/19th C., w/ engraved ivory, an incised memorial monument w/ willow branch flanked by split columns & polychrome embellishments, minor imperfections, ht. 5¾in. **$8,225**

DECOYS

Decoys are choice items of collectors and decorators these days. They diligently search for these pieces of floating and sitting sculpture, realizing that many have found their way into antique shops, or are still roosting quietly in old abandoned sheds, waterfront shacks and barns. Floaters are the most popular, followed by shorebird stickups which were never widely made beyond the Atlantic coastal area. In 1918 a Federal law prohibited shooting these diminutive shorebirds; therefore, early stickups are rare. Fish decoys have also become choice collectibles. They are used for ice fishing during the winter months, especially around the Great Lakes.

Many producers of decoys claimed that the most effective decoy was a realistic one, carved and painted to resemble a particular type of bird, while others believed that details didn't really matter; so the difference of opinions resulted in a great variety of decoy styles made from wood, metal, papier-mâché, canvas and rubber. Most found today were made during the late 19th and 20th centuries. Wooden and tin decoys were produced by small manufacturers such as the Mason and Dodge factories.

Most professional carvers marked their birds and examples of their work is extremely valuable. Although many decoys are unsigned, carvers can oftentimes be identified by their style, while others will remain anonymous. Serious collectors prefer to collect the early hand-carved varieties which have become very scarce and expensive.

PG 11 #20

A-ME Apr. 2003   Guyette & Schmidt Inc.

#20 Pintail Drake, Mason Factory, hollow, early 1st qtr. 20th C., w/ orig. paint, premier grade. **$4,000**

PG 11 #21

A-ME Apr. 2003
Guyette &
Schmidt Inc.

#21 Mallards, pair, Mason Factory, 1st qtr. 20th C., hollow challenge grade w/ orig. premier grade paint, minor wear & discoloration. **$1,350**

PG 14 #31, #32

A-ME Apr. 2003   Guyette & Schmidt Inc.

#31 Bobtail Canvasbacks, pair, Mason Factory, premier grade, both w/ orig. paint & moderate flaking & wear. Hen lightly hit by shot. **$2,500**

PG 12 #22, #23

A-ME Apr. 2003   Guyette & Schmidt Inc.

#22 Bluewing Teal Drakes, pair, Mason

Factory, 1st qtr. 20th C., w/ orig. paint, minor wear & dents. **$1,350**

#23 Bluewing Teal Drake, Mason Factory,

1st qtr. 20th C., standard grade w/ cracks, glass eyes, orig. paint & minor wear. **$1,200**

PG 18 #51

A-ME Apr. 2003   Guyette & Schmidt Inc.

#51 **Redheads,** early hollow pair, ca.last qtr. 19th C., w/ dry orig. paint, show minor wear, drake has small chip in tail. **$18,000**

PG 24 #76, #77

A-ME Apr. 2003   Guyette & Schmidt Inc.

#76 **Mallard Drake,** w/ slightly turned head, near mint orig. paint, tiny dents. **$1,500**

#77 **Greenwing Teal Hen,** orig. paint w/ minor discoloration & small dents. **$800**

PG 24 #75

A-ME Apr. 2003   Guyette & Schmidt Inc.

#75 **Canvasback Hen & Drake,** near mint w/ orig. paint, small spots of in use touch up on underside of drake, tiny dents. **$4,200**

PG 12 #24, #25, #26, #27, #28, #29

A-ME Apr. 2003   Guyette & Schmidt Inc.

First Row

#24 **Bluewing Teal Drake,** Mason Factory, standard grade w/ tack eyes & orig. paint, tiny dents & cracks. **$900**

#25 **Bluebill,** Mason Factory, 1st qtr. 20th C., challenge grade w/ orig. paint, minor wear, 3 cracks in body. **$650**

#26 **Black Duck,** Mason Factory, 1st qtr. 20th C., challenge grade, orig. paint w/ minor discoloration, small cracks & dents. **$750**

Second Row

#27 **Bluebill Drake,** Mason Factory, premier grade w/ traces of premier stamp on underside. Orig. paint w/ moderate discoloration & wear, dents. **$1,600**

#28 **Canvasback Hen,** Mason Factory, 1st qtr. 20th C., premier grade w/ orig. paint, moderate wear, small dents & cracks. **$1,200**

#29 **Canvasback Hen,** Mason or Hays Decoy Factory, standard grade with glass eyes. Orig. paint w/ minor flaking; small shot mark in bill & crack on underside. **$500**

DECOYS

PG 28 #92-95

A-ME Apr. 2003   Guyette & Schmidt Inc.

Fish Decoys

#92 **Trout,** western NY State, w/ orig.

paint, flaking, lg. approx. 7¾in. **$3,600**
#93 **Trout,** Lake Chautauqua, NY, metal fins & tail, orig. paint w/ minor flaking and wear, lg. 6¼in. **$2,200**
#94 **Trout,** Lake Chautauqua, NY, metal

fins & leather tail, orig. paint w/ minor flaking, lg. approx. 7in. **$3,150**
#95 **Fish,** Lake Chautauqua, NY, metal fins & tail, orig., excellent, lg. 7¼in. **$1,200**

PG 29 #96-97

A-ME Apr. 2003   Guyette & Schmidt Inc.

Fish Decoys

#96 **Trout,** Lake Chautauqua, NY, metal fins, leather tail, approx. ⅓ tail missing, orig., good, lg. 6in. **$200**
#97 **Trout,** Lake Chautauqua, NY, metal fins, leather tail, orig., very good, lg. 7½in. **$1,900**

PG 29 #98-99

A-ME Apr. 2003   Guyette & Schmidt Inc.

Fish Decoys

#98 **Pan Fish,** Lake Chautauqua, NY, metal fins, leather tail, worn paint, tail replaced, lg. approx. 7in. **$700**
#99 **Fish,** western NY State, metal fins & tail, orig. paint, darkened, excellent, lg. approx. 9in. **$650**

PG 57 #223-225

A-ME Apr. 2003   Guyette & Schmidt Inc.

Spearing Decoys

#223 **Red & White Sunfish,** attrib. to Leroy

Howell, 1st to 2nd qtr. 20th C., tiny chip to tail, orig. excellent, lg. 4¼in. **$300**
#224 **Red & Cream Fish,** attrib. to Leroy Howell, 1st to 2nd qtr. 20th C., minor

wear, orig. excellent, lg. 7¼in. **$350**
#225 **Green Fish,** attrib. to Leroy Howell, 1st to 2nd qtr. 20th C., minor wear to edges, orig. excellent, lg. 7in. **$1,800**

PG 57 #220-222

A-ME Apr. 2003   Guyette & Schmidt Inc.

Spearing Decoys

#220 **Green Fish,** attrib. to Leroy Howell,

1st to 2nd qtr. 20th C., orig. excellent, lg. 7in. **$1,750**
#221 **Gold Fish,** attrib. to Leroy Howell, 1st to 2nd qtr. 20th C., minor paint

chips, orig. excellent, lg. 5in. **$300**
#222 **Green Fish,** attrib. to Leroy Howell, 1st to 2nd qtr. 20th C., minor wear to edges, orig. excellent, lg. 6½in. **$1,450**

PG 29 #100

A-ME Apr. 2003   Guyette & Schmidt Inc.

#100 **Fish Decoys,** two, western NY State, both w/ metal fins, one w/ leather tail, orig. paint, wear. **$1,400**

PG 57 #226

A-ME Apr. 2003   Guyette & Schmidt Inc.

#226 **Fish Decoys,** two, attrib. to Leroy Howell, larger w/ mint orig. paint, minor discoloration on metal fins, other w/ significant wear, lg. approx. 7¼ in & 6½in. **$400**

PG 58 #227, #228-229

A-ME Apr. 2003 Guyette & Schmidt Inc.

#227 **Wood Ducks,** two, Gloucester, MA, 2nd qtr. 20th C., orig. paint w/ good patina, both w/ carved wing tips, minor wear, hairline cracks & tiny dents. **$3,000**

#228 **Bluewing Teal Drake,** Gloucester, MA, 2nd qtr. 20th C., relief wing carving w/ carved wing tips. **$850**

#229 **Merganser Drake,** Mason Factory, challenge grade, repainted by Elmer Crowell, good patina & minor wear, small chip missing from neck filler. **$4,400**

PG 67 #255-256

A-ME Apr. 2003   Guyette & Schmidt Inc.

#255 **Canada Goose,** attrib. to Ed Phillips, early 2nd qtr. 20th C., dry orig. paint w/ old working touchup, drying cracks in body & breast. **$5,250**

#256 **Highhead Canada Goose,** attrib to Ed Phillips, early 2nd qtr. 20th C., dry crackled orig. paint, minor wear, cracks in body, orig. filler unstable in one crack, fractures in lower neck. **$2,000**

PG 76 #303
A-ME Apr. 2003   Guyette & Schmidt Inc.
#303 **Canada Goose,** attrib. to Ben Schmidt, 2nd qtr. 20th C., hollow, detachable head w/ small metal plate at neck seam, near mint orig. paint w/ good patina, tiny chip and crack in tail. **$5,000**

PG 100 #509-511
A-ME Apr. 2003   Guyette & Schmidt Inc.
Shorebirds

#509 **Yellowlegs,** balsa body, carved in running pose, orig. paint w/ minor wear, chip in tail. **$275**
#510 **Yellowlegs,** NJ, orig. paint w/ minor

discoloration and wear, tiny dents. **$350**
#511 **Sandpipers,** pair, flat sided, NJ, ca.1900, orig. paint w/ minor wear, one w/ old varnish. **$400**

PG 100 #512-513
A-ME Apr. 2003   Guyette & Schmidt Inc.
Shorebirds

#512 **Yellowlegs,** two, silhouettes, NJ, ca.1900, one has incised wing carving, orig. paint w/ minor wear, good patina, tiny dents. **$500**

#513 **Black Bellied Plovers,** two, fall plumage, last qtr. 19th C., dry orig. paint w/ minor wear, shot marks; one w/ chip on tail. **$1,000**

PG 100 #514-517
A-ME Apr. 2003   Guyette & Schmidt Inc.
Shorebirds
#514 **Yellowlegs,** NJ, 1st qtr. 20th C., cedar body w/ inserted wood bill, orig. paint w/ flaking & wear, bill scraped

down. **$550**
#515 **Black Bellied Plover,** NJ, ca.1900, slightly flat sided, orig. paint in spring plumage, breast overpainted in winter plumage. **$400**
#516 **Yellowlegs,** running silhouette, NJ,

ca.1900, orig. paint w/ minor to moderate wear, several small cracks. **$450**
#517 **Black Bellied Plover,** incised wing carving, 1st qtr. 20th C., orig. paint, minor wear, rest., small crack on underside. **$400**

DOLLS & DOLL-HOUSES

Dolls come in an incredible variety ranging from the exquisitely dressed French fashion dolls to the fine German bisque dolls made in Meissen, Germany, to humble American folk dolls. Only in recent years have collectors' tastes broadened to include these charming old whimsical dolls which have a timeless quality.

Most dolls sold in America from 1900 to 1910 came from Europe. The First World War practically halted the production of French and German dolls and again during the Second World War dollmaking was disrupted. It wasn't until 1949 that a breakthrough invigorated the doll industry with the invention of hard plastic which quickly solved many problems that had plagued dollmakers. By the 1950s the introduction of soft vinyl resulted in the production of even more realistic dolls.

Modern and vintage dolls, like many toys these days, are throwbacks to dolls made years ago. Trends have a tendency to become fashionable again, only to lose their popularity after a few years and then reappear years later, different but reminiscent of the originals. An example would be cloth advertising dolls that became popular during the early 1900s.

Dolls delight children, but they serve primarily as a very gentle friend on whom they can project their fantasies and to whom they can turn in times of adversity. Today these childhood memories literally set records at auctions across America. Pristine condition contributes significantly to their value.

The earliest doll-houses were made in Germany and Holland. American doll-houses date from the late 1800s and were generally modeled after popular contemporary styles of architecture. The invention of lithography during the mid-19th century supplied manufacturers of doll-houses with an inexpensive means of mass-producing these toys. The R. Bliss Manufacturing Co., Pawtucket, RI, became a major manufacturer round 1904, and the Morton E. Converse Co, Winchendon, MA, one of America's largest manufacturers of toys during the early 1900s, produced a few doll-houses which appeared in the company's 1913 catalog. During the late 1920s A. Schoenhut & Co., Philadelphia, offered an array of colorful doll-houses in various styles and sizes, all of which are prized collectibles these days.

A-NY Mar. 2003

Willis Henry Auctions, Inc.

#10 Jumeau Doll w/ swivel neck, bisque socket head, wrap-around paperweight eyes, orig. mohair wig, kid body, ht. 12in. **$1,667**

A-NY Mar. 2003

Willis Henry Auctions, Inc.

#1 Simon & Halbig K*R Bisque Socket Head Doll w/ mohair wig, fully jointed comp. body, orig. finish, ht. 23in. **$517**

A-NY Mar. 2003

Willis Henry Auctions, Inc.

#25 French Fashion Doll w/ swivel head, painted features, paperweight eyes, mohair wig, not orig., kid body, arms repl., French fashion boots mkd. "I", ht. 16in. **$1,495**

A-NY Mar. 2003
Willis Henry
Auctions, Inc.

#36 Kestner, Bisque Socket Head Doll, early German, eight ball jointed body, ht. 18in. **$2,645**

A-NY Mar. 2003   Willis Henry Auctions, Inc.
#32 **Belton Bisque Socket Head Doll**, late 19th C., w/ mohair wig, paperweight eyes, one repl. upper arm, antique undergarments, French shoes mkd. "I", ht. 14in. **$1,380**

A-NY Mar. 2003 Willis Henry Auctions, Inc.
#53 **Bisque Black Doll** w/ socket head, imp. "12", plaster pate, repl. skin wig, pegged one-piece limbs, kid lined joints, eyes reset, ht. 8in. **$3,220**

A-ME June 2003   James D. Julia, Inc.
#1 **Simon & Halbig Doll**, "A-14T", bisque on repainted comp. body, clothing & repl. wig, ht. 28in. **$258**

A-ME June 2003 James D. Julia, Inc.
#2 **Kestner 146 Doll**, ball jointed comp. body, repl. clothing, bisque head has tiny chip in corner of doll's left eye, ht. 24in. **$300**

A-ME June 2003 James D. Julia, Inc.
#3 **C.M. Bergmann Doll**, German, antique dress w/ orig. shoes, wig & socks repl., ht. 22in. **$345**

A-ME June 2003 James D. Julia, Inc.
#4 **S.P.B.H. Doll**, German, ball jointed comp. body, repl. clothing & human hair wig, body has been repainted, ht. 30in. **$420**

A-ME June 2003 James D. Julia, Inc.
#5 **D.E.P. Doll**, German made for French market on French comp. body, new costume, paint rest. to body, ht. 30in. **$517**

A-ME June 2003 James D. Julia, Inc.
#6 **Simon & Halbig Doll**, German, comp. body is orig. finish but has craquelure, redressed, repl. wig, ht. 30in. **$488**

A-ME June 2003 James D. Julia, Inc.
#7 **Unis France**, French child doll on a ball joint comp. body, re-dressed & repl. wig, ht. 31in. **$805**

A-ME June 2003   James D. Julia, Inc.

#31 K*R Doll, pale bisque, doll has pull strings that say "Mama," "Papa," ht. 29in. $1,495

A-ME June 2003   James D. Julia, Inc.

#32 K*R Doll, comp., ball jointed body, re-dressed & repl. wig, ht. 29in. $575

A-ME June 2003   James D. Julia, Inc.

#33 German Doll, bisque w/ turned-head, kid body, repl. clothes, orig. wig, ht. 18in. $977

A-ME June 2003   James D. Julia, Inc.

#34 German Fashion Doll w/ swivel neck on bisque shoulder plate, all kid body, repl. clothing & wig, retains orig. shoes, reset eyes & body repr., ht. 32in. $1,200

A-ME June 2003   James D. Julia, Inc.

#35 Bergmann/Simon & Halbig Doll w/ jointed comp. body, clothing & repl. wig, ht. 30in. $517

A-ME June 2003   James D. Julia, Inc.

#36 Bergmann/Simon & Halbig Doll w/ ball jointed comp. body, clothing & repl. wig, ht. 32in. $480

A-ME June 2003   James D. Julia, Inc.

#37 A.B.G. Doll w/ ball-jointed comp. body, wired for leg activation, head turning & voice box, clothing repl., ht. 34in. $600

A-ME June 2003   James D. Julia, Inc.

#38 Simon & Halbig Doll w/ jointed German comp. body, restoration to head & comp. hands, ht. 32in. $600

A-ME June 2003   James D. Julia, Inc.

#39 K*R Baby Doll, life-size w/ orig. clothing & wig, prof. restor. body & one finger glued, ht. 39in. $690

A-ME June 2003   James D. Julia, Inc.

#41 Heubach Kopplesdorf Doll w/ ball jointed comp. body, redressed & repl. wig, ht. 33in. **$575**

A-ME June 2003   James D. Julia, Inc.

#42 Kestner Doll, early Kestner on chunky comp. body, dressed in antique white clothing, repl. human wig ht. 31in. **$2,645**

A-ME June 2003   James D. Julia, Inc.

#40 Portrait Jumeau Doll, 1st series, mkd., w/ orig. eight ball jointed body, repainted, clothing & repl. wig, doll has slight nose rub & minute scuff to right cheek, ht. 14½in. **$8,625**

A-ME June 2003   James D. Julia, Inc.

#43 A.M. Doll, German w/ ball jointed comp. body, redressed & repl. wig, body all orig. except hands, ht. 40in. **$1,667**

A-ME June 2003   James D. Julia, Inc.

#30 Bru Doll w/ pristine kid body & remnants of orig. wig, but now repl., rear of head mkd. w/ "I" w/ circle dot crescent below, clothes later repl., ht. 17in. **$13,512**

A-ME June 2003   James D. Julia, Inc.

#44 Handwerck/Halbig Boy Doll w/ ball jointed comp. body, re-dressed & repl. wig, ht. 41in. **$4,025**

A-ME June 2003   James D. Julia, Inc.

#45 Handwerck/Simon & Halbig Doll w/ jointed comp. body, re-dressed & new wig, pate is glued tight & left leg detached, ht. 42in. **$5,290**

A-ME June 2003   James D. Julia, Inc.

#46 Simon & Halbig 1906 Doll w/ brown human hair wig, re-dressed, mkd. w/ date, ht. 40in. **$2,070**

A-ME June 2003   James D. Julia, Inc.

#55 **German Doll** w/ jointed comp. body, repl. clothing & wig, ht. 23in. **$201**

A-ME June 2003   James D. Julia, Inc.

#56 **French Fashion Doll** w/ bisque socket head, kid body & orig. silk dress & underclothes, repair to right arm, ht. 12½in. **$1,440**

A-ME June 2003   James D. Julia, Inc.

#57 **Simon & Halbig Doll** w/ jointed comp. body, orig. blond human hair wig & dressed in antique white dress & baby shoes, ht. 34in. **$1,552**

A-ME June 2003   James D. Julia, Inc.

#63 **Jumeau Doll,** body restored, repl. clothing & wig, retains orig. spring in head, ht. 22in. **$3,335**

A-ME June 2003   James D. Julia, Inc.

#64 **German "Viola" Doll** w/ jointed comp. body w/ repl. clothing & wig, ht. 24in. **$316**

A-ME Nov. 2002   James D. Julia, Inc.

#259 **Doll Carriages,** one w/ hinged top & plastic windows, wire & wood wheels, wood handle, ht. 25in., one w/ small wicker carriage w/ hinged hood, wire & rubber wheels, ht. 23in. **$230**

A-ME Nov. 2002   James D. Julia, Inc.

#260 **Wicker Rolled Edge Doll Carriage** by Whitney Carriage Co., painted white, undercarriage in metal w/ brown paint, ht. 37in. **$172**

A-ME Nov. 2002   James D. Julia, Inc.

#261 **Doll Carriage,** painted & lithographed w/ simulated leather seat & fringed canopy. Wood frame w/ red paint w/ black & gold stenciling, wear to paint, ht. 27in. **$345**

A-ME Nov. 2002   James D. Julia, Inc.

#262 **Doll Trunks,** dome top w/ paper covering, fitted interior w/ one lid missing & some damage to covering together w/ flat top trunk w/ compartmented tray & lid, key is present & two leather straps for securing, ht. 9in. **$150**

A-ME Nov. 2002

James D. Julia, Inc.

#263 Painted Doll Carriage w/ wood wheels, blue body w/ wood & spring under carriage, the tall fringed canopy is supported by metal brackets, repair to top area, ht. 23in. **$373**

A-ME Nov. 2002

James D. Julia, Inc.

#264 Doll Carriage, Metal Padded by Prince Products w/ swinging hood, wheel fenders w/ rubber tires & metal spoke wheels, one tear to inside upholstery, nicks & scrapes to paint, ht. 28in. **$90**

A-ME Nov. 2002

James D. Julia, Inc.

#201 Two Child's Press-Back Rocking Chairs, old finish, ht. approx. 28in. **$345**

A-ME Nov. 2002

James D. Julia, Inc.

#202 Child's Oak Combination High Chair, baby walker or rocking chair w/ collapsible pressed back device by Waite Chair Co., pat. 3/17/1885, ht. approx. 42in. **$258**

A-ME June 2003

James D. Julia, Inc.

#20 French Closed Mouth Bebe Doll, mkd. "A.14 T" (A. Thullier) on rear of head, antique shoes mkd. "Bebe Jumeau 12", comp. body repainted, w/ pepper flakes on chin & jaw, ht. 30in. **$21,275**

A-ME Nov. 2002

James D. Julia, Inc.

#273 Shirley Temple Doll, composition w/ orig. wig & dress, mkd. "Shirley Temple Ideal," w/ pin, slight crazing on face, ht. 18in. **$360**

A-ME Nov. 2002

James D. Julia, Inc

#283 High Brow China Head Doll w/ old dress, cloth body soiled, hands repaired, ht. 21in. **$460**

A-ME Nov. 2002   James D. Julia, Inc.

#154 Doll-house, German by Gottschalk, new brick paper applied many years ago, some paint rest. to white woodwork & base, most of interior orig., ht. 29, wd. 22, dp. 15in. **$1,560**

A-ME Nov. 2002   James D. Julia, Inc.

#158 Doll-house, paper litho, attrib. to Moritz Gottschalk, German, w/ some discoloration to paper & loss, ht. 25, wd. 18, dp. 11in. **$1,035**

A-ME Nov. 2002   James D. Julia, Inc.

#161 Bliss Doll-house, paper litho simulating stone, brick & clapboard w/ eisenglass windows, interior all orig. except 2nd floor, minor paper loss & some fading, ht. 13in. **$600**

The furnishings of America's past had a particular flair... functionalism that was the natural design expression of a country where practicality meant survival. The bulk of the early furniture was utilitarian and commonplace, made to serve a useful purpose. The earliest cabinetmakers were generally itinerant craftsmen who borrowed their ideas from several periods, oftentimes adding a bit of individuality of their own. Therefore, furniture produced in America was a combination of Yankee ingenuity in adopting revered Old World styling to New World materials, resulting in furniture having a timeless appeal in uniqueness that is purely American, with simplicity of line being its most characteristic feature.

As our population increases and collectors become more knowledgeable, no other field has attracted more attention than furniture from all periods. This chapter includes a variety of case pieces... that is furniture that encloses a space such as cabinets, chests of drawers, cupboards, desks, sideboards and the linen press. In addition, a variety of many other furnishings are included. Each illustrated entry describes the object, its condition and provides historical background information when available. Surprisingly, even restoration and repairs have become more acceptable these days. However, when the original finish or decoration has been removed from a period – or just an elderly – piece of furniture, it reduces the value substantially.

Because of the quality of much mass-produced furniture today, combined with the demand for and unavailability of quality, there has become an increased demand for custom-made furniture from all periods by well recognized cabinetmakers. Many of these pieces will become the sought-after antiques of tomorrow.

A-NH Nov. 2002   Northeast Auctions
#645 **Sheraton Canopy Bed,** N.H., red paint, footposts w/ reeding, ht. 67in., wd. 55in., lg. 78in. **$4,000**

A-NH Aug. 2003   Northeast Auctions
#616 **Canopy Bed,** NH, Sheraton, orig. red, probably Portsmouth, footposts w/ delicate ring turnings, pencil-post headposts, ht. 85in., lg. 75in. **$3,500**
#617 **Toile Curtains,** partial set, red & white "Am. Presenting at the Altar of Liberty...", six curtains, lg. 7ft.5in., plus additional panel. **$1,200**

A-NH Nov. 2002   Northeast Auctions
#661 **Sheraton Tall-Post Bedstead** w/ canopy, birch, urn turned finials & reeded baluster & foliate carving tapering to feet, incl. rails & canopy, ht. 74in. lg. 75in. **$2,250**

FURNITURE

#271 Four-Poster Bed, PA, ca.1820, retains old green painted surface, ht. 81in., wd. 53in., lg. 78in. **$3,450**

#272 Trundle Bed, early 19th C., retains an old salmon painted surface, ht. 13in., wd. 43½in., lg. 65in. **$460**

Biedermeier & Parian Figures

#247 Daybed, fruitwood & ebonized, ends inlaid w/ panels of stylized flowers & foliage, lg. 73in. **$1,900**

#248 Parian Figures of Paul & Virginia, each imp. "Copeland" behind base, ref: "The Parian Phenomenon", pg. 150, hts. 15in. & 13½in. **$300**

#249 Commode, inlaid-beech w/ different

geometric designs, ht. 30in., wd. 31in. **$2,000**

#250 Empire Dressing Table, fruitwood & ebonized, ht. 57¾in., wd. 42in. **$3,000**

A-NH Aug. 2003   Northeast Auctions

#1039 Canopy Bedstead, N. Eng., Sheraton, tiger maple w/
ring turnings, ht. w/ canopy 85in., wd. 57in., lg. 77in.
$4,000

A-NH Aug. 2003   Northeast Auctions

#807 Tester Bedstead, Philadelphia, Hepplewhite, mah. w/
acanthus drapery, cord & tassel carving on sq. tapered legs, ht.
91in., wd. 63in., lg. 80in. **$9,500**

A-PA May 2003   Pook & Pook Inc.

#125 Tall Post Bed, Sheraton, PA, bird's-eye maple, ca.1830
w/ bold turned posts & orig. flat tester, ht. 8ft.7in., wd. 54in.
$2,530

A-NH Mar. 2003   Northeast Auctions

#561 Hepplewhite Bedstead, N. Eng., birch, pencil post in red
paint, incl. rails, ht. 85in., wd. 52½in. **$5,500**

FURNITURE

A-NH Nov. 2002

Northeast Auctions

#159 Sheraton Pine Harvest Table w/ drawer, ht. 29½in., lg. 96½in., wd. 43½in. $10,000

#160 Rodback Windsor Side Chairs, N. Eng., w/ plank seats & box stretchers. $1,500

A-NH Mar. 2003   Northeast Auctions

#540 Q.A. Side Chairs, set of six, w/ molded crests & arched shoulders, Spanish feet. $18,000

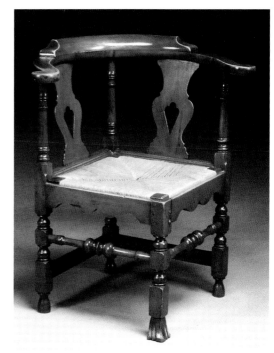

A-NH Nov. 2002   Northeast Auctions
#635 **Q.A. Side Chair,** N. Eng., walnut w/ slip seat. **$6,000**
#636 **Q.A. Side Chair,** N. Eng., walnut w/ slip seat, **$4,800**

A-NH Nov. 2002   Northeast Auctions
#630 **Corner Chair,** CT, ca.1720-1740, cherry w/ rush slip-seat & Spanish feet. **$2,400**

A-NH Nov. 2002   Northeast Auctions
#518 **Fanback Windsor Side Chairs** w/ bamboo raked legs, N. Eng., ht. 39½in. **$2,000**

481

A-SC Dec. 2002
                          Charlton Hall Galleries, Inc.
#481 **Q.A. Corner Chair,** MA, ca.1750, mah. w/ old rest., ht. 34in., wd. 16½in. **$3,600**

A-PA Feb. 2003   Pook & Pook Inc.
#100 **Chippendale Dining Chairs,** DE Valley, walnut, ca.1770, cabriole legs w/ shell carved knees, ball & claw feet. **$29,900**

FURNITURE

A-NH Aug. 2003

Northeast Auctions

#920 Bowback Windsor Chairs, set of 12 w/ braces, incl. 4 armchairs w/ incised outlines. **$30,000**

A-NJ Dec. 2002   **Treadway Gallery Inc.**

#406 Settle, Lifetime w/ orig. finish, sgn. w/ paper label, recovered leather cushions, wd. 82in., dp. 33in., ht. 31in. **$3,750**

A-NJ Dec. 2002   **Treadway Gallery Inc.**

#408 Settle, Lifetime w/ orig. finish, sgn. w/ paper label, recovered cushion, wd. 62in., dp. 29in. ht. 31in. **$2,400**

Opposite

A-IA Oct. 2002

Jackson's International Auctioneers

#793 Mammy Bench, pine & maple, painted black w/ gilt pinstripes, early 19th C., lg. 4in. **$201**

#794 Immigrants Chest, 19th C. w/ polychrome dec. & wrought iron hardware, lg. 61in., ht. 22in. **$143**

#795 Pine Settee, 19th C. w/ applied dec. & lift top seats, lg. 46in. **$230**

#796 Bread Maker's Table, 19th C. w/ wood pegged const., wear, ht. 34in. **$431**

#797 Pine Settle w/ scrolled back & later dec., lg. 74in., ht. 35in. **$172**

#798 Maple Field Cradle w/ bent ribs & iron wheels, 19th C., orig. lg. 44in. **$143**

#799 Mission Oak Rocker w/ orig. finish, mkd. "Limbert", ht. 30in. **$258**

#800 Mission Oak Rocker w/ repl. leather seat, mkd. Knaus. **$201**

#801 Victorian Writing Desk, oak w/ tambour top, orig. cond., ht. 53in. **$345**

#802 Oak Hall Tree, ca.1915 w/ oval beveled mirror, iron hooks & umbrella

rests, ht. 79in. **$258**

#803 Oak Ice Box w/ orig. finish & in excellent condition, ht. 38in., wd. 19in. **$402**

#804 Sectional File Cabinet, three sections, six drawers of various sizes, ht. 46in., wd. 18in. **$373**

#805 Music Cabinet, ca.1925 w/ layered pine wood strip const. in a concentric rectangle patt., ht. 38in., wd. 15in. **$948**

#806 Drop-Front Secretary, Victorian w/ mirror, mah. finish, ht. 48in. **$258**

#793

#794

#795

#796

#797

#798

#799

#800

#801

#802

#803

#804

#805

#806

FURNITURE

A-NH Nov. 2002

Northeast Auctions

#498 Captain's Chairs, assembled set of 8, N. Eng., orig. rosewood graining & mustard striping, some w/ initials "O.B" under seats. **$4,750**

A-NH Nov. 2002

Northeast Auctions

#649 Banister-Back Armchair, early Am. w/ sausage turnings, double arched crest above four split banisters w/ flanking knopped stiles, double box stretcher. **$1,500**
#650 Brass Candlesticks, pr., Eng. on dished octagonal bases, ht.5½in. **$500**
#651 Candlestand, pine & birch, N. Eng., sq. top above pedestal w/ urn turning, cabriole legs w/ pad feet, ht. 25½in., top 13½in. x 15½in. **$650**
#652 Banister-Back Armchair, early Am. w/ sausage turnings, shaped rails & rush seat, double box stretcher w/ modified front paired baluster & reel turning. **$2,000**

A-NH Nov. 2002   Northeast Auctions

#665 Fanback Windsor Side Chairs, set of 6, arched crest w/ upturned ears, shaped seat on raked legs. **$2,500**

A-NH Nov. 2002   Northeast Auctions

#654 **Banister-Back Armchair,** early Am., w/ shaped crest & sausage turned legs, split banisters, double box stretcher. **$2,000**

#655 **English Brass Candlesticks,** set of 4, ea. w/ ringed candlecup & sq. cut corner base w/dished tray, ht. 6in. **$750**

#656 **Q.A. Dish-Top Stand,** mah., N. Eng., raised molded edge, flaring pedestal, arched cabriole legs w/ pointed pad feet on platforms, ht. 28in., dia. 10 ½in. **$800**

#657 **Banister-Back Armchair,** early Am. w/ arched crest, turned posts w/ urn finials, rush seat, block turned legs, front paired baluster & reel turning. **$2,000**

A-NH Nov. 2002   Northeast Auctions

#733 **Q.A. Wing Chair,** mah., Eng., bowed seat cushion, carved knees & scrolling returns on pad feet w/ disks, ht. 46½in. **$4,500**

A-NH Nov. 2002   Northeast Auctions

#1175 **George III Side Chairs,** pr., walnut, ea. w/ slightly arched crest, over-upholstered seat, recessed box stretcher. **$1,300**

#1176 **Q.A. Gaming Table,** walnut w/ outset sq. corners, front cabriole legs w/ leaf carved knees, scrolled returns on pad feet, ht. 28½in., top 15¾in. x 32in. **$2,400**

#1177 **Q.A. Side Chair,** mah., raised yoke rest, vasiform splat, slip-seat, front cabriole legs, pad feet. **$700**

#1178 **Q.A. Drop-Leaf Table,** walnut, hinged leaves w/ rounded ends, arcaded apron on turned legs w/ pad feet on disks, ht. 27in., lg. 27in. **$1,200**

#1179 **Candlesticks,** pr., heavy brass, now w/ tin shades, ht. 20½in. **$1,100**

#1180 **Q.A. Wall Mirror,** walnut w/ two glass plates, ht. 21½in. **$1,800**

FURNITURE

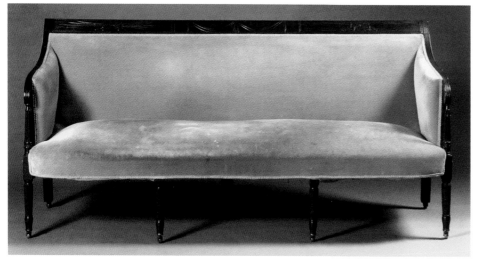

A-NH Mar. 2003   Northeast Auctions

#565 **Sheraton Sofa,** NY by Duncan Phyfe, mah., crest w/ bowknot & thunderbolts centering a panel w/ swagged drapery, reeded arms & legs, brass casters, lg. 77½in. **$13,000**

A-MA Nov. 2002   Skinner, Inc.

#730 **Federal Mah. Easy Chair,** possibly PA, ca.1790, sq. tapering front legs w/ inlaid panels, ht. 43½in., dp. 27in. **$7,050**

A-NH Aug. 2003   Northeast Auctions

#727 **Windsor Settee,** bamboo turned, possibly PA, scribed borders above turned spindles, plank seat, lg. 45in. **$12,000**

A-MA Aug. 2003
   Robert C. Eldred Co., Inc.
#1002 **Lolling Chair,** Am., mah. w/ molded arms & box stretcher. **$3,680**

1002

A-NH Aug. 2003

Northeast Auctions

#1048 **Sofa,** MA, Sheraton, mah. w/ carved shoulders on curved supports on swelled reeded legs, upholstered (new), lg. 75in. **$1,750**

A-MA Nov. 2002   Skinner, Inc.

#576 **Windsor Painted Arm Chair,** N. Eng., late 18th C., w/ old surface, imper., ht. 38½in. **$7,050**

A-MA Nov. 2002   Skinner, Inc.

#605 **Comb-back Windsor Armchair,** CT, ca.1780-90 w/ old surface, ht. 37in. **$3,819**

A-MA Nov. 2002   Skinner, Inc.

#750 **Transitional Cherry Sofa,** late 18th to early 19th C., CT, old refinish, rest., ht. 42in., lg. 80in. **$12,925**

A-NH Aug. 2003   Northeast Auctions

#765 **Sheraton Sofa,** N. Eng., mah., w/ loose seat cushion above a conforming upholstered rail & ring turned tapering reeded front legs, ht. 32in., lg. 72in. **$12,000**

FURNITURE

A-MA June 2003   **Skinner, Inc.**

#7 Roundabout Chair, Chippendale mah., Newport RI, 1760-90, similar rear leg does not have carving, old ref., rest., ht 31¼in. **$8,813**

A-NH Aug. 2003   **Northeast Auctions**

#1051 Sofa, MA, Sheraton, bird's eye maple & mah. w/ flat upholstered (new) back, lg. 75in. **$4,250**

A-SC June 2003

      Charlton Hall Galleries, Inc.

Stools

#598 Georgian, mah., late 19th C., w/ needlework top & padded snake feet, ht. 19½in. **$500**

#599 George III, mah., pair, each w/ crewel-work upholstery w/ scroll feet, ht. 18in. **$425**

#600 Victorian, early 20th C., w/ needlepoint top, stained, ht. 14in. **$125**

A-NH May 2003   **Northeast Auctions**

Late Biedermeier

#242 Stool, mah. w/ square slip seat, ht. 16½in., top 19½in. sq. **$500**

#243 Bedside Cabinets, pr., mah. &

ebonized, ht. 28in., wd. 18¾in. **$2,000**

#244 Recamier, walnut, adjustable, the left side w/ folding footrest, lg. closed 52¼in., open 66in. **$1,500**

#245 Stools, neo-classical style, walnut

curule-form stools, ht. 18¾in. **$3,000**

#246 Sewing Stand, walnut w/ a pincushion on cover, ht. 29½in. **$500**

A-NH Aug. 2003 **Northeast Auctions**
#690 **Arrowback Chairs,** set of four, N. Eng. Sheraton, green painted & dec. w/ shaped rush seat on ball & rib turned tapering legs on ball feet, incl. an armchair w/ scrolled arms. **$1,750**
#691 **Chest of Drawers,** N. Eng. pine in yellow painted w/ grape & vine dec., ring turned columns supported by turned feet, ht. 43in., wd. 43in. **$3,000**

A-NH Aug. 2003

Northeast Auctions
#732 **Q.A. Candlestand,** Salem, MA, mah., w/ serpentine edge, ht 26½in., dia. 17in. **$6,000**
#733 **Lolling Chair,** Chippendale, MA, mah. w/ molded legs joined by a box stretcher. **$6,000**

168

169

1

A-MA Nov. 2002   Skinner, Inc.

#1011 **Windsor Rocking Chair,** thumb-back, N. Eng., ca.1830 w/ all-over mustard yellow paint w/ polychrome dec., orig. surface, minor surface imper., ht. 30in. **$470**

A-MA Aug. 2003   Fontaine's Auctions, LLC

Belter Laminated Furniture
Rosalie w/ Grapes Pattern, ca.1855
#168 **Armchair** w/ carved crest, ht. 43in. **$3,200**
#169 **Armchair** w/ carved crest, ht. 43in. **$4,200**
#170 **Sofa** w/ carved crest, ht. 42in., wd. 83in. **$6,000**

Opposite

A-IA Mar. 2003

Jackson's International Auctioneers

#698 **Pump Organ,** Story & Clark, w/ pink & white porcelain pulls, bellows need repr. **$57**
#699 **Pump Organ,** by Smith, walnut case w/ orig. finish, includes stool. **$86**
#700 **Victorian Chair,** Louis XV style w/ pink floral silk upholstery, mid-20th C. **$345**
#701 **Side Chair,** Victorian Renaissance Revival style. **$149**

#702 **Victorian Arm Chair,** Louis XV style, mid-20th C., w/ foot stool. **$201**
#703 **Eastlake Center Table** w/ rectangular top. **$86**
#704 **Marble Top Table,** mid-Victorian w/ spoon carved decoration on flat surfaces. **$257**
#705 **Continental Table** w/ ormolu dec. & satin-lined curio cabinet in top. **$201**
#706 **Drop Leaf Kitchen Table,** walnut, ht. 30in. **$80**
#707 **Sofa** w/ medallion back, Louis XV

style, ca.mid-20th C. **$517**
#708 **Side Chairs,** pr., Louis XV style, ca.mid-20th C. **$517**
#709 **Bench,** oak, Arts & Crafts style, lg. 41in. **$632**
#710 **Table,** oak w/ three leaves & octagon pedestal, ht. 30in., dia. 50in. **$431**
#711 **Dining Chairs,** oak, set of 6, ht. 41in. **$287**

#698

#699

#700

#701

#702

#703

#704

#705

#706

#707

#708

#709

#710

#711

FURNITURE

A-MA June 2003   Skinner, Inc.

#78 Windsor Fan-Back Side Chairs, set of 4, painted, CT, late 18th C., old black paint, one repr. spindle, ht. 37½in. **$4,700**

A-NH Aug. 2003   Northeast Auctions

#182 Settee, N. Eng., Sheraton, tiger maple double chairback, ht. 27in., lg. 36in. **$3,600**

#183 Blanket Chest, N. Eng., tiger maple w/ drawer, ht. 32in., top 37in. x 17in. **$3,750**

A-PA Nov. 2002   Pook & Pook Inc.

#348 Daybed, N. Eng., Wm. & Mary, ca.1720, maple w/ carved crest over vasiform splat flanked by square styles supported by blocked legs joined by stretchers, some rest., lg. 72in. **$1,380**

A-NH May 2003

Northeast Auctions

#166 Dining Chairs, George II, mah., set of 6 w/ legs carved at knees w/ leaftips & ending in hairy paw feet. **$16,000**

A-PA Sept. 2003   Pook & Pook Inc.

Banister Back Chairs
#121 Armchair, N. Eng., maple, ca.1740 w/ carved crest & ram's horn arms. **$633**
#122 Armchair, N. Eng., figured ash & maple, ca.1740. **$2,070**
#123 Armchair, N. Eng., maple & figured maple, ca.1740. **$1,035**

423

424

A-MA Feb. 2003
Skinner, Inc.

#423 Classical Sofa, carved mah., probably N. Eng., 1830-40, w/ flattened ball feet on casters, old surface, imper., ht. 35¾in., lg. 88in. **$1,175**
#424 Classical Center Table, mah. w/ marble top, Boston, ca.1830, imper., ht. 28in., dia. 35in. **$2,233**

A-PA Sept. 2003
        Pook & Pook Inc.
#425 Sofa, Philadelphia Chippendale, mah., ca.1785, w/ Marlborough legs joined by stretchers, ht. 42in., wd. 89in. **$27,600**

A-PA May 2003   Pook & Pook Inc.

#130 **Dower Chest** by Johann Rank, dated 1798 w/ all brown stippled ground & dec. w/ three salmon & ivory double arched tombstone panels enclosing five stylized tulips arising from an urn incised w/ the maker's name & date. ht. 22½in., wd. 51in. dp. 22¼in. **$20,700**

A-PA Oct. 2002   Pook & Pook Inc.

#206 **Spice Chest,** ca.1760, Chester Co., PA, walnut w/ herringbone, line & berry inlaid door opening to an int. w/ 11 sm. spice drawers, ht. 18in., wd. 15½in. **$115,000**

A-PA Feb. 2003   Pook & Pook Inc.

#278 **Dower Chest,** Lebanon County, PA, ca.1810, dec. w/ ivory tombstone panels, red ground, straight bracket feet, ht. 20½in., wd. 47in. **$1,380**

A-PA Sept. 2003   Pook & Pook Inc.

#450 **Blanket Chest,** PA, pine w/ painted dec., attrib. to David Y. Ellinger (1913-2003), ht. 28½in., wd. 41½in. **$14,950**

A-PA Sept. 2002   Pook & Pook Inc.

#250. **Dower Chest,** Dauphin County, PA, dated 1803, molded lift lid, inscription of Anna Marie Harman, overall dec., black ogee bracket feet, red moldings, underside of lid retains remnants of fraktur drawing, ht. 27in., wd. 48½in. **$280,000**

A-PA Feb. 2003   Pook & Pook Inc.

#173 Blanket Chest, PA, poplar, ca.1820, dov. case, drawers w/ orig. brass pulls, ogee bracket feet, orig. salmon & ochre grained surface, ht. 30in., wd. 48in. **$5,175**

A-PA Sept. 2003   Pook & Pook Inc.

#290 Dower Chest, Lancaster, PA, by the Embroidery Artist, dated 1788, ht. 27in., wd. 52in. dp. 23in. **$55,200**

007   *008*

A-SC Dec. 2002   Charlton Hall Galleries, Inc.

#007 Miniature Chest of Drawers, mah., early 19th C., w/ partial separation to top, ht. 11½in., wd. 13in. **$550**

#008 Miniature English Chest of Drawers, mah., sgn. S. Towne & dated Feb. 4, 1823, ht. 13½in., wd. 12½in. **$1,600**

A-SC June 2003   Charlton Hall Galleries, Inc.

#633 Blanket Chest, Am., pine, painted, early 19th C., old repr., ht. 39in., wd. 40in. **$750**

A-OH Oct. 2003   Garth's Arts & Antiques

#24 Soap Hollow Chest, poplar w/ orig. black over red grained dec. & yellow line borders around the drawers, mkd. w/ initials "J.W." & dated 1850, side panels dec. w/ vases of tulips & roses, back splash is missing, ht. 46in., wd. 36¾in. **$6,900**

FURNITURE

A-PA Feb. 2003   Pook & Pook Inc.

#110 **Blanket Chest,** PA, painted pine, ca.1820 w/ lift lid, turned feet, ht. 29½in., wd. 39in. **$2,070**

336

A-PA Feb. 2003   Pook & Pook Inc.

#336 **Blanket Chest,** PA, poplar, vibrant red & black grain dec., paneled case on turned feet, ht. 24 in., wd. 39in. **$3,163**

A-NH Mar. 2003   Northeast Auctions

#460 **Chippendale Chest of Drawers,** N. Eng., cherry, serpentine front, beaded dividers, ht. 33¾in., wd. 39in. **$3,750**

A-NH Mar. 2003   Northeast Auctions

#461 **Chippendale Chest of Drawers,** walnut & yellow pine, possibly Southern, ogee bracket feet, ht. 35½in., wd. 39¾in. **$4,400**

A-NH Mar. 2003   Northeast Auctions
#531 Chippendale Chest of Drawers, MA, mah. oxbow, serpentine front w/ molded edge, drawers w/ beaded dividers, base molding, cabriole legs on ball & claw feet, ht. 35in., wd. 34½in. **$35,000**

A-NH Mar. 2003   Northeast Auctions
#547 Chippendale Chest of Drawers, Salem, birch, top w/ serpentine front, center drop w/ carved ends, central demilune shell on cabriole legs, ball & claw feet, ht. 33½in., wd. 36in. **$17,000**

A-NH Mar. 2003   Northeast Auctions
#597 Chippendale Chest of Drawers, N. Eng., birch, molded edge, bracket base w/ shaped returns, orig. bail brasses. **$3,000**

A-NH Mar. 2003   Northeast Auctions
#445 Chippendale Chest of Drawers, CT, cherry, scratch beaded outline on base molding w/ ogee bracket feet, ht. 37in., wd. 38½in. **$4,750**

FURNITURE

A-NH Mar. 2003   Northeast Auctions

#637 Federal Chest of Drawers, mah., inlaid edge, drawers w/ crossbanding, stringing & beaded edge, base molding w/ straight bracket feet, ht. 35¼in., wd. 39¾in. **$3,800**

A-NH Nov. 2002   Northeast Auctions

#642 Chippendale Chest of Drawers, Boston or Salem, MA, mah. oxbow, blocked ends, serpentine front w/ molded edge, base molding on ogee bracket feet, ht. 32¼in., wd. 34¾in. **$8,000**

A-NH Mar. 2003   Northeast Auctions

#648 Hepplewhite Chest of Drawers, N. Eng., mah., bowfront, inlaid edge, drawers & skirt w/ contrasting banding, French feet, ht. 36¼in., wd. 41in. **$4,750**

A-NH Mar. 2003   Northeast Auctions

#686 Federal Chest of Drawers, MA, mah., bowfront, contrasting banding edge, drawers w/ beading & stringing, raised French feet, silvered brasses marked "H&B", ht. 38¼in. wd. 39¼in. **$5,000**

A-MA Nov. 2002   Skinner, Inc.

#726 Federal Bowfront Chest of Drawers, mah. veneer, NH, early 19th C., top w/ bowed front & cockbeaded drawers, inlays, old refinish, repl. brass, imper., ht. 38in., wd. 43in., dp. 21¾in. **$1,880**

A-NH Aug. 2003   Northeast Auctions

#762 Sheraton Chest of Drawers, MA, mah. w/ turret ends, Seymour School, banded & inlaid knobs & contrasting escutcheon, reeded & ring turned stiles over tapering feet, ht. 39in. wd., 43in. **$6,000**

A-NH Nov. 2002   Northeast Auctions

#706 Chippendale Lowboy, PA, walnut, ball & claw feet, thumbmolded drawers, elaborate apron on cabriole legs, ht. 29½in. wd. 32in., top 20in. x 36½in. **$13,000**

A-MA June 2003   Skinner, Inc.

#44 Chest of Drawers, Federal, cherry & maple w/inlay, ca.1815, each drawer w/an elongated cherry oval set in mitered mah. panels w/ivory urn escutcheon, old refinish, minor imper., ht. 42in., wd. 44in. **$8,225**

A-NH Mar. 2003   Northeast Auctions

#513 **Q.A. High Chest,** cherry wood, secondary wood pine, carved maple flat-top, shaped skirt outlined by beaded edge above cabriole legs, Spanish feet, sgn., ht. 76in., wd. 39in. **$35,000**

A-PA Feb. 2003   Pook & Pook Inc.

#117 **Federal Chest of Drawers,** PA, tiger maple w/ drawers flanked by chamfered stiles, flaring French feet, ht. 45½in. wd. 36in. **$3,680**

A-SC Dec. 2002   Charlton Hall Galleries, Inc.

#011 **Miniature Chest of Drawers,** mah., ca.1830, beveled top above frieze w/ hidden drawer, moulded base w/ shaped feet, nicks, separation to top. **$700**

#012 **Letter Box,** mah., English, ca.1850, in the form of a slant-front desk, top w/ compartments & tray, lower has fitted int. w/ glass & brass inkwells, brass feet, repr. & wear, ht. 10¾in., wd. 12½in., dp. 7¼in. **$250**

#013 **Miniature Chest of Drawers,** mah., English, 19th C., molded edge top w/ 12 narrow drawers, molded base w/ acorn feet, minor scuffs, ht. 10in., wd. 14½in. **$325**

A-NH Nov. 2002

Northeast Auctions

#626 Chippendale Chest-On-Chest, closed bonnet top, CT, ca.1770-1780, attrib. to Aimeon Pomeroy, orig. brasses, ht. 81½in., wd. 36in., dp. 19½in. **$30,000**

A-OH Jan. 2003

Garth's Auctions, Inc.

#56 Q.A. High Chest, two pieces, birch & pine w/ old deep red wash, w/ dov. drawers incl. one hidden inside cornice, ht. 71in., 39in. at waist molding. **$33,000**

180

A-PA Feb. 2003

Pook & Pook Inc.

#180 Chippendale Tall Chest, CT, cherry, ca.1770, two parts, upper w/ compass & herringbone inlays, base w/ cabriole legs & ball & claw feet, ht. 84in., wd. 43¾in. **$20,700**

A-PA Feb. 2003

Pook & Pook Inc.

#255 Chippendale High Chest, PA, walnut, ca.1780, stepped cornice, flanked by fluted quarter columns, ogee feet w/ shaped returns, lacking sm. frieze molding, ht. 67in., wd. 40in. **$9,200**

FURNITURE

A-NH Mar. 2003

Northeast Auctions

#532 Q.A. Highboy, MA, figured maple, dark finish, two parts, upper w/ five drawers, lower w/ center drawer & finely carved fan, brasses orig., ht. 72¾in., wd 38¼in. $50,000

A-NH Mar. 2003

Northeast Auctions

#598 Q.A. Highboy, Long Island, NY, walnut, two part, upper w/ molded cornice, lower w/ thumbmolded drawers, sq. pad feet, ht. 66½in., wd. 41in. $4,750

A-NH Mar. 2003

Northeast Auctions

#546 Chippendale Chest-On-Chest, N. Eng., cherry, two parts, upper w/ molded swan's neck crest, thumbmolded drawers, lower section w/ base molding & bracket feet, ht. 89in., wd. 39½in. $25,000

A-NH Mar. 2003

Northeast Auctions

#586 Q.A. Highboy, N. Eng., maple, in two parts, upper w/ cove molding, lower w/ cabriole legs & pad feet, ht. 66in., wd. 37in. $5,750

A-NJ Dec. 2002   Treadway Gallery Inc.
#421 **Chest,** Prairie School w/ orig. finish, minor roughness, wd. 48in., dp. 30in., ht. 35in. **$500**

A-PA Feb. 2003   Pook & Pook Inc.
#398 **Chippendale Tall Chest,** PA, walnut, ca.1780, cover & reeded cornice, fluted quarter columns, ogee bracket feet, rest. feet, ht. 67½in., wd. 41in. **$4,313**

A-NH Nov. 2002   Northeast Auctions
#666 **Flat Top Highboy,** cherry, N. Eng., two parts, upper w/ cove molding & pin wheel carving, lower w/ arched apron & cabriole legs, ht. 73in., wd. 36 ¾in. **$11,500**

A-NH Mar. 2003   Northeast Auctions
#517 **Q.A. Lowboy,** PA, walnut, molded edge & notched front corners, thumbmolded drawers, shaped skirt on cabriole legs w/ shell carved knees & trifid feet, ht. 28½in., top 19in. x 36in. **$5,000**

FURNITURE

A-NH Nov. 2002   Northeast Auctions
#673 Chippendale Tall Chest, N. Eng., maple, top w/ cove molding & fan carving, bracket base, ht. 48in., wd. 36in. **$6,000**

A-MA Aug. 2003   Skinner, Inc.
#87 Cupboard, painted poplar, Fulton Co. OH, ca.1865, top section w/ raised panel doors w/ chamfered corners, lower on bracket feet, salmon-red painted surface w/ green & gilt dec., imper., ht. 86in., wd. 57in. **$12,925**

A-NH Nov. 2002   Northeast Auctions
#646 Q.A. Highboy, MA, tiger maple, two parts, upper w/ cove molding over graduated drawers, lower w/ arched apron w/ pendant drops, cabriole legs w/ pad feet, incl. copy of "Danforth Family" genealogy, ht. 69in., wd. 39in. **$28,000**

A-MA June 2003
Skinner, Inc.
#111 Chippendale Chest on Chest, Woodbury, CT area, 1770-90, cherry w/ flame finials, two pcs., some orig. & some repl. brass, old refinish, ht. 83½in. wd. 36in. dp. at lower case 19in. **$22,325**

A-NH Aug. 2003
Northeast Auctions
#736 Q.A. Flat-Top Highboy, DE River Valley, tiger maple w/ Spanish feet, two parts, upper w/ stepped cornice, lower w/ midmolding & angular cabriole legs w/ Spanish feet & cuffs, ht. 71¼in., wd 41in. **$32,500**

A-NH Aug. 2003
Northeast Auctions
#728 Q.A. Chest on Frame, NH, tiger maple, molded cornice & frame w/ scalloped skirt, banded cabriole legs w/ pad feet on disks, ht. 61in., wd. 35in. **$25,000**

A-NH Aug. 2003
Northeast Auctions
#744 Bonnet-Top Chest-On-Chest, cherry, Newport area, Chippendale, in two parts, brasses are of pine tree form, ht. 87in., wd. 38½in. **$18,000**

A-PA May 2003   Pook & Pook Inc.

#217 **Pillar & Scroll Clock,** Federal, by Seth Thomas, ca.1810, ht. 31in. **$2,415**

#218 **Chest,** Chippendale, walnut, ca.1780 w/ dentil molded cornice & acanthus carved quarter columns, ht. 59½in., wd. 36¾in. **$8,050**

#219 **Corner Cupboard,** Federal, two-piece, ca.1810 w/ cut-out bracket feet, ht. 86in. wd. 44in. **$4,255**

75

A-PA Sept. 2002   Pook & Pook Inc.

#75 **Chippendale Schrank,** PA, walnut, ca.1770, Greek key & dentil molded cornice, fluted plinths, orig. H-hinges, paneled sides & stiles w/ fluted qtr. columns, thumbmolded drawers, ogee bracket feet, ht. 83½in, wd. 61in. **$26,450**

A-NJ Dec. 2002   Treadway Gallery, Inc.

#453 **China Cabinet,** L & JG Stickley w/ orig. strap hardware, orig. finish, sgn. w/ Handcraft decal, wd. 50in., dp. 17in. ht. 70in. **$36,000**

A-PA June 2003   Conestoga Auction Company, Inc.
#616 Schrank, Chippendale, walnut, PA w/ rattail hinges & dov. drawers, repl. ogee bracket feet, ht. 82in., wd. 76in. **$12,650**

A-PA June 2003   Conestoga Auction Company, Inc.
#618 Pie Safe, walnut w/ 12 pinwheel patt. punched tin panels, ht. 52½in., wd. 40in. **$2,310**

635

A-NH Aug. 2003   **Northeast Auctions**
#784 Kas, William & Mary, NY, Hudson River Valley area, gumwood & mah. w/ ebonized feet, ht. 81in., wd. 76in. dp. 28½in. **$9,500**

A-PA June 2003   Conestoga Auction Company, Inc.
#635 Spice Cabinet in kas form w/ "H" hinges & compartmented int., ht. 23in., wd. 26in., dp. 9¾in. **$4,620**

A-OH Oct. 2003   Garth's
Arts & Antiques
**#253 Q.A. Chest on
Frame,** walnut w/ old
refinish, poplar secondary
wood, repl. brasses,
base repl., ht. 59in., wd.
46½in. **$2,400**

A-MA Aug. 2003
    Robert C. Eldred Co., Inc.
#1004 Chest-On-Chest,
Am., tiger maple, two
sections w/ repl. brasses
in orig. holes, ht. 69in.
wd. 49in. **$12,650**

1004

A-PA June 2003   Conestoga Auction Company, Inc.
#619 Wardrobe, 19th C., w/ blue & grain paint dec. & paneled
doors, ht. 72½in., wd. 50½in. **$20,900**

A-PA Sept. 2003   Pook & Pook Inc.
#225 High Chest, Chippendale, PA, ca.1775 w/ Greek key
molding, ht. 63¾in., wd. 39in. **$12,650**

A-NH Mar. 2003

             Northeast Auctions

#474 Chippendale Corner Cupboard, PA, walnut, beaded cupboard doors over mid molding & base molding, ht. 85in., wd. 41in. **$3,500**

A-NH Mar. 2003 Northeast Auctions

#514 Corner Cupboard, Federal, inlaid walnut, possibly VA, two parts, swan's neck molded crest, inlaid pinwheel terminals, inlaid dec., lower w/ molded base & shaped bracket feet, ht. 98in., wd 51½in. **$25,000**

A-PA Feb. 2003   Pook & Pook Inc.

#67 Federal Secretary Linen Press, PA, mah., ca.1810, upper w/ molded cornice, lower w/ pull out desk w/ fitted interior, French feet, ht. 93½in., wd. 42¾in. **$2,875**

A-PA Sept. 2002   Pook & Pook Inc.

#151 Corner Cupboard, PA, poplar, ca.1850, two parts, upper w/ ogee molded cornice, orig. vibrant red & salmon grained surface, lower section w/ scalloped skirt on scrolled cut out feet, ht. 90in., wd. 38in., dp. 26½in. **$23,000**

151

FURNITURE

A-PA Sept. 2003   Pook & Pook Inc.

#305 **Corner Cupboard,** Federal, PA, one-piece, ca.1810 w/ convex molded & paneled cornice over conforming case, ht. 87in., wd. 48in. **$21,850**

A-NH Aug. 2003   Northeast Auctions

#921 **Corner Cupboard,** tiger maple, N. Eng., Salem, shaped shelves & spurred bracket feet, ht. 80in. wd. 50in. **$12,000**

A-PA Feb. 2003   Pook & Pook Inc.

#85 **Apothecary Cupboard,** N. Eng., painted pine, mid 19th C., retains ochre grain dec., ht. 39in., wd. 43in., dp. 13in. **$9,200**

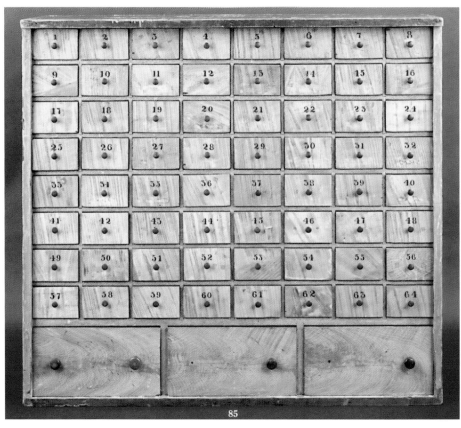

175

A-PA Feb. 2003   Pook & Pook Inc.

#175 Q.A. Dressing Table, DE Valley, walnut, ca.1760, orig. chased brasses, cabriole legs, Spanish feet, ht. 31in., wd. 30in. **$21,850**

A-NJ Dec. 2002   Treadway Gallery Inc.

#454 Dressing Table, English Arts & Crafts w/ tall tapered candle stands w/ brass holder bobeche, refinished, wd. 42in., dp. 20in., ht. 61in. **$1,200**

A-SC Mar. 2003
        Charlton Hall Galleries,
                                    Inc.

#187 Vitrine, Louis XV style, a kingwood & gilt-bronze mounted case w/ glazed panel door & sidelights, resting on cabriole legs, ht. 63in., wd. 27in. **$800**

A-SC June 2003
        Charlton Hall Galleries,
                                    Inc.

#278 Welsh Dresser, English, late 19th C., oak w/ inlay, minor scratches, ht. 82in., wd. 53in., dp. 19½in. **$1,200**

278

A-NH Aug. 2003   **Northeast Auctions**

#654 Dressing Table, N. Eng., yellow paint & dec., bowed front & sides, sq. tapering legs, ht. 38in., lg. 36in. **$2,750**

A-NH Aug. 2003   **Northeast Auctions**

#930 Bowfront Dressing Glass, Sheraton, flame birch veneer, brass rim, ht. 24in., wd. 18in. **$17,000**

#931 Bowfront Chest of Drawers, Sheraton, inlaid mah., coastal N.H., stiles w/ bird's-eye maple panels, ht. 39in., wd. 41in. **$6,500**

A-NH Mar. 2003   **Northeast Auctions**

#516 Hepplewhite Sideboard, NY, inlaid mah., rope twist geometric inlay, stiles w/ diamond - over-oval stringing, sq. tapering legs w/ line inlay & cuffs, ht. 41½in., lg. 73¼in. **$18,000**

Opposite

A-IA Mar. 2003

Jackson's International Auctioneers

#277 Chest of Drawers, Victorian, walnut, ca.1890, ht. 42in., wd. 43in. **$259**

#278 Chest of Drawers, Victorian, walnut, ca.1890, ht. 40in., wd. 38in. **$115**

#279 Dresser, Victorian, oak, ca.1900 w/ wishbone mirror, ht. 74in., wd. 44in. **$259**

#280 Chest, Victorian, ca.1900 w/ serpentine drawers & hat box, ht. 48in., wd. 36in. **$316**

#281 Drop Front Desk, ca.1810, ash w/ interior pigeon hole compartments, ht. 40, wd. 26in. **$144**

#282 Rocker, child's, ca.1890 w/ caned seat & back, ht. 27in. **$126**

#283 Rocker & later foot rest, ca.1890 w/ caned seat & back, ht. 40in. **$80**

#284 Hall Tree, oak, w/ marble top, contemporary, ht, 75in. **$316**

#285 Console Table w/ marble top, Victorian style, mah., contemporary, ht. 30in. **$144**

#286 Side Table, Victorian style, mah., ht. 28in. **$46**

#287 Parlor Table, Victorian style, mah. w/ marble top, ht. 29in. **$115**

#288 Wash Stand, Victorian, ca.1880, walnut, ht. 29in. **$120**

#289 Nesting Tables w/ Oriental scenes carved in deep relief. **$374**

#290 Library Table, Empire period, mah., lowered in height, 24in. **$69**

#291 Console Table w/ pierced floral designs in skirt. **$80**

#277

#278

#279

#280

#281

#282

#283

#284

#285

#286

#287

#288

#289

#290

#291

FURNITURE

A-NH Nov. 2002   **Northeast Auctions**

#702 **Sideboard,** N. Eng. Federal, inlaid mah. w/ serpentine front, each drawer w/ double line oval & circular line inlay, all w/ applied beaded edge, sq. tapering legs, stringing & cuffs, ht. 42in., wd. 70in. **$8,000**

A-NH Mar. 2003   **Northeast Auctions**

#587 **Hepplewhite Sideboard,** N. Eng., inlaid mah., top w/ inset ovolo corners, black inlaid outline, sides w/ bowed drawers, one over bottle drawer, one over cupboard door, ht. 42¾in., wd. 71½in. **$6,250**

A-NJ Dec. 2002   **Treadway Gallery Inc.**

#500 **Sideboard,** Limbert, w/ mirrored back over base cabinet, orig. copper hardware, refinished, branded, wd. 45in., dp. 19in., ht. 50in. **$2,600**

Opposite

A-IA Oct. 2002

Jackson's International Auctioneers

#777 **Secretary Bookcase,** Victorian, oak w/ curved glass door & beveled mirror, ht. 72in., wd. 38in. **$1,610**

#778 **Gentleman's Dresser,** oak w/ applied carvings & beveled mirror, ht. 82in., wd. 44in. **$460**

#779 **Kitchen Cupboard,** 19th C., oak, repl. hardware, ht. 82in., wd. 40in. **$920**

#780 **Victorian Hotel Commode,** ash w/ mirror & towel bar, ht. 72in., wd. 34in. **$345**

#781 **Pine Cupboard,** 19th C. w/ two-door paneled top on three bin base w/ slanted covers, ht. 82in., wd. 62in. **$517**

#782 **Country Wardrobe,** early 19th C. w/ later polychrome floral dec., & 1802 date on cornice, ht. 72in., wd. 50in. **$431**

#783 **Food Safe,** 19th C., mixed woods w/ screened front, ht. 70in., wd. 41in. **$287**

#784 **Country Pine Hutch,** 19th C., w/ two door scalloped top, ht. 82in., wd. 51in. **$350**

#785 **Country Pine Kitchen Cupboard,** ht. 75in., wd. 47in. **$258**

#786 **Sectional Bookcase,** ca.1920 by Globe-Wernicke, four units over two, ht. 81in., wd. 34in. **$1,092**

#787 **Estey Parlor Organ,** walnut, ca.1875, orig. cond., ht. 71in., wd. 44in. **$115**

#788 **Victorian Dresser,** walnut w/ hankie boxes, no hardware, ht. 81in., wd. 39in. **$230**

#789 **Round Dining Table,** oak, ca.1920 w/ scrolled pedestal base, four leaves, dia. 54in. **$258**

#790 **Poker Table,** oak w/ beverage shelves below on iron paw footed pedestal, ht. 30in., top 34in. sq. **$345**

#791 **Blanket Chest,** pine, ca.1850 w/ scalloped base, ht. 37in., wd. 36in. **$201**

#792 **Gateleg Kitchen Table,** oak w/ carved floral end panels, ht. 28in. **$287**

#777

#778

#779

#780

#781

#782

#783

#784

#785

#786

#787

#788

#789

#790

#791

#792

A-MA Nov. 2002   Skinner, Inc.

#320 Federal Sideboard, mah. & mah. veneer, serpentine inlay, ca.1790-1810, w/ inlays, lozenges & stringing, old ref., imper., ht. 40½in., wd. 71¾in., dp. 28½in. **$16,450**

49

A-PA Nov. 2002   Pook & Pook Inc.

#49 Sideboard, Federal, mah., North Shore, MA, ca.1815, ht. 43½in., wd. 72½in. **$7,475**

A-MA Nov. 2002   Skinner, Inc.

Tramp Art
#406 Gilt Carved Frame, Am., 19th C., minor edge losses, 70in. x 70in. **$5,405**
#407 Floor Lamp, chip-carved, Am., early 20th C., w/ hidden compartment, black conical paper shade, loose door, ht. 59in. **$1,763**
#408 Mirrored Sideboard, Am., late 19th C., cupboard w/ interior shelf, brass pulls & latch, wear, ht. 67½in., wd. 42in., dp. 22¾in. **$3,055**

A-NH Mar. 2003

Northeast Auctions

#555 Secretary Bookcase, early Am., cherry & walnut, two parts, upper section w/ cove molding, lower section w/ slant-lid opening to serpentine drawers, reeded qtr. columns, & ogee bracket feet, ht. 85in., wd. 41in. **$6,250**

A-NH Aug. 2003   **Northeast Auctions**

#796 Library Bookcase, probably Portsmouth, NH, ca.1800-1810, Sheraton, mah., two parts, upper w/ gothic shaped mullions, lower w/ hinged writing flap, solid cupboard doors, int. w/ bookshelves, French bracket feet, ht. 100¼in., wd. 60½in. **$20,000**

A-NH Aug. 2003

Northeast Auctions

#760 Secretary Bookcase, Federal, Portsmouth, NH, mah. & flame birch, attrib. to Langley Boardman, ht. 72in., wd. 38in., dp. 19in. **$21,000**

A-NH Aug. 2003

Northeast Auctions

#674 Hepplewhite Secretary, N. Eng., mah. & bird's-eye maple, central sq. panel, urn finials, shelfed compartments behind glazed doors, fold-out lid w/ inlaid oval dec., sq. tapering legs w/ spade feet, ht. 72in., wd. 40in. **$9,000**

A-MA Nov. 2002   Skinner, Inc.

#375 **Tramp Art Child's Mirrored Bureau,** Am., 19th C. w/ applied lithograph paper cut-outs of flowers, birds & figures, drawers w/ wire pulls, ht. 32¾in., wd. 14⅜in., dp. 11in. **$382**

A-PA Sept. 2003   Pook & Pook Inc.

#448 **Bureau,** Federal, Baltimore, ca.1810, mah. w/ serpentine front, ht. 47¾in., wd. 39¼in. **$4,830**

A-NH Mar. 2003   Northeast Auctions

#639 **Chippendale Desk,** Hartford, CT, cherry, attrib. school of George Belden, dov. top, interior w/ drawers & cubbyholes, thumbmolded drawers, base molding w/ ogee bracket feet, ht. 42in., wd. 44in. **$3,000**

A-NH Mar. 2003   Northeast Auctions

#520 **Chippendale Slant-Lid Desk,** CT, cherry, pilastered document drawers & valanced pigeonholes over drawers, cabriole legs w/ ball & claw feet, center drop w/ carved pinwheel, ht. 44in., wd. 38in. **$14,000**

325

065

A-PA Feb. 2003   Pook & Pook Inc.
#325 Chippendale Desk, Boston, MA, mah., ca.1770, lid encloses fitted int. w/ arched & raised panel door, document drawers w/ fluted columns, pigeon holes & 12 sm. drawers, orig. Chinese brasses, short cabriole legs, ht. 44½in., wd. 40in., dp. 23in. **$21,850**

A-SC Mar. 2003   Charlton Hall Galleries, Inc.
#065 Davenport Desk, mah., fall front w/ leather insert, bird's eye maple, fitted interior & brass gallery, stress cracks & new hinges, ht. 33in., wd. 21in. **$950**

A-NH Aug. 2003   Northeast Auctions
#184 Fall-Front Desk of sm. size, N. Eng., Country Sheraton, in two parts, ht. 50in., wd. 34½in. **$700**
#185 Stepback Chest & Bookcase, N. Eng., Sheraton, bird's-eye maple & flame birch, in two parts, ht. 83in., wd. 44½in., **$1,400**
#186 Hooded Cradle, N. Eng., bird's eye maple, dov., ht. 26in., lg. 45in. **$1,500**

A-MA Nov. 2002   Skinner, Inc.

#333 Federal Tambour Lady's Desk, mah. veneer, Boston, MA, ca.1790 w/ fold-down writing surface, refinished, orig. brasses, imper., ht. 46¼in., wd. 42in., dp. 21in. **$3,819**

A-MA June 2003   Skinner, Inc.

#91 Chippendale Slant-Lid Desk, tiger maple, probably southeastern N. Eng., w/ old mellow surface & brown stained int., minor imper., ht. 41in., wd. 36¼in. dp. 18½in. **$36,425**

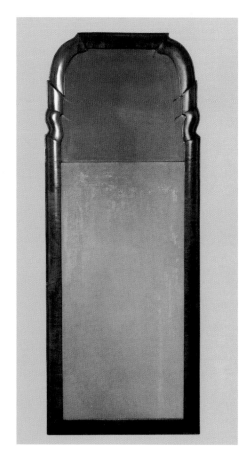

A-NH Mar. 2003   Northeast Auctions

#558 Q.A. Mirror, walnut, two-part beveled, ogival top & applied molded edge, 50in. x 19½in. **$2,200**

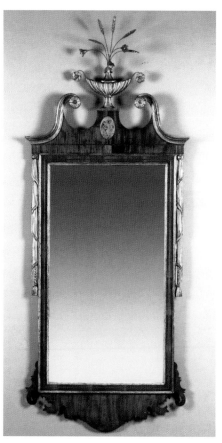

A-NH Nov. 2002   Northeast Auctions

#742 Wall Mirror, Am. w/ Am. eagle on pediment, inlaid mah. & giltwood, urn & wheat center finial, 68in. x 27½in. **$7,000**

A-NH Mar. 2003   Northeast Auctions

#638 Chippendale Mirror, walnut & parcel gilt, molded frame, 44¾in. x 24in. **$3,000**

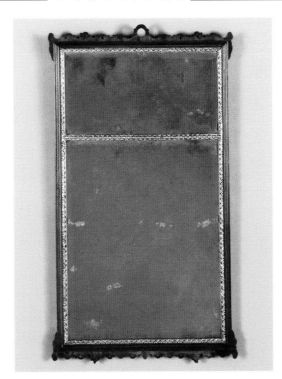

A-PA Feb. 2003   Pook & Pook Inc.
#396 Chippendale Mirror, PA, mah.,
ca.1780, labeled "Wayne & Biddle",
ht. 30in., wd. 15½in. **$3,450**

A-NH Mar. 2003

Northeast Auctions
#519 Chippendale Mirror, mah.
& giltwood, two-part, openwork
shallow crest w/ cut-outs,
beveled edge mirrors w/
narrow apron & row of
openwork teardrops, 35in. x
20in. **$5,000**

A-MA June 2003   Skinner, Inc.
#20 Mirror, Federal gilt gesso, N. Eng.,
ca.1825, w/ tablet depicting three
buildings, minor imper., ht. 35in., wd.
16in. **$881**
#21 Classical Split Mirror, N. Eng.,
ca.1825, w/ tablet showing man

fishing w/ sailboat on pond, ht. 36¾in.,
wd. 17in. **$2,115**
#22 Mirror, Federal, gilt gesso, ca.1815-
20 w/ tablet showing an Am. flag &
schooner, minor imper., ht. 37½in., wd.
18in. **$2,223**
#23 Bowfront Bureau, Federal, cherry w/

inlay, old repl. brasses, w/ bird's eye
maple veneered panels, minor imper., ht.
30½in., wd. 39in., dp. 22in. **$7,638**
#24 Federal Bureau, cherry & bird's eye
maple w/ stringing & mah. crossbanding,
ca.1815-20, refinished & imper., ht.
39in., wd. 39in. dp. 20in. **$7,050**

A-MA Aug. 2003   Robert C. Eldred Co., Inc.
#1009 **Convex Mirror,** Federal period, gilt wood w/ foliate drop & entwined dolphin pediment, ht. 42in. **$8,500**

348

A-SC Jan. 2003

Charlton Hall Galleries, Inc.
#348 **Cheval Mirror,** mah., 20th C., ht. 71½in., wd. 33in., dp. 20½in. **$500**

A-SC Dec. 2002   Charlton Hall Galleries, Inc.
#565 **Q.A. Parcel-Gilt Looking Glass,** walnut, first qtr. 19th C. w/ beveled edge glass (repl.), w/ normal wear veneer separations, ht. 47in., wd. 16¾in. **$800**

A-NH Mar. 2003   Northeast Auctions
#595 **Q.A. Candlestand,** MA, mah., tilt-top, molded edge, ridged pointed slipper feet on pads, ht. 27½in., top 18¼in. x 17¾in. **$2,500**

A-NH Mar. 2003   Northeast Auctions
#473 **Q.A. Candlestand,** New London, CT, cherry, black paint, ht. 27¾in., dia. 14in. **$16,000**

A-NH Mar. 2003   Northeast Auctions
#550 **Tray-Top Stand,** Federal, N. Eng., inlaid cherry, molded edge w/ inlaid oval patera, & slipper feet on pads, ht. 27¼in., top 13½in. x 13¾in. **$3,750**

A-PA Feb. 2003   Pook & Pook Inc.

#185 **Q.A. Candlestand,** PA, ca.1765, top tilts & turns on birdcage support, cabriole legs & pad feet, ht. 27¼in., dia. 17½in. **$28,750**

A-NH Aug. 2003   Northeast Auctions

#735 **Q.A. Tilt-Top Candlestand,** PA, walnut, molded edge, turned pedestal on cabriole legs w/ pad feet on platforms, ht. 27in., dia. 18in. **$5,500**

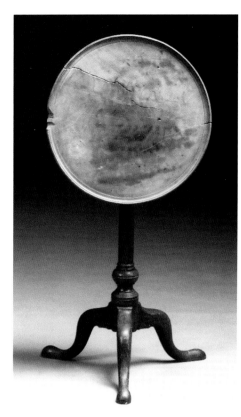

A-NH Nov. 2002   Northeast Auctions

#676 **Q.A. Dish-Top Candlestand,** PA, walnut, w/ orig. patina in as-found condition, ca.1760, ht. 26⅜in., dia. 17in. **$3,250**

A-NH Aug. 2003   Northeast Auctions

#787 **Q.A. Candlestand,** PA, walnut w/ birdcage support, molded raised rim, tripod cabriole legs w/ platformed pad feet, ht. 28¼in., dia. 20½in. **$8,500**

A-NJ Dec. 2002   Treadway Gallery Inc.

#527 **Plant Stand** w/ ebony inlay, orig. finish, two repl. corbels, Limbert branded signature, wd. 14in., dp. 14in., ht. 34in. **$1,800**

A-NH Nov. 2002   Northeast Auctions

#622 **Sheraton Work Table,** NY, mah. w/ three drawers, ca.1800-1810, w/ orig. brasses, by Duncan Phyfe, top drawer fitted as a desk compartment, contemporary of equal rank, ht. 30½in., top 16½in. x 20¾in. **$12,000**

FURNITURE

A-NH Mar. 2003   Northeast Auctions

#596 **Chippendale Card Table,** mah., hinged top w/ sq. outset corners, carved knees & ball & claw feet, ht. 28½in., wd. 32½in. **$6,750**

A-NH Mar. 2003   Northeast Auctions

#636 **Sheraton Pembroke Table,** MA, mah., sq. drop leaves, single drawer, reeded legs, ht. 28½in., lg. 36in. **$5,000**

A-NH Mar. 2003   Northeast Auctions

#615 **Sheraton Work Table,** NY, mah., half-round corners & reeded edge, drawers w/ beaded edge, turned feet on casters, ht. 30¾in., top 13in. x 19¼in. n/s

#616 **Federal Candlestand,** mah., tilt-top, banded w/ inlay on spider legs w/ cuffs, ht. 29¼in., top 17½in. x 26in. **$2,000**

#617 **Federal Card Table,** Boston, MA, mah., rounded corners & edges w/ inlay, legs w/ inlay & cuffs, ht. 29¼in., top 35½in. x 17¾in. **$4,200**

A-NH Mar. 2003   Northeast Auctions
#455 Card Table, N. Eng., mah., serpentine front, hinged top, contrasting sawtooth inlay, apron w/ satinwood veneer panels, center bird's-eye maple w/ zebrawood oval, ht. 29¼in. **$13,000**

A-NH Mar. 2003   Northeast Auctions
#646 Sheraton Card Table, MA, mah. & bird's-eye maple, hinged serpentine top w/ turret ends, spool turned stiles, ht. 29in., wd. 34in. **$2,500**

A-MA Nov. 2002   Skinner, Inc.
#752 Q.A. Drop-Leaf Table, cherry, probably MA, ca.1740-60, refinished, imper. & repr., ht. 28½in., wd. 48½in., dp. 49in. **$3,290**

A-NH Mar. 2003

Northeast Auctions
#746 Cellarette, Eng., mah., fitted on stand, interior compartments, ht. 30½in., lg. 21½in. **$1,600**
#747 Bedsteps, mah. & tooled leather, pull out section fitted w/ enameled chamberpot, ht. 27¼in., lg. 32½in. n/s
#748 Hepplewhite Corner Washstand, mah., bowfront & cut-outs, apron w/ line inlay, sq. legs curving to feet, ht. 40¾in., wd. 25in. **$1,100**

#551 **Q.A. Tea Table,** N. Eng., maple, black paint over old blue, molded edge, pad feet, ht. 27½in., top 20½in. x 29½in. **$13,000**

#459 **Gateleg Dining Table,** Wm. & Mary, MA, w/ drawers, maple, oval top w/ hinged leaves, ht. 26in., lg. 44in. **$5,250**

#497 **Dropleaf Table,** Limbert, gateleg form w/ arched corbels at apron, thru-tenon const., four 9in. leaves in orig. case, orig. finish, branded, wd. 45in., dp. 25in., ht. 30in. **$1,800**

#307 **Federal Academy Painted Work Table,** tiger maple, Boston, MA, ca.1790-1810, top w/ ovolo corners, cockbeaded drawers, top has free-hand dec., paint loss, ht. 29½in., wd. 20¾in., dp. 16¾in. **$12,925**

#581 **Sheraton Sewing Table,** Charleston, MA, Jacob Forster, 1764-1838, orig. finish, dated "1814" in ink, compartmented drawers, bag drawer on side w/ lock, used by John Seymour, orig. brass knobs, ht. 28¾in., top 20in. x 16in. **$18,000**

#795 **Q.A. Game Table,** Eng., mah., triple fold top, plain playing surface, baize-lined playing surface & backgammon board, pad feet on casters, ht. 29¾in., wd 33½in. **$6,500**

A-SC Mar. 2003   Charlton Hall Galleries, Inc.
#624 Victorian Bedroom Suite, walnut & burl, 4th qtr. 19th C., three pieces consisting of a marble-top dresser w/ mirror, marble-top washstand w/ mirror & half-tester bed, each w/ floral carved & reeded design, the marble top on dresser has old repr. & crack, bed ht. 99in., dresser & washstand 80½in. **$6,250**

A-MA June 2003   Skinner, Inc.

#32 Stand Table, Federal, cherry, CT River Valley, ca.1800 w/ shaped top & square tapering legs, refinished, possible height loss, ht. 26¾in., wd. 20½in. **$1,116**

#33 Candlestand, Federal, cherry, ca.1790 w/ square top & ovolo corners by inlaid stringing on vase & ring-turned support, refinished, repr., ht. 27in., top 15¾in. x 15½in. **$1,175**

#34 Candlestand, Federal, cherry, N.

Eng., early 19th C., old surface, minor repr., ht. 27in., dia. 19½in. **$2,938**

#35 Candlestand, Federal, cherry w/ inlay, MA, ca.1790, refinished, ht. 26in., top 14¾ in x 14½in. **$4,994**

FURNITURE

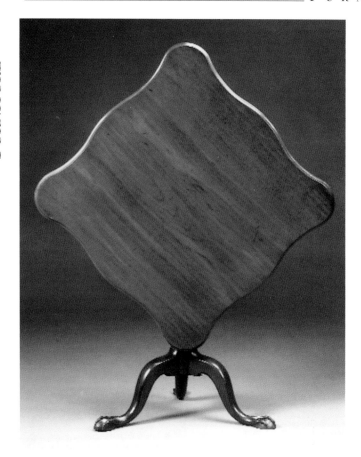

A-NH Nov. 2002   Northeast Auctions

#724 Chippendale Tilt-Top Tea Table, mah., MA, Salem-Newburyport area, molded edge, spiral turned urn on arched cabriole legs, ht. 29½in., top 32in. sq. **$2,300**

A-NH Nov. 2002   Northeast Auctions

#726 Sheraton Card Table, inlaid mah., Portsmouth, N.H., w/ brand of Lewis Barnes, 1776-1856, bowed front, turret corners, bird's-eye maple banded edges, reeded legs w/ ringed cuffs, ht. 30¼in., wd. 39¼in. **$32,000**

A-NH Nov. 2002   Northeast Auctions

#869 Q.A. Tilt-Top Table, mah., piecrust top, fluted baluster-turned standard carved w/ leaf-tips, ht. 28½in. dia. 30½in. **$1,000**

#870 Chippendale Bird-Cage Tea Table, Eng., carved mah., piecrust edge,

carved knees & feet, ht. 28in., dia. 28in. **$900**

#871 Q.A. Tilt-Top Tea Table, Eng., carved mah., serpentine molded edge, pedestal w/ swirl carved urn, carbriole legs w/ pad feet, ht. 27in. dia. 25in. **$1,900**

#872 Tilt-Top Tea Table, Eng., mah., top

w/ dished rings & shell carving, tripod base, ht. 28in., dia. 30in. **$2,000**

#873 Chippendale Tilt-Top Tea Table, carved mah., shaped circular top on reeded urn pedestal w/ leaf carved knees, elongated ball & claw feet on pads, ht. 29½in., dia. 31in. **$500**

A-PA Feb. 2003   Pook & Pook, Inc.

#120 **Child's Drysink,** PA, ca.1820, painted pine, retains overall ochre grain painted surface, ht. 24½in., wd. 32in. **$1,265**

A-MA Nov. 2002   Skinner, Inc.

#700 **Walnut Gate-leg Table,** Chowan County, NC, early 18th C., old surface, rest., ht. 29¾in., wd. 50in. x 49in. **$4,113**

A-NH Nov. 2002   Northeast Auctions

#698 **Q.A. Tea Table,** Rhode Island, mah. w/ pad feet on disks, ht. 27in., top 22in. x 31in. **$4,500**

A-MA Nov. 2002   Skinner, Inc.

#707 **Carved Mah. Card Table** w/ mah. veneer, Salem, MA, ca.1820-30, refinished, imper., ht. 29in., wd. 36in. **$1,645**

A-NH Aug. 2003   Northeast Auctions

#913 **Q.A. Tea Table,** walnut w/ tray top, ht. 26in., top 19in. x 28in. **$24,000**

FURNITURE

A-NH Aug. 2003   Northeast Auctions

#763 **Sheraton Work Table,** MA, mah., shaped top w/ turret corners, drawers w/ shield shaped ivory escutcheon, ringed stiles, reeded legs w/ cuffs ringed, ht. 30in., top 20½in. x 17¾in. **$3,000**

A-MA Nov. 2002   Skinner, Inc.

#744 **Federal Tiger Maple Pembroke Table,** probably NY, ca.1810, reeded legs, refinished, minor imper., ht. 28⅜in. wd. 23¼in., dp. 36¾in. **$1,880**

A-NH Aug. 2003   Northeast Auctions

#764 **Sewing Table,** N. Eng., Sheraton, w/ two drawers, the top w/ checkered inlay, the lower one w/ silk bag, on tapering legs w/ ringed cuffs, ht. 28½in., top 16in. x 22in. **$7,000**

A-MA Nov. 2002   Skinner, Inc.

#342 **Federal Card Table,** mah. & flame-birch veneer, Portsmouth, NH, ca.1790 w/ bowed front & ovolo corners, refinished, imper., ht. 29½in., wd. 37in., dp. 18in. **$19,975**

A-NH Aug. 2003   Northeast Auctions

#761 Dining Table, Am., two-part Federal, inlaid mah., edge bordered w/ contrasting stringing, hinged deep drop leaves, sq. tapering legs w/ stringing, ht. 30in., wd. 48in., ea. leaf 24in. **$11,000**

778

779

776 (table)

777 (set of chairs)

A-MA Nov. 2002   Skinner, Inc.

#776 Table, N. Eng., 2nd qtr. 19th C., w/ pine scrubbed two-board top, orig. red paint, imper., ht. 30in., wd. 66in., dp. 36in. **$2,233**

#777 Windsor Chair, thumb-back, set of 6, Lancaster County, PA, 1st half 19th C., crest rails have polychrome dec. showing fruit & flowers w/ brown ground paint, orig. surface, minor imper., ht. 33in. **$823**

#778 Wood Bowl, carved, early Am. w/ two handles applied w/ pegs, wear, cracks, ht. 7in., dia. 21in. **$646**

#779 Candlesticks, wood, pr., Am., early 20th C. w/ mustard colored paint & smoke dec., minor wear, ht. 11¼in. **$176**

A-NH Mar. 2003

Northeast Auctions

#515 Sheraton Dining Table, MA, two-part, drop leaf raised on circular fluted ring-turned legs, ht. 29½in., lg., extension 7ft., wd. 48in. **$4,000**

FURNITURE

A-MA Nov. 2002   Skinner, Inc.
#780 Q.A. Drop-Leaf Table, maple, MA or RI, ca.1780, refinished, imper., ht. 27¼in., wd. 44in. **$881**

A-MA Nov. 2002   Skinner, Inc.
#783 Q.A. Porringer-top Tea Table, maple, N. Eng., ca.1740-60, refinished, imper., ht. 26in., wd. 32in., dp. 25in. **$3,055**

A-MA Nov. 2002   Skinner, Inc.
#936 Basin Stand, N. Eng., ca.1830 w/ all-over black & red graining simulating rosewood w/ yellow highlights, orig. surface, repl. glass pulls, minor imper., ht. 36in., wd. 18¼in. dp. 16in. **$470**
#935 Slat-back Armchair, probably, CT, 1st half 18th C., early split rush seat w/ 19th C. brown paint highlighted w/ yellow striping, surface wear, ht. 43½in. **$823**

311

A-PA Nov. 2002

Pook & Pook Inc.

#311 Dining Table, NY, Federal, mah., two-part, ca.1810, inlaid skirt w/ brass banding, three leaves, acanthus carved & line inlaid legs w/ brass animal paw castors, ht. 30¼in., wd. 48¼in., lg. 117¼in. **$12,650**

A-MA June 2003 Skinner, Inc.

#40 Work Table, Federal, mah. w/ mah. veneer, N. Eng., ca.1820 w/ shaped top, old ref., minor imper, ht. 30⅛in., wd. 20in. **$3,525**
#41 Candlestand, Federal, mah. w/ tilt-top, N. Eng., ca.1810-15, refinished & imper., ht. 29¾in., top 22½in. x 14¾in. **$1,175**
#42 Candlestand, Federal, cherry tilt-top, N. Eng., ca.1820, refinished w/ minor imper., ht. 29¾in., top 21in. x 15¾in. **$1,116**
#43 Work Table, Federal, N. Eng., carved mah. & mah. veneer, refinished & imper., ht. 29in., wd. 17½in. **$1,528**

A-MA June 2003 Skinner, Inc.

#52 Chamber Stand, Federal, mah. & cherry, N. Eng., ca.1825, refinish & minor imper., ht. 39in. **$1,410**
#53 Pembroke Table, Federal, mah., probably MA, 1815-20, w/ beaded drawer, vase & ring-turned reeded legs, refinished & minor imper. ht. 29in., wd. 38in., closed dp. 19½in. **$1,410**
#54 Chamber Stand, classical, cherry & bird's eye maple, ca.1825, refinish & minor imper., ht. 38¾in. **$999**

A-MA June 2003
Skinner, Inc.
#90 **Gate-Leg Table,** William & Mary, tiger maple, MA, 1740-60, falling leaves w/ gate supports, baluster-shaped & turned feet, old refinish, old repl. drawer, minor imper., ht. 29in., top 48in. x 53in. **$47,000**

A-NH Aug. 2003
Northeast Auctions
#339 **Dining Table,** Hepplewhite inlaid mah., three-part, ht. 29½in., wd. 50in., lg. closed 69in., open 135in. **$6,750**

Opposite

A-IA Mar. 2003
Jackson's International Auctioneers
#662 **Work Table,** mid-1800s, walnut w/ single drawer, ht. 29in., wd. 32in. **$460**
#663 **Game Table,** Empire, walnut w/ lyre shape support, ht. 29in., wd. 36in. **$258**
#664 **Rocker & Arm Chair,** matching, ca.1910 w/ orig. upholstery. **$488**
#665 **Dresser, Renaissance Revival,** walnut, ca.1880 w/ marble top, ht. 95in., wd. 41in. **$747**
#666 **Chest of Drawers,** Chippendale style, cherry, early 19th C. w/ repl. pulls, ht. 43in. wd. 40in. **$632**
#667 **Parlor Table** w/ marble top, Victorian, walnut w/ finger mold carving & turned dec., ht. 29in., dia. 32in. **$517**
#668 **Dining Room Suite** consisting of 6-legged table, 6 chairs, buffet & china cabinet, walnut, ca.1920. **$2,070**
#669 **Pressback Chairs,** oak, set of 4, ca.1900 w/ scrolled floral designs & caned seats, ht. 40in. **$143**
#670 **Victorian Side Chairs,** walnut, set of 4, ca.1800 w/ black horsehair upholstery, ht. 35in. **$287**
#671 **Victorian Arm Chair,** ca.1800 w/ carved walnut frame & black horsehair upholstery, matches above lot. **$287**

#662

#663

#664

#665

#666

#667

#668

#668

#669

#670

#671

#680

#681

#682

#683

#684

#685

#686

#687

#688

#689

#690

#691

#692

#693

#694

#695

#696

#697

Opposite

A-IA Mar. 2003

Jackson's International Auctioneers

#680 Oriental Table, carved w/ red marble insert in top, ht. 32in. **$431**

#681 Chest of Drawers, French style w/ overall inlaid dec. & ormolu pulls, ht. 40in., wd. 27in. **$373**

#682 Dresser, mah. w/ mirror, orig. glass & brass pulls, ht. 78in., wd. 56in. **$373**

#683 Beds, pr., 4-poster, mah. w/ pinecone finials, ca.1915-1920, lg. 59in. **$460**

#684 Gothic Revival Chair, walnut w/ needlepoint seat & brass casters. **$138**

#685 Baker Shelves, wrought iron & brass w/ iron scrolls, iron casters. **$600**

#686 What-Not-Shelf, walnut, ht. 60 in. **$86**

#687 What-Not-Shelf, walnut w/ flat back in graduating length, ht. 69in. **$143**

#688 What-Not-Shelf, walnut, ht. 6in. **$103**

#689 Victorian Center Table w/ turned pedestal, ht. 30in. **$258**

#690 Sewing Machine, an early Wheeler & Wilson, walnut cabinet w/ footprint pedals. **$143**

#691 Victorian Platform Rocker, Eastlake.

$103

#692 Arm Chair, figural carved walnut, ca.1890, ht. 53in. **$201**

#693 French Lacquer Chair, 19th C. w/ MOP inlay. **$140**

#694 French Side Chair, splat inlaid w/ MOP inlay. **$316**

#695 Victorian Style Chair w/ medallion back & carved rose crest, ca.1950. **$201**

#696 Birdcage & Stand, solid brass, adjustable, restored, ht. 70in. **$379**

#697 Bentwood Rocker, Austrian, ca.1890, ht. 36in. **$230**

A-MA May 2003   Fontaine's Auction, LLC

#524 Trestle Table, oak, unsigned, ht. 30in., wd. 48in. lg. 108in. **$6,250**

A-OH Oct. 2003   Garth's Arts & Antiques

#821 Sheraton Stand Table, cherry w/ old refinish, poplar secondary wood, dov. drawers retain orig. wooden pulls, ht. 28½in., top 23in. x 25in. **$316**

A-PA Sept. 2003   Pook & Pook Inc.

#535 Trestle Table, 18th C., Lancaster Co., PA, retains old dry surface, ht. 29½in., wd. 80in. **$18,400**

A-MA Nov. 2002   Skinner, Inc.

#706 Carved Mah. Pedestal Dining Table w/ mah. veneer, ca.1825, old refinish, imper., w/ two 23in. freestanding leaves, ht. 30in., wd. 48in., full extension dp. 138in. **$19,975**

A-NJ Dec. 2002   **Treadway Gallery Inc.**

#449 Desk, L & JG Stickley w/ orig. finish, sgn. w/ Handcraft decal, minor stains to top, wd. 40in., ht. 36in. **$1,200**

A-NJ Dec. 2002   **Treadway Gallery Inc.**

#455 Bed, Gustav Stickley w/ orig. finish, sgn. w/ red decal, wd. 41in., lg. 79in., ht. 45in. **$2,100**

A-MA May 2003   **Fontaine's Auctions, LLC**

#12 Settle, Gustav Stickley, oak w/ orig. finish, ht. 40in., wd. 60½in. **$14,500**

A-NJ Dec. 2002   **Treadway Gallery Inc.**

#469 Settle, Stickley Brothers, w/ orig. finish, repl. cushion, metal tag, wd. 72in., dp. 32in., ht. 35in. **$2,500**

A-NJ Dec. 2002
Treadway Gallery Inc.

#477 **Sewing Table,** Gustav Stickley w/ orig. hardware, orig. finish, branded signature, wd. 18in., dp. 18in., ht. 28in. **$4,750**

A-NJ Dec. 2002
Treadway Gallery Inc.

#443 **Table,** Gustav Stickley, orig. finish, unsgn., minor repr. to apron, dia. 36in., ht. 29in. **$1,400**

A-NJ Dec. 2002   Treadway Gallery Inc.

#444 **Dining Table,** Gustav Stickley, w/ orig. finish, sgn. w/ paper label, dia. 48in., ht. 31in. **$2,000**

A-NJ Dec. 2002   Treadway Gallery Inc.

#445 **Dining Table,** Limbert, orig. finish w/ branded signature, dia. 54in., ht. 30in. **$4,000**

A-NJ Dec. 2002
Treadway Gallery Inc.

#467 **Lunch Table,** Stickley Brothers, w/ orig. finish, unsgn., wd. 36in., dp, 36in., ht. 30in. **$1,400**

#464 **Library Table,** L & JG Stickley, w/ orig. finish, sgn., wd. 48in., dp. 30in., ht. 29in. **$1,700**

FURNITURE

A-NJ Dec. 2002
**Treadway Gallery
Inc.**

#499 Costumer,
Gustav & Stickley,
ca.1904, single
pole w/ 8 unique
spaded orig. iron
hooks, orig. finish,
red decal, wd.
26in., ht. 75in.
$3,900

A-NJ Dec. 2002   Treadway Gallery Inc.
#523 Rocker, Stickley Brothers, drop-in cushions, repl. leather, refinished, wd. 28in., dp. 24in., ht. 36in.
$500
#524 Tabouret, Stickley Brothers, w/ three leg base having keyed-tenon const., orig. finish, sgn., ht. 17in.,
dia. 15in. n/s
#525 Chair, Stickley Brothers w/ drop-in cushion, repl. leather, refinished, wd. 28in., dp. 23in., ht. 40in.
$450

A-NJ Dec. 2002   Treadway Gallery Inc.
#458 Morris Chair, Stickley Brothers, w/ recovered cushion, orig.
pegs & finish, sgn. w/ red decal, wd. 33in., dp. 38in., ht.
42in. **$11,000**

A-NJ Dec. 2002   Treadway Gallery Inc.
#460 Morris Chair, Stickley Brothers, 17 spindles, repl. seat
foundation & cushion, refinished, unsgn., wd. 30in., dp.
36in., ht. 37in. **$5,000**

A-NJ Dec. 2002   Treadway Gallery Inc.

#407 **Footstool,** Gustav Stickley, x-shaped frame on curled foot w/ orig. leather & finish, remnant of paper label, tear to leather, wd. 21in., dp. 14in., ht. 13in. **$4,500**

A-NJ Dec. 2002   Treadway Gallery Inc.

#544 **Trestle Table,** Gustav Stickley, w/ double keyed tenon const. above a shoe foot, base orig. finish, wd 48in., dp. 30in. ht. 28in. **$3,000**

A-NJ Dec. 2002   Treadway Gallery Inc.

#545 **Library Table,** Gustav Stickley w/ orig. leather, thru-tenon const., orig. finish, sgn. w/ red decal, wd. 54in., dp. 32in. ht. 30in. **$6,500**

A-NJ Dec. 2002
Treadway Gallery Inc.

#456 **Dresser,** Gustav Stickley w/ Harvey Ellis influence, orig. iron hardware , orig. mirror w/ butterfly joint const., refinished, sgn. w/ red decal, wd. 48in., dp.22in., ht. 67in. **$2,800**

A-NJ Dec. 2002
Treadway Gallery Inc.

#476 **Dresser,** Gustav Stickley, w/ Harvey Ellis influence, orig. finish, sgn. w/ red decal & paper label, wd. 36in., dp. 20in., ht. 52in. **$7,500**

Agata Glass was patented by Joseph Locke of the New England Glass Company of Cambridge, Massachusetts, in 1877. The application of a metallic stain left a mottled design characteristic of agata, hence the name.

Amber Glass is the name of any glassware having a yellowish-brown color. It became popular during the last quarter of the 19th century.

Amberina Glass was patented by the New England Glass Company in 1833. It is generally recognized as a clear yellow glass shading to a deep red or fuchsia at the top. When the colors are opposite, it is known as reverse amberina. It was machine-pressed into molds, free blown, cut and pattern molded. Almost every glass factory here and in Europe produced this ware, but few pieces were ever marked.

Amethyst Glass – The term identifies any glassware made in the proper dark purple shade. It became popular after the Civil War.

Art Glass is a general term given to various types of ornamental glass made to be decorative rather than functional. It dates primarily from the late Victorian period to the present day and, during the span of time, glassmakers have achieved fantastic effects of shape, color, pattern, texture and decoration.

Aventurine Glass The Venetians are credited with the discovery of aventurine during the 1860s. It was produced by various mixes of copper in yellow glass. When the finished pieces were broken, ground or crushed, they were used as decorative material by glassblowers. Therefore, a piece of aventurine glass consists of many tiny glittering particles on the body of the object, suggestive of sprinkled gold crumbs or dust. Other colors in aventurine are known to exist.

Baccarat Glass was first made in France in 1756, by La Compagnie des Cristelleries de Baccarat – until the firm went bankrupt. Production began for the second time during the 1820s and the firm is still in operation, producing fine glassware and paperweights. Baccarat is famous for its earlier paperweights made during the last half of the 19th century.

Bohemian Glass is named for its country of origin. It is ornate, overlay, or flashed glassware, popular during the Victorian era.

Bristol Glass is a lightweight opaque glass, often having a light bluish tint, and decorated with enamels. The ware is a product of Bristol, England – a glass center since the 1700s.

Burmese – Frederick Shirley developed this shaded art glass at the now famous old Mt. Washington Glass Company in New Bedford, Massachusetts, and patented his discovery under the name of "Burmese" on December 15, 1885. The ware was also made in England by Thomas Webb & Sons. Burmese is a hand-blown glass with the exception of a few pieces that were pattern molded. The latter are either ribbed, hobnail or diamond quilted in design. This ware is found in two textures or finishes: the original glazed or shiny finish, and the dull, velvety, satin finish. It is a homogeneous single-layered glass that was never lined, cased, or plated. Although its color varies slightly, it always shades from a delicate yellow at the base to salmon-pink at the top. The blending of colors is so gradual that it is difficult to determine where a color ends and another begins.

Cambridge glasswares were produced by the Cambridge Glass Company in Ohio from 1901 until the firm closed in 1954.

Cameo Glass can be defined as any glass in which the surface has been cut away to leave a design in relief. Cutting is accomplished by the use of hand-cutting tools, wheel cutting and hydrofluoric acid. This ware can be clear or colored glass of a single layer, or glass with multiple layers of clear or colored glass.

Although cameo glass has been produced for centuries, the majority available today dates from the late 1800s. It has been produced in England, France and other parts of Europe, as well as the United States. The most famous of the French masters of cameo wares was Emile Gallé.

Carnival Glass was an inexpensive, pressed iridescent glassware made from about 1900 through the 1920s. It was made in quantities by Northwood Glass Company, Fenton Art Glass Company and others, to compete with the expensive art glass of the period. It was originally called "taffeta" glass during the 1920s, when carnivals gave examples as premiums or prizes.

Chocolate Glass, sometimes mistakenly called caramel slag because of its streaked appearance, was made by the Indiana Tumbler & Goblet Company of Greentown, IN, from 1900 to 1903. It was also made by the National Glass Company factories, and later by Fenton from 1907 to 1915.

Consolidated Lamp & Glass Co. of Coraopolis, PA, was founded in 1894 and closed in 1967. The company made lamps, art glass and tablewares. Items made after 1925 are of the greatest interest to collectors.

Coralene – The term coralene denotes a type of decoration rather than a kind of glass – consisting of many tiny beads, either of colored or transparent glass, decorating the surface. The most popular design used resembled coral or seaweed, hence the name.

Crackle Glass – This type of art glass was an invention of the Venetians which spread rapidly to other countries. It is made by plunging red-hot glass into cold water, then reheating and reblowing it, thus producing an unusual outer surface which appears to be covered with a multitude of tiny fractures, but is perfectly smooth to the touch.

Cranberry Glass – The term "cranberry glass" refers to color only, not to a particular type of glass. It is undoubtedly the most familiar colored glass known to collectors. This ware was blown or molded, and often decorated with enamels.

Crown Milano glass was made by Frederick Shirley at the Mt. Washington Glass Company, New Bedford, Massachusetts, from 1886-1888. It is ivory in color with a satin finish, and was embellished with floral sprays, scrolls and gold enamel.

Crown Tuscan glass has a pink-opaque body. It was originally produced in 1936 by A.J. Bennett, president of the Cambridge Glass Company of Cambridge, Ohio. The line was discontinued in 1954. Occasionally referred to as Royal Crown Tuscan, this ware was named for a scenic area in

Italy, and it has been said that its color was taken from the flash-colored sky at sunrise. When trans-illuminated, examples do have all of the blaze of a sunrise – a characteristic that is even applied to new examples of the ware reproduced by Mrs. Elizabeth Degenhart of Crystal Art Glass, and Harold D. Bennett, Guernsey Glass Company of Cambridge, Ohio.

Custard Glass was manufactured in the United States for a period of about 30 years (1885-1915). Although Harry Northwood was the first and largest manufacturer of custard glass, it was also produced by the Heisey Glass Company, Diamond Glass Company, Fenton Art Glass Company and a number of others.

The name custard glass is derived from its "custard yellow" color which may shade light yellow to ivory to light green glass that is opaque to opalescent. Most pieces have fiery opalescence when held to the light. Both the color and glow of this ware came from the use of uranium salts in the glass. It is generally a heavy type pressed glass made in a variety of different patterns.

Cut Overlay – The term identifies pieces of glassware usually having a milk-white exterior that have been cased with cranberry, blue or amber glass. Other examples are deep blue, amber or cranberry on crystal glass, and the majority of pieces have been decorated with dainty flowers. Although Bohemian glass manufacturers produced some very choice pieces during the 19th century, fine examples were also made in America, as well as in France and England.

Daum Nancy is the mark found on pieces of French cameo glass made by August and Jean Daum after 1875.

Durand Art Glass was made by Victor Durand from 1879 to 1935 at the Durand Art Glass Works in Vineland, New Jersey. The glass resembles Tiffany in quality. Drawn white feather designs and thinly drawn glass threading (quite brittle) applied around the main body of the ware, are striking examples of Durand creations on an iridescent surface.

Findlay or Onyx art glass was manufactured about 1890 for only a

short time by the Dalzell Gilmore Leighton Company of Findlay, Ohio.

Flashed Wares were popular during the late 19th century. They were made by partially coating the inner surface of an object with a thin plating of glass of another, more dominant color – usually red. These pieces can readily be identified by holding the object to the light and examining the rim, as it will show more than one layer of glass. Many pieces of "rubina crystal" (cranberry to clear), "blue amberina" (blue to amber), and "rubina verde" (cranberry to green), were manufactured in this way.

Francisware is a hobnail glassware with frosted or clear glass hobs and stained amber rims and tops. It was produced during the late 1880s by Hobbs, Brockunier and Company.

Fry Glass was made by the H.C. Fry Company, Rochester, Pennsylvania, from 1901, when the firm was organized, until 1934, when operations ceased. The firm specialized in the manufacturing of cut glassware. The production of their famous "foval" glass did not begin until the 1920s. The firm also produced a variety of glass specialties, oven wares and etched glass.

Gallé glass was made in Nancy, France, by Emile Gallé at the Gallé Factory, founded in 1874. The firm produced both enameled and cameo glass, pottery, furniture and other art nouveau items. After Gallé's death in 1904, the factory continued operating until 1935.

Greentown glass was made in Greentown, Indiana, by the Indiana Tumbler and Goblet Company from 1894 until 1903. The firm produced a variety of pressed glasswares in addition to milk and chocolate glass.

Gunderson Peachblow is a more recent type of art glass produced in 1952 by the Gunderson-Pairpoint Glass Works of New Bedford, Massachusetts, successors to the Mt. Washington Glass Company. Gunderson pieces have a soft satin finish shading from white at the base to a deep rose at the top.

Hobnail – The term "hobnail" identifies any glassware having "bumps" – flattened, rounded or pointed – over the

outer surface of the glass. A variety of patterns exists. Many of the fine early examples were produced by Hobbs, Brockunier and Company, Wheeling, West Virginia, and the New England Glass Company.

Holly Amber, originally known as "golden agate," is a pressed glass pattern which features holly berries and leaves over its glossy surface. Its color shades from golden brown tones to opalescent streaks. This ware was produced by the Indiana Tumbler and Goblet Company for only 6 months, from January 1 to June 13, 1903. Examples are rare and expensive.

Imperial Glass – The Imperial Glass Company of Bellaire, Ohio, was organized in 1901 by a group of prominent citizens of Wheeling, West Virginia. A variety of fine art glass, in addition to carnival glass, was produced by the firm. The two trademarks which identified the ware were issued in June 1914. One consisted of the firm's name, "Imperial," by double-pointed arrows.

Latticino is the name given to articles of glass in which a network of tiny milk-white lines appear, crisscrossing between two walls of glass. It is a type of filigree glassware developed during the 16th century by the Venetians.

Legras Glass – Cameo, acid cut and enameled glasswares were made by August J.F. Legras at Saint-Denis, France, from 1864-1914.

Loetz Glass was made in Austria just before the turn of the century. As Loetz worked in the Tiffany factory before returning to Austria, much of his glass is similar in appearance to Tiffany wares. Loetz glass is often marked "Loetz" or "Loetz-Austria."

Lutz Glass was made by Nicholas Lutz, a Frenchman, who worked at the Boston and Sandwich Glass Company from 1870 to 1888, when it closed. He also produced fine glass at the Mt. Washington Glass Company. Lutz is noted for two different types of glass – striped and threaded wares. Other glass houses also produced similar glass, and these wares were known as Lutz-type.

Mary Gregory was an artist for the Boston and Sandwich Glass Company during the last quarter of the 19th century. She decorated glassware with white enamel figures of young children engaged in playing, collecting butterflies, etc., in white on transparent glass, both clear and colored. Today the term "Mary Gregory" glass applies to any glassware that remotely resembles her work.

Mercury Glass is a double-walled glass that dates from the 1850s to about 1910. It was made in England as well as the United States during this period. Its interior, usually in the form of vases, is lined with flashing mercury, giving the items an all over silvery appearance. The entrance hole in the base of each piece was sealed over. Many pieces were decorated.

Milk Glass is an opaque pressed glassware usually of milk-white color, although green, amethyst, black, and shades of blue were made. Milk glass was produced in quantity in the United States during the 1880s, in a variety of patterns.

Millefiori – This decorative glassware is considered to be a specialty of the Venetians. It is sometimes called "glass of a thousand flowers" and has been made for centuries. Very thin colored glass rods are arranged in bundles, then fused together with heat. When the piece of glass is sliced across, it has a design like that of many small flowers. These tiny water-thin slices are then embedded in larger masses of glass, enlarged and shaped.

Moser Glass was made by Ludwig Moser at Karlsbad. The ware is considered to be another type of art nouveau glass, as it was produced during its heyday – during the early 1900s. Principal colors included amethyst, cranberry, green and blue, with fancy enameled decoration.

Mother-of-Pearl, often abbreviated in descriptions as M.O.P., is a glass composed of two or more layers, with a pattern showing through to the other surface. The pattern, caused by internal air traps, is created by expanding the inside layer of molten glass into molds with varying designs. When another layer of glass is applied, this brings out the design. The final layer of glass is then acid dipped, and the result is mother-of-pearl satin ware. Patterns are numerous. The most frequently found are the diamond quilted, raindrop and

herringbone. This ware can be one solid color, a single color shading light to dark, two colors blended or a variety of colors which include the rainbow effect. In addition, many pieces are decorated with colorful enamels, coralene beading, and other applied glass decorations.

Nailsea Glass was first produced in England from 1788 to 1873. The characteristics that identify this ware are the "pulled" loopings and swirls of colored glass over the body of the object.

New England Peachblow was patented in 1886 by the New England Glass Company. It is a single-layered glass shading from opaque white at the base to deep rose-red or raspberry at the top. Some pieces have a glossy surface, but most were given an acid bath to produce a soft, matte finish.

New Martinsville Peachblow Glass was produced from 1901-1907 at New Martinsville, Pennsylvania.

Opalescent Glass – The term refers to glasswares which have a milky white effect in the glass, usually on a colored ground. There are three basic types of this ware. Presently, the most popular includes pressed glass patterns found in table settings. Here the opalescence appears at the top rim, the base, or a combination of both. On blown or mold-blown glass, the pattern itself consists of this milky effect–such as Spanish lace. Another example is the opalescent points on some pieces of hobnail glass. These wares are lighter weight. The third group includes opalescent novelties, primarily of the pressed variety.

Peking Glass is a type of Chinese cameo glass produced from the 1700s well into the 19th century.

Phoenix Glass – The firm was established in Beaver County, Pennsylvania, during the late 1800s, and produced a variety of commercial glasswares. During the 1930s the factory made a desirable sculptured gift-type glassware which has become very collectible in recent years. Vases, lamps, bowls, ginger jars, candlesticks, etc., were made until the 1950s in various colors with a satin finish.

Pigeon Blood is a bright reddish-orange glassware dating from the early 1900s.

Pomona Glass was invented in 1884 by Joseph Locke at the New England Glass Company.

Pressed Glass was the inexpensive glassware produced in quantity to fill the increasing demand for tablewares when Americans moved away from the simple table utensils of pioneer times. During the 1820s, ingenious Yankees invented and perfected machinery for successfully pressing glass. About 1865, manufacturers began to color their products. Literally hundreds of different patterns were produced.

Quezal is a very fine quality blown iridescent glassware produced by Martin Bach, in his factory in Brooklyn, New York, from 1901-1920. Named after the Central American bird, quezal glassware has an iridescent finish, featuring contrasting colored glass threads. Green, white and gold colors are most often found.

Rosaline Glass is a product of the Steuben Glass Works of Corning, New York. The firm was founded by Frederick Carter and T.C. Hawkes, Sr. Rosaline is a rose-colored jade glass or colored alabaster. The firm is now owned by the Corning Glass Company, which is presently producing fine glass of exceptional quality.

Royal Flemish Art Glass was made by the Mt. Washington Glass Works during the 1880s. It has an acid finish which may consist of one or more colors, decorated with raised gold enameled lines separating into sections. Fanciful painted enamel designs also decorate this ware. Royal Flemish glass is marked "RF," with the letter "R" reversed and backed to the letter "F," within a four-sided orange-red diamond mark.

Rubina Glass is a transparent blown glassware that shades from clear to red. One of the first to produce this crystal during the late 1800s was Hobbs, Brockunier and Company of Wheeling, West Virginia.

Rubina Verde is a blown art glass made by Hobbs, Brockunier and Company, during the late 1800s. It is a transparent glassware that shades from red to yellow-green.

Sabino Glass originated in Paris, France, in the 1920s. The company was founded by Marius-Ernest Sabino, and was noted for art deco figures, vases, nudes and animals in clear, opalescent and colored glass.

Sandwich Glass – One of the most interesting and enduring pages from America's past is Sandwich glass produced by the famous Boston and Sandwich Glass Company at Sandwich, Massachusetts. The firm began operations in 1825, and the glass flourished until 1888, when the factory closed. Despite the popularity of Sandwich Glass, little is known about its founder, Deming Jarvis. The Sandwich Glass house turned out hundreds of designs in both plain and figured patterns in colors and crystal, so that no one type could be considered entirely typical – but the best known is the "lacy" glass produced there. The variety and multitude of designs and patterns produced by the company over the years is a tribute to its greatness.

Silver Deposit Glass was made during the late 19th and early 20th centuries. Silver was deposited on the glass surface by a chemical process so that a pattern appeared against a clear or colored ground. This ware is sometimes referred to as "silver overlay."

Slag Glass was originally known as "mosaic" and "marble glass" because of its streaked appearance. Production in the United States began about 1880. The largest producer of this ware was Challinor, Taylor and Company.

Spanish Lace is a Victorian glass pattern that is easily identified by its distinct opalescent flower and leaf pattern. It belongs to the shaded opalescent glass family.

Steuben – The Steuben Glass Works was founded in 1904, by Frederick Carder, an Englishman, and T.G. Hawkes, Sr., at Corning, New York. In 1918, the firm was purchased by the Corning Glass Company. However, Carder remained with the firm, designing a bounty of fine art glass of exceptional quality.

Stevens & Williams of Stourbridge, England, made many fine art glass pieces covering the full range of late Victorian ware between the 1830s and 1930s. Many forms were decorated

with applied glass flowers, leaves and fruit. After World War I, the firm began producing lead crystal and new glass colors.

Stiegel-Type Glass – Henry William Stiegel founded America's first flint glass factory during the 1760s at Manheim, Pennsylvania. Stiegel glass is flint or crystal glass; it is thin and clear, and has a bell-like ring when tapped. The ware is quite brittle and fragile. Designs were painted free-hand on the glass – birds, animals and architectural motifs, surrounded by leaves and flowers. The engraved glass resulted from craftsmen etching the glass surface with a copper wheel, then cutting the desired patterns.

It is extremely difficult to identify, with certainty, a piece of original Stiegel glass. Part of the problem resulted from the lack of an identifying mark on the products. Additionally, many of the craftsmen moved to other areas after the Stiegel plant closed, producing a similar glass product. Therefore, when one is uncertain about the origin of this type of ware, it is referred to as "Stiegel type" glass.

Tiffany Glass was made by Louis Comfort Tiffany, one of America's outstanding glass designers of the art nouveau period, from about 1870 to the 1930s. Tiffany's designs included a variety of lamps, bronze work, silver, pottery and stained glass windows. Practically all items made were marked "L.C. Tiffany" or "L.C.T." in addition to the word "Favrile".

Tortoiseshell Glass – As its name indicates, this type of glassware resembles the color of tortoiseshell, and has deep, rich brown tones combined with amber and cream colored shades. Tortoiseshell glass was originally produced in 1880 by Francis Poh, a German chemist. It was also made in the United States by the Sandwich Glass Works and other glass houses during the late 1800s.

Val St. Lambert Cristalleries – The firm is located in Belgium, and was founded in 1825. It is still in operation.

Vasa Murrhina glassware was produced in quantity at the Vasa Murrhina Art Glass Company of Sandwich, Massachusetts, during the late 1800s. John C. Devoy, assignor to

the firm, registered a patent on July 1, 1884, for the process of decorating glassware with particles of mica flakes coated with copper, gold, nickel or silver, sandwiched between an inner layer of clear or transparent colored glass. The ware was also produced by other American glass firms and in England.

Vaseline Glass – The term "vaseline" refers to color only, as it resembles the greenish-yellow color typical of the oily petroleum jelly known as Vaseline. This ware has been produced in a variety of patterns both here and in Europe – from the late 1800s. It has been made in both clear and opaque yellow, vaseline combined with clear glass, and occasionally the two colors are combined in one piece.

Verlys Glass is a type of art glass produced in France after 1931. The Heisey Glass Company, Newark, Ohio, produced identical glass for a short time, after having obtained the rights and formula from the French factory. French produced ware can be identified from the American product by the signature. The French is mold marked, whereas the American glass is etched script signed.

Wavecrest Glass is an opaque white glassware made from the late 1890s by French factories and the Pairpoint Manufacturing Company at New Bedford, Massachusetts. Items were decorated by the C.F. Monroe Company of Meriden, Connecticut, with painted pastel enamels. The name wavecrest was used after 1898 with the initials for the company "C.F.M. Co." Operations ceased during World War II.

Webb Glass was made by Thomas Webb & Sons of Stourbridge, England, during the late Victorian period. The firm produced a variety of different types of art and cameo glass.

Wheeling Peachblow – With its simple lines and delicate shadings, Wheeling Peachblow was produced soon after 1883 by J.H. Hobbs, Brockunier and Company at Wheeling, West Virginia. It is a two-layered glass, lined or cased inside with an opaque, milk-white type of plated glassware. The outer layer shades from a bright yellow at the base to a mahogany red at the top. The majority of pieces produced are in the glossy finish.

GLASS

A-OH Jan. 2003   Early Auction Company

Darners

#343 Steuben Gold Aurene ball on baluster handle w/ open snapped pontil, lg. 6in. **$300**

#349 Rouge Flambé, free blown w/ open ground pontil, lg. 6in. **$125**

#350 Peachblow, N. Eng. Glass Co., w/ glossy surface & another glossy peachblow w/ cracked handle n/s.

#346 Peachblow, N. Eng. Glass Co., free blown w/ sheared pontil, lg. 6in. **$200**

#348 Steuben Gold Aurene ball on baluster handle w/ open snapped pontil, lg. 6 ½in. **$375**

#344 Steuben Blue Aurene ball on baluster handle, w/ open snapped pontil, lg. 6in. **$350**

#345 Nailsea free blown cased darner, white ground w/ pulled maroon loop strings & sheared pontil, lg. 6in. **$75**

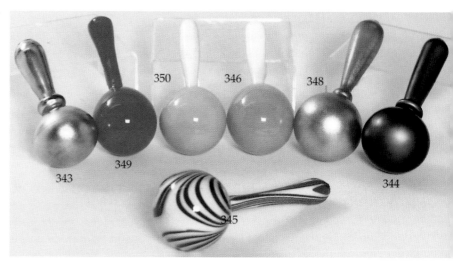

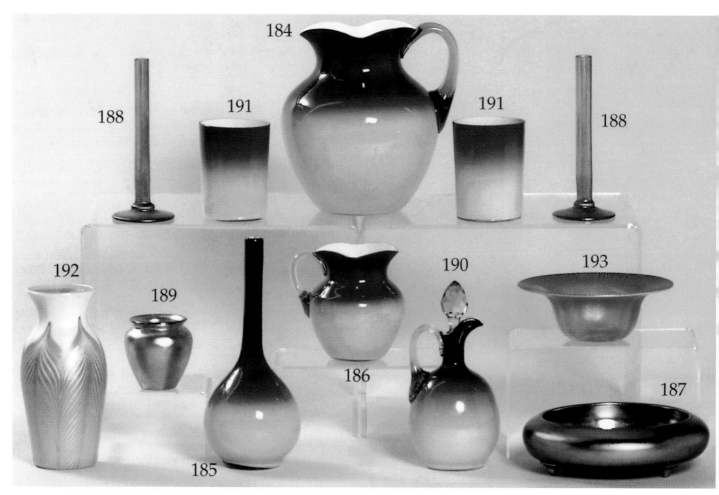

A-OH Jan. 2003   Early Auction Company

Art Glass

First Row

#188 Steuben Bud Vases, pr. sgn. "Aurene", ht. 6in. **$300**

#191 Wheeling Peachblow Tumblers, ht. 3¾in. **$600**

#184 Wheeling Peachblow Water Pitcher w/ applied amber handle, ht. 7¼in. **$1,450**

Second Row

#189 Steuben Vase, classic form, sgn. "Aurene", ht. 2½in. **$550**

#186 Wheeling Peachblow Creamer w/ applied amber handle, ht. 4in. **$825**

#193 Tiffany Favrile Bowl w/ stretch border & opal feathering, sgn., dia. 6in. **$500**

Third Row

#192 Quezal Vase w/ pulled feather dec. & gold liner, ht. 6½in. **$1,100**

#185 Wheeling Peachblow Stick Vase, ht. 8½in. **$700**

#190 Wheeling Peachblow Cruet w/ applied reeded handle, ht. 6¾in. **$1,450**

#187 Steuben Aurene Bowl, deep blue w/ applied feet, sgn. dia. 7½in. **$500**

A-SC Dec. 2002   Charlton Hall Galleries, Inc.

#410 Perfume Flask, early 20th C., by Tiffany & Co., rose cut to clear flask w/ 18 karat gold top, lacking stopper, lg. 7in. **$3,450**

A-NJ May 2003   Craftsman Auctions

#221 Daum Nancy Bowl on tortoiseshell ground, sgn., ht. 2½in., dia. 7¾in. **$1,200**

A-IA Mar. 2003

Jackson's International Auctioneers

Carnival Glass

First Row

#191 Basket, Grape patt. by Imperial, ht. 9¾in. **$115**

#192 Tumblers, pair, w/ three rose panels, vertical rib, ht. 4¼in. **$34**

#193 Candlesticks, pair, by Imperial, Crackle patt. **$34**

#194 Footed Bowl by Imperial, Double Dutch patt., dia. 9½in. **$46**

#195 Footed Bowl, Waterlily patt., dia. 9in. **$46**

#196 Vase, Feathers patt., mkd. Northwood, ht. 7in. **$56**

#197 Tumblers, set of six, Floral & Grape Patt., w/ minor loss to one piece. **$57**

Second Row

#198 Bowl by Fenton in Holly patt., dia. 9in. **$184**

#199 Bowl mkd. Northwood, Three Fruits patt., dia. 9in. **$161**

#200 Tumblers, three Peacock at the Fountain patt. by Northwood, Waterlily & Cattails, & Grape patt., unmarked. **$46**

#201 Epergne, Wide Panel patt., w/ minor damage, ht. 17in. **$259**

#202 Bowl by Northwood, Wild Strawberry patt., mkd. dia. 9in. **$230**

#203 Bowl, Star of David patt., dia. 8in. **$126**

#204 Sherbet & Vase, Holly patt. **$34**

Third Row

#205 Bowl in Good Luck patt., w/ Northwood mark, dia. 9in. **$287**

#206 Two-Handled Footed Bonbon in Floral & Wheat patt. **$57**

#207 Bowl, Dragon & Lotus patt. **$57**

#208 Compote, Horse's Heads patt. w/ minor loss from broken bubble, dia. 7in. **$57**

#209 Bowl in Stippled Rays patt. w/ Northwood mark, dia. 10in. **$34**

#210 Bowl, Fishscale patt. w/ opalescent edge, dia. 9in. **$23**

A-OH Jan. 2003 Early Auction Company

#75 Epergne w/ trumpet vase at top & three red satin ruffled bowls resting in silver plated base, ht. 23in. **$1,300**

#74 Steuben Rosaline Plates, three, one w/ floral cutting, dia. 8½in. **$250**

A-OH Jan. 2003 Early Auction Company

#536 Royal Flemish Vase, "Garden of Allah", Mt. Washington Glass Co., w/ gold dec. & an aperture in base, ht. 13¾in. **$5,750**

A-OH Jan. 2003   Early Auction Company

Art Glass

First Row

#512 Wheeling Tumbler w/ tiny nick at rim, ht. 3¾in. **$300**

#501 Agata Lemonade, N. Eng. Glass Co., ht. 5in. **$650**

#497 Agata Lily Vase w/ light wear, ht. 8in. **$1,000**

#500 Agata Lemonade w/ strong blue & amber staining, N. Eng. Glass Co., ht. 5in. **$1,900**

#516 Wheeling/Creamer w/ applied amber handle, ht. 3¼in. **$600**

Second Row

#496 Wheeling Peachblow Pitcher w/ sq. mouth & applied amber handle, ht. 5⅜in. **$950**

#514 Wheeling Peachblow Pitcher w/ sq. mouth & applied amber handle, ht. 4in. **$900**

#532 Plated Amberina Tumbler, ht. 3¾in. **$1,700**

#533 Plated Amberina Tumbler, ht. 3¾in. **$1,800**

Third Row

#515 Wheeling Peachblow Cruet w/ applied amber reeded handle & amber

faceted stopper w/ roughness, ht. 7in. **$875**

#513 Wheeling Peachblow Tumbler, ht. 3¾in. **$200**

#534 A Plated Amberina Creamer w/ distinct ribbing patt., ht. 2¼in. **$3,600**

#535 Plated Amberina Tumbler, ribbed, w/ horizontal crack, ht. 3¾in. **$150**

#534 Plated Amberina Cruet w/ applied amber handle w/ annealing line at top, ht. 7in. **$2,650**

A-OH Jan. 2003   Early Auction Company

First Row

#21 Pigeon Blood Oil Lamp, two parts w/ gold floral dec., ht. 8in. **$625**

Second Row

#20 Blue Satin Glass Vase, D.Q. patt. w/ ruffled top, ht. 9½in. **$155**

#38 Cranberry Pickle Castor, Inverted Thumbprint patt. w/ silverplate holder, mkd. Homan. **$300**

#18 Cut Velvet Bowl, butterscotch ground w/ spider webs & floral dec. in amethyst. silver plate frame original. **$450**

Third Row

#22 Burmese Bride's Bowl w/ ruffled top & enameled spider mum dec. in two colors, dia. 10in. **$900**

#23 Amethyst Opalescent Rose Bowl w/ applied glass flowers & loop crystal handle, ht. 8in. **$150**

Fourth Row

#19 Mt. Washington Burmese Mustard Pot in conforming silverplate holder. **$300**

#26 Sterling Silver Flask w/ crystal body chased in scrolled sterling overlay, cap dented, ht. 5½in. **$50**

#35 Satin Glass Lamp Shade w/ three faceted jewels inserted in body, deep

yellow shading lighter, ht. 6in. w/ butterscotch satin glass vase D.Q. patt. – at right, ht. 7in. **$200**

#30 Greentown Chocolate Glass Tumbler in File patt. **$50**

#37 Peg Lamp, DQMOP blue satin glass on brass base. **$725**

#13 Favrile Nut Dish, flower form sgn. LCT together w/ Tiffany vase. **$250**

#36 Vasa Murrhina Bride's Basket, cranberry shading to pink w/ silver metallic inclusions, w/ rope handle, dia. 10in., ht. 8in. **$300**

#15 Cruet, Prussian blue, Inverted Coin Spot patt. w/ floral dec., ht. 5in. **$80**

497
501
500
516
512
496
514
515
532 533
534
534A 535
513

21
38
37
20
18
22
23
36
19
30
15
26 35
35
33

A-OH Jan. 2003   Early Auction Company
Water Pitchers

First Row

#6 **Cranberry Opalescent,** Fern patt. by Beaumont, ht. 8½in. **$150**

Second Row

#8 **Sapphire Blue** w/ inverted Coin Spot patt. w/ enamel dec., ht. 9in. **$175**

#3 **Prussian Blue** w/ scrolled opalescent Arabian Nights patt., ht. 9in. **$30**

Third Row

#11 **DQMOP Satin Glass** shading from satin red to white w/ reeded handle, ht. 8½in. **$225**

#10 **Amberina** w/ overall quilted patt., clear reeded handle, ht. 9in. **$50**

Fourth Row

#1 **Cranberry** w/ opalescent hobnails by HB&C, ht. 8in. **$300**

#5 **Cut Velvet Type** w/ cranberry stripes on white ground, ht. 9in. **#275**

#4 **Cranberry Swirl Opalescent** w/ clear applied handle, ht. 8½in. **$175**

#7 **Cranberry Swirl** w/ spatter dec., frosted handle, ht. 9in. **$300**

#2 **Francisware** by HB&C w/ roughness to 3 hobs, ht. 8in. **$225**

#12 **DQMOP Satin Glass** shading from pink w/ frosted handle, ht. 7½in. **$325**

#9 **Royal Ivy** by Northwood shading from cranberry to clear, ht. 8½in. **$150**

A-IA June 2003
Jackson's International
Auctioneers

Daum Nancy Cameo Glass

#651 **Vase,** ca.1910, sgn. w/ Cross of Lorraine, ht. 8in. **$2,760**

#642 **Vase,** ca.1900, sgn. w/ Cross of Lorraine, ht. 8½in. **$4,600**

#643 **Vase,** ca.1900, sgn. w/ Cross of Lorraine, ht. 9in. **$4,140**

#654 **Vase,** ca.1900 footed, sgn. w/ Cross of Lorraine, ht. 6in. **$4,600**

GLASS

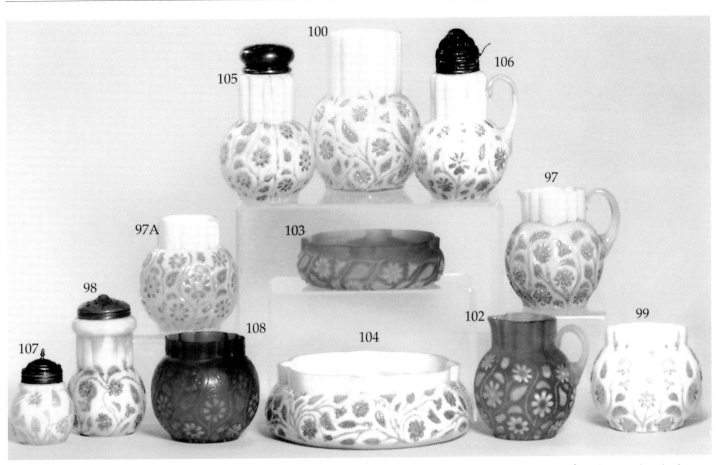

Findlay Onyx Glass

First Row

#105 Sugar Shaker w/ sterling cap, roughness to rim, ht. 6¼in. **$1,150**

#100 Celery w/ strong lustre dec., ht. 6¼in. **$200**

#106 Syrup Pitcher w/ applied fiery opalescent handle, ht. 6¾in. **$425**

Second Row

#97A Spooner w/ strong color, ht 4½in.

$550

#103 Floradine Bowl, red satin ground w/ white frosted flowers, dia. 5¾in. **$1,400**

#97 Creamer w/ strong lustre dec., ht. 4¾in. **$375**

Third Row

#107 Mustard Pot w/ metal cap, ht. 3½in. **$800**

#98 Sugar Shaker w/ orig. cap, ht. 5¼in. **$255**

#108 Sugar Bowl, red ground w/ white flowers, ht. 4in. **$300**

#104 Low Bowl w/ rim roughness, dia. 8in. **$630**

#102 Floradine Pitcher w/ frosted flowers & leaves on red satin ground, ht. 4¾in. **$1,900**

#99 Sugar Bowl w/ strong color, ht. 4in. **$350**

A-IA June 2003

Jackson's International Auctioneers

Victorian Brides Bowls

First Row

#800 Clear Glass Bowl, dec. w/ swirled cranberry & yellow pull-up patt. under threaded & rigoree surface, in period quadruple frame. **$287**

#801 Enameled & Cased Bowl, late 19th C., in emerald green glass cased w/ translucent peach & opal enamel w/ gilt scrolls & silvered frame. **$920**

#802 Cased Satin & Enameled Bowl, late 19th C., on silvered base. **$402**

Second Row

#803 Cased Glass Bowl, late 19th C., on silvered base, **$258**

#804 Enameled & Cased Glass Bowl, late 19th C., in later Pairpoint frame. **$402**

#805 Enameled & Cased Glass Bowl in opal glass w/ Aurora silvered frame. **$287**

#189 **Gallé Vase** w/ detailed raised leaf & berry design, frosted ground, ht. 9in. $4,500

A-OH Dec. 2002
Treadway Gallery, Inc.

#188 **Gallé Vase**, swollen & footed form w/ carved cameo clematis blossoms, sgn., ht. 14½in. $4,000

#190 **Le Verre Francais Vase** w/ elaborate cameo design of stylized plant, mkd. w/ embedded cane, ht. 20in. $2,900

A-IA June 2003

Jackson's International Auctioneers

Klondike Glass, 19th C.
Satin Finish Panels & Amber Stain

#869 **Vase**, ht. 8in. $258
#870 **Water Pitcher**, ht. 10in. $1,092

#871 **Condiment Set** consisting of a 7in. cruet – repl. stopper – toothpick holder, salt & pepper & tray, 5½in. sq. $1,035
#872 **Oval Bowl**, lg. 9¼in. $86
#873 **Large Celery**, ht. 5½in. $115
#874 **Bowl**, ht. 3in., 7¼in. sq. $115

#875 **Covered Butter**, minor chips on base, 7in. sq. $258
#876 **Punch Cups**, set of 6, roughness on base of one & ground chip on base of another, ht. 2½in. $258

#609 Gallé Vase w/ detailed cameo floral design in multiple tones, frosted ground, sgn., ht. 11in. $2,900

A-OH Dec. 2002
Treadway Gallery, Inc.

#608 Gallé Vase w/ carved & enameled floral design & incised sgn. at base, ht. 18in. $2,200

#610 Austrian Vase, organic form w/ handles in an iridescent blue & green glaze, repr. chip on handle, ht 11½in. $500

A-IA June 2003

Jackson's International Auctioneers

Art Glass

#785 Wheeling Amberina Morgan vase, late 19th C., w/ minor rim flake, ht. 8in. $431

#786 Amberina Pitcher, late 19th C., w/ Inverted Thumbprint w/ applied handle, ht. 7½in. $172

#787 Gunderson Peachblow Footed Cup & Saucer, mid-20th C. $103

#788 Mt. Washington Colonial Ware Vase, late 20th C., w/ polychrome dec., red crown & wreath mark, ht. 13¾in. $2,070

#789 Satin Glass Bowl, Stevens & Williams w/ applied mat-so-nu-ke dec. & English Registry mark, dia. 5½in. $402

#790 Burmese Footed Vase, late 19th C., w/ diamond quilted patt. & applied prunt on pontil, ht. 7½in. $345

#791 Large Burmese Vase, late 19th C., ht. 11½in. $431

806　807　808　809　810　811　812

A-IA June 2003
Jackson's International Auctioneers

Art Glass

First Row

#806 Mt. Washington Biscuit Jar, w/ enameled dec., late 19th C., stamped "M.W.", ht. 7½in. **$488**

#807 Austrian Enameled Vase, ca.1900 w/ stylized floral panels & gilt dec., ht. 10¾in. **$201**

#808 Czech Art Glass Basket Lamp, ca.1920 w/ applied floral & fruit forms, minor disrepair, ht. 10½in. **$431**

Second Row

#809 Harrach Bohemian Vase, ca.1900, cased w/ fern dec., ht. 5in. **$143**

#810 Bohemian Vase, ca.1870 w/ applied handles, white enameled dec. & rigoree, minor loss, ht. 9¼in. **$143**

#811 Mary Gregory Beverage Set, 7 pc. w/ enameled dec., **$575**

#812 Bristol Mantle Urns, ca.1885, w/ transfer dec. of angels & children, ht. 15¼in., pair. **$373**

220

A-NJ May 2003　　　**Craftsman Auctions**

#220 Daum Nancy Gourd-Shaped Vase etched w/ branches of chestnuts, small nick to base, marked, ht. 7½in. **$1,200**

222

A-NJ May 2003
Craftsman
Auctions

#222 Degue Chalice-Shaped Vase w/ etched cobalt leaves on mottled pink ground, ht. 11¼in. **$900**

A-NJ May 2003
Craftsman
Auctions

#223 Le Verre Francais Vase etched w/ orange foxglove on pink mottled ground, a few pock marks to base, sgn., ht. 19in. **$1,600**

223

A-MA Feb. 2003   Skinner, Inc.

Sandwich Glass by Boston & Sandwich Glass Co., Sandwich, MA ca.1825-50

First Row

#320 Salt, Gothic Arch patt., med. blue w/ white striations, chips, ht. 1⅝in. **$529**

#321 Salt, amber, oblong w/ chips, ht. 1⅝in. **$499**

#322 Oval Salt in the Peacock Eye patt., w/ white striations, chips, ht. 1½in. **$1,410**

#323 Salt, silvery opaque light blue, chips, ht. 2in. **$1,880**

#324 Salt, dark blue w/ light striations, chips, ht. 1⅞in. **$1,880**

#325 Salt, Boat patt., cobalt blue w/ rim & base chips, ht. 1⅝in. **$705**

#326 Opalescent Salt, Crown patt., edge chips, ht. 2½in. **$764**

Second Row

#327 Lacy Cup Plates, two, one violet-blue, Shell Border patt., & one opalescent, Shell Border patt., rim chips, dia. 3in. **$294**

#328 Salt, Shell patt., green-blue w/ edge roughness & loss to one corner, ht. 1⅝in. **$646**

#329 Nappy, Roman Rosette patt., dia. 6in. n/s

#330 Cup Plates, three, one Roman Rosette patt., two Heart patt., rim chips, dia. 3⅜in. & 3½in. **$382**

Third Row

#331 Cup Plates, two, Eagle patt., an amethyst & cobalt blue, dia. 2⅞in. **$588**

#332 Plate, red amber in the Roman Rosette patt., w/ rim chips, dia. 5⅜in. **$353**

#333 Plate, cobalt blue w/ scalloped rim w/ disk & rosette designs, surface wear & rim chip, dia. 6in. **$112**

#334 Cup Plates, two, Roman Rosette patt., an amethyst & blue, minor rim chips, dia. 3in. **$323**

Fourth Row

#335 Colognes, blown molded glass, two (L&R), w/ chips, ht. 5⅞in. & 5⅜in. **$176**

#336 Lacy Glass Cup Plate, Heart patt., chips, dia. 3⅜in. **$441**

#337 Plate, dark amethyst pressed glass, Rosette patt., rim chips, dia. 5⅜in. **$294**

#338 Lacy Glass Cup Plate w/ rough surface & rim chips, dia. 3½in. **$294**

Bottom Row

#339 Lacy Glass Plates, two (L&R), a blue-green w/ trefoil design & a yellow-green plate in Gothic Arch patt., rim chips, dia. 5⅝in. **$100**

#340 Colognes, two, yellow blown molded glass, edge chips, Sandwich, w/ edge chips, ht. 5⅝in. & 5¼in. **$206**

#341 Cologne, ruby cased blown molded w/ oval panel designs, ht. 5¼in. **$118**

GLASS

A-NJ May 2003
Craftsman Auctions

#216 Emile Gallé Vase etched w/ branches of sweet peas on chartreuse/yellow ground, sgn., ht. 14½in. **$1,300**

A-NJ May 2003
Craftsman Auctions

#217 Emile Gallé Vase w/ branch of olive green eucalyptus against a pearl gray ground, sgn., ht. 25½in. **$2,700**

A-NJ May 2003
Craftsman Auctions

#218 Emile Gallé Vase w/ flaring cupped rim, etched w/ orange spider mums on pearl gray ground, sgn., ht. 15in. **$1,400**

A-IA Mar. 2003

Jackson's International Auctioneers

Cut Glass

#1456 Tall Compote, mid 20th C., w/ scalloped rim & fan design, ht. 9in. **$92**

#1457 Wine Jug, early 20th c., w/ buzzsaw patt., ht. 11½in. **$218**

#1458 Vase, early 20th C., w/ engraved floral designs, ht. 12in. **$115**

#1459 Vase, last half 20th C., w/ hobstar band & engraved florals, ht. 12in. **$138**

#1460 Vase, first half 20th C., w/ buzzsaw floral design, ht. 12in. **$149**

#1461 Vase, early 20th C., w/ gravic cut florals & scrolls, ground pontil, ht. 13in. **$69**

#1462 Pitcher, last half 20th C., w/ Button & Daisy & Rosette patt., ht. 10in. **$126**

#1463 Bottle, first half 20th C., w/ gravic cut Thistle & Flower patt., ht. 9½in. **$80**

#1464 Candlesticks, early 20th C., w/ zipper & diamond point cutting, ht. 10in. **$259**

#1465 Bowl, last half 20th C., w/ etched pear & leaves, mkd. "Clark", lg. 12in. **$184**

#1466 Dresser Box, first half 20th C., w/ buzzsaw design, minor flake, dia. 6¼in. **$46**

#1467 Console Bowl, last half 20th C., w/ acid etched pear dec., dia. 9in. **$144**

#1468 Covered Box, first half 20th C., w/ hobstar & horizontal rib design, sgn., "Hawkes", dia. 4in. **$138**

#1469 Pair of Water Bottles, last half 20th C., w/ hobstar & etched florals, ht. 8in. **$69**

#1470 Handled Nappy, first half 20th C., four part divided form w/ hobstar, lg. 11in. **$126**

#1471 Bowl, first half 20th C. w/ hobstar & arches, dia. 9in. **$207**

#1472 Dresser Box, ca.1900 w/ hobstar & panels, sgn. "P&B" (Pitkin & Brooks), lg. 5½in. **$259**

#1473 Table Lamp, first half 20th C., cut w/ diamond point & floral designs, ht. 21in. **$1,150**

#1474 Whisky Jug, first half 20th C., w/ hobstar & fan designs, ht. 7¼in. **$172**

#1475 Dresser Box, first half 20th C., w/ buzzsaw dec., dia. 5½in. **$144**

#1476 Charger, ca.1900 w/ scrolling thistle & flower design, sgn. "Libbey", dia. 12in. **$374**

#1477 Plate, early 20th C., w/ hobstar & paneled arches, 7in. sq. **$126**

#1478 Celery, early 20th C., w/ hobstar & fan design, lg. 11½in. **$34**

#1479 Pedestal, early 20th C., w/ button & daisy rosettes & fanned arches, minor flakes, dia. 9in. **$57**

#1480 Decanter, first half 20th C., w/ hallmarked silver rim, flakes on stopper, ht. 16½in. **$103**

#1481 Nappy, first half 20th C., w/ center handle & buzzsaw designs, dia. 6¼in. **$92**

#1482 Ice Cream Tray, first half 20th C., w/ buttons, fans & buzzsaw designs, chips, lg. 13½in. **$115**

#1483 Dresser Bottle, first half 20th C., w/ etched Sunflower patt., ht. 5½in. **$57**

#1484 Pair of Nappies, last half 20th C., w/ hobstar designs, dia. 5in. & 6in. **$69**

#1485 Auto Vase, first half 20th C., w. floral design & nickel plate hardware, lg. 11½in. **$161**

#1486 Sandwich Tray, first half 20th C., w/ button & etched designs, lg. 12in. **$115**

#1487 Celery, first half 20th C., w/ hobstar & buzzsaw designs, lg. 12in. **$115**

#1488 Cruet w/ silver overlay, early 20th C., w/ gravic cut florals, ht. 6in. **$69**

1456 1457 1458 1459 1460 1461 1462 1463 1464 1465 1466 1467 1468 1469 1470 1471 1472 1473 1474 1475 1476 1477 1478 1479 1480 1481 1482 1483 1484 1485 1486 1487 1488

GLASS

987

988

989

990

991

992

993

994

995

996

996

997

998

999

1000

1001

1002

1003

1004

1005

1006

1007

1008

1009

1010

1011

1012

A-MA Feb. 2003   Skinner, Inc.

Paperweights

First Row

#342 Two, N. Eng. Glass Co., 1850-80, one scrambled w/ bits of multicolored ribbon twists; the other w/ red, white & blue canes in quatrefoil patt. on white latticinio cushion, scratches & sm. bruises, ht. 1⅞in. & 1⅝in. **$235**

#343 Faceted Millefiore, England, composed of red/white & blue floral canes in concentric circle, minor scratch, ht. 1⅝in. **$147**

#344 Sandwich Weedflower, 1870-87, the blossom composed of two blue petals over three pink & white striped petals on stem, scratches & nicks, ht. 1⅝in. **$646**

#345 Faceted Millefiori, attrib. to Whitefriars, England, composed of predominantly red, white & blue canes w/ one round facet cut on top & five on sides, ht. 1⅝in. **$294**

#346 Floral Bouquet Miniature, N. England Glass Co., w/ flat bouquet centered w/ three different colored florets & leaves, scratched & nicks, ht. 1½in. **$176**

#347 Saint-Louis Crown, France, mid-19th C., composed of green, red & white ribbon twists, capped by a floret, scratches & nicks, ht. 1½in. **$1,116**

Second Row

#348 Sandwich Poinsettia, pinkish-red flower petals on stem w/ leaves, & few scratches, ht. 2in. **$499**

#349 Glass Fruit, depicting pears, cherries & leaves on white latticinio basket, w/ scattered surface scratches, ht. 2in. **$176**

#350 Multifaceted Floral Bouquet & Garland Glass, Saint-Louis, France, mid-19th C., w/ flat bouquet of four multicolored florets bordered by a pink & white floral garland w/ 19 cut facets on top & 8 around sides, scratches, ht. 1⅞in. **$558**

#351 Glass Fruit, N. England Glass Co., depicting pears & cherries surrounded by leaves on white latticinio basket, scratches, ht. 2¼in. **$353**

#352 Baccarat Pansy Glass, France, 1845-55, depicting purple & yellow pansy blossom & bud on stem w/ leaves, sm. internal crack, ht. 2¼in. **$529**

Opposite

A-IA Mar. 2003   Jackson's International
Auctioneers

Carnival Glass

#987 Bowl, Strawberry patt., Northwood w/ emb. mark w/ flakes on foot rim, dia. 9in. **$92**

#988 Bowl, Leaf Chain patt., Fenton, dia. 9in. **$103**

#989 Bowl, Peacock & Urn patt., Fenton, dia. 9in. **$149**

#990 Bowl, Three Fruits Medallion patt., Northwood w/ emb. mark, dia. 9in. **$138**

#991 Bowl, Holly patt., Fenton, dia. 9in. **$80**

#992 Tree Jar – chip on base – creamer & two tumblers, late 20th C. **$46**

#993 Bowl, Orange Tree patt., Fenton, together w/ Continental bowl. **$46**

#994 Bowl Heart & Vine patt., dia. 9in. **$92**

#995 Bonbon, Persian Medallion patt., lg. 7½in. **$103**

#996 Vases, Rustic patt., ht. 9½in., by Fenton, Northwood Drapery patt., ht. 8½in. **$92**

#997 Bowl, Thistle patt., by Fenton, dia. 8in., together w/ pickle dish, Pansy patt., by Fenton. **$115**

#998 Hat Shape Dish, Blackberry Spray patt., by Fenton, dia. 7in. **$69**

#999 Hat Shape Dish, Blackberry Spray patt. by Fenton, early. **$230**

#1000 Bowls, Grape & Cable by Fenton & Grape Delight patt. by Dugan. **$138**

#1001 Footed Bowl w/ water lily & grape design w/ scrolled feet, dia. 6¼in. **$103**

#1002 Table Setting, 4-piece, Alaska patt. by Northwood, ca.1900, incl. spooner, sugar, creamer & water pitcher, ht. 7¼in. **$776**

#1003 Bowls, Heart & Vine patt. & Heavy

Grape patt. bowl - chips, by Fenton. **$57**

#1004 Footed Compote, Question Marks patt. by Dugan, dia. 6½in. **$69**

#1005 Bowls, three by Fenton, Vintage Leaf patt., dia. 7in. & 6in. **$92**

#1006 Tumblers, Grape patt., early, ht. 4in. **$69**

#1007 Bowl, Stippled Rays patt. w/ hat vase in Peacock Tail patt. – flakes – by Fenton. **$34**

#1008 Footed Bowl, Panther patt. by Fenton, dia. 6in. **$57**

#1009 Plates, pair, Garden Path patt. by Dugan, early, dia. 6½in. **$431**

#1010 Bonbon Dish Butterflies w/ a bowl in the Stippled Rays patt. by Fenton. **$69**

#1011 Bowl, Persian Medallion by Fenton, dia. 6in. **$57**

#1012 Bowl, Pine Cone patt., by Fenton, dia. 5½in. **$92**

A-MA Feb. 2003   Skinner, Inc.

Paperweights

First Row

#353 **Clematis Blossom,** attrib. to Baccarat, France, 1845-50, composed of veined white petals surrounded by leaves on stem, star cut base, ht. 2⅛in. **$940**

#354 **Sandwich Poinsettia,** Boston & Sandwich, pinkish-red flower petals on stem w/ three leaves, on double swirl white latticinio ground, minor bruise on base, ht. 2¼in. **$411**

#355 **Red Rose Blossom,** Millville, NH,

1905-12, red shaded upright blossom surrounded by leaves, ht. 3⅛in. **$470**

#356 **Poinsettia,** Boston & Sandwich Glass Co., w/ pinkish-red flower petals on stem w/ bud & leaves on double-swirl white latticinio cushion, ht. 2⅛in. **$558**

Second Row

#357 **Red Rose Blossom,** footed, Millville, NJ, w/ red shaded blossom surrounded by leaves, sm. bruise on foot, ht. 3¾in. **$558**

#358 **Sandwich Weedflower,** Boston & Sandwich Glass Co., w/ flower composed of two shaded pink petals

over three pink, blue & white striped petals, surface wear, ht. 2in. **$646**

#359 **Yellow Water Lily,** footed, Millville, NJ, upright shaded yellow blossom surrounded by four leaves, round facet on top, few scratches, ht. 3⅝in. **$1,923**

#360 **Floral Garland,** attrib. to Baccarat, France, composed of blue, green, red & white interlaced garland of millefiori canes, ht. 2⅛in. **$648**

#361 **Yellow Rose Blossom,** footed, Millville, NJ, w/ yellow blossom surrounded by three leaves & raised on pedestal, scratches, ht. 3¾in. **$1,057**

A-IA Mar. 2003

Jackson's International Auctioneers

#1425 **Cut Glass Compote** w/ thumbnails & stars on blown hollow base, ht. 10in. **$34**

#1426 **Cut Glass Vase** w/ florals & spiral ribs, ht. 10in. **$57**

#1427 **Cut Glass Pitcher** w/ etched floral designs, ht. 10in. **$57**

#1428 **Heisey Crystal Martini Server** w/ figural rooster head stopper, ht. 14in. **$51**

#1429 **Cut Glass Vase** w/ gravic cut flowers, ht. 12in. **$69**

#1430 **Cut Glass Pitcher** w/ etched floral blossoms, ht. 10in. **$149**

#1431 **Cut Glass Vase** w/ buzzsaw dec., ht. 10in. **$92**

#1432 **Heisey Basket** w/ gravic cut floral dec. & emb. diamond mark, ht. 10in. **$218**

#1433 **Cut Glass Dresser Bottle** w/ silver collar, ht. 7½in. **$69**

#1434 **Victorian Glass Bowl** w/ handle in silvered basket w/ serving spoon, mkd.

Reed & Barton, lg. 10½in. **$138**

#1435 **Engraved Glass Group,** 19th C., incl. two stoppered bottles & jug w/ applied twist handle, ht. 10in. **$57**

#1436 **Waterford Wine Set,** 7 pc., Kenmare patt., sgn., ht. 12½in. **$373**

#1437 **Dresser Bottles,** 3, one mkd. Czechoslovakia, ht. 4½in. & 5½in. **$115**

#1438 **Waterford Glass Compote** in Glendore patt., sgn., ht. 6½in. **$126**

#1439 **Cut Glass Ferner,** footed in Hobstar & Fan patt., some flakes, ht. 7in. **$57**

#1440 **Cut Glass Biscuit Jar** w/ buzzsaw design, lid absent, ht. 5½in. **$34**

#1441 **Baccarat Crystal Figure** of a stylized porcupine, sgn., lg. 5in. **$115**

#1442 **Cut Glass Covered Cake Stand** w/ domed top, wheel cut & floral designs, chip on rim, ht. 11½in. **$161**

#1443 **Waterford Juice Pitcher** in the Glendore patt., sgn., ht. 6½in. **$161**

#1444 **Paperweight Candle Holder** w/ suspended bubbles & cut shoulder bank, sgn. "Thos. Webb, England", ht. 3in. **$46**

#1445 **Orrefors Crystal Vase** depicting little girl, moon & stars, sgn., lg. 6¼in. **$103**

#1446 **Cut Glass Box & Sugar Bowl,** ht. 4in. **$23**

#1447 **Cut Glass Plates,** set of 10 w/ hobstar designs, dia. 5¾in. **$138**

#1448 **Cut Glass,** 4 pcs., cruet, knife rest, salt & pepper. **$46**

#1449 **Waterford Cut Glass Bowl** in large Waffle patt., sgn. dia. 8in. **$138**

#1450 **Heisey Crystal Figure** of a standing colt, ht. 5in. **$69**

#1451 **Crystal Figures,** 3, incl. pair of New Martinsville seals w/ ball & whale. **$92**

#1452 **Cut Glass Dresser Bottles,** one w/ losses & one stopper repl. **$69**

#1453 **Crystal Dresser Bottles** incl. a cornucopia & figural bird. **$80**

#1454 **Cut Glass Bowls,** pair w/ buzzsaw dec., dia. 8in. **$172**

#1455 **Crystal & Silver Mounted Wines,** set of 8 w/ gravic cut, mkd. "Robert Anstead .800", ht. 5in. **$138**

1425 1426 1427 1428 1429 1430 1431 1432
1433 1434 1435 1436 1437
1438 1439 1440 1442 1443 1444 1445 1446
1441
1447 1448 1449 1450 1451 1452
1453 1454 1455

1393

1399

1400

1408

1409

1393

1394

1402

1401

1411

1410

1419

1418

1395

1403

1396

1404

1405

1397

1398

1406

1407

1412

1413

1414

1415

1416

1417

1420

1421

1422

1423

1424

A-IA Mar. 2003

Jackson's International Auctioneers

#1393 **Bohemian Art Glass Vase** in Tree of Life patt., ht. 7in. **$115**

#1394 **Satin Glass Vase** w/ applied rigoree handle, ground pontil, ht. 12in. **$103**

#1395 **Enameled Satin Glass Mantle Ewer** w/ ormolu handle & base, ht. 16in. **$126**

#1396 **Bohemian Art Glass Vase** w/ pulled purple loops, rim w/ flakes, ht. 12in. **$149**

#1397 **Bohemian Art Glass Vase** w/ applied coiled snake, ht. 10½in. **$144**

#1398 **Satin Glass Vase**, rim appears to have been ground, ht. 8in. **$23**

#1399 **Peachblow Syrup Pitcher** w/ enameled flowers & applied handle, ht. 7in. **$138**

#1400 **Chocolate Glass Nappy** in Leaf Bracket patt., lg. 6in. **$11**

#1401 **Cambridge Glass Jug** w/ clear glass stopper, ht. 7in. **$34**

#1402 **Green Crystal Compote** w/ etched bird & urn, ht. 7in. **$23**

#1403 **Victorian Epergne** w/ silvered swan base & opalescent glass to green glass vases, ht. 20in. **$719**

#1404 **Crystal Glass Basket** w/ wheel cut floral designs, ht. 10in. **$69**

#1405 **Imperial Art Glass Basket**, ht. 6in. **$287**

#1406 **Heisey Crystal Basket** w/ emb. diamond mark, ht. 8½in. **$103**

#1407 **Austrian Glass Goblet**, 19th C., flashed w/ enameled florals, ht. 5¼in. **$23**

#1408 **Czech Art Glass Vase** w/ minor flakes, ht. 9in. **$46**

#1409 **Sabino Glass Figure** of two love birds, mkd. lg. 5in. **$69**

#1410 **Crystal Basket** w/ amber flashed rim & cut designs, ht. 7½in. **$92**

#1411 **Czech Figural Glass Dresser Lamp** ca.1920 w/ partly nude woman, shade has minor damage, ht. 18in. **$287**

#1412 **Stretch Glass Compote** w/ iridized finish, dia. 7½in. **$11**

#1413 **MOP Rose Bowl** w/ quilted pattern, ht. 5½in. **$201**

#1414 **Sandwich Glass Museum Bowl** in ruby cut to clear, dia. 9in. **$172**

#1415 **Albert French Crystal Paperweights** w/ portraits, one sgn., dia. 3in. **$57**

#1416 **Figural Stem Wine Glasses**, pair, ht. 5¼in. **$57**

#1417 **Victorian Toothpick** in Colorado patt., ht. 3in. **$34**

#1418 **Copper Lustre** Pcs., mid-19th C., incl. 3 cream jugs & 3 mugs. **$103**

#1419 **Czech Glass Accent Lamp**, ca.1920 w/ art deco designs, mkd., ht. 8½in. **$431**

#1420 **Victorian Bride's Basket** w/ enameled bowl in silvered frame, bowl repr., ht. 13in. **$149**

#1421 **Bohemian Glass Miniatures**, 5 pieces, two cordials, salt, vase & handled cup. **$92**

#1422 **Opaque Glass Compote** in variegated glass, dia. 7¼in. **$11**

#1423 **Cambridge Glass Compote** w/ acid etched & iridized designs, dia. 6½in. **$57**

#1424 **Perfume Bottles**, pair, ht. 7in. **$80**

A-IA June 2003

Jackson's International Auctioneers

First Row

#724 **French Bowl** early 20th C. w/ enameled wintry scene of a minstrel, sgn. "Perlam", ht. 5¼in. **$195**

#725 **French Cameo Vase**, ca.1920, sgn. "Muller Fres Luneville", ht. 4¾in. **$517**

#726 **Devez Cameo Perfumer**, ca.1900, sgn. "DeVez", no atomizer, ht. 6in. **$632**

#727 **French Enameled Cabinet Vases**, 3, ca.1900, ea. sgn. "Peynaud", ht. 4¼in. **$201**

Second Row

#728 **French Enameled Covered Box**, ca.1900, sgn. "Peynaud", dia. 5in.

$172

#729 **Daum Nancy Vase**, ca.1915, sgn. w/ Cross of Lorraine, ht. 6½in. **$258**

#730 **French Enameled Finger Bowl**, ca.1900, sgn. "Peynaud", dia. 4¼in. **$115**

#731 **French Enameled Bowl**, ca.1900, sgn. "Peynaud", dia. 3¾in. **$195**

A-IA June 2003   Jackson's International Auctioneers

#833 **Mary Gregory Vases** w/ enameled dec.,
ca.1885 w/ cut scalloped rim, ht. 7¼in. **$2,070**

A-NJ May 2003   Craftsman Auctions

#38 **Tiffany Twisted Candlesticks** w/ cupped bobeches in gold lustered
glass, mkd. L.C.T., ht. 5in. **$1,100**

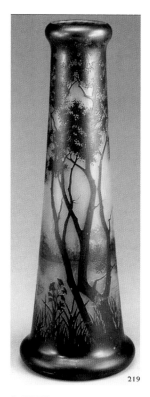

A-NJ May 2003

Craftsman Auctions

#37 **Tiffany Floriform Vase**
in gold lustered finish, mkd.
L.C.T., ht. 15½in. **$3,750**

A-NJ May 2003

Craftsman Auctions

#219 **Daum Nancy Vase**
w/ cupped rim, etched
w/ trees by river, sgn.,
ht. 24in. **$3,500**

A-IA Oct. 2003   Jackson's International Auctioneers

#799 **Mother-of-Pearl Satin Glass Ewers,** mid-20th C., w/ diamond
quilt patt., ht. 12½in. **$431**
#800 **Mother-of-Pearl Satin Glass Vase,** late 19th C., w/ diamond quilt
patt., ht. 9in. **$143**

HALLOWEEN

Halloween was introduced into the United States by immigrants from England, Ireland, and Scotland during the late 1800s. It was a celebration of the end of the harvest season. Originally it was known as All Saints Day, and after a period of time came to be known as All Hallows Eve, and later as Halloween. By the first decade of the new century, publishers capitalized on the new holiday with a variety of postcards and books. This material inspired manufacturers to produce a variety of party decorations during the 1920s and Halloween parties with an array of colorful decorations were all the rage. But it was not until later that Halloween became linked with children and the tradition of "trick or treating" became popular. It was at this time that two merchandising magnates, Frank W. Woolworth and Sebastian S. Kresge, began exporting a variety of German Halloween items for the growing American holiday market until the late 1930s.

Collectors became serious about collecting Halloween memorabilia in the 1970s. Values remained moderate until the early 1990s when antique dealers began specializing in these vintage collectibles. When articles began to appear in antiques trade magazines, prices for the seasonal collectibles literally escalated to lofty levels. Today, Halloween collectibles are second only to Christmas collectibles, and the variety is enormous.

A-PA May 2003   Noel Barrett Antiques & Auctions Ltd.

#1 Lipstick Mouth Jack-O'-Lantern, German pressed cardboard, wear & wire repl., ht. 4¾ in. **$110**

#2 Jack-O'-Lantern, German pressed cardboard w/ original insert, repairs to insert, ht. 7½in. **$198**

#3 Jack-O'-Lantern, glazed, German pressed cardboard w/ original insert, some damage to insert, ht. 5½in. **$77**

#4 Jack-O'-Lantern Pole Mount, hand painted tin, early U.S. made, ht. 9in. **$742**

#5 Jack-O'-Lantern w/ Goatee, German pressed cardboard w/ shredded tissue eyebrows & goatee, dimensional nose, ht. 4½in. **$880**

#6 Jack-O'-Lantern, pressed cardboard mkd. Germany, slight damage one side & rear of base, ht. 4½in. **$22**

#7 Tin Jack-O'-Lantern, hand painted, mkd. w/ pat. May 13, 1902, Toledo Metal Sign Co., OH, damage to insert, ht. 7½in. **$990**

#8 Jack-O'-Lantern, German, pressed cardboard w/ repl. insert & base, ht. 2¾ in. **$176**

#9 Two Mini Jack-O'-Lanterns, pressed cardboard, both mkd. Germany, ht. 2½ in. **$440**

#10 Four Jack-O'-Lanterns, U.S. paper pulp, includes lg., med., & two mini closed eye & mouth lanterns/candy containers, ht. from 5¾in. to 2½in. **$153**

#11 Double Faced & Singing Jack-O'Lanterns, both American paper pulp, smaller w/ two-sided image, larger missing insert w/ black glitter highlights, edge wear & cracked bottom, largest ht. 7in. **$55**

#12 Three Cardboard Lanterns, all double sided, two Jack-O'-Lanterns along w/ black cat, damage to inserts & wear on cat features, largest ht. 7¾in. **$177**

#13 Skull Lantern, U.S. made papier-mâché w/ repl. insert, back edge has singed rim, ht. 4¼in. **$302**

#14 Jack-O'-Lanterns on Cat Body, U.S. paper pulp w/ repl. insert, amusing details include tail in back, slight wear to rim, ht. 7¾in. **$357**

#15 Glass Jack-O'-Lantern, painted, U.S. made w/ metal rim & handle, some overpainting, ht. 4½in. **$357**

#16 Jack-O'-Lantern Man, w/ full body, U.S. paper pulp w/ great detail, ht. 7in. **$330**

A-PA May 2003   Noel Barrett Antiques & Auctions Ltd.

#17 Jack-O'-Lantern, open nose, U.S. glazed paper pulp w/ green highlights, slight dent in back, ht. 8in. **$159**

#18 Jack-O'-Lantern, U.S. made glazed paper pulp in original cellophane w/ toys & candy, Caruth Candy Co. label, slight cracking of cellophane, overall ht. 13in. **$295**

#19 Jolly Jack-O'-Lantern, U.S. paper pulp w/ repl. insert, ht. 7in. **$253**

#20 Jack-O'-Lantern w/ Arched Brows,

U.S. glazed paper pulp, ht. 6in. **$165**

#21 Jack-O'-Lantern w/ Stem, U.S. paper pulp w/ repl. insert, pencil scribbling on back, ht. 7½in. **$99**

#22 Smiling Jack-O'-Lantern, U.S. paper pulp, damage/repair to insert, ht. 5½in. **$77**

#23 Jack-O'-Lantern in Cellophane, U.S. paper pulp w/ orig. wrap, cellophane cracked & split, ht. 4in. **$154**

#24 Drum Lantern, oil cloth on wood rim covered w/ paper, minor cracking &

splits to oil cloth, ht. 4¾in. **$413**

#25 Full Bodied Cat Lantern, orange, U.S. paper pulp w/ repl. insert, repair to left ear, lg. 7in., ht. 6½in. **$385**

#26 Full Bodied Cat Lantern, black, U.S. paper pulp w/ original insert, ear tip missing, other cracked, lg. 7in., ht. 6½ in. **$318**

#27 Black Cat Candy Container, painted papier-mâché, slight chip on ear, ht. 7in. **$143**

#28 Black Cat Lantern, German, pressed cardboard w/ dimensional ears, small repair to insert, ht. 3½in. $660

#29 Glass Jack-O'-Lantern, painted glass w/ straight eyes & triangle nose, light ear & scratching, ht. 4in. $412

#30 Cat Jack-O'-Lantern, molded painted cardboard w crepe collar & bow tie, eye inserts repaired, ht. 5½in. $522

#31 Glass Jack-O'-Lantern, U.S. made w/ metal rim & handle, ht. 4½in. $302

#32 Cat Lantern, molded & painted cardboard w/ crepe bow tie, stamped Germany on base, ht. 3½in. $715

#33 Black Cat on Fence Lantern, U.S. glazed paper pulp w/ repl. insert, ht. 7½in. $220

#34 Cat Face Lantern, orange, U.S. paper pulp w/ repl. insert, edge wear & slight cracking, ht. 5in. $93

#35 Owl Candy Container, papier-mâché w/ plastic eyes, damaged ears, light water spotting on back, ht. 10in. $93

#36 Orange Cat on Fence Lantern, U.S. glazed paper pulp w/ repl. insert, edge wear to ears & nose, ht. 7¼in. $66

#37 Small Jack-O'-Lantern w/ nose, U.S. paper pulp, ht. 4¼in. $77

#38 Singing Jack-O'-Lantern, U.S. paper pulp by Pulpco, battery operated light & original .29¢ tag, ht. 4½in. $187

#39 Two Smiling Jack-O'-Lanterns, both U.S. paper pulp, one w/ repl. insert, has slight burn, both approx. ht. 4½in. $82

#40 Two Open Mouth Jack-O'-Lanterns, both U.S. colored paper pulp, larger w/ repaired tissue insert, largest ht. 5in. $220

#41 Witch w/ Broom Candy Container, painted composition w/ crepe paper hair & broom, removable head, stamped Germany, tip of hat damaged, ht. 6in. $385

#42 Pumpkin Girl Nodder, painted composition figure on wood base w/ bobbing spring head, slight warp to base, ht. 6in. $467

#43 Witch Nodder, detailed painted composition figure on wood base w/ spring bobbing head, slight crease to brim of hat, ht. 7in. $687

#44 Smiling Witch Candy Container, painted composition & cardboard w/ crepe paper collar, slide in bottom stamped Germany, paint chipping on hat, ht. 4¾in. $412

#45 Squash Head Candy Container, painted composition, wood & cardboard mkd. Germany on base, ht. 5in. $203

#46 Veggie Man & Turnip Candy Container, painted composition w/ cardboard slide mkd. Germany in base, ht. 4¼in. $944

#47 Glass Witch Candy Container, hand painted w/ screw cap on base retains much orig. detailed paint, ht. 4¾in. $1,062

#48 Two Pumpkin Head Men, painted composition figures on cardboard disks, both mkd. Germany, slight paint chipping on top of yellow man, both ht. 2¼ in. $220

#49 Witch in Pumpkin, very early painted composition piece believed to be German, possible candy container, minor paint loss, ht. 3in. $522

#50 Jack-O'-Lantern Candy Container, painted composition w/ cardboard slide in bottom, small repair to edge of disk, ht. 2½in. $306

#51 Veggie Witch on Candy Box, composition, cardboard & cotton figure on crepe covered box, light staining & discoloration to crepe, lg. 3½ in., ht. 3in. $143

#52 Cat Squeaker Candy Container, painted composition & cloth dressed figure on paper covered cardboard, chimney is squeaker, mkd. Germany on inside of slide, ht. 5¾in. $531

#53 Witch w/ Black Cat Candy Container, painted composition figure w/ removable head mkd. Germany, ht. 4in. $522

#54 Veggie Man on Candy Box, painted composition figure on paper covered cardboard base w/ slide, small repair to tip of one foot, ht. 3in. $275

#55 Pumpkin Face & Gourd Man Candy Boxes, composition & stuffed crepe figures on paper & crepe covered cardboard containers, both approx. ht. 2in. $121

#56 Devil on Candy Container Box, painted plaster & cardboard mkd. Germany, intricate detail on face, paint chip to one horn, ht. 3½in. $154

#57 Pumpkin Head Man on Candy Container, painted composition figure on crepe covered base w/ slide, ht. 3¼in. $306

#58 Tomato Head Veggie Man Candy Container, painted composition w/ cardboard slide in base mkd. Germany, two small holes on head, ht. 4in. $165

#59 Black Cat & Broom Candy Container, painted composition figure w/ spring tail on paper covered cardboard box, ht. 2in. $110

#60 Veggie Man on Candy Container, painted composition figure mkd. Made in Germany, ht. 2¾in. $357

#61 Crouching Black Cat Candy Container, painted plaster figure retains original ribbon, some paint crazing, lg. 6in. $990

#62 Sitting Pretty Black Cat Candy Container, flock covered composition figure has slide in neck, plastic eyes & great detail, ht. 5¼in. $1,210

#63 Swinging Cat Face Candy Container, painted composition figure on cardboard box, head mounted on wire & cross post to cause swinging, paint chipping on ears, missing bottom slide, ht. 5½in. $137

#64 Cross Eyed Cat Candy Container, flocked composition figure on paper covered cardboard box, flock loss in small areas, ht. 5in. $440

#65 Scared Black Cat Candy Container, mohair covered composition & wood figure w/ removable head, slight edge wear to one ear, ht. 5in. $385

#66 Two Mini Black Cats, painted composition figures, mkd. "Made in U.S. zone Germany", slight paint crazing on one figure, ht. 1¾in. $110

#67 Hissing Black Cat Candy Container, painted & flocked composition figure w/ slide in neck, ht. 3in. $275

HALLOWEEN

A-PA May 2003   Noel Barrett Antiques & Auctions Ltd.

#68 Witch & Cat Candy Containers, printed cardboard w/ tab & slot construction, wood wheels w/ tree stump all by Fibro Toy Co., some bends & fraying to outer edges, largest lg. 8¼in. **$165**

#69 Two Witch Candy Containers, painted pressed cardboard w/ cotton, felt & chenille accents both made in western Germany, paint flaking on berry noses, largest ht. 7½in. **$106**

#70 Two Cat & Pumpkin Candy Containers, painted pressed cardboard w/ felt, chenille & straw accents, all mkd. western Germany, slight paint crazing to largest head, largest ht. 6¾in. **$88**

#71 Sugar Jack-O'-Lantern & Two Candy Boxes, crystallized sugar w/ elaborate scene of cat in Halloween field made of royal icing w/ 2 cardboard candy boxes, all ca.1950, all approx. ht. 4in. **$44**

#72 Witch Squeak Toy, painted composition head on cloth & cardboard body, probably early German piece, slight fading on orange cloth, ht. 6½in. **$1,265**

#73 Cat Squeak Toy, cardboard & cloth, ht. 5½in. **$137**

#74 Surprise Ball & Candle Squeaker, printed paper & crepe covered cardboard w/ toy inside mkd. Japan along w/ litho paper & crepe candle squeak toy, both approx. ht. 3¼in. **$88**

#75 Two Jack-O'-Lantern Squeakers, printed paper face w/ squeaker & holly berry eyes on hexagonal box along w/ wood & cardboard squeaker that roll eyes when pressed, largest wd. 2¾in. **$220**

#76 Black Cat Candy Container, molded & painted full body papier-mâché figures, ht. 7in. **$330**

#77 Two Stichler Co. Candy Containers, stuffed felt & flocked plastic figures w/ original cellophane covered candy boxes w/ company labels, candy slightly melted, largest ht. 5½in. **$88**

#78 Grinning Witch Candy Container, painted pressed cardboard figure w/ great detail & strands of cotton hair, small area of overpaint, ht. 9in. **$577**

#79 Pumpkin Head w/ Pilgrim Hat Nodder, printed paper on cardboard face w/ "loofa" body, mkd. "Made in Germany", ht. 5½in. **$203**

#80 Pumpkin Head Corn Man Candy Container, painted composition head & moveable arms on cardboard body w/ slide in base, ht. 5in. **$440**

#81 Jack-O'-Lantern Candy Container, painted pressed cardboard mkd. "Germany D.R.G.M. registered", wd. 3¼in. **$165**

#82 Witch on Jack-O'-Lantern Candy Container, painted pressed cardboard w/ crepe, wood & composition face w/ slide in base, slight paint loss on top of hat, ht. 4¼in. **$577**

#83 Two Crepe Candy Containers, one paper covered straw & cardboard w/ slide in bottom & other w/ composition head w/ elaborate crepe removable collar, slight crushing on ruffled collar, largest ht. 3½in. **$99**

#84 Witch & Cat on Pumpkins Candy Containers, painted composition figures w/ cardboard bases mkd. made in U.S. zone Germany, paint chipping to brim of hat & tips of cat ears, ht. 4¼in. & 4½in. **$198**

#85 Three Devils & Veggie Man, all are bisque, veggie man stamped made in Japan, two seated devils are salt & pepper shakers, chipping on standing devil, largest ht. 3¾in. **$176**

#86 Two Veggie Men, bisque figure stamped Japan on back, w/ composition figure w/ spring neck, largest ht. 3in. **$198**

#87 Three Pumpkin Head Men, bisque figures, chipping to base on two smallest, largest ht. 3½in. **$176**

#88 Pumpkin Head Ratchet, painted composition head w/ crepe collar on wooden ratchet, ht. 6in. **$104**

#89 Cat Face Squeaker, painted composition head & felt dressed figure on stick squeaks when shaken, ht. 10¼in. **$522**

#90 Witch Head Ratchet, painted composition head on wood, some discoloration to face, ht. 7in. **$100**

#91 Jack-O'-Lantern Face Ratchet, pressed cardboard head on wooden device, slight discoloration to face, ht. 7in. **$143**

#92 Black Cat Ratchet, painted composition full bodied cat on wooden triple ratchet, ht. 9¼in. **$121**

#93 Cruciform Ratchet Clacker, pressed cardboard face on wooden toy, two hand operation, stamped Germany on bottom, wd. 6½in. **$148**

#94 Devil Ratchet, painted composition head on wood crepe dressed body, great bobbing action when ratchet is turned, small chip to one ear, ht. 8½in. **$302**

#95 Two Scissor Toys & Ratchet, all made in Japan, scissor toys w/ printed cardboard cat & pumpkin faces, some bends on faces, ratchet wd. 6in. **$55**

#96 Printing Block & Planchette, printing plate on wood block w/ holiday images along w/ fortune telling planchette w/ great imagery, fortune board has water staining on bottom & some warping of paper, wd. 5½in. & 6¼in. **$88**

#97 Two Sets Cookie Cutters, in original box, 3 pc. set made in Germany, 6 pc. set w/ brightly colored idea sheet, smaller box has water staining, largest box 5½ x 8¼in. **$55**

#98 Double Sided Paddle w/ Horn, wooden handle which is also a horn has printed paper cat image on one side & Jack O'-Lantern on other, mkd. made in Czechoslovakia, slight wear & staining to cat image, ht. 11¾in. **$118**

#99 Double Ended Wood Paddle, printed paper Jack-O'-Lantern faces on both sides, both ends & sides mkd. Made in Boston U.S.A., lg. 14in. **$118**

#100 Three Candy Molds, ceramic group includes witch & pumpkin molds mkd. I.B. Davis Co. & salesman sample from J. Frauenberger Co., largest wd. 3½in., ht. 4¼in. **$53**

#101 Three Chocolate Molds, embossed tin group w/ skeleton, flying witch & Jack-O'-Lantern stamped Germany, small areas of corrosion on pumpkin mold, largest ht. 6in. **$121**

#102 Jack-O'-Lantern Rattle, printed paper w/ cardboard & crepe accents retains original C.A. Reed Co. label, ht. 8¼in. **$82**

#103 Four Tambourines, lithographed tin, all by Chein & Co., several dents, missing a few disks, ht. 6¾in. **$715**

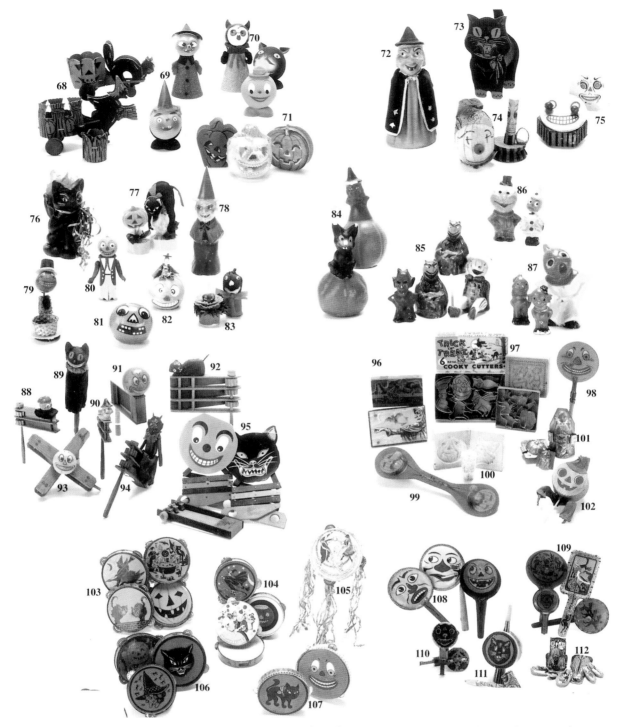

#104 Four Assorted Tambourines, lithographed tin, one w/ cardboard drum by T. Cohn Inc., party imaged one by Kirchhof, other unmarked, tape repair to cardboard drum, missing one set of disks, dia. 6¼in. **$192**

#105 Hand Painted Tambourine, elaborate kid skin & maple wood tambourine personalized w/ guest's name, given as party favor described by Phila. society clipping pasted on inside rim, dia. 7in. **$354**

#106 Three Tambourines, lithographed tin, one by T. Cohn, J. Chein & other is by Kirchhof, largest dia. 7in. **$275**

#107 Two Paper Head Tambourines, printed paper & wood w/ metal disks, both mkd. Made in Germany, largest dia. 7½in. **$224**

#108 Three German Noisemakers, lithographed tin & wood group includes two double faced clangers, one is ratchet type picture w/ cigarette, other is painted tin w/ printed paper face in middle w/ clanger on back, largest lg. 8¾in. **$198**

#109 Four Assorted Clangers, lithographed tin & wood group includes an unmarked mini., one rectangular by Kirchhof, convex clanger made in Japan, other unmarked, mini. missing tip of

handle, largest lg. 8½in. **$121**

#110 Two Sparklers, lithographed tin w/ spring activated levers, lg. 4¾in. **$112**

#111 Jack-O'-Lantern Pipe & Drum/Horn, cardboard, wood & tissue pipe mkd. Germany along w/ printed paper & wood horn w/ black cat image on drum, small tear & slight loss of covering to back of drum, largest lg. 7in. **$112**

#112 Seven Assorted Size Clickers, lithographed tin group includes larger owl printed on toad shape, large insect, three mini & two med. size all by Kirchhof; largest lg. 3¼in. **$35**

A-PA May 2003   Noel Barrett Antiques & Auctions Ltd.

#113 Three Spool-Turned Wooden Toys, believed to be from teens or twenties, creatures have arms attached by elastic string, ht. 6½in. **$209**

#114 Jack-O'-Lantern & Tambourine, lithographed tin both by U.S. Metal Toy, wear & fading on top side of Jack-O'-Lantern, both approx. dia. 6in. **$121**

#115 Skeleton Couple, painted composition figure w/ springy arms & legs, made in occupied Japan, female missing foot, ht. 4in. **$38**

#116 Two Double Sided Glass Lanterns, painted glass battery operated lamps, same design w/ one made in Japan & other by Wales made in Hong Kong, areas of paint loss on Wales version, ht. 5¼in. **$49**

#117 Ghost Candy Container, painted composition & cloth figure w/ slide in base, cloth soiled, ht. 4½in. **$198**

#118 Skull Lantern, in original box, battery operated milk glass lamp, made in Hong Kong, double action switch, box slightly warped, ht. 5¾in. **$106**

#119 Early Czech Devil, painted wood demon has holes for horns & tail, stamped Made in Czechoslavakia, ht. 6¼in. **$27**

#120 Five Assorted Clackers, lithographed tin, four by T. Cohn & one by U.S. Metal Toy, all approx. dia. 4in. **$76**

#121 Four Frying Pan Clangers, lithographed tin & wood, three by T. Cohn, other by Kirchhof, two w/ cat images & two w/ Jack-O'-Lanterns, one missing wood clanger ball in back, largest lg. 8in. **$188**

#122 Eleven Assorted Noisemakers, group includes seven cardboard, wood & tissue horns, two metal & plastic horns, kazoo by Kirchhof & cylindrical noise maker which makes siren noise when opened & closed, largest lg. 10in. **$71**

#123 Five Witch Frying Pan Noisemakers, lithographed tin w/ wood by U.S. Metal Toy, Kirchhof & T. Cohn, all depict various witch imagery, all approx. lg. 8in. **$110**

#124 Eight Assorted Clickers, lithographed tin group includes three toad shaped clickers by T. Cohn, three Kirchhof & two by U.S. Metal Toy Co., largest lg. 4¼in. **$33**

#125 Seven Drum Rattles, lithographed tin w/ wood handles, two by T. Cohn, one by Kirchhof, one U.S. Metal Toy, others unmarked, all lg. 3¼in. **$88**

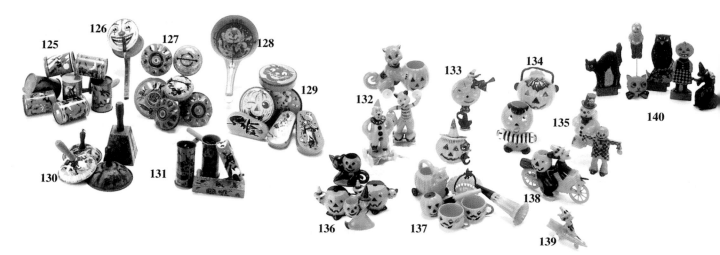

#126 Double Cymbal Noisemaker, lithographed tin w/ wood handle mkd. M.B. Co., lg. 10in. **$154**

#127 Six Assorted Rattles, lithographed tin w/ wood handles, two by T. Cohn, one by Kirchhof, others unmarked, edge wear & spots of corrosion especially

smaller, largest dia. 4¼in. **$66**

#128 Large Frying Pan Clanger, lithographed tin & wood embossed "pat. June 1906" on handle, slight pitting on back, lg. 10¾in. **$49**

#129 Six Assorted Clackers, lithographed

tin, three elongated, two by U.S. Metal Toy & one by Kirchhof, & three round by Kirchhof, largest lg. 5½in. **$112**

#130 Four Bell Noise Makers, lithographed tin w/ wood handles, one square & three round, smallest mkd. U.S. Metal Toy, largest ht. 6in. **$220**

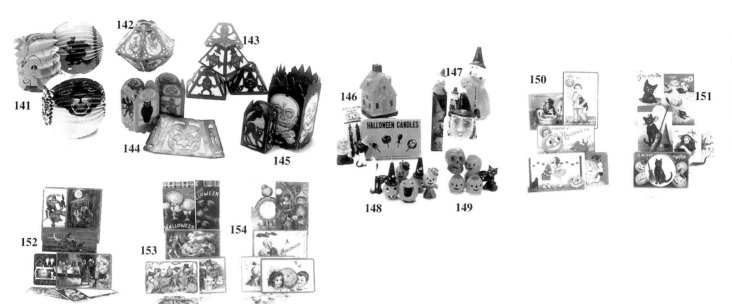

#131 Four Assorted Noise Makers, lithographed tin w/ wood handles, two unmarked tin ratchets & two clackers, one mkd. U.S. Metal Toy, largest lg. 4¾in. $76

#132 Clown & Two Cats on Wheels, all hard plastic, large pumpkin cracked, damage to pull hole & one corner on waving cat, all approx ht. 6in. $188

#133 Two Cake Decoration Pieces, hard plastic includes Jack-O'-Lantern w/ black cat & cat under pumpkin face moon w/ witch on spring, largest ht. 6½in. $165

#134 Two Jack-O'-Lantern Candy Containers, hard plastic, largest ht. 5in. $60

#135 Scarecrow & Snowman, hard plastic candy containers, ht. 4¼in. & 5in. $110

#136 Four Witch & Cat Candy Containers, all hard plastic, includes two witch & cat lollipop holders & witch & black cat candy containers, black cat has crack in front, largest ht. 3¾in. $82

#137 Four Candy Containers & Two Noise Makers, all hard plastic which includes basket, two cups, cat head pumpkin on wheels, horn & Jack-O'-Lantern whistle pipe, pipe lg. 5¼in., cat on wheels ht. 3½in. $247

#138 Witch Riding Motorcycle, hard plastic, missing small piece of foremost point of cycle, lg. 7in. $212

#139 Witch on Rocket Pull Toy, hard plastic w/ white wheels, lg. 4½in. $141

#140 Six Assorted Halloween Items, lead witch on log, cat ring, three mini German diecut stand ups & a Jack-O'-Lantern stick pin, largest ht. 2¾in. $132

#141 Three Pleated Paper Lanterns, two German globe style lanterns w/ cat & witch images & tubular Japanese shade, hinge wire missing from one side of one globe, open dia. 8in. $77

#142 Large Hexagonal Lantern, die cut cardboard w/ German printed tissue paper transparencies, slight fading on top, larger of this size produced, dia. 9in. $192

#143 Set of Four Lampshades, hand cut cardboard & tissue backed shades each w/ different four sided image, one shade w/ heavier wear & torn, ht. 4in. $33

#144 Three Diecast Lanterns, cardboard & tissue w/ assorted holiday images, largest wd. 7in. $27

#145 Two Cardboard Lanterns, both have tissue paper lining behind holiday images, larger w/ skull & crossbones on all sides has edge wear & damage to points, smaller has four different images – witch, owl, cat & pumpkin face, ht. 10in. & 6in. $47

#146 Lot of Assorted Candles, includes large house by Capri, two cats by Gurley, one package of Jack-O'-Lantern candles by Halo & boxed set of 12 assorted candles on toothpicks by Pressner & Co., house ht. 6½in. $112

#147 Five Witch Candles, includes large, two small & square carved image candles, all by Gurley along w/ hard wax candle holder where candle glows thru witch face, largest ht. 8in. $44

#148 Six Figural Candles, all by Gurley Co., includes two Jack-O'-Lanterns w/ hats, two pumpkin men, cat w/ tail candle & cat in pumpkin, largest ht. 4in. $22

#149 Four Jack-O'-Lanterns, Cat & Skull, all made of hard wax probably candy containers, largest ht. 2½in. $11

#150 Postcards 30 w/ Children, assorted greeting cards mostly w/ images of children, some are used, some embossed, 3½ x 5½in. $472

#151 Postcards 30 w/ Black Cats, assorted cards featuring mostly images of cats, some are used & embossed, 3½ x 5½in. $560

#152 Postcards 30 w/ Witches, assorted cards w/ mostly images of witches, some are used w/ amusing holiday messages, 3½ x 5½in. $560

#153 Assorted 30 Postcards, varied holiday images, some are used & embossed, 3½ x 5½in. $590

#154 Postcards 30 w/ Children & Other Images, assorted cards featuring mostly images along w/ other varied holiday imagery, great graphics, some used & embossed, 3½ x 5½in. $501

A-PA May 2003   Noel Barrett Antiques &
Auctions Ltd.

#155 Postcards 35 w/ Couples, assorted cards featuring images of holiday couples & Victorian ladies, some are used w/ amusing greetings, 3½ x 5½ in. **$442**

#156 Three Party Games, Cat & Witch by Whitman, The Witch of Endor Fortune Telling Game, both in original box & Witch Party Game which is actually a pin the eyes on the Jack-O'-Lantern game, not all games complete, larger game target 20 x 20in. **$55**

#157 Owen's Halloween Tales Book, 1931, 2nd edition printing of Ethel Owen's amusing Halloween Tales, w/ original dust jacket, 6 x 8in. **$93**

#158 Halloween Party Book & Festival Book, very colorful 1930 Festival book by American tissue Mills along w/ Beistle party book, some cut-outs detached, largest 7 x 12in. **$154**

#159 Early Boogie Book & Two Magazines, Dennison's 1916 Boogie Book & 1937 & 1938 issues of Children's Play Mate Magazine, 6 x 9in. **$99**

#160 Two Dennison Gala Books, 1925 & 1926 books w/ festive suggestions for several holidays, 5 x 7in. **$5**

#161 Three Dennison Boogie Books, 1916, 1921 & 1925 editions w/ many ideas using Dennison products, cover detached from 1925 edition, 5½ x 8¼in. **$412**

#162 Two Early Boogie Books, 1914 & 1915 versions of the famous Dennison Party Books, 5 x 7½in. **$467**

#163 Four Advertising Halloween Books, two Weeny Witch party books by Farmer Boy Frankfurters, Morgan's Sapolio magic book & Dr. Miles' Signs & Omens book, largest 6½ x 9in. **$55**

#164 Four Party Books, two Weeny Witch cut-out books by Essex Packers, Dennison's 1931 Boogie Book & Whitman's party book w/ assorted cut-outs, largest 9¼ x 14in. **$71**

#165 Two Party Magazines, Dennison's 1927 Oct-Nov Party Magazine & 1934 Halloween Parties, some pencil markings in one book, 7 x 10in. **$143**

#166 Two Early Dream & Fortune Books, Egyptian Witch ca.1920s & Gypsy Witches Dream book ca.1890, edge wear & small spot of cover missing on smaller, largest 9 x 12in. **$93**

#167 Assorted Stunt Games, three punch-out stunt boards, two dial games & boxed game complete w/ all cards & instructions, largest 12 x 9in. **$129**

#168 Six Fortune Games, five spin wheel boards w/ amusing fortunes, some w/ stunts & a boxed Gypsy Fortune telling game w/ pull-up tabs, largest 9 x 13in. **$330**

#169 Four Halloween Magazine Pages, all from The Ladies' Home Journal dating to 1912-1917, includes two witch fortune games, masquerade designs & paper dolls w/ multiple costumes, all

10½ x 15½in. **$1**

#170 Assorted Halloween Advertising, 11 pcs. include pages from Ladies' Home Journal, Saturday Evening Post, etc. featuring brands such as Ford, Wrigley's, Real Silk Hosiery, etc., 10 x 14in. **$1**

#171 Six Cat Musician Die Cuts, embossed cardboard by H.E. Luhrs, one large & five smaller, two on original

packaging card, largest ht. 18in. **$253**

#172 Four Cat Die Cuts, embossed cardboard, three mkd. Germany & other by H.E. Huhrs, edge wear, some tape repairs, ht. 15½in. **$33**

#173 10 H.E. Luhrs Die Cuts, embossed cardboard w/ traditional holiday images, some w/ tape marks, all approx. ht. 9in. **$16**

#174 Witch & Devil Die Cuts, heavily embossed cardboard mkd. Germany, some edge creasing, especially on witch, largest ht. 9½in. **$188**

#175 Three Owl Die Cuts, embossed cardboard mkd. Germany, some surface wear, largest ht. 15½in. **$55**

#176 Two Die Cut Tiaras, embossed cardboard mkd. Germany w/ great details, slight edge wear, 10 x 5½in. **$1,045**

#177 Two Flying Witch Die Cuts, embossed cardboard mkd. Germany, brooms creased, edge wear, largest ht. 13in. **$118**

#178 Four Moon & Figure Die Cuts, embossed cardboard mkd. Germany includes witch, cat, owl & Jack-O'-Lantern, tape repair to larger, largest ht. 11in. **$141**

#179 German Cat Fan, wood w/ tissue fur body & printed cardboard face & tail, tissue slightly faded, face & tail reinforced, ht. 12in. **$154**

#180 Two Cat Stand-Ups, embossed cardboard mkd. Germany w/ glossy highlights, male missing top of hat, ht. 18½in. **$118**

#181 Ten Assorted Hats, German & Japanese honeycomb tissue w/ varied holiday images including pirate hat, clown faces & Jack-O'-Lanterns, largest approx. ht. 12in. **$224**

#182 Large Square Die Cut, heavily embossed cardboard made in Germany w/ great detail, edge wear, repair to small area near hat, sq. 12¾in. **$354**

#183 Ten Jack-O'-Lantern Die Cuts, two med. & one mini. German embossed, five Beistle including cardboard lantern w/ tissue inserts, & two Jack-O'-Lanterns by Luhrs, edge wear & some w/ tape damage, largest ht. 15in. **$77**

#184 Three Jack-O'-Lantern People, embossed cardboard mkd. Germany, includes two clowns & lady w/ cat, feet repaired one clown, small areas of water damage on others, ht. 15½in. **$198**

#185 Assorted Decorations, w/ original packaging, four Beistle Co. items include two complete party packs, Halloween pumpkin cut-outs, Flaming Halloween fortune envelope & Gold Seal Co. wax stencil package, not all complete, largest 10 x 12in. **$605**

#186 Eight Candy/Nut Cups, crepe & cardboard w/ assorted printed images, largest ht. 4½in. **$59**

#187 Candy Boxes & Party Crackers, five crepe & cardboard party crackers along w/ candy corn box & slot & tab box w/ image of skeleton pulling cart by G.M. Co., crackers lg. 8in. **$66**

#188 Assorted Blowouts & Horns, cardboard, wood & waxed paper lot, includes six German & Japanese blowouts, an odd double mustache blowout, a pressed cardboard Jack-O'-Lantern & double sided witch blowers & a striped crepe dressed German pumpkin man horn, some blowers fatigued, largest lg. 11¾in. **$82**

#189 Decorated Toothpicks & Favors,
numerous cotton & crepe decorated toothpicks, most made in Japan along w/ crepe witch & dancing girl, figures ht. 5in. **$55**

#190 Six Honey Centerpieces, witch on
flying saucer, two black cats, dancing witch w/ skirt & large spider, some edge wear, largest ht. 16in. **$53**

#191 Collecting Guide & Honeycomb,
holiday paper honeycomb book by Jeannette Lasansky, along w/ witch & caldron honeycomb pictured on cover, honeycomb w/ some fading, book has some highlight marks, book 8½ x 10in. **$17**

#192 Five Assorted Honeycombs,
includes two dancing witches, one cat & two scarecrows & cornstalk centerpieces, some wear & fatigue to crepe especially on dancing items, largest 10 x 12in. **$27**

#193 Two Dennison Jack-O'-Lanterns,
crepe fringed images w/ suggestions for use on back-games, decorations etc., some creasing & fatigue to crepe, wd. 29in x ht. 23in. **$47**

#194 Four Elaborate Crepe Horns,
cardboard & wood horns w/ detailed crepe accents & assorted printed images including Betty Boop figure made in Germany, largest lg. 14in. **$94**

#195 Five Honeycomb Arm Figures,
includes three in original package, owl, witch & scarecrow along w/ larger owl & ghoul, ghoul ears repaired, largest ht. 12in. **$129**

#196 Two Die Cut Garlands, both
believed to be by Beistle, five cat face festoon & a seven varied image garland featuring center scarecrow, tape marks & repairs, largest lg. 7ft. **$112**

#197 Assorted Die Cuts, 11 unmarked
cardboard images along w/ boxed set of 10 cut-outs, largest ht. 9½in. **$33**

#198 Two Stand-Ups & Crepe Witch, two
Beistle Jack-O'-Lantern stand ups & a handmade crepe & die cut centerpiece, edge wear, repair to largest figure, largest ht. 20in. **$110**

#199 Seven Dancing Skeletons,
cardboard jointed figures include among others a glow in the dark, a cat skeleton & one in the original paper envelope, some w/ repairs, largest ht. 25in. **$60**

#200 Four Early Decorations, black &
white images Am. & believed to date to early 1900s along w/ two paper doilies, diecuts ht. 9½in., doilies dia. 9in. & 7in. **$38**

#201 Costume w/ Candy Bag, early
hand made suit of glazed cotton w/ crepe pumpkins & coordinating Jack-O'-Lantern candy bag, lg. 44in. **$121**

#202 Three Crepe Costume Accessories,
hostess apron w/ strong image along w/ two child's hats w/ German diecut stickers, some fading on hats, apron 20½ x 18in. **$55**

#203 Six Large Die Cuts, tape & edge
damage. **$77**

#204 16 Crepe Party Hats, assorted
crepe designs some w/ honeycomb tissue & printed images, ht. 12in. **$77**

Native American Indian collectibles have attracted collectors from the late 19th century, but it has only been within the latter half of the 20th century that the demand reached the present fever pitch. The major areas of Indian collectibles are rugs, blankets, pottery, beadwork, basketry, wood carvings, leather work and jewelry. Each tribe has its own distinctive designs.

Blankets and rugs have had a great attraction for collectors. The Hopi and Zuni tribes have produced some very appealing examples. However, many collectors search for examples made by Navajo weavers. They worked on an upright loom of their own invention, using natural dyes and wool from their sheep. Today, examples of their early creations are considered art forms.

Perhaps the best known pottery is the black-on-black pieces that were made at the San Ildefonso pueblo, near Santa Fe, New Mexico, by the Martinez family. Julian and Maria signed pieces are especially sought by collectors. Other fine examples of pottery were made at the pueblos of Santo Domingo, Santa Clara and Acoma in New Mexico. And the Hopi Indians in Arizona made fine pottery.

The finest baskets, and the ones most sought by collectors, are those of the Southwest. Their light and durable Indian baskets were made in large quantities, for both personal use and as something to be sold to tourists.

This chapter also includes interesting kachinia dolls of the Southwestern pueblos. Because several hundred known examples were made, many great dolls can still be found. Kachinias represent figures from the Indian spirit world.

A-PA May 2003   Pook & Pook, Inc.

First Row

#430 MicMac quill, birch bark & sweet grass oval box w/ floral decor., ht. 2½, lg. 9in. **$173**

#431 MicMac colorful quill & birch bark round box, ca.1880 w/ geometric decor., losses, ht. 4, dia. 6in. **$489**

#432 MicMac birch bark & quill rectangular box w/ flower & leaf decor., ht. 3¾, wd. 7in. **$201**

#433 MicMac early quill & birch box w/ dome lid & intricate star & geometric patt., ht. 5½, wd. 8¾in. **$805**

#434 MicMac quill & birch box, mid 19th C., w/ geometric design, ht. 4¾, wd. 6¼in. **$633**

Second Row

#435 Plains Beaded & Quilled Hide Moccasins together w/ pair of Woodlands beaded moccasins, losses. **$690**

#436 Cree Beaded Hide Moccasins w/ leaf & floral decor. & brass buttons. **$748**

#437 Great Lakes Beaded Hide Moccasins w/ another beaded pair. **$474**

#438 Kiowa Child's Boots, beaded w/ brass buttons. **$2,530**

A-PA May 2003   **Pook & Pook, Inc.**

#549 Plains Hide Female Doll, ca.1890 w/ orig. beaded clothes, ht. 12¾in. **$6,325**

#550 Cree Indian Male Doll, ca.1890-1900 w/ orig. beaded clothes, ht. 17in. **$230**

A-PA May 2003   **Pook & Pook, Inc.**

#529C Navajo Rug, w/ grey, red, black & cream zigzag, diamond & stripe patt., 66 x 55in. **$5,175**

A-PA May 2003   **Pook & Pook, Inc.**

#581 Navajo Silver & Turquoise Concha Belt, w/ 11 conchas. **$345**

#582 Silver Bracelet w/ 3 inset turquoise stones together w/ a silver & turquoise belt buckle. **$316**

#583 Silver Cuff w/ 6 turquoise stones,

sgn. "R". **$460**

#584 Turquoise & Red Coral Necklace w/ silver catch, together w/ a silver & turquoise bolo. **$633**

#585 Silver Cuff w/ large turquoise stone. **$460**

#586 Squash Blossom Necklace, silver &

turquoise. **$546**

#587 Silver Cuff w/ 4 turquoises in a flower setting. **$403**

#588 Silver Cuff w/ inset turquoise, onyx, agate & jade, sgn. **$920**

#589 Silver & Turquoise Cuffs, two, one signed. **$460**

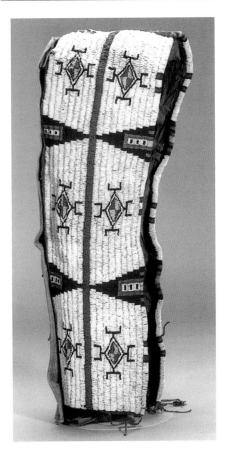

A-MA Jan. 2003   Skinner, Inc.

#126 **Plains Hide Coat,** beaded, last qtr. 19th C., lg. incl. fringe, 46in. **$4,994**

A-MA Jan. 2003   Skinner, Inc.

#131 **Plains Cloth Cradle,** beaded hide, Cheyenne, ca.1880s, some stiffness to hide, lg. 26½in. **$8,813**

A-MA Jan. 2003   Skinner, Inc.

#132 **Hide Pipe Bag,** Central Plains, beaded & quilled, Lakota, late 19th C., lg. 35in. **$2,468**

#133 **Hide Double Saddlebags,** beaded, Lakota, ca.1870, panels slit at center & down one side for storage, some stiffness to hide, lg. 35in. **$9,400**

#134 **Pipe Bag,** Central Plains, beaded & quilled, Lakota, ca.last qtr. 19th C., w/ minor bead & quill loss., lg. 43in. **$2,703**

A-MA Jan. 2003   Skinner, Inc.

#218 **Beaded Cloth Sash,** probably Choctaw, mid-19th C., bead loss & minor damage to cloth, lg. 45in. **$7,638**

#219 **Beaded Wool Sash,** finger woven, Great Lakes, early 19th C., w/ wool loss & minor fading of wool, lg. incl. fringe 72in. **$9,400**

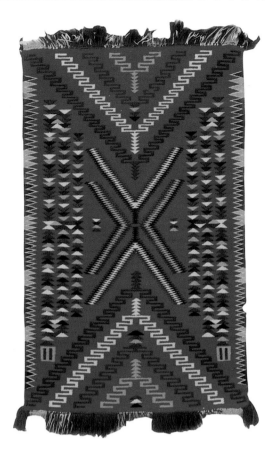

A-MA Jan. 2003   Skinner, Inc.

#512 Navajo Saddle Blanket, Southwest Germantown weaving, late 19th C., w/ wool loss & minor damage, 40 x 25½in. **$3,525**

A-MA Jan. 2003   Skinner, Inc.

#499 Navajo Blanket, Southwest weaving, last qtr. 19th C., 68 x 54in. **$11,163**

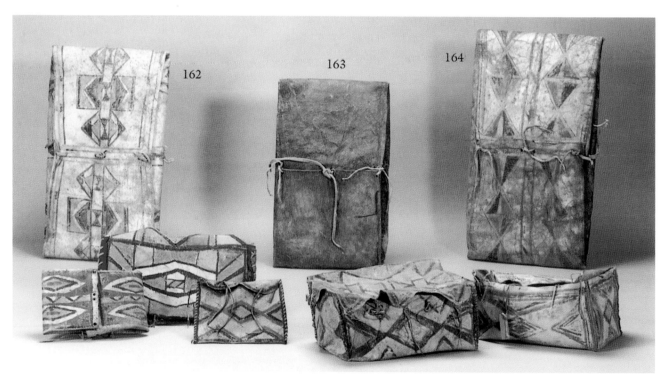

A-MA Jan. 2003   Skinner, Inc.

#162 Plateau Parfleche Envelope, last qtr. 19th C., w/ minor paint loss, lg. 26½in. **$940**

#163 Plains Buffalo Rawhide Parfleche Envelope, mid-19th C., w/ thick buffalo hide ties, old repair, lg. 23in. **$1,116**

#164 Buffalo Rawhide Parfleche Envelope, Northern Plains, Blackfoot, 3rd qtr. 19th C., w/ hide ties., lg. 28½in. **$3,819**

#165 Three Plains Polychrome Parfleche Containers, Lakota, ca.1900, two flat wallets & one small envelope, lg. to

17in. **$2,585**

#166 Two Plains Parfleche Trunks, Lakota, late 19th C., w/ bold painted geometric designs, misshapen, paint loss, ht. 8½, lg. 15in. **$823**

A-MA Jan. 2003   Skinner, Inc.

Pipe Bowls

#200 Ojibwa, Great Lakes w/ lead inlay, 19th C., w/ bold checkered & linear devices, lg. 7¼in. **$1,175**

#201 Pawnee (possibly), early 19th C., w/ incised linear decor., lg. 5in. **$1,528**

#202 Ojibwa, Great Lakes, w/ inlaid lead & red pipestone geometric designs, lg. 8in. **$1,116**

#203 Plains Red Pipestone Pipe, ca.first half 19th C., lg. 3¾in. **$940**

#204 Plains Lead Inlaid Red Bowl, first half 19th C., w/ inlay on both shank & bowl, repr. n/s

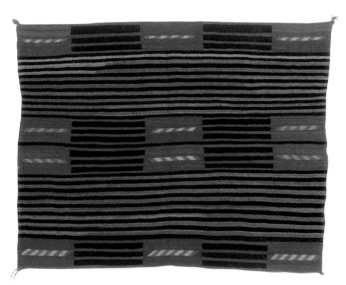

A-MA Jan. 2003   Skinner, Inc.

#523 Navajo Blanket, Southwest weaving, last qtr. 19th C., commercially dyed homespun wool, in style of a woman's "second phase" blanket, minor stains, 64 x 51in. **$11,750**

A-MA Jan. 2003   Skinner, Inc.

#527 Navajo Blanket, Southwest weaving, last qtr. 19th C., dyed homespun & raveled wool in a "second phase" chief's patt., w/ minor wool loss & old reprs., 66 x 57in. **$31,725**

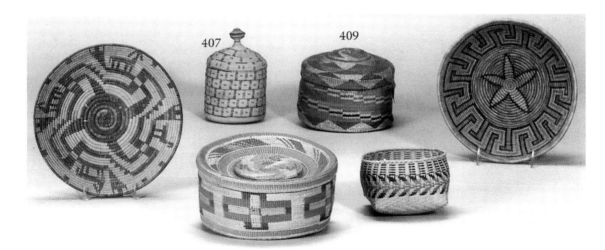

A-MA Jan. 2003   Skinner, Inc.

#406 Southwest Coiled Basketry Tray, Pima, early 20th C., w/ 2 small holes, dia. 9½in. **$558**

#407 Northwest Twined Rattle Top Basket, Aleut, decor. w/ polychrome yarns, ht.

6in. **$2,350**

#408 Northwest Coast Twined Rattle Top Basket, Tlingit, ca.1900, w/ colorful decor., dia. 8½in. **$1,763**

#409 Northwest Coast Twined Lidded Basket, Tlingit, late 19th C., w/ decor.,

slightly misshapen, dia. 6½in. **$585**

#410 Louisiana Twilled Bowl, Chitimacha, w/ decor., ht. 3¼, dia. 5¼in. **$294**

#411 California Coiled Bowl, Mission, late 19th C., w/ decor., dia. 9½in. **$1,880**

A-MA Jan. 2003 Skinner, Inc.

#269 Inuit Cribbage Board, ivory, engraving depicts a hunter in a kayak, walrus, a dwelling, fish & seal, w/ bone end cap, 25½in. **$704**

#270 Inuit Walrus Tusk, depicting whale hunting scenes, lg. 12in. **$529**

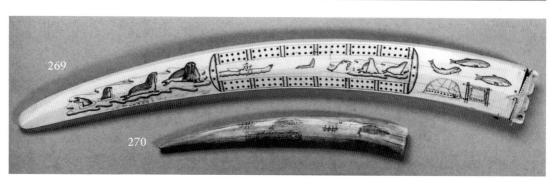

A-MA Jan. 2003   Skinner, Inc.

#476 S.W. Pottery Olla, San Juan, globular body w/ polished black slip, surface abrasions, ht. 10, dia. 10in. **$353**

#477 S.W. Pottery Bowl, San Ildefonso, Marie, globular form w/ matte geometric designs on polished black ground, scratches & abrasions, dia. 9½in. **$588**

A-MA Jan. 2003   Skinner, Inc.

#481 S.W. Pottery Plate, San Ildefonso, Maria/Popovi, flared form w/ matte abstract feather decor. on polished ground, dia. 9½in. **$4,994**

#482 S.W. Pottery Jar, San Ildefonso, Marie, lidded cylindrical form w/ matte geometric designs on polished black ground, ht. 5½in. **$2,703**

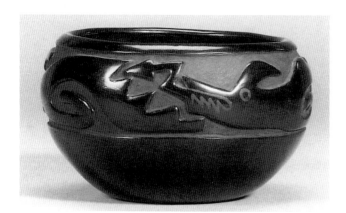

A-MA Jan. 2003   Skinner, Inc.

#483 S.W. Carved Pottery Bowl, Santa Clara, Margaret Tafoya, globular bowl w/ deep relief carved "Avanyu" polished black surface w/ matte design, ht. 4¾, dia. 8¾in. **$3,055**

A-MA Jan. 2003   Skinner, Inc.

#478 S.W. Pottery Bowl, San Ildefonso, Marie & Julian, w/ gun-metal finish & band of matte design, minor scuffs, ht. 2¾, dia. 4½in. **$588**

#479 S.W. Pottery Bowl, San Ildefonso, Maria & Santana, round form w/ bank of matte abstract foliate design, small chip at rim, dia. 3½in. **$470**

#480 S.W. Pottery Bowl, San Ildefonso, Marie & Julian, black on black globular form, from the Pueblos of Santa Clara, ht. 2, dia. 3¾in. **$588**

KITCHEN COLLECTIBLES

Of all the many types of kitchen collectibles, woodenware has the greatest appeal. It has been produced in America from the earliest times. From the Indians the colonists learned the art of making utilitarian objects such as trenchers, porringers, noggins and bowls. The completely hand-shaped pieces are prized by collectors, as no two were ever alike. Oftentimes cutting lines, copper, pewter and iron, left by the craftsman are clearly evident on the surface of an object. Even vessels may bear signs of crude decoration, having an incised geometric design, wiggle work, initials, a date or name... which, of course, enhances the value.

Although numerous kinds of wood were available to the colonists, it was the bulgy growth scar tissue found at the base of certain trees that was favored. This is known as "burl". Its grain, instead of running in the usual parallel lines, was twisted and coiled and produced an unusually attractive grain. In this field, it is the interesting early burl examples that fetch the highest prices when sold.

There are almost countless examples of many types of early kitchen utensils and gadgets... from the hearth to the cookstove... still available for a price, because "waste not, want not" was a favorite maxim. Recycling was simply a natural way of life for our ancestors. Objects were well made and designed to be functional. During the mid-1800s, when mass production was in full gallop, every imaginable device for the refinement of the culinary art was patented. Therefore, most of us have a few old or inherited items in our modern-day kitchens, and these old "classics" are treasured.

Because of the scarcity of early objects, many collectors have become interested in collecting not only gadgets but utensils dating from the second half of the 20th century, including appliances.

A-ME June 2003
James D. Julia, Inc.
#833 **Coffee Mill,** twin wheel grinder w/ "Enterprise Mfg. Co., Philadelphia, USA" embossed on wheel castings, No. 7, repainted w/ repl. wooden drawer, copper hopper missing lid & finial, ht. 24in. **$373**

A-ME June 2003
James D. Julia, Inc.
#834 **Coffee Mill,** Parker No. 502 202, w/ "The Cha's Parker Co., Meriden, Conn. USA" on wheel castings, ht. 16in. **$480**

A-ME June 2003
James D. Julia, Inc.
#835 **Coffee Mill,** No. 200 w/ "The Cha's Parker Co., Meriden, Conn. USA" embossed on wheel, orig. drawer w/ "Pat'd. No 200, March 9, 1897", repainted, ht. 12½in. **$540**

A-ME June 2003
James D. Julia, Inc.
#836 **Coffee Grinder** w/ one wheel mkd. "Lane Bros., Paughkeepsie, NY, repainted, ht. 14in. **$690**

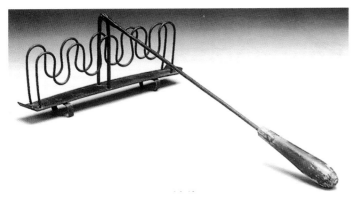 

0360

A-NC May 2003   Brunk Auction Services, Inc.
#0362 **Hinged Iron Toaster** w/ wooden handle, scattered light surface rust, lg. 21in. **$225**

A-NC May 2003   Brunk Auction Services, Inc.
#0360 **Revolving Gridiron** w/ tripod base & handle, scattered light rust, lg. 22½in. **$375**

A-IA Oct. 2002

Jackson's International Auctioneers

#44 Red Wing Pitcher dec. w/ emb. cars & planes, crazing, ht. 9in. **$103**

#45 Enamel Container w/ floral dec., ht. 16in. **$57**

#46 Red Wing Lily Pitcher & Bowl, has damage, pitcher ht. 11in. **$345**

#47 Agateware Coffeepot, swirl green, losses, ht. 12in. **$69**

#48 Red Wing Pitcher w/ blue & white band, ht. 12in. **$103**

#49 Salt Crock, blue & white w/ lid, daisy on snowflakes dec., hairline, ht. 6in. **$92**

#50 Boston Bean Pot & Lid w/ cobalt dec., lid has losses, ht. 7½in. **$103**

#51 Buckeye Root Beer Mug, blue & white, hairlines, ht. 5in. **$99**

#52 Red Wing Pitcher, blue & white band, ht. 6in. **$253**

#53 Blue & White Stoneware Bowl w/ hairline, ht. 6in. **$115**

#54 Jug, one qt., adv. Tobey Polish, ht. 6¼in. **$23**

#55 Mug, adv. Supreme Malt Extract Co., ht. 5¼in. **$92**

#56 Butter Crock, 5lb., w/ lid & handle, minor losses, ht. 6¼in. **$57**

#57 Red Wing Beater Jar, ht. 4¾in. **$92**

#58 Salt Crock & Lid, daisy on snowflakes dec., minor losses, ht. 6in. **$57**

#59 Salt Crock w/ blue & white dec., ht. 3in. **$80**

#60 Wesson Oil Beater Jar, ht. 5½in. **$80**

#61 Agateware Colander, blue swirl, losses, ht. 4in. **$28**

#62 Butter Crock, adv. Lord & Jackson Dairies, ht. 4in. **$51**

#63 Beater Jug, adv. Farmers Union, ht. 5in. **$126**

#64 Red Wing Pitcher w/ cherry band dec., ht. 8¼in. **$115**

#65 Butter Crock w/ blue & white butterfly dec., handle & lid losses, ht. 4½in. **$86**

#66 Red Wing Pitcher w/ cherry band dec., hairline, ht. 9¼in. **$34**

#67 Beater Jar w/ blue band, store adv., ht. 5½in. **$207**

#68 Agateware Shaded Blue Coffeepot, losses, ht. 9in. **$51**

#69 Small Blue & White Bowl, ht. 1¾in. **$34**

#70 Stoneware Butter Crock w/ blue band, ht. 3½in. **$57**

#71 Agateware Blue Swirl Colander w/ losses, ht. 5in. **$40**

#72 Red Wing Beater Jar, store adv., ht. 5in. **$126**

#73 Agateware Coffeepot, blue swirl, losses, ht. 8in. **$115**

#74 Red Wing Sponge Dec. Bowls, set of seven, one w/ hairline, ht. of tallest 11in. **$920**

#75 Agateware Blue Swirl Coffeepot w/ chrome lid & wood handle, ht. 9in. **$195**

#76 Agateware Blue & Hole Muffin Pan, losses, lg. 14½in. **$69**

#77 Stoneware Rolling Pin w/ blue band, adv., lg. 8¼in. **$661**

#78 Cookbook Holder, adv. of Sleepy Eye Milling Co. **$115**

#79 Stoneware Chamber Pot w/ blue band, losses, ht. 6½in. **$69**

#80 Stoneware Soap Dish w/ blue sponge dec., losses, ht. 1in. **$126**

#81 Pickle Crock, Heinz adv., w/ hairline, ht. 5½in. **$92**

#82 Stoneware Rolling Pin w/ blue band, lg. 8in. **$115**

#83 Stoneware Mugs, two, blue & white, ht. 5in. **$103**

#84 Stoneware Mug w/ embossed cattails, ht. 4¼in. **$103**

0363

A-NC May 2003 Brunk Auction Services, Inc.

#0363 Iron Roasting Rack, vertical gridiron w/ one side hinged, notched clasp at top, stretcher base & penny feet, ht. 18½in. **$1,200**

0358

A-NC May 2003   Brunk Auction Services, Inc.

#0358 Iron Roasting Stand, adjustable w/ scroll top above adjustable fork & pan for grease, ht. 23½in. **$1,300**

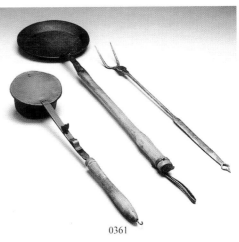

0361

A-NC May 2003   Brunk Auction Services, Inc.

#0361 Iron Cooking Implements incl. **roaster** w/ hinged lid & twist lock, wooden handle has repairs, lg. 28in.; **skillet** w/ long handle mkd. "Stahl", lg. 41¼in.; and **fork** w/ shaped tip, polished surface, lg. 34¼in. **$600**

A-PA Feb. 2003　　　　　Pook & Pook, Inc.

Lehnware

First Row

#133 **Egg Cup** w/ strawberry vines dec., ht. 3½in. **$920**

#134 **Egg Cup** w/ strawberry vine design w/ pedestal base, ht. 3in. n/s

#135 **Covered Sugar Bucket** w/ lid on red ground w/ three iron bands w/ fine dec., ht. 9¾in. **$2,530**

#136 **Footed Bowl** w/ strawberry vines on salmon ground w/ pedestal base, ht. 3in. **$1,380**

#137 **Lidded Cup** w/ strawberry vine design on salmon ground w/ fine dec., ht. 4in. **$1,265**

Second Row

#138 **Saffron Box** w/ strawberry vines on salmon ground, ht. 5¼in. **$575**

#139 **Saffron Box** w/ foliate dec. on tan ground w/ red, green & yellow bands. **$518**

#140 **Cup & Saucer** w/ freehand & stencil design on salmon ground w/ black rim. **$460**

#142 **Footed Saffron Box** w/ black finial above strawberry vines on salmon ground, repair, crack in base, ht. 5in. **$633**

#143 **Lidded Saffron Cup** w/ strawberry vines on salmon ground, red & green bands, repr., crack in base, ht. 5½in. **$1,035**

A-IA Oct. 2002

Jackson's International Auctioneers

#85 **Agateware Coffeepot**, shaded blue, ht. 11¼in. **$86**

#86 **Agateware Coffeepot** w/ blue & white swirl dec., minor losses, ht. 12in. **$103**

#87 **Stoneware Pitcher & Bowl Set**, blue & white, ht. 12in. **$201**

#88 **Agateware Coffeepot** w/ cobalt swirl dec., ht. 10in. **$92**

#89 **Agateware Coffeepot** w/ light blue mottled dec., ht. 8in. **$57**

#90 **Stoneware Butter Crock** w/ lid & blue sponge dec., ht. 6in. **$103**

#91 **Katina Cheese Crock**, no lid or handle, hairlines, ht. 7in. **$34**

#92 **Stoneware Salt Crock** w/ cover, losses, ht. 5in. **$57**

#93 **Red Wing Mixing Bowl**, blue & white w/ Greek key molded dec., dia. 12in. **$115**

#94 **Red Wing Panel Bowl** w/ sponge dec., ht. 4¼in. **$89**

#95 **Stoneware Butter Crock** w/ lid & handle, hairline & losses, ht. 6¼in. **$92**

#96 **Stoneware Bowls**, pair w/ blue bands, ht. 6¼in. **$69**

#97 **Beater Jar** w/ blue bands, adv., ht. 5in. **$253**

#98 **Red Wing Adv. Jar** w/ minor chips, ht. 5in. **$195**

#99 **Chamber Pot**, blue & white w/ emb. apple blossom dec. **$80**

#100 **Agateware Coffeepot** w/ goose neck, blue speckled & tin lid. **$92**

#101 **Tea Canister**, blue & white, no lid, ht. 6in. **$34**

#102 **Stoneware Pitcher**, blue & white w/ emb. Dutch images, ht. 7in. **$28**

#103 **Red Wing Bowl** w/ blue sponged dec., minor flake on base, ht. 9in. **$28**

#104 **Salt Crock** w/ blue dec., wood lid, ht. 5in. **$92**

#105 **Agateware Chamber Pot**, blue & white swirl, losses, repl. lid, ht. 6in. **$69**

#106 **Stoneware Bowl** w/ blue band, adv., ht. 4in. **$69**

#107 **Butter Crock**, adv., ht. 5in. **$69**

#108 **Salt Crock**, blue & white w/ emb. dec., ht. 4in. **$149**

#109 **Salt Crock**, blue & white, no lid, ht. 4in. **$57**

#110 **Agateware Coffeepot**, green swirl dec., minor base losses, ht. 10in. **$80**

#111 **Wesson Oil Jar & Beater**, ht. 5½in. **$126**

#112 **Two Jars**, each w/ blue band, ht. 5in. & 5½in. **$57**

#113 **Butter Crock**, tan & brown dec., hairline, ht. 5in. **$34**

#114 **Red Wing Bowl** w/ blue sponge dec., ht. 4¼in. **$632**

#115 **Butter Crock**, blue & white w/ bail handle, losses to lid, ht. 7in. **$92**

#116 **Butter Crock & Lid**, gray & blue, adv., ht. 5½in. **$345**

#117 **Pitcher**, blue & white w/ cattail dec., ht. 7in. **$126**

#118 **Butter Crock**, no lid, blue & white, ht. 5¼in. **$46**

#119 **Butter Crock** w/ bail handle & lid, blue & white, ht. 5¼in. **$103**

#120 **Butter Crocks**, two w/ blue dec. of cows, no handles or lids, ht. 3¼in. & 5¼in. **$46**

#121 **Hot Water Bottle** w/ salt glaze, ht. 6½in. **$92**

#122 **Bowls**, two w/ blue bands, ht. 3in. & 4in. **$57**

#123 **Red Wing Framed Letter**, dated 1934. **$57**

#124 **Stoneware Rolling Pin** w/ blue bands, lg. 8in. **$138**

#125 **Stoneware Rolling Pin** w/ blue cherry dec., lg. 8in. **$103**

#126 **Blue Sponge Dec. Lid**, dia. 9¼in. **$28**

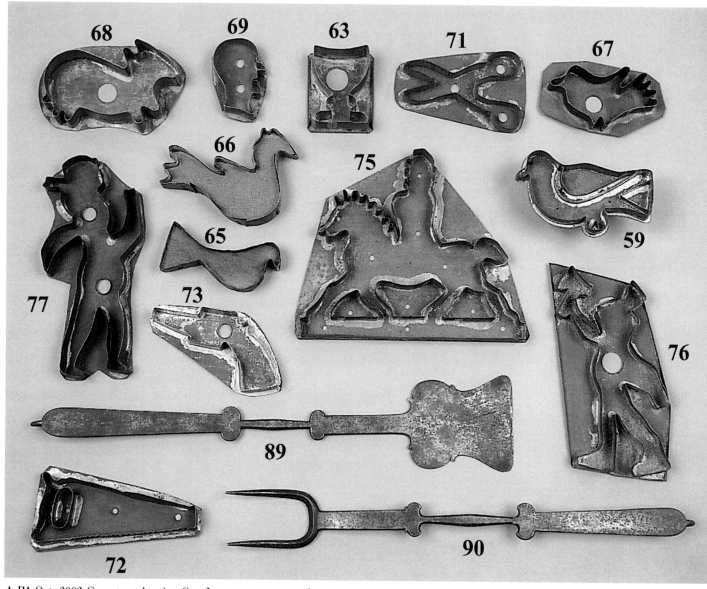

A-PA Oct. 2002 Conestoga Auction Co., Inc.

Tin Cookie Cutters

#68 Rabbit Form Cutter, lg. 5¾in. **$77**

#69 Two Figural, one w/ bust of man's head, ht. 3in. together w/ a miniature dog form, not illus., ht. 2½in., both missing handles. **$104**

#63 Chalice Form Cutter mounted on a sq. back plate, ht. 3¾in. **$22**

#71 Scissors Form, lg. 5¼in. **$165**

#67 Two Bird Cutters, one w/ missing handle, lg. 2½in. & 5in. **$55**

#77 Protesting Pioneer Cutter, ht. 8½in. **$440**

#66 Swan Form, wood banded by tin, ht. 5¼in. **$247**

#65 Bird Form, wood banded by tin, ht. 4½in. **$132**

#73 Revolver Form Cutter, lg. 5½in. **$110**

#75 Man On Horse Cutter, ht. 7¼in., lg.

9in. **$1,430**

#59 Bird Cutter w/ reinforced loop handle & wing, tail & eye details, lg. 5¼in. **$165**

#89 Wrought Iron Spatula w/ shaped handle & hanging hook, lg. 18¼in. **$660**

#72 Carpenter's Saw Form Cutter, lg. 6in. **$165**

#90 Wrought Iron Flesh Fork w/ shaped handle & hanging hook, lg. 17¾in. **$660**

A-PA Oct. 2003   **Conestoga Auction Company, Inc.**

#38 Toleware Gooseneck Coffeepot w/ lid & sunburst dec., ht. 11in. **$1,300**

#39 Red Toleware Gooseneck Coffeepot w/ lid & stylized flower & leaf dec., ht. 11in. **$1,750**

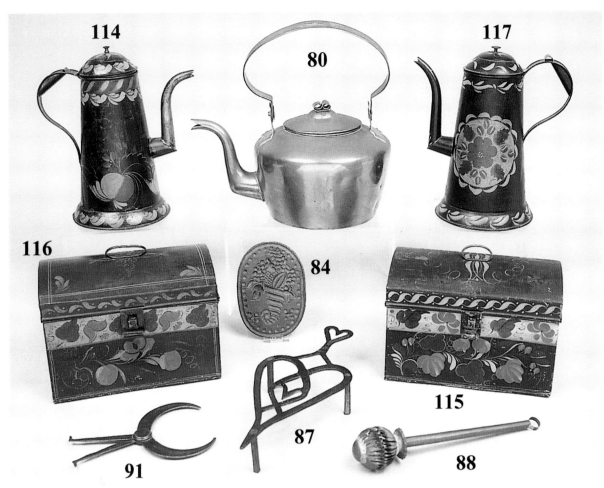

A-PA Oct. 2002 Conestoga Auction Co., Inc.

#114 Toleware Coffeepot w/ gooseneck spout & dome lid w/ brass button, polychrome dec., wear, ht. 10¼in. **$495**

#80 Copper Tea Kettle w/ gooseneck spout, sgn. "G. Youse", ca.1797, w/ repl. rivet in handle. **$990**

#117 Toleware Coffeepot w/ gooseneck spout, dome lid w/ brass button, polychrome dec., minor touch ups, ht. 10½in. **$605**

#116 Toleware Document Box, PA., 19th C., w/ polychrome dec., ht. 6¾in., wd. 9½in. **$880**

#84 Cast Iron Pastry Mold, oval form cornucopia, ht. 5¾in., wd. 4¼in. **$71**

#115 Toleware Document Box w/ polychrome dec. & ring swing handle,ht. 6⅜in., wd. 9¼in. **$1,650**

#91 Iron Caliper, sgn. "J. Lyons & W. George", lg. 7½in. **$38**

#87 Wrought Iron Trivet, heart shaped w/ heart handle, lg. 12½in. **$110**

#88 Dimensional Tin Whisk w/ loop hanging handle, lg. 10½in. **$440**

A-PA Oct. 2003   Conestoga Auction Company, Inc.

#58 Punched Tin Strainer, 19th C., Lancaster Co., PA, w/ pin wheel design, ht. about 11in. x 14½in., lg. 22½in. **$400**

A-PA Feb. 2003   Pook & Pook, Inc.

#132 Bucket by Joseph Lehn, Elizabethtown, Lancaster Co., PA, mid 19th C. w/ overall salmon & orange dec. & iron bands w/ trailing vine, ht. 8¼in. **$9,200**

A-NH Aug. 2003   **Northeast Auctions**

Decorated Toleware

#448 **Canisters,** three w/ lids, one w/ sloping shoulders, hts. 6½in. to 8in. **$550**

#449 **Tray with Cut Corners,** together w/ sander & crochet needle holder, tray 8½in. by 6in. **$550**

#450 **Tray** w/ canted sides & curved side handles, marbleized center, lg. 12½in., wd. 7½in. **$900**

#451 **Document Box** w/ embellishments & hoop handle, ht. 5½in. **$850**

#452 **Tumbler, Mug & Syrup Pitcher,** ht. 4½in. **$1,100**

A-PA June 2003   Conestoga Auction Co., Inc.

Agateware

#1 **Coffeepot,** green & white w/ blue handle & trim, losses, ht. 11in. **$495**

#2 **Pie Pan,** green & white, minor loss, dia. 10in. **$82**

#3 **Milk Pail** w/ bail handle, green white, losses, ht. 10¼in. **$935**

A-PA June 2003   Conestoga Auction Co., Inc.

Agateware

#4 **Cream Pail,** blue & white w/ bail handle, loss on lid & bottom, 7½in. **$357**

#5 **Funnel,** squatty form, blue & white w/ black handle, minor loss, ht. 3¼in. **$104**

#6 **Pitcher** w/ dark blue & white swirl, ht. 3in. **$687**

A-PA June 2003   Conestoga Auction Co., Inc.

Agateware

#12 **Bunt Pan** gray, dia. 10in. **$27**

#15 **Milk Pail,** gray w/ tin lid and bail handle, minor loss, ht. 9in. **$82**

#16 **Coffeepot** w/ tin lid, gray, mkd. on base "L. & G. Mfg. Co.", ht. 6¾in. **$165**

A-PA June 2003   Conestoga Auction Co., Inc.

Agateware

#19 **Teapot,** gray w/ pewter trim, ht. 10¼in. **$330**

#20 **Covered Syrup,** gray w/ pewter trim, ht. 5½in. **$412**

#21 **Sugar Bowl,** gray w/ pewter trim, ht. 5½in. **$165**

A-PA June 2003   Conestoga Auction Co., Inc.

Agateware
#93 Coffeepot, brown & white w/ tin lid, edge wear, ht. 9in. **$38**
#94 Coffeepot, light blue & white, ht. 8½in. **$94**
#95 Coffeepot, cobalt blue & white, ht. 8¾in. **$247**

A-PA June 2003   Conestoga Auction Co., Inc.

Copper
#357 Tea Kettle, 3 gal. w/ gooseneck spout & sgn. "John Getz" (1780-1841), w/ crown handle & tomahawk tab base & cramped seam tabs, overall ht. 16in. **$9,350**
#358 Sauce Pan, one gal., w/ orig. lid & sgn. "John Lay, York" (PA) w/ tubular handle & heart shaped copper riveted tab base & dovetailed seam const., overall ht. 11in. **$14,300**
#359 Cream Pitcher, 19th C., w/ loop handle & riveted spout, ht. 5in. **$110**

A-PA June 2003   Conestoga Auction Co., Inc.

Copper
#360 Turk's Head Mold, fluted copper w/ tin lined interior & brass hanging ring, ht. 4½in., dia. 11in. **$3,575**
#361 Tankard, pint size w/ loop handle, brass collar & base w/ medallion mkd. "Pint, W.O. Hickok, Harrisburg, 1811" & six pointed star, ht. 4½in. **$3,575**
#362 Tea Kettle, 24 oz. w/ gooseneck spout, sign. "W. Cummings" (Phil. PA, 1780-1806), w/ finial knob & dovetailed seam, overall ht. 6¾in. **$5,500**

A-PA June 2003 Conestoga Auction Co., Inc.

Copper
#366 Covered Sauce Pan, 1½ gal., sgn. "Henry Trottman, Philad.", w/ riveted wrought iron handles & tapered tab const., ht. 7in., dia. 9in. **$247**
#367 Tea Kettle, 50 oz. w/ gooseneck spout, sgn. "W. Heiss, No. 213 North 3rd. St, Phila.", w/ crown handle, brass finial & rectangular seam tabs, overall ht. 8½in. **$8,250**
#368 Pitcher, one gal., sgn. "D. Bentley & Sons, Phila." w/ tab seams, ht. 9½in. **$330**

A-PA May 2003   **Pook & Pook, Inc.**

Nutmeg Graters

First Row

#176 Melon Form, Am. silver, lg. 2in., together w/ a shell form by Hilliard & Thomason, Birmingham, 1856, lg. 1¾in. **$1,495**

#177 Treenware Acorn Form, three, together w/ a basket form example, ht. 2in. to 4½in. **$920**

#178 Egg Shaped Grater, Eng., cut silver mkd. "MS", together w/ a similar example by D. Field, London, mid-18th C., & one by T. Mallison, London, ca.1810, lg. 1in. to 2in. **$1,380**

#179 Silver-Gilt Octagonal Grater, Continental, mkd. "AK", together w/ an English silver oval cylinder form mkd. "CR", & an English round cylinder form, 18th C., w/ incised dec., ht. 2½in. **$1,840**

#180 Silver-Gilt elliptical grater by Phipps & Robinson 1789, together w/ an English oval example by J. Holloway, London 1793, & an English silver shield form grater, ca.1800, lg. 1½in. by 2in. **$3,919**

#181 Dutch, two-part cylinder form silver fitted grater w/ outer shaker, ca.1830, together w/ a cylinder form telescoping silver grater, attrib. to P. Robertson, Edinburgh, 1789, a Dutch cylinder form grater, G. Kristian, ca.1742, & a Sheffield plate grater, ca.1780, 2¾in. to 3½in. **$1,840**

#182 Continental Cylinder Form Graters, silver, early 18th C., lg. 2⅜in. to 3¼in. **$2,185**

#183 Tear Shaped Grater, silver, by H. Bunk, Longon, CA, 1745, together w/ a silver rectangular form by T. Shaw, Birmingham, 1829, and a footed silver urn form by Massey, London, 1787, lg. 1½in. by 1⅞in. **$2,530**

#184 Pear-Shaped Grater, silver by Hilliard & Thomason, Birmingham, 1859, together w/ a bobbin form silver grater by Samuel Pemberton, 1801, two egg form w/ repoussé & incised dec., & a cylinder form, lg. 1¼in. by 2in. **$3,220**

Second Row

#185 Silver Coffin-Form Grater by Durgin, ca.1900, together w/ an oval silver grater mkd. "IW", London 1791, an oval shaped silver example, ca.1810, & a silver oval cylinder form by Rawlings & Summers, London, 1831, lg. 2in. to 3in. **$2,300**

#186 Silver Rectangular Form w/ cut corners & bright dec. by Phipps & Robinson, London, ca.1795 together w/ a rectangular form, London, ca.1800 and an oval by S. Pemberton, Birmingham, 1801 and another silver form, ht. 1¼in. to 2in. **$3,680**

#187 Treenware Graters, three, pear, long handled skillet & a chip carved cylinder, together w/ a silver mounted wooden form by J. Reily, late 19th C., ht. 1½in. to 3¾in. **$1,380**

#188 Bone Cylinder Form Grater together w/ an egg shaped ivory & three black toleware graters of oval & rectangular form, lg. 1⅛in. to 2in. **$863**

#189 Silver Barrel Form by J. Taylor, ca.1800, together w/ an oval engraved silver grater and a silver acorn form by S. Pemberton, 1801. **$1,495**

A-PA June 2003   **Conestoga Auction Co., Inc.**

Agateware

#89 Mixing Bowl, green & white swirl, losses, ht. 2⅝in., dia. 6in. **$82**

#90 Mixing Bowl, dark green & white swirl, ht. 3in., dia. 7¼in. **$165**

#91 Mixing Bowl, dark green & white, mkd. w/ paper label "Emerald Ware No. 24, The Strong Enamel Co., Bellaire, OH", minor wear, ht. 4in., dia. 10in. **$412**

#92 Bowl, green & white, ht. 5⅛in., dia. 11¼in. **$412**

LIGHTING

The commodities for producing light in colonial America were splints of wood, animal or vegetable oils, depending upon their availability. The oils were used for burning fluids in various forms of shallow flat grease lamps. Because domestic animals were not plentiful in America until the late 1600s, finding a substitute for beef tallow was a major difficulty. Substitutes included beeswax, found on stems of the bay shrub, and "spermaceti" from the head of the sperm whale.

An enormous variety of candlesticks were made of wood, tin and pewter. Candlemolds were made in quantity, as well as sconces with backplates of pewter and tin. Those made with bits of looking glass that reflected the candlelight are extremely desirable. Candlestands soon became fashionable which permitted height adjustments. But, it was not until the 1700s that lanterns, portable and fixed, and fitted with candles became popular.

The availability of whale oil transformed lamp designs during the late 1700s, and remained the most important type of fuel for lamps well into the 1800s. Camphene lamps came into use during the second quarter of the 19th century. They resemble the whale oil lamps, but their wick tubes are set at opposing angles… "V" … shape to compensate for the extreme combustibility of the fuel. From the 1830s until the 1860s the Argand whale oil burner dominated lamp designs. It was not until the 1860s that kerosene eventually replaced all fuels.

Between the rush light holders of the early settlers and the fancy kerosene lamps of the late Victorian era, to the very pricey colorful Art Deco creations, there still exists a seemingly endless variety of very fine lighting collectibles and accessories. Many are readily adaptable for modern decorative and functional usage.

A-ME Nov. 2002

James D. Julia, Inc.

#300 **Satin Glass Mini. Lamp** w/ melon ribbed base & pansy ball shade w/ nutmeg burner, ht. 7in. **$1,150**

A-ME Nov. 2002

James D. Julia, Inc.

#311 **Owl Mini. Lamp** w/ white glass shade painted in black & gray w/ yellow eyes & acorn burner, ht. 7¾in. **$747**

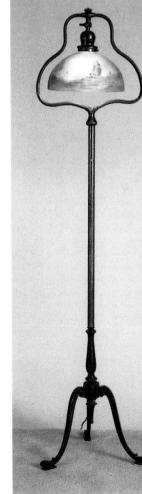

A-ME Nov. 2002

James D. Julia, Inc.

#313 **Blue Satin Mini. Lamp** w/ embossed ribs & nutmeg burner, ht. 8½in. **$517**

A-ME Nov. 2002

James D. Julia, Inc.

#321 **Artichoke Mini. Lamp** in white milk glass w/ green & yellow paint, nutmeg burner, chip on edge of shade, ht. 8in. **$143**

A-ME Nov. 2002

James D. Julia, Inc.

#600 **Floor Lamp** sgn. "Handel" w/ reverse painted shade dec. w/ harbor scene, the bronze three-footed base has single light socket & harpshade holder, dia. of shade 10in., ht. 57in. **$7,475**

A-ME Nov. 2002

James D. Julia, Inc.

#580 **Puffy Orange Tree Table Lamp,** sgn. on inside of 14in. dia. shade "The Pairpoint Corp." in gold, ht. 24in. **$51,740**

A-OH Dec. 2002   Treadway Gallery, Inc.
#576 Arts & Crafts Bronzed Metal Lamp w/ adjustable arm & orig. glass shade, minor crack, & orig. patina, ht. 12in., wd. 13in.
$900

A-OH Dec. 2002   Treadway Gallery, Inc.
#577 Arts & Crafts Table Lamp in the style of Limbert w/ wooden twin base supporting a rectangular shade in hammered copper w/ cut-out leaf design backed w/ mica, all orig. ht. 18in., shade 24in. by 16in. **$3,250**

A-ME Nov. 2002   James D. Julia, Inc.
#601 Floor Torchère w/ reverse painted shade dec. w/ yellow daisies w/ yellow centers, blue sky & green stems, sgn. "Handel", dia. 10in., overall ht. 57in. **$7,475**

183

A-OH Dec. 2002   Treadway Gallery, Inc.
#578 Floor Lamps, pair w/ shades of Oriental poppy design, supported by ornate holders of ram's heads & swag chains w/ tassels on twisted column of painted metal & wood, some tassels missing, ht. 68in. **$3,500**

A-MA Dec. 2002   Fontaine's Auction Gallery
#183 Adjustable Handel Overlay Desk Lamp w/ weighted foot, ht. 14in. **$1,765**

184

A-MA Dec. 2002   Fontaine's Auction Gallery
#184 Desk Lamp by Handel w/ overlay of leaves & vines w/ weighted foot, ht. 10in. **$2,012**

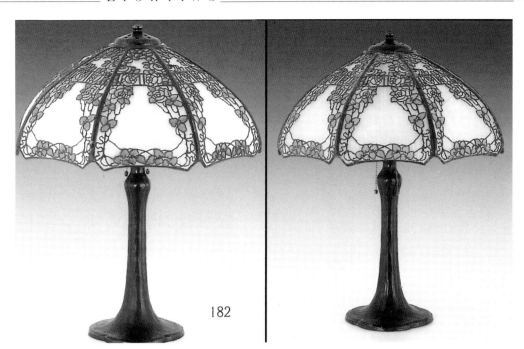

A-MA Dec. 2002

Fontaine's Auction Gallery

#186 **Harp Desk Lamp** w/ slag shade by Handel, ht. 5½in., dia. shade 18in. **$1,955**

A-MA Dec. 2002

#182 **Table Lamps,** pair by Handel w/ metal overlay of yellow roses on trellis, w/ simple bronze bases, shade sgn. ht. 23in., dia. of shade 18in., pair. **$10,350**

Fontaine's Auction Gallery

A-IA June 2003

Jackson's International Auctioneers

#834 **Hanging Parlor Lamp,** glass & bronze, ca.1880 w/ satin diamond quilt opalescent shade & font, red jeweled pull-down frame. **$3,450**

A-ME May 2003

James D. Julia, Inc.

#381 **Rayo Kerosene Floor Lamp,** kerosene font sgn. "Rayo" w/ green & caramel slag, crown of shade & border backed w/ ruby red glass, lamp has never been wired, ht. 69in. **$1,140**

A-IA June 2003

Jackson's International Auctioneers

#836 **Hanging Parlor Lamp,** glass & bronze, ca.1880 w/ satin diamond quilt opalescent shade & font in bronze frame w/ opalescent jewels. **$8,337**

LIGHTING

A-ME Nov. 2002   James D. Julia, Inc.

Hanging Hall Lamps

#407 Hobnail Shade w/ chips, electrified w/ incomplete brass frame, dia. of shade 14in. **$287**

#408 Hobnail Shade w/ electrified drop-in font, brass frame missing evener ring & replaced crown ring on shade, dia. 14in. **$575**

#409 Ball Shape Shade w/ optically ribbed glass, in antiqued brass frame, complete w/ smoke bell. **$172**

#410 Optic Ribbed Swirl Shade in yellow brass frame, complete. **$230**

#411 Melon Ribbed Shade, complete w/ font, burner & chimney. **$345**

#412 Cranberry Hobnail Cone Shaped Shade, complete w/ brass frame. **$201**

#413 Ribbed Opalescent Cylindrical Shade w/ brass frame, complete. **$373**

#414 Cranberry Paneled Shade w/ brass frame, complete. **$143**

#415 Melon Ribbed Amber Shade w/ brass frame, complete. **$143**

#416 Tapered Cranberry Shade, optically paneled in ribbed swirl patt., w/ brass frame, complete. **$143**

A-OH Jan. 2003

Early Auction Company

#563 Steuben Acid Cutback Table Lamp in pussy willow design w/ gold aurene over opal geometric cutting, mounted on reticulated brass base, ht. 10¼in. **$1,400**

A-IA June 2003   Jackson's International Auctioneers

#571 Steuben Glass & Bronzed Metal Chandelier, ca.1900 w/ brown aurene bell-shape shades, ea. sgn., one w/ minor chip, ht. of shades 5in., matching ceiling cap not shown. **$4,887**

A-NH Mar. 2003   Northeast Auctions

#257 **Tiffany Lily Lamp** w/ 10 favrile glass lily form shades hanging from a patinated bronze stem base w/ imp. lily pads, mkd. "Tiffany Studios, New York", one shade damaged, 2 repl., ht. 20in. **$17,250**

A-IA June 2003   Jackson's International Auctioneers

#626 **Muller Cameo Glass Table Lamp,** ca.1910, sgn. "Muller Freres Luneville", ht. 23in. **$16,675**

A-NH Mar. 2003   Northeast Auctions

#271 **Tiffany Leaded Glass Table Lamp** w/ bronze footed base, mkd. "Tiffany Studios, New York", ht. 26in. **$31,050**

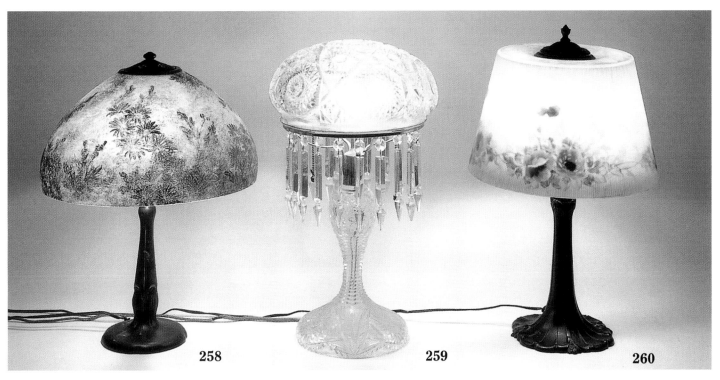

258

259

260

A-NH Mar. 2003   Northeast Auctions

#258 **Handel Table Lamp** w/ reverse painted sand-finished glass shade, bronze base mkd. "Handel", ht. 20in. **$3,220**

#259 **Cut Glass Table Lamp** w/ spear prisms, one missing, minor roughness, ht. 20½in. **$1,840**

#260 **Reverse Painted Table Lamp** w/

hand painted flowers & leaves, mkd. "Jefferson", on bronzed base w/ leaf carved shaft & petal base, ht. 21½in. **$1,150**

LIGHTING

A-OH Jan. 2003　　Early Auction Company
#509 Handel Table Lamp, w/ curved slag glass panels dec. w/ floral overlay, sgn. at top & retains green felt w/ stitched label on base, ht. 21in. **$2,350**

A-OH Jan. 2003　Early Auction Company
#149A Table Lamp w/ leaded glass slag shade dec. w/ stylized tulips, on detailed patinated art nouveau base, ht. 30in. **$2,300**

A-OH Jan. 2003　Early Auction Company
#508 Hanging Lamp w/ brass frame, opalescent shade, dia. 14in. **$1,600**

A-OH Jan. 2003　Early Auction Company
#132A Table Lamp w/ green slag panels bordered w/ red & green bands, the base w/ raised lily pads & feathers & mkd. Handel on base, ht. 24in. **$900**

A-OH Jan. 2003　Early Auction Company
#444 Table Lamp w/ leaded glass shade radiating geometric caramel slag panels w/ stylized ruby & green floral band, dia. shade 18in., sgn. under cap – C&C Co. w/ orig. base, ht. 24in. **$750**

A-OH Jan. 2003　Early Auction Company
#563A Quezal Chandelier, 6 light, w/ pulled feather dec. tipped in gold iridescence on ribbed opal ground, acanthus leaf covers over sockets. **$2,000**

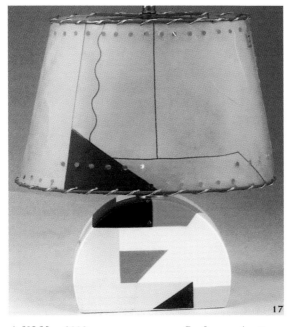

A-OH Jan. 2003

Early Auction Company

#365 **Daum Nancy Lamp** w/ mushroom shade & base w/ stylized yellow flowers on internally mottled ground, shade & base sgn., ht. 14in. **$10,100**

A-NJ May 2003   **Craftsman Auctions**

#175 **Art Deco Lamp** by Susie Cooper, w/ geometric pat., topped by its original "Doumerque" laced parchment shade, small chip on base, both pieces mkd., ht. 15in. **$1,000**

A-OH Jan. 2003   **Early Auction Company**

#413 **Table Lamp, Art Nouveau** style w/ goose neck, shade sgn. Quezal, dia. 5in. **$400**

A-NJ May 2003

Craftsman Auctions

#13 **Oil Candlelamp** by Tiffany Studios, gold lustered candlestick base & pierced pine needle shade & silver beaded trim, dia. of shade 5½in., ht. 9in., **$1,300**

A-OH Jan. 2003

Early Auction Company

#563B **Cranberry Hobnail Hanging Lamp** w/ perfect hobs, shade dia. 13½in. **$1,000**

A-MA Nov. 2002   Skinner, Inc.

#33 **Double Overlay Fluid Lamps** w/ cut overlay standards, Sandwich, w/ brass connectors, chips to basses marble edges, ht. 15⅜in. **$8,813**

#34 **Double Overlay Glass Vases,** w/ oval & vesica cuts & scrolled foliate gilt embellishments, minor wear, ht. 11⅞in. pr. **$940**

#35 **Cut Overlay Glass Fluid Lamp** w/ cut overlay standard & marble base, & brass connector, ht. 15⅞in. **$3,524**

LIGHTING

A-MA Nov. 2002   Skinner, Inc.

First Row

#156 Ship's Lanterns, iron, pair (L&R), by Nathaniel Tufts Maker, Boston, Mass., 19th C., labeled "Port," the other "Starboard," retain orig. brass maker's tags w/ weathered surface, ht. 22in. n/s

#157 Sand-Weighted Push-Up Candlesticks, early 19th C. w/ corrosion, pr. n/s

#158 Policeman's Lanterns, Am. 19th C., w/ pressed glass lenses, 8, mkd. Dietz Flashlight Police Lantern, pat'd. April 13, '86, wear, ht. 6⅝in. **$441**

#159 Ufford Tin Lard Lamps, two, Boston, one w/ adjustable reflector shade, the other has a hogscraper type push-up mechanism, dents & minor corrosion, ht. 12in. & 9¼in. **$411**

Second Row

#160 Tin Candlestick, adj., painted green w/ notched cylindrical shaft & weighted base, ht. 11½in. **$235**

#161 Tin Chamber Lamp, early 19th C., w/ quilted tin standard, ring handle, dents, ht. 6¾in. **$235**

#162 Tin Betty Lamp on a tin tidy stand, early 19th C., minor corrosion, ht. 14¼in. **$294**

#163 Tin Barn Lantern, mid-19th C., w/ ring handle w/ pierced air vent & two glass panels, wear, ht. 15½in. **$264**

#164 Redware Lard Oil Lamp, slip-glazed, PA, 19th C. w/ single spout & handle, ht. 6⅝in. **$235**

#165 Fixed Cranberry Glass Onion Globe Lantern w/ pierced tin frame, tin ring handle, wire guard & metal font w/ burner, ht. 18¼in. **$1,293**

#166 Tin Camphene Lamp, Pratt's Buggy Lamp & Feeder Co., Pat. Sept. 10, 1858, mkd. on base, minor corrosion, ht. 8in. **$881**

#167 Fixed Globe Lantern w/ black painted pierced tin frame, 19th C., w/ molded hobnail-style font, ring handle & whale oil burners, ht. 15in. **$881**

#168 Pewter Lamps, two, Capen & Molineux, NY, 1848-54 w/ round dish bases & maker's mark, ht. 8⅝in. & 8in. **$470**

#169 Fixed Onion Globe Lantern w/ pierced tin frame, mid-19th C., w/ ring handle, glass fluid lamp & whale oil burners, ht. 11in. **$176**

#170 Two Small Lanterns, 19th C., one a whale oil signal lantern & a magic lantern w/ extended pressed glass lens, ht. 4in. & 5in. **$82**

Third Row

#171 Pewter Whale Oil Lamps, two, mid-19th C., both w/ urn-form fonts on baluster shafts, applied handles & burners, ht. 7in. & 8½in. **$353**

#172 Barn Lantern, half-round, painted & pierced tin, 19th C. w/ hinged glass panel, topped w/ ring handle, another at rear, fitted w/ candle holder, ht. 14¾in. **$264**

#173 Pewter Candlestick, adjustable, 18th C., w/ spiral shaft, round domed base, w/ impr. "R", ht. 8in. **$206**

#174 Hogscraper Candlesticks, brass & sheet iron, w/ push-up plates & spun brass bands around candlecups, midshaft & lower shaft, wear & losses, ht. 9¼in. pr. **$1,293**

#175 Tin Candlestick, 18th C., w/ tall notched shaft w/ mid-drip pan, applied handle, ht. 16¾in. **$118**

#176 Iron Stable Candlestick on carved wooden base, Eng., mid-18th C., w/ wire cage surrounding candle holder, ht. 6½in. **$558**

#177 **Tin & Glass Barn Lantern,** mid-19th C., painted black w/ three glass panels, one hinged, interior fitted w/ kerosene lamp & glass chimney, wear, ht. 15¼in. **$206**

#178 **Sheet Iron Candlestick,** adjustable, early 19th C., w/ notched tubular shaft on footed base, ht. 6½in. **$264**

#179 **Wrought Iron Rush Light** on carved wooden base, early 19th C., ht. 10¾in. **$558**

#180 **Tin Candlestick/Tinderbox,** early 19th C., w/ ring handle & drip pan which lifts to reveal covered tinderbox w/ striker, wear, ht. 3in. **$558**

#181 **Wrought Iron Rush Holders,** three, late 18th early 19th C., two w/ combination rush & candle holders, another w/ wedge jaws, arched legs on a sprocket-edge ring base, ht. 9 in, 12in. & 19⅜in. **$1,175**

#182 **Fixed Onion Globe Lantern** w/ pierced tin frame, 19th C., w/ asphaltum burner on tin w/ ring handle, tin font & whale oil burner, wear, ht. 11¼in. **$382**

A-MA Nov. 2002 Skinner, Inc.

First Row

#132 **Fluid Lamps,** Sandwich, 19th C., blue pressed loop glass, w/ minor base edge chips, ht. 9⅞in. pr. **$2,350**

#133 **Pattern Glass Fluid Lamps,** Sandwich, pressed Star & Punty patt., w/ whale oil burners, gilt wear, base chips, ht. 11¼in. **$1,116**

#134 **Fluid Lamp,** canary yellow, Sandwich, Star & Punty patt., w/ brass camphene burners, ht. 11⅛in. **$999**

Second Row

#135 **Pressed Glass Fluid Lamp,** Sandwich, Three-Printie Block patt., font on hexagonal base w/ chips, ht. 8¼in. **$823**

#136 **Pressed Glass Kerosene Lamp,** ca.1860 w/ elaborate scroll oval Cartouche & Diamond patt., ht. 10¼ in. **$176**

#137 **Fluid Lamp,** pressed glass, Sandwich, in Loop patt., minor base chips, ht. 7⅞in. **$823**

Third Row

#138 **Pressed Glass Fluid Lamps** w/ frosted cut glass shades, Sandwich, giant Sawtooth patt. font w/ hexagonal base, shades cut w/ floral sprays w/ brass kerosene burners & glass chimneys, chips to bases, fitter rims on shades, ht. 20⅛in. pr. **$764**

#139 **Colorless Blown Fluid Lamps,** Sandwich, w/ free blown painted fonts w/ leaf motifs, whale oil burners, included, ht. 11in. **$235**

#140 **Cut Overlay Fluid Lamp** on columnar brass standard, ht. 8⅛in. **$141**

A-MA Feb. 2003   Skinner, Inc.

First Row

#301 Dolphin Candlesticks, blue & clamshell, Boston & Sandwich Glass Co., 1845-70, w/ petal-form socket, chips, ht. 10¼in. **$1,763**

#302 Cut Double Overlay Glass Kerosene Lamp, probably Sandwich w/ brass burner, chips to marble base, ht. 18¼in. **$1,293**

#303 Cobalt Pressed Glass Vase, Mt. Washington Glass Co., 1840-60, Arch patt., w/ gauffered rim, chips, ht. 11⅝in. **$764**

#304 Fluid Lamp w/ spiraling blue & white stripes in font, brass connector, base cracks & chips, ht. 9⅝in. **$999**

#305 Clambroth & Translucent Blue Lamps, Acanthus Leaf patt., Boston & Sandwich Glass Co. w/ overall rough textured surface, chips & crack at lower font & wafer area, ht. 11¼in. **$764**

Second Row

#314 Cut Double Overlay Fluid Lamp, Boston & Sandwich Glass Co., w/ opaque white cut to clear, cut to green font, brass connector & clambroth base w/ gilt highlights, minor edge chips, ht. 13¼in. **$2,938**

#315 Clambroth Dolphin Candlesticks, pr., Sandwich, w/ petal-form & candle cups, both w/ cracks & chips, ht. 10⅛in. **$499**

#316 Blue & Clambroth Petal & Loop Candlesticks, Sandwich, chips to rim petals, one w/ repair top of base, ht. 7in. **$823**

#317 Two Colored Cut Overlay Glass Fluid Lamps, opaque white to cranberry; the other w/ cranberry cut to clear font, not illus., both w/ minor imperfections, ht. 13⅞in. & 9in. **$999**

#318 Sapphire Blue Candlesticks, Sandwich, petal-form sockets on hexagonal bases, w/ minor base chips, ht. 7⅜in. **$1,645**

#319 Cut Double Overlay Glass Fluid Lamp, opaque rosy pink cut to white, on opalescent white glass base, surface scratches & base chips, ht. 13¾in. **$881**

The number of small objects made of metal and used in American households that were treated in such a way to attract collectors in this field is enormous. The pleasure of pewter lies not only in its softly rounded forms, but in its glowing surface. Copper has been used essentially for utilitarian articles since the 18th century. Pots, pans, molds and kettles for example are difficult to identify as American, because few were marked and American styles closely resemble European styles. Iron was the most commonly used metal because it was low in cost and high in strength. Early brass pieces, especially candlesticks, are very decorative and are becoming scarcer and more expensive with each passing year. Because tin-plate was a cheap and flexible medium, a tremendous variety of objects were produced. It is the early custom-made objects produced by tinsmiths that are sought after by collectors… such as decorative little cookie cutters and unusual candlemolds and sconces. It is the gaily decorated tinware known as "toleware" that is so popular among collectors. It dates from the 19th century. (Examples of toleware are included in the Kitchenware Chapter.) Although it dates from the nineteenth century, a great number of decorated pieces were produced by talented artists.

A century after America was settled, every center of population had a number of silversmiths to supply the needs of the wealthier colonist. Therefore, early American silver is understandably very rare, but on occasion a fine piece will surface. The majority of objects included in this chapter include silver plate, sterling and English old Sheffield plate. Silver plate is not solid silver, but a ware made of metal such as copper or nickel. The objects are simply covered with a thin coating of silver, whereas the term "sterling" refers to an object of solid silver, conforming to the highest standard. The term "Sheffield" refers to fused plate (a thin sheet of silver fused by heat to a thicker copper ingot), a process discovered by a Sheffield (England) man. Sheffield plate was, however, also produced in Birmingham (England), France and Russia. Lastly, it should be included that between 1836 and 1838 the English firm of G.R. & H. Elkington, of Birmingham, are credited with the invention of electroplating. By the 1840s, the first successful plating techniques were achieved in America.

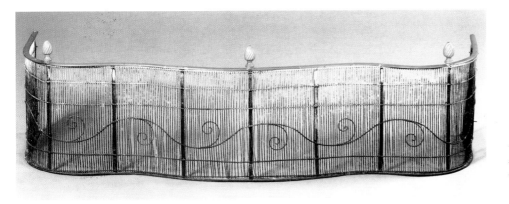

A-NH Aug. 2003   Northeast Auctions
#1802 **Brass Fender** w/ serpentine wirework w/ brass trim & scrolling motif, lg. 52½in. **$5,000**

A-NH Aug. 2003   Northeast Auctions

#1799 **Brass Candlesticks,** ea. w/ circular base & repoussé dec., pr. **$2,000**

#1800 **English Brass Candlesticks** w/ reeded baluster standards & stepped bases, the bobeches w/ gadrooned edges, ht. 9in. **$1,700**

#1801 **French Rococo Brass Candlesticks** w/ dome bases & intertwined swirls supporting urn-form & knopped posts, ht. 10in. **$1,750**

METALS

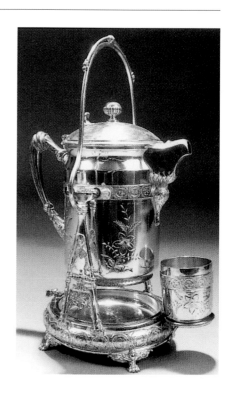

A-NH Aug. 2003

Northeast Auctions

#1797 Bell-Metal Lemon Top Andirons, ea. w/ a tapered stand above a plinth on spurred cabriole legs w/ ball & claw feet, fitted w/ matching log stops, together w/ matching shovel & tongs, not illus., ht. 20in. **$3,250**

A-IA June 2003　Jackson's
International Auctioneers

#1024 Victorian Water Pitcher ca.1875 w/ insulated pot on stand & removable drip pan w/ orig. cup., mkd. "Wilcox", ht. 16½in. **$345**

A-NH Mar. 2003　　　**Northeast Auctions**

Pewter

First Row

#150 Irish Haystack Measures, set of four w/ touchmark of "Austen & Son (act. 1828-33), Cork, 94 North Main Street", image of a lion, crown & "Imperial", ht. of tallest 7½in. **$500**

#151 Continental Oil Lamps, possibly German, late 18th C., **Whale oil lamp,** ht. 9¾in., together w/ ribbed glass **font**

lamp, raised on a cylindrical standard, ht. 12¾in. **$325**

#152 French Glass Hour Lamp, early 19th C., raised on a cylindrical standard & circular dish, ht. 15½in. **$175**

#153 French Flagons, 19th C., w/ touchmarks of a fox's head & urn, hts. 9¼in. & 6½in. **$200**

Second Row

#154 English Mugs, ca.1805, one w/

touchmarks "CC", a wheat sheaf & "Imperial", ht. 6in., other w/ touchmark of two lions, rectangles & crosses, ht. 6½in. **$425**

#155 Continental Pricket Candlesticks, probably French, ht. 12½in. **$425**

#156 Metric Measures, assembled set of eight w/ a Danish example. **$150**

#157 Measures, three English "Belly" type mkd. quart, pint & half pint; the three tankards w/ flat cover covers & factory touch marks. **$1,400**

A-IA June 2003

Jackson's International Auctioneers

#1025 **Victorian Table Castor,** ca.1880 w/ five etched glass bottles mkd. "Pairpoint", ht. 16½in. **$201**

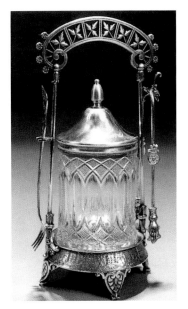

A-IA June 2003

Jackson's International Auctioneers

#1026 **Victorian Glass Pickle Castor,** ca.1875 w/ pattern glass insert, mkd. "Meriden", ht. 10½in. **$287**

A-IA June 2003

Jackson's International Auctioneers

#1027 **Victorian Sugar Bowl,** ca.1880 w/ cranberry glass insert & silvered spoons, ht. 8½in. **$517**

A-NH Mar. 2003　　　Northeast Auctions

Pewter

First Row

#139 **Flagons (R & L),** by Thomas Danforth Boardman (act. 1805-50), ea. w/ molded bands & rims w/ touchmarks, ht. 12in. **$1,700**

#140 **Coffeepots** by James H. Putnam (act. 1830-35), & Rufus Dunham, ea. w/ molded base & ebonized C-scroll handle, the first w/ touchmark "Putnam;" & the second "R. Dunham" (act. 1837-61), hts. 10¾in. & 11¾in. **$450**

#141 **Coffeepot** by Roswell Gleason (act. 1822-71) w/ his touchmark, together

w/ Queen Anne teapot of pear form w/ domed cover, hts. 9½in. & 6¾in. **$850**

Second Row

#142 **Four Plates** w/ touch marks of Samuel Pierce (act. 1792-1830), Nathaniel Austin, Richard Austin (act. 1763-1800) & Thomas Badger (act. 1737-1815), dia. 8in. & 8½in. **$1,300**

#143 **Porringers** by Samuel Hamlin, Sr. (act. 1767-1801), one w/ keyhole handle & touchmark of eagle clutching arrows above "Hamlin", together w/ four w/ keyhole handles & two w/ Richard Lee-type handles. **$1,200**

#144 **Whale Oil Lamps,** Am., ea. mkd. "Patent", together w/ reflectors, ht. 8¾in. & 9in. **$1,300**

#145 **Deep Dish** by Blakslee Barns w/ touchmark of eagle beneath "B. Barnes", (act. 1812-17) together w/ three graduated bowls w/ worn touchmarks. **$800**

#146 **Oil Lamps by Roswell Gleason** (act. 1822-71), two pairs w/ touchmarks, & Freeman Porter (act. 1835-60s), hts. 8in. & 6¼in. **$650**

#147 **Two-handled Cups** by P. Edgar & Son, Bristol, Eng. (act. 1845-52) w/ touchmark of Edward & Son, ht. 4¾in. **$150**

A-SC Dec. 2002 Charlton Hall Galleries, Inc.

#420 Silver, Plated & Sterling Coin Silver Tea Service, Am., ca.1840 by John & James Cox, NY, ht. of teapot 11½in. **$2,500**

420

A-NH Mar. 2003   **Northeast Auctions**

PEWTER

First Row

#164 Whale Oil Lamp, Roswell Gleason (act. 1822-71) w/ touchmark, together w/ whale oil lamp w/ touchmark of Smith & Co., hts. 6½in. & 7¾in. **$600**

#165 Whale Oil Lamps, group of three, one mkd. Houghton & Wallace, Patent Nov. 15, 1843, together w/ similar lamp by R. Dunham (act. 1861-62) w/ touchmark, & an unmarked example, ht. of first 5⅛in. **$600**

#166 Double Bull's-Eye Whale Oil Lamp ca.1850 w/ touchmark of Fuller & Smith, Poquonock Bridge, New London, ht. 10in. **$650**

#167 Mug w/ engraved bands & side spout, by G. Richardson, Sr., (act. 1818-

28) and Cranston (1828-45), w/ Richardson touchmark, ht. 4½in. **$500**

#168 Gimbal Whale Oil Lamp by Henry Yale & Stephen Curtis (act. 1858-67) w/ touchmark, ht. 5⅛in. **$250**

Second Row

#169 Candlesticks by Roswell Gleason (act. 1822-71) w/ molded circular base & detachable nozzles & touchmark, together w/ single candlestick, pair illus., ht. 7in. **$750**

#170 Continental Porringers, Eng. w/ touchmarks, two illus. **$500**

#171 Whale Oil Lamps, eight by various makers. **$650**

#172 Plates, four w/ touchmarks by D. Melville (act. 1755-93); G. Jones (act. 1774-1809); W. Billings (act. 1791-

1806) and W. Calder (act. 1817-56). **$1,100**

#173 Pitchers, one by Daniel Curtis (act. 1822-40) w/ touchmark, together w/ pitcher by Freeman Porter (act. 1835-60's), hts. 6¾in. & 6¼in. **$700**

#174 Plates by Thomas Danforth I, Taunton, MA (act. 1727-33) & Norwich, CT (act. 1733-73), ea. w/ touchmarks of a rampant lion w/ scrolls, "T&I" & "TD", dia. 8in. **$700**

#175 Whale Oil Lamps, two w/ touchmarks of "Morey & Ober/Boston/I" & "Smith/Warranted/Boston/I", hts. 3¾in. & 3⅞in. **$400**

#176 Plates, three by various makers w/ touchmarks of Jacob Whitmore, Thomas Danforth III & Thomas Danforth Boardman & partners, dia. 7¾ & 8in. **$800**

#720 Running Horse Weathervane, stamped by A.J. Harris & Co., copper w/ rod & stand, lg. 29½in. **$5,750**

#723 Trotting Horse Weathervane w/ full body, copper & cast-zinc in gilt, mounted on stand, lg. 28in. **$10,000**

#939 Running Horse Weathervane by J.W. Fiske Manufacturer, NY, mkd. Ethan Allen Running Horse, lg. of rod 29¼in. **$4,000**

Candlesticks
#1060 Two Pairs, brass & a snuffer on stand, larger pair on spreading sq. base,

ht. 10½in.; the second pair w/ cut corner base, ht. 6¼in. & snuffer ht. 7½in. **$900**
#1061 Two Similar Pairs w/ petal bases,

ea. w/ trumpet turned pedestal, ht. 7½in. & 7¾in. **$900**

METALS

A-NH Aug. 2003

Northeast Auctions

#721 **Rooster Weathervane**, painted cast-iron & sheet-iron, base mkd., Venus Model Co., NY, overall ht. 69in., lg. 32½in. **$3,500**

A-NH Aug. 2003

Northeast Auctions

#722 **Full-Bodied Rooster Weathervane**, gilded w/ detailed feathering, on rod & stand, ht. 26½in. **$5,250**

A-NH Aug. 2003   **Northeast Auctions**

#719 **Rooster Weathervane**, full bodied w/ gilt surface & red highlights on sphere w/ midband, on stand, overall ht. 31in. **$5,250**

A-IA Mar. 2003

Jackson's International Auctioneers

Silver, Plated & Sterling

#917 **Sheffield Humidor** w/ hand chased designs, early 20th C., ht. 8in. **$46**

#918 **Pickle Castor** w/ amber pressed glass insert, ht. 11in. **$258**

#919 **Candelabra**, pair, mid-20th C., w/ embossed floral designs, ht. 13in. **$195**

#920 **Table Castor** w/ 6 etched glass bottles in turn-table frame, ht 16 in **$218**

#921 **Compote**, early 20th C., w/ embossed scenic band, ht. 13in. **$69**

#922 **Candlesticks**, two, early 20th C., mkd. "Sterling", ht. 8in. & 10in. **$57**

#923 **Sugar Bowl Caddy** w/ bird finial lid displaying 12 period sugar shells, 6 matching, ht. 8in. **$184**

#924 **Hair Brush** w/ Art Nouveau design of a woman, lg. 7in. **$34**

#925 **Candelabra**, pair, mid-19th C., mkd. "Newport Sterling", ht. 10in. **$356**

#926 **Sheffield Tray**, mid-20th C., w/ deep embossed floral designs, mkd., dia. 12in. **$57**

#927 **Table Castor** w/ three etched glass bottles, mkd. "Rogers & Co", ht. 12in. **$57**

#928 **Candlesticks**, English, 19th C., pair, hallmarked, ht. 6in. **$92**

#929 **Candlesticks**, early 20th C., together w/ bud vase mkd. "Sterling", ht. 8in. **$115**

#930 **Compotes**, group of three, mid-20th C., one w/ enamel bowl, ea. mkd. "Sterling", ht. 6in. **$126**

#931 **Victorian Tea Set**, 4-pcs., w/ chased dec., mkd. "Homan Quadruple Plate". **$80**

#932 **Sweet Meat Castor** w/ Mary Gregory style cranberry glass insert, ht. 10½in. **$276**

#933 **Cigarette Box & Hand Mirror**, Continental silver, ea. mkd. "835", lg. 11in. **$46**

#934 **Victorian Basket** w/ figural branch handle, mkd. "James Tufts", lg. 9½in. **$92**

#935 **Candle Holders**, pair, Salt & Pepper & Tray, ea. mkd. "Sterling". **$172**

#936 **Victorian Bread Basket**, ca.1850

w/ classical portraits, mkd. "Reed & Barton", lg. 11½in. **$69**

#937 **Sheffield Plate Serving Tray**, "SM" hallmark, early 20th C., w/ embossed scrolls & chased foliate designs, lg. 26½in. **$575**

#938 **Nut Set**, 7pc., first half of 20th C., w/ pierced foliate designs, Gorham hallmarks & "Sterling". **$230**

#939 **Silver & Cut Glass Toilette Set**, ca.1900, w/ toothbrush holder, 2 bottles & 3 jars, worn hallmarks. **$201**

#940 **Pickle Castor** w/ replaced clear insert, ht. 11in. **$149**

#941 **Napkin Rings**, 12 w/ two pairs of salt/pepper shakers, mkd. "Reed & Barton, Sterling". **$230**

#942 **Tea Set**, 6-pcs., early 20th C., mkd. "Silver on Copper". **$143**

#943 **Bowl**, mid-20th C., mkd. "Towle Sterling", dia. 9in. **$92**

#944 **Candle Holders**, set of 9, 1907-08, w/ embossed scrolled dec. & mkd. "W&H" in pennant hallmark, some damage. **$253**

METALS

A-IA Mar. 2003
Jackson's International Auctioneers

Silver, Plated & Sterling

#888 Pitcher, early 20th C., "Renaissance" patt., w/ chased designs, mkd. "Whiting & Co. Sterling", ht. 10½in. **$517**

#889 Pair of Candelabra, early 20th C., w/ scrolled socket arms, mkd. "Alvin Sterling", ht. 12½in. **$172**

#890 Continental Silver, mid 20th C., consisting of a 16in. server, covered dish & underplate w/ matching designs, mkd. "Anstead Sterling" & 800. **$488**

#891 Continental Compote, silver & crystal, mid-20th C., w/ pierced & chased foliate design, mkd. "800", glass damaged, dia. 6in. **$143**

#892 Vase, crystal & silver, mid-20th C., w/ chased designs, mkd. "800 Anstead", ht. 12in. **$431**

#893 Bowl, ca.1900 w/ deep repoussé & chased Art Nouveau florals, mkd. "Sterling" w/ unidentified hallmark, dia. 11in. **$287**

#894 Continental Compote, silver & crystal, mid-20th C., w/ repoussé foliate & bird designs, mkd. "800 Anstead L.A.", ht. 5in. **$201**

#895 Continental Cream & Sugar, mid-20th C., w/ swirled rib & chased designs, w/ worn hallmarks, ht. 5in.

$115

#896 Bowl, mid-20th C., "Marie Antoinette" patt., mkd. "Gorham Sterling", dia. 10in. **$172**

#897 Ash Receptacle, Continental, mid-20th C., w/ wheel-cut scrolls & silver holder, mkd. "800", dia. 5½in. **$34**

#898 Coffee & Tea Pot, mid-20th C., w/ repoussé & chased scroll designs, mkd. "J.S. Kaufmann. 800", ht. 10in. & 7in. **$391**

#899 Silver Tazza, early 20th C., w/ deep repoussé Art Nouveau florals, mkd. "Sterling", dia. 6in. **$126**

#900 Continental Cigar Box, mid-20th C., w/ repoussé scene of couple courting, stamped "800", lg. 8in. **$264**

#901 Bowl, early 20th C., w/ repoussé Art Nouveau florals, mkd. "Sterling", dia. 5½in. **$126**

#902 Tumblers, set of 8, 20th C., mkd. "Sterling", ht. 5in. **$316**

#903 Italian Cigarette Box, mid-20th C., mkd. "Anstead .800", made in Italy, lg. 7½in. **$201**

#904 Bowl & Server, Am., mid-20th C., w/ embossed stylized handles, mkd. "Sterling", lg. 12in. **$267**

#905 German Silver Trays, pair, mid-20th C., w/ chased foliate designs, mkd. "800 Made in Germany, Anstead", dia.

10in. & 7½in. **$218**

#906 Cartier Tea Set, mid-20th C., incl. teapot, cream & sugar, mkd. "Cartier Sterling", ht. 7in. **$402**

#908 Candelabra, mid-20th C., w/ chased floral designs, mkd. ".800", ht. 8in. **$230**

#909 Cream & Sugar Set, 3-pcs., mid-20th C., "Prelude" patt., mkd. "Prelude International Sterling", lg. 8¾in. **$201**

#910 Stemware, Am., 19pcs., mid-20th C., 6 goblets, 8 sherbets & 5 cordials, mkd. "Sterling". **$345**

#911 Chester Muffineer, ca.1908-09 w/ pierced openwork, hallmarks, ht. 6¾in. **$115**

#912 Pair of Trays, ca.1900 w/ repoussé Art Nouveau designs, ea. mkd. "Sterling", dia. 6in. & 5½in. **$230**

#913 Dresser Set, ca.1910 w/ mirror, 2 brushes ea. mkd. "Sterling" & cut glass dresser box. **$143**

#914 Continental Bread Bowl, mid-20th C., w/ pierced scrollwork & florals, mkd. ".800", lg. 10½in. **$517**

#915 Dresser Set, 6 pc. Art Nouveau, ca.1900 w/ deep repoussé designs of poppies, mkd. "Sterling". **$345**

#916 Whiting Silver Tazzas, early 20th C., w/ repoussé floral urns & foliage, mkd. "Sterling", dia. 8in. **$258**

A-NH Aug. 2003   **Northeast Auctions**

#1065 Two Pairs, brass, ea. w/ shaped base, taller ones w/ beading & faceted stem, ht. 10in.; other pair w/ trumpet turned stem, ht. 8¼in. **$2,200**

#1066 Petal Base Candlesticks & Two Related Examples, all w/ petal form bobeche, the two singles w/ faceted petal turning on trumpet pedestal, ht. of pair 8in., other two 7in. & 9¼in. **$1,200**

During the past year a remarkable number of exceptionally important original American artwork has sold. Although professional artists did flourish in the more populated areas, most of our early American paintings fall under the heading of amateur work, painted by itinerant artists during the 18th and 19th centuries. Their inability to create a cohesive composition, and their lack of skill in depicting a true likeness or correct perspective, resulted in many naïve paintings. No one speaks more eloquently for our heritage than the folk artist. Their portraits of sober-faced children – especially those with their favorite toy or dog – are very valuable these days because all serve as a surviving link to a vital and fascinating past. These paintings with juvenile quality are extremely appealing to collectors.

Today there are available to collectors many charming and beautiful paintings, drawings and prints, from all schools and periods of art. As with all fields of collecting, values vary greatly and many factors – quality, size, an artist's signature, and condition – determine value. But, in general, a beautiful original work of art can be found to fit almost every budget.

Many charming works of art are available, including portraits, still-life, historical, and religious paintings. However, folk art paintings and pictures are in a class all of their own. They include paper cuttings, tinsel pictures, theorems on velvet, cotton or paper, calligraphic drawings, needlework pictures and silhouettes.

Collectors should never overlook artwork by an unknown artist, or an unsigned work if it is good. It will not only bring the owner the aesthetic pleasure of owning something beautiful, but it also offers the practical quality of generally being a good investment. However, it is the signed and dated pieces that will fetch substantially high prices in the marketplace.

A-NH Aug. 2003   **Northeast Auctions**

#826 **Portrait,** attrib. to Albert Gallatin Hoit, Am. (1809-1856) of young boy & his dog, oil on canvas, inscription on stretcher, "George Otis Lawrence, born, 1843, painted 1849, 45in. x 32in. **$12,000**

A-NH Aug. 2003   **Northeast Auctions**

#715 **Portrait,** Am., of Sarah Benham seated in CT landscape, oil on canvas, 34in. x 33in. **$15,000**

A-PA May 2003   **Pook & Pook, Inc.**

#61 **Theorem,** by David Y. Ellinger (1913-2003), oil on velvet of a bird perched atop a basket of fruit, sgn. "D. Ellinger", 13¾in. x 17⅛in. **$2,300**

A-PA Nov. 2002   **Pook & Pook, Inc.**

#90b **Theorem** of a basket of flowers, watercolor & pencil on paper, Am. 19th C., sgn. & dated 1857, 7½in. x 9½in. **$9,200**

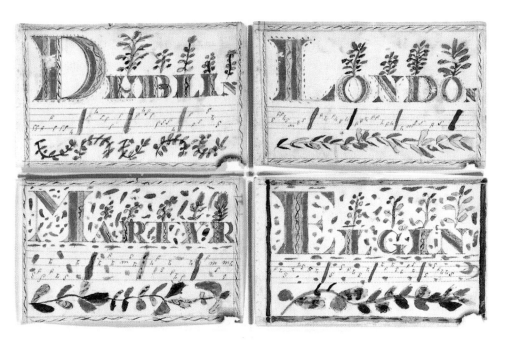

A-PA Nov. 2002   Pook & Pook, Inc.
#90c **Song Book Plates,** four, watercolor, in overall red, yellow & green colors within floral & fine dec., each w/ inscription, 7in. x 12in. **$1,380**

A-MA Mar. 2003   Robert C. Eldred Co., Inc.
#277 **Framed Painting** of strawberries & hydrangeas, sgn. "A. Laux", (August Laux, Am 1847-1921), oil on canvas, 10in. x 14¼in. **$3,450**

A-PA Oct. 2002   Conestoga Auction Company, Inc.
#550 **Autumn Harvest Day** sgn. Hattie Brunner, watercolor, 1972, 13½in. x 17¾in. **$3,025**

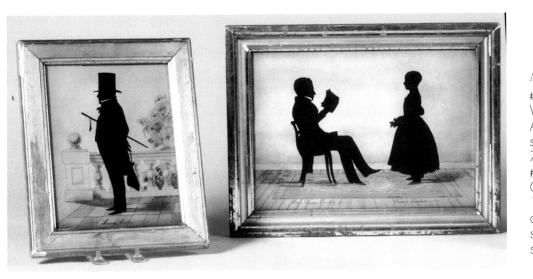

A-NH Aug. 2003 Northeast Auctions
#298 **Silhouette,** of Simon Fisher Wearing Top Hat, 1837 by Auguste Edouart (1818-1892), sgn. & dated, sight size 9¼in. x 7¼in. **$2,750**
#299 **Silhouette** of Hon. Isaac Carlson & Phoebe, Baltimore, 1841, by Edouart. Each paper cut applied on paper w/ Oriental scatter rug, sgn. & dated, sight size 11in. x 7in. **$2,750**

A-NH Aug. 2003   Northeast Auctions

#364 **Audubon Elephant-Folio** of a Turkey Hen, by J.J. Audubon, hand colored aquatint by R. Havell, London, sight size 25in. x 38in. **$9,500**

A-SC Dec. 2002   Charlton Hall Galleries

#475 **KPM Porcelain Plaque**, ca.1895, oval portrait of young girl w/carved giltwood frame (repairs), ht. 7in. wd. 5in. **$1,600**

A-PA Oct. 2002   Pook & Pook, Inc.

#30 **Mount Vernon**, watercolor & ink drawing on paper, inscribed "James W. Queen Jan 1, 1820 Mount Vernon" the Seat of the late Gen. G. Washington w/ figures & horses on the lawn, 16 in x 20in. **$11,500**

A-PA Oct. 2002   Conestoga Auction Company, Inc.

#260 **Painting**, "Down Loudle Creek Way" by David Y. Ellinger (1913-2003), oil on board, sgn. "D. Ellinger", 22in. x 29in. **$31, 625**

A-NH Mar. 2003   Northeast Auctions

#534 **Memorial picture** attributed to Mary Balch's School of Providence, RI. Worked in chenille & silk threads, ca.1780, w/family genealogy, 19 x 25in. **$10,000**

ABC Plates – Alphabet plates were made especially for children as teaching aids. They date from the late 1700s and were made of various material including porcelain, pottery, glass, pewter, tin and ironstone.

Amphora Art Pottery was made at the Amphora Porcelain Works in the TeplitzTurn area of Bohemia during the late 19th and early 20th centuries. Numerous potteries were located there.

Anna Pottery – The Anna Pottery was established in Anna, IL, in 1859 by Cornwall and Wallace Kirkpatrick, and closed in 1894. The company produced utilitarian wares, gift wares and pig-shaped bottles and jugs with special inscriptions, which are the most collectible pieces.

Battersea Enamels – The name "Battersea" is a general term for those metal objects decorated with enamels, such as pill, patch, and snuff boxes, doorknobs, and such. The process of fusing enamel onto metal – usually copper – began about 1750 in the Battersea district of London. Today the name has become a generic term for similar objects – mistakenly called "Battersea".

Belleek porcelain was first made at Fermanagh, Ireland, in 1857. Today this ware is still being made in buildings within walking distance of the original clay pits, according to the skills and traditions of the original artisans. Irish Belleek is famous for its thinness and delicacy. Similar wares were also produced in other European countries, as well as in the United States.

Bennington Pottery – The first pottery works in Bennington, Vermont, was established by Captain John Norton in 1793, and for 101 years it was owned and operated by succeeding generations of Nortons. Today the term "Bennington" is synonymous with the finest in American ceramics because the town was the home of several pottery operations during the last century – each producing under different labels. Today items produced at Bennington are now conveniently, if inaccurately, dubbed "Bennington". One of the popular types of pottery produced there is known as "Rockingham". The term denotes the rich, solid brown glazed pottery from which many household items were made. The ware was first produced on the Marquis of Rockingham's estate in Swinton, England – hence the name.

Beswick – An earthenware produced in Staffordshire, England, by John Beswick in 1936. The company is now a part of Royal Doulton Tableware Ltd.

Bisque – The term applies to pieces of porcelain or pottery which have been fired but left in an unglazed state.

Bloor Derby – "Derby" porcelain dates from about 1755 when William Duesbury began the production of porcelain at Derby. In 1769 he purchased the famous Chelsea Works and operated both factories. During the Chelsea-Derby period, some of the finest examples of English porcelains were made. Because of their fine quality, in 1773 King George III gave Duesbury the patent to mark his porcelain wares "Crown Derby". Duesbury died in 1796. In 1810 the factory was purchased by Robert Bloor, a senior clerk. Bloor revived the Imari styles which had been so popular. After his death in 1845, former workmen continued to produce fine porcelains using the traditional Derby patterns. The firm was reorganized in 1876 and in 1878 a new factory was built. In 1890, Queen Victoria appointed the company "Manufacturers to Her Majesty" with the right to be known as Royal Crown Derby.

Buffalo Pottery – The Buffalo Pottery of Buffalo, New York, was organized in 1901. The firm was an adjunct of the Larkin Soap Company, which was established to produce china and pottery premiums for that company. Of the many different types produced, the Buffalo Pottery is most famous for its "Deldare" line, which was developed in 1905.

Canary Luster earthenware dates to the early 1800s, and was produced by potters in the Staffordshire district of England. The body of this ware is a golden yellow and decorated with transfer printing, usually in black.

Canton porcelain is a blue-and-white decorated ware produced near Canton, China, from the late 1700s through the last century. Its hand-decorated Chinese scenes have historical as well as mythological significance.

Capo-di-Monte, originally a soft paste porcelain, is Italian in origin. The first ware was made during the 1700s near Naples. Although numerous marks were used, the most familiar to us is the crown over the letter N. Mythological subjects, executed in either high or low relief and tinted in bright colors on a light ground, were a favorite decoration. The earlier wares had a peculiar grayish color as compared with the whiter bodies of later examples.

Carlsbad porcelain was made by several factories in the area from the 1800s and exported to the United States. When Carlsbad became a part of Czechoslovakia after World War I, wares were frequently marked "Karlsbad". Items marked "Victoria" were made for Lazarus & Rosenfeldt, importers.

Castleford earthenware was produced in England from the late 1700s until around 1820. Its molded decoration is similar to Prattware.

Celadon – Chinese porcelain having a velvet-textured greenish-gray glaze. Japanese and other Oriental factories also made celadon glazed wares.

Chelsea – An early soft paste porcelain manufactured at Chelsea in London from around 1745 to 1769. Chelsea is considered to be one of the most famous of English porcelain factories.

Chelsea Keramic Art Works – The firm was established in 1872, in Chelsea, MA, by members of the Robertson family. The firm used the mark CKAW. The company closed in 1889, but was reorganized in 1891, as the Chelsea Pottery U.S. In 1895, the factory became the Dedham Pottery of Dedham, MA, and closed in 1943.

Chinese Export Porcelain was made in quantity in China during the 1700s and early 1800s. The term identifies a variety of porcelain wares made for export to Europe and the United States. Since many thought the product to be of joint Chinese and English manufacture, it has also been known as "Oriental" or "Chinese Lowestoft".

As much of this ware was made to order for the American and European market, it was frequently adorned with seals of states or the coat of arms of individuals, in addition to eagles, sailing scenes, flowers, religious and mythological scenes.

Clarice Cliff Pottery – Clarice Cliff (1889-1972) was a designer who worked at A.J. Wilkinson Ltd.'s Royal Staffordshire Pottery at Burslem, England. Cliff's earthenwares were bright and colorful Art Deco designs which included squares, circles, bands, conical shapes and simple landscapes incorporated with the designs. Cliff used several different printed marks, each of which incorporated a facsimile of her signature – and generally the name of the pattern.

Clews Pottery – (see also, Historical Staffordshire) was made by George Clews & Co., of Brownhill Pottery, Tunstall, England, from 1806-1861.

Clifton Pottery – William Long founded the

Clifton Pottery in Clifton, NJ, in 1905. Pottery was simply marked CLIFTON. Long worked until 1908, producing a line called Crystal Patina. The Chesapeake Pottery Company made majolica marked Clifton Ware, which oftentimes confuses collectors.

Coalport porcelain has been made by the Coalport Porcelain Works in England since 1795. The ware is still being produced at Stoke-on-Trent.

Coors Pottery – Coors ware was made in Golden, CO, by the Coors Beverage Co. from the turn of the century until the pottery was destroyed by fire in the 1930s.

Copeland-Spode – The firm was founded by Josiah Spode in 1770 in Staffordshire, England. From 1847 W.T. Copeland & Sons Ltd. succeeded Spode, using the designation "Late Spode" to its wares. The firm is still in operation.

Copper Luster – See Lusterwares.

Cordey – Boleslaw Cybis was one of the founders of the Cordey China Company, Trenton, NJ. Production began in 1942. In 1969, the company was purchased by the Lightron Corporation, and operated as the Schiller Cordey Company. Around 1950, Cybis began producing fine porcelain figurines.

Cowan Pottery – Guy Cowan produced art pottery in Rocky River, OH, from 1913 to 1931. He used a stylized mark with the word COWAN on most pieces. Also, Cowan mass-produced a line marked LAKEWARE.

Crown Ducal – English porcelain made by A.G. Richardson & Co. Ltd. since 1916.

Cup Plates were used where cups were handleless and saucers were deep. During the early 1800s, it was very fashionable to drink from a saucer. Thus, a variety of fancy small plates were produced for the cup to rest in. The lacy Sandwich examples are very collectible.

Davenport pottery and porcelain was made at the Davenport Factory in Longport, Staffordshire, England, from 1793 until 1887 when the pottery closed. Most of the wares produced there – porcelains, creamwares, ironstone, earthenwares and other products – were marked.

Dedham (Chelsea Art Works) – The firm was founded in 1872, at Chelsea, Massachusetts, by James Robertson & Sons, and closed in 1889. In 1891, the pottery was reopened under the name of The Chelsea Pottery, U.S. The first and

most popular blue underglaze decoration for the desirable "Cracque Ware" was the rabbit motif – designed by Joseph L. Smith. In 1893, construction was started on the new pottery in Dedham, Massachusetts, and production began in 1895. The name of the pottery was then changed to "Dedham Pottery," to eliminate the confusion with the English Chelsea Ware. The famed crackleware finish became synonymous with the name. Because of its popularity, more than fifty patterns of tableware were made.

Delft – Holland is famous for its fine examples of tin-glazed pottery dating from the 16th century. Although blue and white is the most popular color, other colors were also made. The majority of the ware found today is from the late Victorian period and when the name Holland appears with the Delft factory mark, this indicates that the item was made after 1891.

Dorchester Pottery was established by George Henderson in Dorchester, a part of Boston, Massachusetts, in 1895. Production included stonewares, industrial wares and, later, some decorated tablewares. The pottery is still in production.

Doulton – The pottery was established in Lambeth in 1815 by John Doulton and John Watts. When Watts retired in 1845, it became known as Doulton & Company. In 1901, King Edward VII conferred a double honor on the company by presentation of the Royal Warrant, authorizing their chairman to use the word "Royal" in describing products. A variety of wares were made over the years for the American market. The firm is still in production.

Dresden – The term identifies any china produced in the town of Dresden, Germany. The most famous factory in Dresden is the Meissen factory. During the 18th century, English and Americans used the name "Dresden china" for wares produced at Meissen which has led to much confusion. The city of Dresden which was the capital of Saxony, was better known in 18th century Europe than Meissen. Therefore, Dresden became a generic term for all porcelains produced and decorated in the city of Dresden and surrounding districts, including Meissen. By the mid-19th century, about thirty factories in the city of Dresden were producing and decorating porcelains in the style of Meissen. Therefore, do not make the mistake of thinking all pieces marked Dresden were made at the Meissen factory. Meissen pieces generally have

crossed swords marks and are listed under Meissen.

Flowing Blue ironstone is a highly glazed dinnerware made at Staffordshire by a variety of potters. It became popular about 1825. Items were printed with Oriental patterns and the color flowed from the design over the white body, so that the finished product appeared smeared. Although purple and brown colors were also made, the deep cobalt blue shades were the most popular. Later wares were less blurred, having more white ground.

Frankoma – The Frank Pottery was founded in 1933, by John Frank, Sapulpa, OK. The company produced decorative wares from 1936-38. Early wares were made from a light cream-colored clay, but in 1956 changed to a red brick clay. This along with the glazes helps to determine the period of production.

Fulper – The Fulper mark was used by the American Pottery Company of Flemington, NJ. Fulper art pottery was produced from approximately 1910 to 1930.

Gallé – Emile Gallé was a designer who made glass, pottery, furniture and other Art Nouveau items. He founded his factory in France in 1874. Ceramic pieces were marked with the initials E.G. impressed, Em. Gallé Faiencerie de Nancy, or a version of his signature.

Gaudy Dutch is the most spectacular of the gaudy wares. Made for the Pennsylvania Dutch market from about 1785 until the 1820s, this soft paste tableware is light-weight and frail in appearance. Its rich cobalt blue decoration was applied to the biscuit, glazed and fired – then other colors were applied over the first glaze – and the object was fired again. No luster is included in its decoration.

Gaudy Ironstone was made in Staffordshire from the early 1850s until around 1865. This ware is heavier than Gaudy Welsh or Gaudy Dutch, as its texture is a mixture of pottery and porcelain clay.

Gaudy Welsh, produced in England from about 1830, resembles Gaudy Dutch in decoration, but the workmanship is not as fine and its texture is more comparable to that of spatterware. Luster is usually included with the decoration.

Gouda Pottery – Gouda and the surrounding areas of Holland have been one of the principal Dutch pottery centers since the 17th century. The Zenith pottery and the Zuid-Hooandsche pottery produced the brightly colored wares marked GOUDA from 1880 to about

1940. Many pieces of Gouda featured Art Nouveau or Art Deco designs.

Grueby – Grueby Faience Company, Boston, MA, was founded in 1897 by William H. Grueby. The company produced hand thrown art pottery in natural shapes, hand molded and hand tooled. A variety of colored glazes, singly or in combinations, were used, with green being the most prominent color. The company closed in 1908.

Haeger – The Haeger Potteries, Inc., Dundee, IL, began making art wares in 1914. Their early pieces were marked with HAEGER written over the letter "H." Around 1938, the mark changed to ROYAL HAEGER.

Hampshire – In 1871, James S. Taft founded the Hampshire Pottery Company in Keene, NH. The company produced redware, stoneware, and majolica decorated wares in 1879. In 1883, the company introduced a line of colored glazed wares, including a Royal Worcester type pink, blue, green, olive and reddish-brown. Pottery was marked with the printed mark or the impressed name HAMPSHIRE POTTERY or J.S.T. & CO., KEENE, N.H.

Harker – The Harker Pottery Company of East Liverpool, OH, was founded in 1840. The company made a variety of different types of pottery including yellowware from native clays. Whiteware and Rockingham type brown-glazed pottery were also produced in quantities.

Historical Staffordshire – The term refers to a particular blue-on-white, transfer-printed earthenware produced in quantity during the early 1800s by many potters in the Staffordshire district. The central decoration was usually an American city scene or landscape, frequently showing some mode of transportation in the foreground. Other designs included portraits and patriotic emblems. Each potter had a characteristic border, which is helpful to identify a particular ware, as many pieces are unmarked. Later transfer-printed wares were made in sepia, pink, green and black, but the early cobalt blue examples are the most desirable.

Hull – In 1905, Addis E. Hull purchased the Acme Pottery Company in Crooksville, OH. In 1917, Hull began producing art pottery, stoneware and novelties, including the Little Red Riding Hood line. Most pieces had a matte finish with shades of pink and blue or brown predominating. After a flood and fire in 1950, the factory was reopened in 1952 as the Hull Pottery Company. Pre-1950 vases are marked Hull USA or HULL ART USA. Post-1950 pieces are simply marked HULL in large script or block letters. Paper labels were also used.

Hummel – Hummel items are the original creations of Berta Hummel, born in 1909 in Germany. Hummel collectibles are made by W. Goebel Porzellanfabrik of Oeslau, Germany, now Rodenthal, West Germany. They were first made in 1934. All authentic Hummels bear both the signature, M.I. Hummel, and a Goebel trademark. However, various trademarks were used to identify the year of production.

Ironstone is a heavy, durable, utilitarian ware made from the slag of iron furnaces, ground and mixed with clay. Charles Mason of Lane Delft, Staffordshire, patented the formula in 1823. Much of the early ware was decorated in imitation of Imari, in addition to transfer-printed blue ware, flowing blues and browns. During the mid-19th century, the plain white enlivened only by embossed designs became fashionable. Literally hundreds of patterns were made for export.

Jackfield Pottery – is English in origin. It was first produced during the 17th century; however, most items available today date from the last century. It is a red-bodied pottery, often decorated with scrolls and flowers in relief, then covered with a black glaze.

Jasperware – is a very hard, unglazed porcelain with a colored ground, varying from blues and greens to lavender, red, yellow or black. White designs were generally applied in relief to these wares, and often reflect a classical motif. Jasperware was first produced by Wedgwood's Etruria Works in 1775. Many other English potters produced jasperware, including Copeland, Spode and Adams.

Jugtown Pottery – This North Carolina pottery has been made since the 18th century. In 1915 Jacques Busbee organized what was to become the Jugtown Pottery in 1921. Production was discontinued in 1958.

King's Rose is a decorated creamware produced in the Staffordshire district of England during the 1820-1840 period. The rose decorations are usually in red, green, yellow and pink. This ware is often referred to as "Queen's Rose".

Leeds Pottery was established by Charles Green in 1758 at Leeds, Yorkshire, England. Early wares are unmarked. From 1775, the impressed mark "Leeds Pottery" was used. After 1880, the name "Hartley, Greens & Co." was added, and the impressed or incised letters "LP" were also used to identify the ware.

Limoges – The name identifies fine porcelain wares produced by many factories at Limoges, France, since the mid-1800s. A variety of different marks identify wares made there including Haviland china.

Liverpool Pottery – The term applies to wares produced by many potters located in Liverpool, England, from the early 1700s, for American trade. Their print-decorated pitchers – referred to as "jugs" in England – have been especially popular. These featured patriotic emblems, prominent men, ships, etc., and can be easily identified, as nearly all are melon-shaped with a very pointed lip, strap handle and graceful curved body.

Lonhuda – In 1892, William Long, Alfred Day, and W.W. Hunter organized the Lonhuda Pottery Company of Steubenville, OH. The firm produced underglaze slip-decorated pottery until 1896, when production ceased. Although the company used a variety of marks, the earliest included the letters LPCP.

Lotus Ware – This thin, Belleek-like porcelain was made by the Knowles, Taylor & Knowles Company of Easter Liverpool, OH, from 1890 to 1900.

Lusterware – John Hancock of Hanley, England, invented this type of decoration on earthenwares during the early 1800s. The copper, bronze, ruby, gold, purple, yellow, pink and mottled pink luster finishes were made from gold painted on the glazed objects, then fired. The latter type is often referred to as "Sunderland Luster". Its pinkish tones vary in color and pattern. The silver lusters were made from platinum.

Maastricht Ware – Petrus Regout founded the De Sphinx pottery in 1835 at Maastricht, Holland. The company specialized in transfer printed earthenwares.

Majolica – The word "majolica" is a general term for any pottery glazed with an opaque tin enamel that conceals the color of the clay body. It has been produced by many countries for centuries. Majolica took its name from the Spanish island of Jamorca, where figuline (a potter's clay) is found. This ware frequently depicted elements in nature: birds, flowers, leaves and fish. English manufacturers marked their wares, and most can be identified through the English Registry mark and/or the potter-designer's mark, while most Continental pieces had an incised number. Although many American potteries produced majolica between 1850 and 1900, only a few chose to identify their wares. Among these were the firm of Griffen, Smith & Hill, George Morely, Edwin Bennett, Chesapeake Pottery Company, and the new Milford-Wannoppe Pottery Company.

Marblehead – This hand thrown pottery had its beginning in 1905 as a therapeutic program by Dr. J. Hall for the patients of a Marblehead, MA, sanitarium. Later, production was moved to another site and the factory continued under the management of A.E. Baggs until it closed in 1936. The most desirable pieces found today are decorated with conventionalized designs.

Matt-Morgan – By 1883, Matt Morgan, an English artist, was producing art pottery in Cincinnati, OH, that resembled Moorish wares. Incised designs and colors were applied to raised panels, and then shiny or matte glazes were applied. The firm lasted only a few years.

McCoy Pottery – The J.W. McCoy Pottery was established in 1899. Production of art pottery began after 1926, when the name was changed to Brush McCoy.

Meissen – The history of Meissen porcelain began in Germany in 1710 in the Albrechtsburg fortress of Meissen. The company was first directed by Johann Boettger, who developed the first truly white porcelain in Europe. The crossed swords mark of the Meissen factory was adopted in 1723.

Mettlach, Germany, located in the Zoar Basin, was the location of the famous Villeroy & Boch factories from 1836 until 1921, when the factory was destroyed by fire. Steins (dating from about 1842) and other stonewares with bas-relief decorations were their specialty.

Minton – Thomas Minton established his pottery in 1793 at Hanley, Stoke-on-Trent, England. During the early years, Minton concentrated on blue transfer painted earthenwares, plain bone china, and cream colored earthenware. During the first quarter of the 19th century, a large selection of figures and ornamental wares were produced in addition to their tableware lines. In 1968, Minton became a member of the Royal Doulton Tableware group, and retains its reputation for fine quality hand painted and gilded tablewares.

Mochaware – This banded creamware was first produced in England during the late 1700s. The early ware was light-weight and thin, having colorful bands of bright colors decorating a body that is cream colored to very light brown. After 1840, the ware became heavier in body and the color was often quite light – almost white. Mochaware can easily be identified by its colorful banded decorations – on and between the bands – including feathery ferns, lacy trees, seaweeds, squiggly designs and lowly earthworms.

Moorcroft – William Moorcroft established the Moorcroft Pottery, in Burslem, England, in 1913. The majority of the art pottery wares were hand thrown. The company initially used an impressed mark, MOORCROFT, BURSLEM, with a signature mark, W. MOORCROFT, following. Walker, William's son, continued the business after his father's death in 1945, producing the same style wares. Contemporary pieces are marked simply MOORCROFT with export pieces also marked MADE IN ENGLAND.

Newcomb – William and Ellsworth Woodward founded Newcomb Pottery at Sophie Newcomb College, New Orleans, LA, in 1896. Students decorated the high quality art pottery pieces with a variety of designs that have a decidedly southern flavor. Production continued through the 1940s. Marks include the letters "NC" and often have the incised initials of the artist as well. Most pieces have a matte glaze.

Niloak Pottery with its prominent swirled, marbelized designs, is a 20th century pottery first produced at Benton, Arkansas, in 1911, by the Niloak Pottery Company. Production ceased in 1946.

Nippon porcelain has been produced in quantity for the American market since the late 19th century. After 1891, when it became obligatory to include the country of origin on all imports, the Japanese trademark "Nippon" was used. Numerous other marks appear on this ware, identifying the manufacturer, artist or importer. The handpainted Nippon examples are extremely popular today and prices are on the rise.

Norse Pottery was founded in 1903 in Edgerton, WI. The company moved to Rockford, IL, in 1904, where they produced a black pottery which resembled early bronze items. The firm closed in 1913.

Ohr Pottery was produced by George E. Ohr in Biloxi, Mississippi, around 1883.

Today Ohr is recognized as one of the leading potters in the American Art Pottery movement. Early work was often signed with an impressed stamp in block letters – G.E. OHR BILOXI. Later pieces were often marked G.E. Ohr in flowing script. Ohr closed the pottery in 1906, storing more than 6,000 pieces as a legacy to his family. These pieces remained in storage until 1972.

Old Ivory dinnerware was made in Silesia, Germany, during the late 1800s. It derives its name from the background color of the china. Marked pieces usually have a pattern number on the base, and the word "Silesia" with a crown.

Ott & Brewer – The company operated the Etruria Pottery in Trenton, NJ, from 1863 to 1893. A variety of marks were used which incorporated the initials O & B.

Owens – The Owens Pottery began production in Zanesville, OH, in 1891. The first art pottery was made after 1896, and pieces were usually marked OWENS. Production of art pottery was discontinued about 1907.

Paul Revere Pottery – This pottery was made at several locations in and around Boston, MA, between 1906 and 1942. The company was operated as a settlement house program for girls. Many pieces were signed S.E.G. for Saturday Evening Girls. The young artists concentrated on children's dishes and tiles.

Peters & Reed Pottery Company of Zanesville, Ohio, was founded by John D. Peters and Adam Reed about the turn of the century. Their wares, although seldom marked, can be identified by the characteristic red or yellow clay body touched with green. This pottery was best known for its matte glaze pieces – especially one type, called Moss Aztec, combined a red earthenware body with a green glaze. The company changed hands in 1920 and was renamed the Zane Pottery Company. Examples marked "Zaneware" are often identical to earlier pieces.

Pewabic – Mary Chase Perry Stratton founded the Pewabic Pottery in 1903 in Detroit, MI. Many types of art pottery were produced here, including pieces with matte green glaze and an iridescent crystaline glaze. Operations ceased after the death of Mary Stratton in 1961, but the company was reactivated by Michigan State University in 1968.

Pisgah Forest Pottery – The pottery was founded near Mt. Pisgah in North Carolina in 1914, by Walter B. Stephen. The pottery remains in operation.

Quimper – Tin-glazed hand-painted pottery has been produced in Quimper, France, dating back to the 17th century. It is named for a French town where numerous potteries were located. The popular peasant design first appeared during the 1860s, and many variations exist. Florals and geometrics were equally popular. The HR and HR QUIMPER marks are found on Henriot pieces prior to 1922.

Redware is one of the most popular forms of country pottery. It has a soft, porous body and its color varies from reddish-brown tones to deep wine to light orange. It was produced in mostly utilitarian forms by potters in small factories, or by potters working on their farms, to fill their everyday needs. The most desirable examples are the slip-decorated pieces, or the rare and expensive "sgraffito" examples which have scratched or incised line decoration. Slip decoration was made by tracing the design on the redware shape, with a clay having a creamy consistency in contrasting colors. When dried, the design was slightly raised above the surface.

Red Wing Art Pottery and Stoneware – The name includes several potteries located in Red Wing, MN. David Hallem established his pottery in 1868, producing stoneware items with a red wing stamped under the glaze as its mark. The Minnesota Stoneware Co. began production in 1883. The North Star Stoneware company began production in 1892, and used a raised star and the words Red Wing as it mark. The two latter firms merged in 1892, producing stoneware until 1920, when the company introduced a pottery line. In 1936, the name was changed to Red Wing Potteries. The plant closed in 1967.

Ridgway – Throughout the 19th century the Ridgway family, through partnerships, held positions of importance in Shelton and Hanley, Staffordshire, England. Their wares have been made since 1808, and their transfer design dinner sets are the most widely known product. Many pieces are unmarked, but later marks include the initials of the many partnerships.

Riviera – This dinnerware was made by the Homer Laughlin Company of Newell, WV, from 1938 to 1950.

Rockingham – See Bennington Pottery.

Rookwood Pottery – The Rookwood Pottery began production at Cincinnati, Ohio, in 1880 under the direction of Maria Longworth Nichols Storer, and

operated until 1960. The name was derived from the family estate, "Rookwood," because of the "rooks" or "crows" which inhabited the wooded areas. All pieces of this art pottery are marked, usually bearing the famous flame.

Rorstrand Faience – The firm was founded in 1726 near Stockholm, Sweden. Items dating from the early 1900s and having an Art Nouveau influence are very expensive and much in demand.

Rose Medallion ware dates from the 18th century. It was decorated and exported from Canton, China, in quantity. The name generally applied to those pieces having medallions with figures of people, alternating with panels of flowers, birds and butterflies. When all the medallions are filled with flowers, the ware is identified as Rose Canton.

Rose Tapestry – See Royal Bayreuth.

Roseville Pottery – The Roseville Pottery was organized in 1890 in Roseville, Ohio. The firm produced utilitarian stoneware in the plant formerly owned by the Owens Pottery of Roseville, also producers of stoneware, and the Linden Avenue Plant at Zanesville, Ohio, originally built by the Clark Stoneware Company. In 1900, an art line of pottery was created to compete with Owens and Weller lines. The new ware was named "Rozanne," and it was produced at the Zanesville location. Following its success, other prestige lines were created. The Azurine line was introduced about 1902.

Royal Bayreuth manufactory began in Tettau in 1794 at the first porcelain factory in Bavaria. Wares made there were on a par with Meissen. Fire destroyed the original factory during the 1800s. Many of the wares available today were made at the new factory which began production in 1897. These include Rose Tapestry, Sunbonnet Baby novelties and the Devil and Card items. The Royal Bayreuth blue mark has the 1794 founding date incorporated with the mark.

Royal Bonn – The trade name identifies a variety of porcelain items made during the 19th century by the Bonn China Manufactory, established in 1755 by Elmer August. Most of the ware found today is from the Victorian period.

Royal Crown Derby – The company was established in 1875, in Derby, England, and has no connection with the earlier Derby factories which operated in the late 18th and early 19th centuries. Derby porcelain produced from 1878 to 1890

carries the standard crown printed mark. From 1891 forward, the mark carries the "Royal Crown Derby" wording, and during the 20th century, "Made in England" and "English Bone China" were added to the mark. Today the company is a part of Royal Doulton Tableware, Ltd.

Royal Doulton wares have been made from 1901, when King Edward VII conferred a double honor on the Doulton Pottery by the presentation of the Royal Warrant, authorizing their chairman to use the word "Royal" in describing products. A variety of wares has been produced for the American market. The firm is still in production.

Royal Dux was produced in Bohemia during the late 1800s. Large quantities of this decorative porcelain ware were exported to the United States. Royal Dux figurines are especially popular.

Royal Rudolstadt – This hard paste ware was first made in Rudolstadt, Thuringen, East Germany, by Ernst Bohne in 1882. The ware was never labeled "Royal Rudolstadt" originally, but the word "Royal" was added later as part of an import mark. This porcelain was imported by Lewis Straus and Sons of New York.

Royal Worcester – The Worcester factory was established in 1751 in England. This is a tastefully decorated porcelain noted for its creamy white lusterless surface. Serious collectors prefer items from the Dr. Wall (the activator of the concern) period of production which extended from the time the factory was established to 1785.

Roycroft Pottery was made by the Roycrofter community of East Aurora, New York, during the late 19th and early 20th centuries. The firm was founded by Elbert Hubbard. Products produced included pottery, furniture, metalware, jewelry and leatherwork.

R.S. Germany porcelain with a variety of marks was produced at the Tillowitz, Germany, factory of Reinhold Schlegelmilch from about 1869 to 1956.

R.S. Prussia porcelain was produced during the mid-1800s by Erdman Schlegelmilch in Suhl. His brother, Reinhold, founded a factory in 1869, in Tillowitz in lower Silesia. Both made fine quality porcelain, using both satin and high gloss finishes with comparable decoration. Additionally, both brothers used the same R.S. mark in the same colors, the initials in memory of their father, Rudolph Schlegelmilch. It has not been determined when production at the two factories ceased.

Ruskin is a British art pottery. The pottery, located at West Smethwick, Birmingham, England, was started by William H. Taylor. His name was used as the mark until around 1899. The firm discontinued producing new pieces of pottery in 1933, but continued to glaze and market their remaining wares until 1935. Ruskin pottery is noted for its exceptionally fine glazes.

Sarreguemines ware is the name of a porcelain factory in Sarreguemines, Lorraine, France, that made ceramics from about 1775. The factory was regarded as one of the most prominent manufacturers of French faience. Their transfer printed wares and majolica were made during the nineteenth century.

Satsuma is a Japanese pottery having a distinctive creamy crackled glaze decorated with bright enamels and often with Japanese figures. The majority of the ware available today includes the mass-produced wares dating from the 1850s. Their quality does not compare to the fine early examples.

Sewer Tile – Sewer tile figures were made by workers at sewer tile and pipe factories during the late nineteeth and early twentieth centuries. Vases and figurines with added decorations are now considered folk art by collectors.

Shawnee Pottery – The Shawnee Pottery Company was founded in 1937 in Zanesville, OH. The plant closed in 1961.

Shearwater Pottery – was founded by G.W. Anderson, along with his wife and their three sons. Local Ocean Springs, MS, clays were used to produce their wares during the 1930s, and the company is still in business.

Sleepy Eye – The Sleepy Eye Milling Company, Sleepy Eye, MN, used the image of the 19th century Indian chief for advertising purposes from 1883 to 1921. The company offered a variety of premiums.

Spatterware is soft paste tableware, laboriously decorated with hand-drawn flowers, birds, buildings, trees, etc., with "spatter" decoration chiefly as a back-ground. It was produced in considerable quantity from the early 1800s to around 1850.

To achieve this type of decoration, small bits of sponge were cut into different shapes – leaves, hearts, rosettes, vines, geometrical patterns, etc. – and mounted on the end of a short stick for convenience in dipping into the pigment.

Spongeware, as it is known, is a decorative white earthenware. Color – usually blue, blue/green, brown/tan/blue, or blue/brown – was applied to the white clay base. Because the color was often applied with a color-soaked sponge, the term "spongeware" became common for this ware. A variety of utilitarian items were produced – pitchers, cookie jars, bean pots, water coolers, etc. Marked examples are rare.

Staffordshire is a district in England where a variety of pottery and porcelain wares has been produced by many factories in the area.

Stickspatter – The term identifies a type of decoration that combines hand-painting and transfer-painted decoration. "Spattering" was done with either a sponge or brush containing a moderate supply of pigment. Stickspatter was developed from the traditional Staffordshire spatterware, as the earlier ware was time consuming and expensive to produce. Although most of this ware was made in England from the 1850s to the late 1800s, it was also produced in Holland, France and elsewhere.

Tea Leaf is a lightweight stone china decorated with copper or gold "tea leaf" sprigs. It was first made by Anthony Shaw of Longport, England, during the 1850s. By the late 1800s, other potters in Stafford-shire were producing the popular ware for export to the United States. As a result, there is a noticeable diversity in decoration.

Teco Pottery is an art pottery line made by the Terra Cotta Tile works of Terra Cotta, Illinois. The firm was organized in 1881, by William D. Gates. The Teco line was first made in 1885, but not sold commercially until 1902, and was discontinued during the 1920s.

UHL Pottery – This pottery was made in Evansville, IN, in 1854. In 1908, the pottery was moved to Huntingburg, IN, where their stoneware and glazed pottery was made until the mid-1940s.

Union Porcelain Works – The company first marked their wares with an eagle's head holding the letter "S" in its beak around 1876; the letters "U.P.W." were sometimes added.

Van Briggle Pottery was established at Colorado Springs, Colorado, in 1900, by Artus Van Briggle and his wife, Anna. Most of the ware was marked. The first mark included two joined "A's," representing their first two initials. The firm is still in operation.

Villeroy & Boch – The pottery was founded in 1841, at Mettlach, Germany. The firm produced many types of pottery including the famous Mettlach steins. Although most of their wares were made in the city of Mettlach, they also had factories in other locations. Fortunately for collectors, there is a dating code impressed on the bottom of most pieces that makes it possible to determine the age of the piece.

Watt Pottery – In 1935 the company began producing dinnerware with freehand decorations that has become very popular with collectors. Their most popular pattern is Apple which was produced in 1952. Early pieces in this pattern can be dated from the number of leaves. Originally, the apples had three leaves, but in 1958 only two leaves were used. Other popular patterns in this ware include Rooster (1955), Starflower and Tulip variations. New patterns were introduced annually until October, 1965, when the factory was destroyed by fire; it was never rebuilt.

Walrath – Frederich Walrath worked in Rochester, NY, New York City, and at the Newcomb Pottery in New Orleans, LA. He signed his pottery items "Walrath Pottery." He died in 1920.

Warwick china was made in Sheeling, W V, in a pottery from 1887 to 1951. The most familiar Warwick pieces have a shaded brown background. Many pieces were made with hand painted or decal decorations. The word ILGA is sometimes included with the Warwick mark.

Wedgwood Pottery was established by Josiah Wedgwood in 1759, in England. A tremendous variety of fine wares has been produced through the years including basalt, lusterwares, creamware, jasperware, bisque, agate, Queen's Ware and others. The system of marks used by the firm clearly indicates when each piece was made.

Weller Pottery – Samuel A. Weller established the Weller pottery in 1872, in Fultonham, Ohio. In 1888, the pottery was moved to Piece Street in Putnam, Ohio – now a part of Zanesville, Ohio. The production of art pottery began in 1893, and by late 1897 several prestige lines were being produced, including Samantha and Dickensware. Other later types included Weller's Louwelsa, Aurora, Turada and the rare Sicardo which is the most sought after and most expensive today. The firm closed in 1948.

Wheatley – Thomas J. Wheatley established the Wheatley Pottery in 1880. The Wheatley mark included joined letters WP with a dash below within a circle.

A-PA Apr. 2003   Pook & Pook, Inc.
Gaudy Dutch

#72 **Plate** in the "Grape" pattern, dia. 9¾in. $1,093

#73 **Cup Plate** in the "Butterfly" pattern, dia. 3⅞in.

$4,830

#75 **Creamer** in the "Single Rose" pattern, ht. 4½in. $1,150

#76 **Plate** in the "Carnation" pattern, dia. 9¾in. $1,840

A-PA Apr. 2003

Pook & Pook, Inc.

Gaudy Dutch

#77 **Plate** in the "Primrose" pattern, mkd. "Riley", dia. 8⅜in. $4,140

#78 **Toddy Plate** in the "Grape" pattern, dia. 4½in. $920

#84 **Plate** in the "Urn" pattern, dia. 6¼in. $690

#79 **Plate** in the "Double Rose" pattern, dia. 8¼in. $690

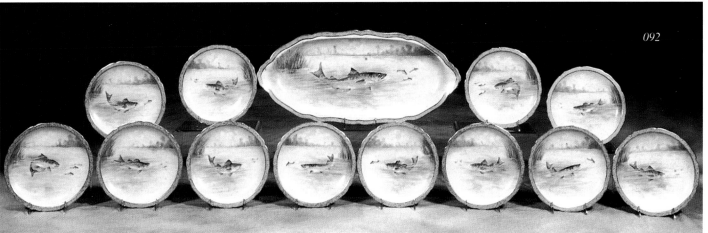

A-SC June 2003   Charlton Hall Galleries, Inc.

#092 **Limoges Porcelain Fish Service,** late 19th C., sgn. Lalans, consisting of 12 plates, dia. 9½in., platter, lg. 24in. $2,000

POTTERY / PORCELAIN

A-PA Apr. 2003   Pook & Pook, Inc.

Spatterware

First Row

#59 **Bowl,** blue w/ rose, ht. 4¼, dia. 6¼in. **$259**

#60 **Sugar Bowl** w/ black brown rainbow spatter, ht. 5in. **$3,450**

#61 **Covered Caddy,** blue & greenish brown spatter, ht. 3¾in. **$1,380**

#62 **Milk Pitcher** w/ red spatter & red &

blue dahlia, ht. 8¼in. **$3,680**

#63 **Paneled Sugar Bowl** w/ teal & orange spatter, ht. 5¼in. **$575**

#64 **Teapot** w/ red spatter & four-sided petal blue flower. **$748**

Second Row

#65 **Mug** w/ teal spatter, ht. 5¼in. **$633**

#66 **Creamer,** red spatter w/ rose & blue bud, ht. 4⅜in. **$316**

#67 **Creamer** w/ black & brown stripes,

ht. 4⅜in. **$2,760**

#68 **Platter** w/ blue & purple mottled spatter, lg. 10⅛in. **$1,150**

#69 **Creamer** w/ brown & black spatter & double sided rose, ht. 4¾in. **$575**

#70 **Waste Bowl** w/ red & green stripes, ht. 3¼in. **$920**

#71 **Creamer** w/ blue spatter & double sided red star, ht. 4½in. **$374**

A-MA Mar. 2003   Robert C. Eldred Co., Inc.

#360 **Rose Medallion Vases,** porcelain w/ mandarin dec. on floral ground w/ gold & salmon ground, ht. 17½in. **$3,680**

A-MA Mar. 2003   Robert C. Eldred Co., Inc.

#354 **Rose Medallion Garden Seats,** porcelain w/ figural design on gilt floral ground, ht. 18½in. **$8,510**

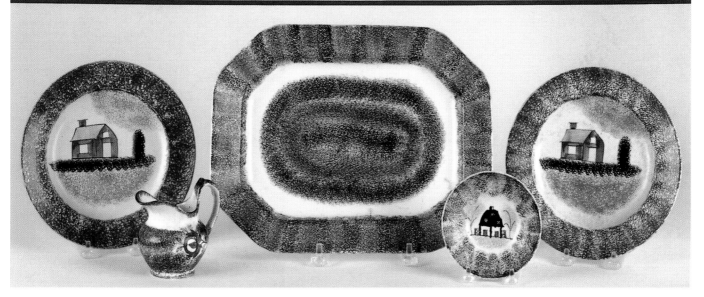

POTTERY / PORCELAIN

A-PA Apr. 2003   Pook & Pook, Inc.

Spatterware

First Row

#326 Milk Pitcher w/ red & blue vertical stripes, ht. 7¼in. $3,912

#327 Paneled Pitcher w/ red, green, yellow, blue & black spatter, ht. 9in. $8,050

#328 Ribbed Rim Pitcher w/ hound form handle in blue, green, orange & red spatter, ht. 6⅞in. $5,750

Second Row

#329 Blue Spatter Plate w/ open body peafowl dec., dia. 8⅜in. $345

#330 Creamer in red spatter w/ yellow & purple tulip, ht. 4½in., together w/ red spatter footed creamer w/ lily of the valley, ht. 5½in. $2,185

#331 Plate w/ green spatter ground & dec. w/ peafowl, dia. 8in. $288

#332 Rainbow Spatter Mini Cup, together w/ 5 misc. rainbow handless cups. $2,070

#333 Paneled Purple Spatter Plate w/ yellow acorn & green leaves, dia. 8in. $1,150

#334 Blue Sponge Plate w/ peafowl dec. & mkd. "Cotton & Barlow", dia. 8¾in., together w/ blue spatter creamware plate

w/ bird on fence, dia. 8⅜in. $1,265

Third Row

#335 Red Spatter Plate w/ red schoolhouse, green & brown lawn & tree, dia. 8¼in. $2,990

#336 Rainbow Spatter Creamer, blue & purple w/ rose, ht. 4in. $40

#337 Platter w/ purple & blue dec., lg. 13½in. $4,600

#338 Saucer w/ red & purple spatter in townhouse pattern, dia. 4⅜in. $6,325

#339 Red Spatter Plate w/ red schoolhouse, green & brown lawn & tree, dia. 8⅜in. $3,680

263   *265*   *264*   *266*

A-SC June 2003   Charlton Hall Galleries, Inc.

Dorothy Doughty & Boehm Birds

#263 Doughty "Blue-Grey Gnatcatchers & Dogwood," sgn. & mkd., Royal Worcester, female bird & leaf re-attached, ht. 11½in., pair. **$2,700**

#265 "Boehm Wood Thrushes," sgn. & mkd. on underside, ht. 16in., pair. **$3,000**

#264 Doughty Oven Bird, ca.1960 & Lady's Slipper Orchid, sgn. & mkd. Royal Worcester, ht. 11in. **$2,400**

#266 Doughty Lark Sparrow, ca.1966, w/ "Red Gild & Twinpod Growing in Volcanic Ash," mkd. Royal Worcester, ht. 6in. **$1,500**

#267 Doughty Oven Bird & Crested Iris, sgn. Royal Worcester, ht. 10½in. **$3,600**

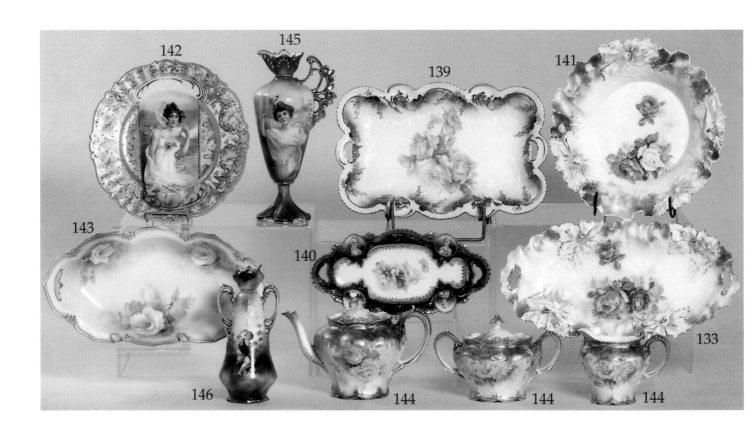

A-NJ June 2003   David Rago Auctions

Roseville

#221 Blue Magnolia, cornucopia vase, ht. 8in., tight line from rim, **ewer,** ht. 6in. & **vase,** raised marks, ht. 9in. **$300**

#222 Peony Vase, ht. 7in., green **White Rose Ewer,** grinding flecks, ht. 6in., & green **White Rose Vase,** raised marks, ht. 6in. **$175**

#223 Jardinière, green Pine Cone, clay pimple to rim w/ fleck, ht. 5½in., & **Vase,** colored-in chip to handle, unmarked, ht. 7in. **$250**

#224 Dahlrose, pair of **candlesticks,** fleck to base of one, one w/ paper label, ht. 8in., **bowl,** chip to handle, chip & bruise to base, dia. 3in. **$250**

#225 Dahlrose unmarked, **vase,** ht. 12in., & **squat vessel,** 6½in. **$475**

#226 Wincraft, pair of blue **ewers,** ht. 8in., **brown tray,** dia. 7in., & **triple candlestick,** several nicks to tops, all marked. **$200**

#227 Primrose Vase, brown, nick to one flower w/ impressed mark, ht. 9in. **$275**

#228 Landscape Pitchers, two, chips, cracks, lines, touchups, unmarked, each ht. 7½in. **$150**

#229 Pitchers, two, one Iris, ht. 8½in., & one w/ Dutchman, lines at rim, several bursts, unmarked, ht. 9in. **$200**

#230 Pitchers, two, one w/ Cow, has a few short lines, & one w/ Tulip, small chip to spout, hairline near handle, unmarked, each ht. 7½in. **$275**

Opposite

A-OH Jan. 2003   Early Auction Company

R.S. Prussia, Red Mark

First Row

#142 Portrait Plate w/ heavy gold encrustation, dia. 8½in. **$1,250**

#145 Portrait Ewer w/ gold highlights & gold handle, ht. 9in. **$1,150**

#139 Scalloped Edge Tray w/ gold highlights. **$135**

#141 Bowl w/ flaring rim & luster highlights, dia. 9¾in. **$150**

Second Row

#143 Oblong Bowl w/ openwork handles, lg. 12in. **$75**

#140 Relish Dish w/ four circular portraits w/ gold highlights, lg. 9¾in. **$650**

#133 Oblong Dish w/ molded floral rim, lg. 13in. **$175**

Third Row

#146 Melon Boy Vase w/ double handles & gold highlights, ht. 7in. **$500**

#144 Tea Service, three piece w/ floral decor. & gold highlights. **$700**

221 222 223 224 225 226 227 228 229 230

A-NJ June 2003   David Rago Auctions

Hull Pottery

#361 Vases, four, ea. w/ a different floral design, nicks overall, all marked, ht. of tallest 9in. **$200**

#362 Vases, four, ea. w/ pink & yellow floral designs, imperfections, all marked, ht. of tallest 11in. **$100**

#363 Vases, four, dec. w/ embossed waterlilies, chip to foot of one, all marked, ht. of tallest 9in. **$175**

#364 Bowl w/ matching **candleholders,** matching **candlesticks, cornucopia vase & ewer,** minor imperfections, ht. of tallest 6½in. **$150**

#365 Cornucopia Shaped Vases & two handled vases, all marked, each w/ different floral designs, ht. of tallest 6¼in. **$150**

#366 Vases, pair, two-handled, one w/ hairline, marked, ht. 8½in. **$125**

Staffordshire

A-MA Apr. 2003   Skinners, Inc.

#47 Creamware Cauliflower Sugar Bowl & Cover, Eng., ca.1775, the bowl w/ scalloped rim & green glazed leaf molding, cover cream glazed w/ molded florets, hairline to cover rim, dia. 4⅜in. **$2,820**

#48 Lead Glazed Creamware Soup Plate, Eng., late 18th C., w/ shallow rim chip, glaze wear, dia. 8½in. **$206**

#49 Lead Glazed Creamware Teapot & Cover, Eng., late 18th C., w/ crabstock handle & spout, set on three mask & paw feet, cover w/ bird finial, restor. to tip of spout & to cover insert rim, chip to bird's beak, ht. 5½in. **$1,058**

#50 Creamware Cauliflower Tea Canister, Eng., ca.1775, w/ shallow rim chip, ht. 4in. **$705**

#51 Lead Glazed Creamware Teapot & Cover, Eng., late 18th C., w/ shallow rim chips to cover & pot, tip of spout restored, ht. 3¾in. **$1,645**

#52 Black Glazed Tea Set, three pieces, Eng., 18th C., each w/ gilt dec. fruits, leaves & vines, incl. covered teapot w/ globular form w/ crabstock handle & spout set on three mask & paw feet, bird finial, missing bird's head, ht. 4⅞in.; cream jug set on three mask & paw feet, nick to spout rim, ht. 4¼in.; & a covered sugar bowl w/ bird finial to cover, rim nicks to bowl, cover w/ rim chips, repr. bird, ht. 4in. **$940**

#53 Lead Glazed Creamware Charger, Eng., late 18th C., paneled border w/ molded rice design, surface wear, dia. 12⅜in. **$1,410**

#54 Lead Glazed Creamware Side Handle Teapot, Eng., ca.1770, strap handle & crabstock molded spout, nicks to spout rim, missing cover, ht. 3⅝in. **$411**

#55 Lead Glazed Creamware Dish, Eng., late 18th C., foliate framed cartouches between dot, star & diapered border, surface wear, slight rim line, dia. 10⅜in. **$588**

#56 Lead Glazed Creamware Tea Canister, Eng., 18th C., mottled tortoiseshell glazes, hairline, ht. 3⅜in. **$499**

#57 Lead Glazed Creamware Cream Jug, Eng., ca.1770, pear shape set on three mask & paw feet, ht. 4⅞in. **$382**

Opposite

A-PA Oct 2002

Conestoga Auction Company, Inc.

Glazed Redware attributed to Jacob Medinger, Montgomery Co., PA, late 19th/early 20th C.

#231 Bulbous Form Pitcher w/ reeded strap handle & coggle wheel band w/ minute glaze chips on edge, ht. 7¾in. **$1,265**

#227 Bulbous Form Vase w/ applied reeded strap handles & coggle wheel dec., ht. 11in. **$1,210**

#234 Plate w/ coggle wheel edge & sgrafitto dec. of two militia men holding muskets, titled "Shoulder Firelock", w/ two lg. chips on edge, dia. 8¼in. **$357**

#232 Bulbous Form Vase w/ applied strap handles & coggle wheel band dec., ht. 11in. **$1,100**

#235 Mottled Glazed Pitcher w/ reeded strap handle & coggle wheel dec., ht. 7¾in. **$660**

#233 Bulbous Pitcher w/ reeded strap handle & coggle wheel dec., chip on inside, ht. 7½in. **$715**

#230 Storage Jar or Vase w/ coggle wheel dec., ht. 7½in. **$825**

#226 Bulbous Pitcher w/ strap handle, eagle & bird sgrafitto dec., tiny chips on edge, ht. 7¾in. **$1,265**

#228 Storage Jar w/ coggle wheel band dec., two edge chips, ht 7¼in. **$440**

#229 Bulbous Pitcher w/ reeded strap handle, coggle wheel dec., glaze flake to tip of spout, ht. 7½in. **$1,045**

A-MA Apr. 2003   Skinners, Inc.
Wedgwood Lustre
#446 **Celtic Ornament Bowl,** Eng., ca.1920, matt black designs to a yellow ground exterior & MOP interior, printed mark, dia. 5in. **$823**

#447 **Lustre Scalloped Bowl,** Eng., ca.1920, lobed body w/ dragons to a mottled blue exterior, MOP interior w/ phoenix surrounding a central "Three Jewel" design, printed mark, dia. 7in. **$1,410**

#448 **Lustre Imperial Bowl,** Eng., ca.1920, polychrome dec. to a black ground exterior, animals & riders in procession to a yellow ground interior, printed mark, slight wear to interior glaze, dia. 8in. **$3,290**

#449 **Lustre Empire Bowl,** Eng., ca.1920, the matt black exterior gilt decorated w/ Gothic circles, mottled orange interior w/ Celtic, printed mark, slight scratch to exterior, dia. 4¼in. **$705**

#450 **Fairyland Lustre Empire Bowl,** Eng., ca.1920, leapfrogging elves to a black exterior, MOP interior w/ elves on a branch, printed mark, dia. 4½in. **$4,406**

#451 **Hummingbird Lustre Compote,** Eng., ca.1920, mottled dark blue exterior w/ hummingbirds surrounding bowl, flying geese to footrim, mottled orange interior w/ flying geese border & hummingbird center, printed mark, dia. 10¾in. **$2,115**

#452 **Two Lustre Bowls,** Eng., ca.1920, one w/ MOP exterior & butterflies, mottled orange interior w/ large central butterfly, dia,. 5in.; & a mottled dark green exterior w/ gilt animals, MOP interior w/ Wu Sun barbarian w/ a Chinese lute, dia. 4in.; printed marks. **$1,175**

#453 **Two Lustre Octagonal Bowls,** Eng., ca.1920, one w/ fruits to a mottled dark blue exterior, orange interior w/ fruit center, together w/ a mottled orange bowl w/ gilt animals, mottled blue/purple interior w/ clouds surrounding a central scarab design, printed marks, dia. 4in. **$1,410**

#454 **Lustre Fruit Bowl,** Eng., ca.1920, mottled deep blue exterior w/ fruits, mottled orange interior w/ berries surrounding a fruit center, printed mark, dia. 8⅛in. **$1,058**

#455 **Dragon Lustre Bowl,** Eng., ca.1920, gilt dragon designs to a mottled green exterior, the interior in MOP w/ a colored & gilt dragon center, printed mark, light center wear, dia. 5½in. **$264**

A-NJ May 2003
Craftsman Auctions
#176 **Clarice Cliff Serving Bowl** in the "Trees & House" patt., w/ stamped mark, ht. 3¼in., dia. 7¾in. **$600**

A-SC Dec. 2002
Charlton Hall Galleries
#534 **Imari Charger,** Japanese, ca.1870 w/ minor wear to rim, dia. 15½in. **$600**

534

A-NH Aug. 2003   Northeast Auctions

Canton

#123 Circular Covered Dishes, two, w/ simple knops & loops for handles, dia. 9¾ & 6in. **$2,250**

#124 Serving Bowl & Scalloped Octagonal Pitcher, ht. 6½in., bowl dia., 9¾in. **$5,500**

#125 Gravy Boat, Pitcher, Tray & Tile, together w/ spoon. 4 pcs. **$2,000**

#126 Three-Piece Covered Soap Dish w/ canted corners, lg. 5½in. **$3,000**

#127 Three-Piece Butter Dish & Gravy Bowl w/ stand. **$5,500**

A-OH Jan. 2003   Early Auction Company

Porcelain Boehm Birds

#93 "Fledgling Western Bluebirds", ht. 5½in. **$125**

#95 "Black-Capped Chickadee", ht. 8½in. **$400**

#94 "A Baby Goldfinch" autographed on bottom "Fondly, E.M. Boehm," ht. 4½in. **$150**

A-IA June 2003   Jackson's International Auctioneers

Buffalo Pottery

#839 Deldare Tankard, ca.1908 w/ scene titled "All You Have to Do to Teach a Dutchman English" & on other side "The Great Controversy", artist sgn. "M. Steiner", ht. 12½in. **$575**

#840 Deldare Chocolate Pot, six sided w/ two cups, ca.1909, dec. w/ scene "Ye Village Street", sgn. "E. Ditmars", cups w/ village street scene, both w/ small rim reprs., pot ht. 10½in. **$1,610**

#841 Deldare Chop Plate, ca.1908, titled "An Evening At Ye Lion Inn", sgn. "W. Foster", dia. 13½in. **$402**

A-NH Aug. 2003   **Northeast Auctions**

#2012 Staffordshire Pearlware "Blue Dragon" patt., ca.1810, incl. sauce tureen; 2 covers & 2 stands; square bowl; 15 soup plates; 21 dinner plates; 16 dessert plates;16 sm. plates; 2 mazarins; a soup tureen, cover & stand; a vegetable dish w/ cover & three platters; a sq. veg. dish & cover, 84 pcs. **$9,500**

#2013 Copeland-Spode Creamware "Aster" patt., incl. platter; center bowl; vegetable dish; sauceboat, stand; large platter, teapot & cover; 10 soup plates; 16 dinner plates; 2 luncheon plates; 15 butter plates; 8 dessert plates & 2 demitasse saucers, 60 pcs. **$700**

#2014 Mottahedeh Porcelain in "The Exotic Plant" patt., w/ botanical dec., 20th C., incl. 12⅛in. & an 8⅛in. bowl, 16 soup plates; 20 dinner plates; 11 dessert plates & saucers, 61 pcs. **$2,250**

A-NH Aug. 2003   **Northeast Auctions**

#1618 Whieldon Creamware Plates, four in the "Royal" patt., w/ tortoiseshell glaze. **$2,250**

#1619 Whieldon Creamware Octagonal Plates w/ beaded edge & tortoiseshell glaze, together w/ two similar pcs., not shown. **$2,250**

A-NH Aug. 2003   Northeast Auctions

Canton

#108 Covered Soup Tureen w/ boar's head handles & stand, lg. 13in. **$2,250**

#109 Tall Cylindrical Vase, ht. 10¼in. **$1,200**

#110 Covered Hot Water Dish, rectangular form w/ berry knop cover, lg. 16¼in. **$350**

#111 Tea Caddy, hexagonal form w/ lid ht. 6¾in. **$1,000**

#112 Covered Punch Pot w/ foo dog finial, lg. 5¾in. **$200**

#113 Teapot, sq. w/ cover on straight feet, lg. 6½in. **$300**

A-NH Aug. 2003   Northeast Auctions

Canton

#14 Candlesticks of tapered form, ht. 10¼in. **$1,175**

#15 Platter, "Well-and-Tree" patt., w/ canted corners, lg. 16½in. **$1,100**

#16 Serving Dishes, three w/ scalloped edges & fluted, dia. of largest 9½in. **$6,500**

#17 Candlesticks of tapered form, ht. 9¾in. **$1,200**

A-NH Aug. 2003   Northeast Auctions

Canton

#19 Covered Hot Water Plates, five, ea. w/ flower-form finials, lg. 10¼in. **$700**

#20 Covered Sauce Tureens, two w/ boar's head handles & stands, lg. 7¼in. & 7½in. **$5,750**

A.-SC Dec. 2002   Charlton Hall Galleries

Staffordshire

#719 Pair of Pugs, ca.1870, wearing painted collar & moulded tag, ht. 11in.**$1,300**

#720 Stag & Dog Spill Vase, 19th C., w/ some small breaks to greenery, ht. 18in. **$150**

#721 Figure of Robin Hood, 19th C., w/ two figures & dog on oval base w/ small side nick, ht. 15in. **$300**

#722 Inkpot & Spill Vase, 19th C., vase in form of castle, ht. 6in. **$250**

Opposite, above

A-IA June 2003

Jackson's International Auctioneers

Deldare by Buffalo Pottery

#842 Calling Card Tray, ca.1908, dec. w/ "Ye Lion Inn" scene, artist sgn., dia. 8in. **$230**

#843 Dresser Tray, ca.1909, dec. w/ "Dancing Ye Minuet" scene, artist sgn., 12 x 9in. **$345**

#844 Fruit Bowl, ca.1908, dec. w/ "Ye Village Tavern" scene, artist sgn., dia. 9in. **$345**

#845 Pine Tray, ca.1909, dec. w/ "Ye Olden Days", artist sgn., lg. 6½in. **$143**

#846 Miniature Mug, ca.1909, dec. w/ "The Fallowfield Hunt" scene, artist sgn., ht. 2¼in. **$287**

#847 Covered Jar, ca.1909, dec. w/ "Ye Village Street" scene, artist sgn., dia.

4¼in. **$230**

#848 Cup & Saucer, ca.1909, dec. w/ "Ye Olden Days" scene, artist sgn. **$143**

#849 Tea Tile, ca.1908, plate set in reticulated metal frame & dec. w/ the "Traveling In Ye Olden Days" scene, artist sgn. dia. 9in. **$373**

#850 Vase, ca.1909 & dec. w/ untitled village scene of Bygone Days, ht. 7in. **$402**

279

280

282

283

A-NJ May 2003
Craftsman Auctions

#279 Rookwood Vase by Katherine Jones, w/ blue bachelor's buttons on blue ground, w/ 1923 flame mark, ht. 7½in. **$800**

A-NJ May 2003
Craftsman Auctions

#280 Rookwood Vase by E. Lincoln, w/ branches of cherry blossoms in black against a shaded red ground w/ 1925 flame mark, ht. 7½in. **$1,100**

A-NJ May 2003
Craftsman Auctions

#282 Rookwood Vase by E. Lincoln, w/ purple berries on green & red leaves over shaded pink ground w/ 1930 flame mark, ht. 6in. **$950**

A-NJ May 2003
Craftsman Auctions

#283 Rookwood Vase by MH McDonald w/ pink leaves on turquoise ground, w/ 1928 flame mark, ht. 5¼in. **$1,000**

A-NH Nov. 2002   Northeast Auctions

#487 Staffordshire Vegetable Dish & Cover, "Woodlands Near Philadelphia," dark blue by Joseph Stubbs, wd. over handles, 11¾in. **$2,750**

Opposite, below

A-IA June 2003

Jackson's International Auctioneers

Deldare by Buffalo Pottery

#851 Tea Tray, ca.1908 & dec. w/ scene titled "Heirlooms", artist sgn., 10¼in. x 13½in. **$488**

#852 Pitcher w/ eight sides, ca.1908 & dec. w/ scenes "This Amazed Me" & "With a Cane Superior Air", artist sgn.,

ht. 9in. **$747**

#853 Hanging Plaque, ca.1909, dec. w/ "Ye Lion Inn scene, artist sgn., dia. 12in. **$373**

#854 Teapot, ca.1909, titled "Village Life in Ye Olden Days", artist sgn., ht. 6in. **$373**

#855 Mustard Jar w/ lid, ca.1909, dec. w/ "Village Life in Ye Olden Days", artist sgn., ht. 4in. **$488**

#856 Creamer & Sugar, ca.1909, dec. w/ "Scenes of Village Life in Ye Olden Days", artist sgn. **$345**

#857 Covered Hair Receiver, ca.1909, dec. w/ "Ye Village Street" scene, artist sgn., dia. 5in. **$316**

#858 Rolled Rim Bowl, ca.1909 w/ "Ye Lion Inn", dec., artist sgn., ht. 4in., dia. 8in. **$431**

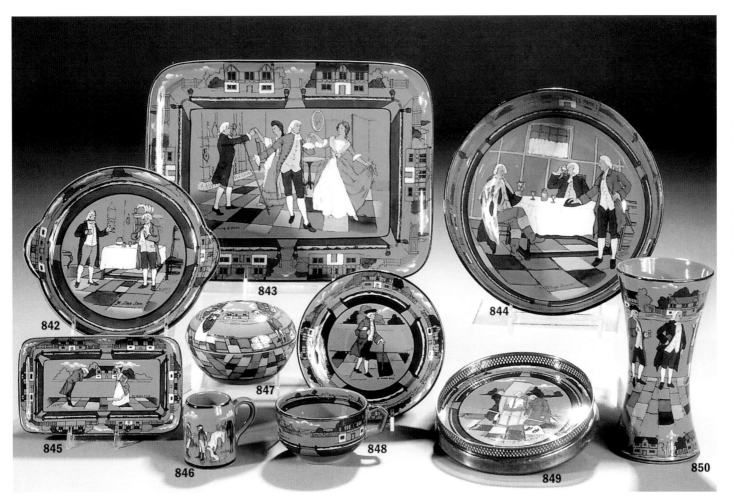

A-NH March 2003   Northeast Auctions

Bennington

#94 **Flint-Enamel Tulip Vases,** unmarked, ht. 10in. pr. **$750**

#95 **Flint-Enamel Coachman Bottle,** now mounted as a lamp, ht. 10½in. **$400**

#96 **Octagonal Doorknobs,** three prs., flint enamel, ht. of each 1¾in. **$600**

#97 **Flint-Enamel Book Flasks,** three, one mottled green/brown/tan, two mottled brown, hts. 8in., 6½in. & 5½in. **$600**

A-NH March 2003   Northeast Auctions

Bennington

#85 **Flint-Enamel Square Tile** in olive-amber glaze on tan ground, w/ imp. mark "1849", sq. 7¼in. **$200**

#86 **Flint-Enamel Uncle Sam Bank** in olive-green & brown, ht. 4¼in. **$200**

#87 **Paperweight** w/ flint-enamel glaze, domed top surmounted by recumbent spaniel, ht. 3in., lg. 4½in. **$900**

#88 **Graniteware Cow Creamer & Cover,** unmarked, ht. 5½in., lg. 7in. **$300**

#89 **Flint-Enamel Cow Creamer & Cover,** unmarked, ht. 5½in., lg. 7in. **$500**

A-NH March 2003   Northeast Auctions

Bennington

#98 **Pie Dishes,** four w/ Rockingham glaze, dia. 11in. **$500**

#99 **Tablewares** incl. oval baking dish, lg. 12in.; four mugs; & two low pitchers, ht. 3⅜in. **$450**

#100 **Pie Dishes,** five w/ flint-enamel glaze, dia. 7⅛ to 13⅛in. **$600**

#101 **Rockingham Mixing Bowls,** set of four in graduated sizes from 7⅛ to 13⅛in. **$1,500**

A-NH March 2003   Northeast Auctions

#90 **Flint-Enamel Candlesticks,** pr. w/ domed base, unmarked, ht. 8½in. **$700**

#91 **Flint-enamel Single Candlestick** w/ olive-green & brown glaze, unmarked, ht. 6½in. **$650**

#92 **Coffeepot & Cover** w/ overall mottled flint glaze, each rib heightened in orange to deep brown, ht. 10in. **$2,900**

A-NH March 2003
Northeast Auctions

#50 **Bennington Flint-Enamel Pitcher & Washbowl Set,** ca. 1849-58, w/ 1849 mark, ht. of pitcher 14¼in., dia. bowl 13¾in., **$1,900**

A-IA Mar. 2003

Jackson's International Auctioneers

Art Pottery

#1489 Group of Art Pottery, three pcs., first half 20th C. consisting of a cornucopia & oil lamp in matt green glaze. lg. 7in. &11in. & a mottled mustard tulip form vase. ht. 8½in. **$57**

#1490 Van Briggle Flower Bowl, "Lady of the Lake" in turquoise w/ blue overspray incised V.B. logo, name, Colo. Springs & USA. ca.1922-1926. **$517**

#1491 Roseville Vase, ca.1940 in "White Rose" on blue ground, emb. mark, ht. 6in. **$80**

#1492 Weller Vase, ca.1940 w/ emb. florals. ht. 5½in. **$34**

#1493 Handel Leaded Glass & Bronze Tulip Lamp, ca.1910, shade w/ alternating layers of green & white leaded glass on orig. hubble socket rising from a lily pad bronze base, base indistinguishably emb. "Handel", ht. 14in. **$1,035**

#1494 Owens Art Pottery Vase, ca.1890 w/ lg. floral blossoms & leaves dec. underglaze, artist initials imp. "Owens", ht. 10½in. **$207**

#1495 Royal Doulton Seriesware Trivet, ca.1900 "Promise Little & Do Much", dia. 6½in. **$144**

#1496 Fiesta Coffee Server, ca.1950 in orange glaze, imp. "Fiesta", ht. 10½in. **$184**

#1497 Van Briggle Art Pottery Vase, ca.1920s "Indian Chief" in chocolate brown glaze w/ green overspray incised "VB" name & Colo. Spgs, minor shallow flake under base, ht. 11in. **$517**

#1498 Fiesta Coffee Server, ca.1950 in green glaze, imp. "Fiesta", ht. 10½in. **$138**

#1499 Van Briggle Art Pottery Vase, mid 20th C. of ovoid form in turquoise w/ blue overspray, incised "V.B." name & "Original", ht. 8in. **$126**

#1500 Weller "Woodland" Vase, ca.1940 w/ emb. apple dec. unmkd. ht. 9in. **$69**

#1501 Warwick Lodge Tankard, ca.1910 w/ scene of an elk, appears to have prof. repr. ht. 12¾in. **$29**

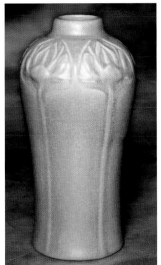

A-OH Dec. 2002   Treadway Gallery, Inc.

#401 Van Briggle Vase, ca.1906 w/ carved floral design under a blue/green matt glaze, incised marks, ht. 8½in. **$1,400**

A-OH Dec. 2002   Treadway Gallery, Inc.

#402 Van Briggle Vase, ca.1907-1912 w/ carved organic design covered w/ multi-tone green matt glaze, incised marks, ht. 6in. **$1,100**

A-OH Dec. 2002   Treadway Gallery, Inc.

#403 Early Van Briggle Vase, ca.1905 w/ carved flowers, vines & leaves covered in a maroon matt glaze w/ blue highlights, incised mark, ht. 6in. **$950**

POTTERY / PORCELAIN

A-IA Mar. 2003

Jackson's International Auctioneers

WATTS WARE

#70 "Apple Bean Pot" w/ chip on inside, #76, ht. 6½in. **$126**

#71 "Apple" Pitcher w/ ice lip, #17, ht. 8in. **$149**

#72 "Apple" Refrigerator Pitcher w/ ice lip & flat sides, minor chips on spout #69, ht. 8in. **$149**

#73 "Starflower" Pitcher w/out ice lip. Marked USA, #17, ht. 8in. **$86**

#74 "Starflower" Bowl advertising "Inter-State Lumber Company", ht. 4½in. **$69**

#75 Pair of Pitchers, one in "Tear Drop", #16, ht. 6½in., #15, ht. 5½in. **$109**

#76 Pair of Bowls "Apple" Advertising, hairline. #63, ht. 4¼in. "Apple" ribbed bowl, #8, ht. 4½in. **$80**

#77 Casserole w/ Lid in "Starflower" marked USA 3/19. Missing rack, dia. 8½in. **$80**

#78 Pair of Ribbed & Covered Bowls in "Apple" series USA #600, dia. 7¾in., ht. 5½in. & USA #601, dia. 8¾in., ht. 6½in. **$195**

#79 Pair of Bowls, in "Apple" series, marked USA #8 dia. 8in., ht. 5in. & USA #9, dia. 9in. ht. 5½in. **$80**

#80 Pair of Mugs, in "Starflower", #501. dia. 2¾in., ht. 4½in. **$172**

#81 Pair of Pitchers, USA, #15. One in "Starflower, & one in "Teardrop". ht. 5½in., wd. 5¾in. **$80**

#82 "Apple" Pitcher, USA #16, ht. 6½in., wd. 6¾in.. Glaze chip. **$46**

#83 "Apple" Advertising Bowl, USA, minor crazing, #7, ht. 4in. **$46**

#84 "Apple" Advertising Pie Dish, Evenbake, USA, #33, dia. 9in. **$138**

#85 "Apple" Advertising Pitcher, USA, minor chip on spout, #15, ht. 5½in. **$69**

#86 "Apple" Nest of Bowls, three, USA, dia. #63, 6½in., #64, dia. 7½in., & #65, dia. 8½in. **$172**

#87 "Apple" Mug, USA, #121, ht. 3¾in., dia. 3¼in. **$149**

#88 Advertising Pie Dish, similar to lot 84. **$138**

#89 "Starflower" Pitcher, USA, #16, ht. 6¾in. **$80**

#90 "Apple" Advertising Ribbed Bowl, USA, #7, ht. 4in. **$69**

#91 "Apple" Bowls, #7, ht. 4½in., #8, ht. 4in. **$115**

#92 "Starflower" Bean Pot, #76, one individual bean pot #75, ht. 6½in. **$34**

#93 "Apple" Ribbed Advertising Bowls, # 5 & #7. **$80**

#94 Three "Apple" Advertising Pitchers, #15. **$92**

#95 Pair of "Apple" Pitchers, #15, ht. 5½in., creamer #62, ht. 4½in. **$103**

#96 "Apple" Advertising Bowl, #8, ht. 5in. **$69**

#97 "Apple" Advertising Pitcher, ht. 5½in. **$57**

#98 "Cherry" Advertising Bowl, # 8, ht. 4in. **$57**

#99 Three Bowls, #5 "Apple," #52 "Cherry," #54 "Starflower". **$138**

#100 "Apple" Bowl, apple on inside, green band on outside, mkd. USA 75, dia. 9½in. **$92**

#101 Two "Apple" Bowls, ht. 5in. **$92**

#102 "Apple" Hour Glass Salt & Peppers, holes in top depict "S" & "P". **$207**

A-IA Mar. 2003

Jackson's International Auctioneers

#1300 Meissen Dinnerware Assembled Service of 79 pcs., 19th/20th C. in purple Indian painted patt. accented w/ gold dots, consisting of 2 coffee pots, 12 tea cups, 9 coffee cups, 13 saucers, 11 9½in. plates, 12 7in. plates, 11 5½in. sauces, 17in. platter, 2 10½in. chop plates, 9in. sq. bowl round & oval covered sugar, 5in. cream jug, 3½in. cream jug, together w/ a 5½in. Kaiser ice bucket in the identical pattern w/ blue crossed sword marks. **$3,910**

POTTERY / PORCELAIN

A-IA Mar. 2003

Jackson's International Auctioneers

#1123 Moriage Handled Vase, ca.1891-1921 w/ raised enameled scrolls on a hand painted ground of poppy florals, unmarked, ht. 9½in. **$460**

#1124 Porcelain Handled Vase, ca.1891-1921 w/ finely painted poppies under a raised gilt shoulder, green "M in wreath" mark, ht. 8½in. **$460**

#1125 Scenic Wine Jug, ca.1891-1921 w/ windmill scene in a woven cover, minor loss to wicker & early repair, stopper absent, blue maple leaf mark, ht. 10in. **$172**

#1126 Scenic Handled Vase, ca.1891-1921 w/ harbor scene raised on embossed gilt feet, green "M in wreath" mark, ht. 10in. **$1,121**

#1127 Handled Vase, ca.1891-1921 w/ cherry blossoms in moriage & raised enamel, unsigned. ht. 9in. **$833**

#1128 Scenic Wine Jug, ca.1891-1921 w/ scene, raised enameled scrolls & foliage, green "M in wreath" mark, stopper repaired, ht. 8in. **$1,063**

#1129 Scenic Handled Vase, ca.1891-1921 w/ harbor scene, green "M in wreath" mark. ht. 6in. **$546**

#1130 Scenic Handled Vase, ca.1891-1921 w/ Egyptian sailboat scene, green "M in wreath" mark. ht. 5¼in. **$603**

#1131 Scenic Handled Vase, ca.1891-1921 w/ man on camel cartoon scene, moriage & enameled details, blue "M in wreath" mark, ground rim w/ minor losses. ht. 7½in. **$690**

#1132 Humidor, ca.1891-1921 w/ smoking motif in moriage & raised enamel. Blue maple leaf mark. ht. 6½in. **$718**

#1133 Handled Bolted Urn, ca.1891-1921 w/ scenic shield form panels & scrolling florals, green "M in wreath" mark. ht. 13¾in. **$862**

#1134 Scenic Plaque, ca.1891-1921 w/ moriage & raised enamel florals, 4 raised beads absent, blue maple leaf mark, dia. 9½in. **$603**

#1135 Coralene Handled Vase, ca.1909, w/ scrolling florals & leafage. U.S. patent mark, very minor loss to beading. ht. 11¾in. **$1,035**

#1136 Coralene Handled Vase, ca.1909, w/ large water lily blossoms & leaves, U.S. patent mark, very minor loss to beading, ht. 7¾in. **$431**

#1137 Coralene Vase, ca.1909 w/ molded buttressed base & stylized florals, U.S. patent mark, very minor loss to beading, ht. 10in. **$1,207**

#1138 Coralene Vase, ca.1909, stylized iris, U.S. patent mark, very minor loss to beading. ht. 5¾in. **$517**

#1139 Coralene Handled Vase, ca.1910 w/ stylized florals on a glazed overshot finish & 1910 Patent "Kinjo" mark, ht. 9¾in. **$603**

#1140 Coralene Footed Rose Bowl, ca.1900 w/ stylized florals "Patent Applied For" mark, minor loss to beading, dia. 5½in. **$575**

#1141 Coralene Handled Vase, ca.1909 w/ stylized florals & leaves. U.S. patent mark, very minor loss to beading. ht. 6in. **$948**

#1142 Coralene Handled Vase, ca.1909 w/ stylized florals on shaded ground, U.S. patent mark, ht. 7in. **$690**

#1143 Coralene Handled Vase, ca.1909 w/ stylized florals & gilt scrolls, U.S. patent mark, very minor loss to beading, ht. 6¾in. **$546**

#1144 Coralene Vase, ca.1909 w/ stylized florals & cobalt blue, U.S. patent mark, minor loss to beading, ht. 4in. **$517**

#1145 Coralene Handled Vase, ca.1909 w/ rose blossoms, U.S. patent mark, ht. 6¾in. **$373**

#1146 Coralene Handled Vases, ca.1909 ea. w/ stylized florals, U.S. patent marks, very minor loss to beading. ht. 5in. **$661**

#1147 Vase w/ coralene dec., ca.1909 w/ cobalt shoulder & base, U.S. Patent mark, ht. 7in. **$977**

#1148 Vase w/ coralene dec., ca.1900, unmarked, ht. 4¾in. **$345**

#1149 Handled Vase w/ coralene dec., ca.1909, minor loss to beading w/ U.S. Patent mark, ht. 9in. **$1,006**

#1150 Handled Vase w/ coralene dec., ca.1909, prof. repr. to handle, U.S. Patent mark, ht. 5½in. **$172**

#1151 Vase w/ coralene dec., ca.1909 w/ U.S. Patent mark, minor loss to beading, ht. 7in. **$948**

#1152 Vase w/ coralene dec., w/ U.S. Patent mark, minor loss to beading, ht. 5in. **$258**

#1153 Vases, pr., ca.1909 w/ U.S. Patent mark, minor losses to beading, ht. 3½in. **$517**

#1154 Handled Vase, ca.1909 w/ U.S. Patent mark, some loss to beading, ht. 6¼in. **$632**

A-PA Oct. 2002   Pook & Pook, Inc.

First Row

#81 Spatter Bowl w/ blue, red & green, dia. 10⅜in. **$10,350**

#82 Cup & Saucer, red, yellow & green "Drape" patt. **$16,000**

#83 Gaudy Dutch Teapot in "Dove" patt. **$920**

#84 Spatter Plate, teal & black w/ tulip buds, dia. 8¼in. **$3,450**

Second Row

#85 Rainbow Spatter Pitcher, red, green, blue, yellow & black, ht. 6⅜in. **$11,500**

#86 Cup & Saucer, yellow spatter w/ cockscomb. **$2,013**

#87 Rainbow Pitcher, red, green, blue, yellow & black, ht. 8¾in. **$4,025**

#88 Sugar w/ red, green, yellow, blue & black spatter. **$19,550**

1123

1124

1125

1126

1127

112

1129

1131

1130

1132

1133

1134

1135

1136

1137

1138

1139

1140

1141

1142

1143

1144

1145

1147

1149

1151

1146

1148

1150

1152

1153

1154

A-IA Mar. 2003

Jackson's International Auctioneers

#1155 **Pottery Vase,** Japanese, unmarked, ht. 12in. **$322**

#1156 **Moriage Vase,** Japanese, mkd. Miyaro Japan, ht. 12in. **$201**

#1157 **Vase,** Japanese pottery w/ raised enamel dec., unmarked, ht. 12in. **$86**

#1158 **Pottery Vase,** Japanese, unmarked, ht. 12in. **$57**

#1159 **Vase,** ca.1900 w/ Royal Nippon mark, ht. 11¾in. **$460**

#1160 **Pottery Vase,** Nippon, ca.1900, unmarked, ht. 11¾in. **$345**

#1161 **Bowl,** ca.1891-1919, Nippon w/ blue "M" in wreath mark, dia. 10¼in. **$115**

#1162 **Humidor,** Noritake, ca.1925 w/ prof. repair to lid, w green "M" in wreath, ht. 5¾in. **$69**

#1163 **Vase,** Nippon, ca.1900, unmarked, ht. 7in. **$201**

#1164 **Mug,** Nippon, ca.1891-1919 w/ green "M" wreath mark, ht. 4¾in. **$69**

#1165 **Posy Basket,** Nippon, ca.1891-1921 w/ moriage dec., unmarked, ht. 5½in. **$126**

#1166 **Milk Pitcher,** Nippon w/ green "M" wreath mark, ht. 8½in. **$103**

#1167 **Bowl & Tray,** Nippon w/ matching dec. & green "M" wreath marks. **$69**

#1168 **Footed Vase,** Nippon w/ moriage dec., ca.1900 w/ printed chop mark, ht. 6in. **$287**

#1169 **Covered Powder Box,** Nippon, footed w/ green "M" wreath dia. 6in. **$92**

#1170 **Covered Jar,** Nippon, dec. w/ violets & blue maple leaf mark, lg. 9in. **$86**

#1171 **Sugar & Creamer,** Nippon, w/ moriage scrolling, unmarked. **$80**

#1172 **Pottery Vase,** ca.1900, hand painted, ht. 16in. **$172**

#1173 **Humidor** w/ stylized florals, "mythical bird" mark, ht. 5½in. **$161**

#1174 **Vase,** Nippon w/ roses on petit point enameled ground, unmarked, ht. 8½in. **$138**

#1175 **Ewer,** Nippon w/ moriage designs, unmarked, ht. 9½in. **$316**

#1176 **Tea Set,** Nippon, unmarked, 3 pcs. **$126**

#1177 **Sugar & Creamer,** Nippon w/ blue maple leaf & crown marks. **$115**

#1178 **Footed Ferner,** Nippon w/ green "M" wreath mark, lg. 6¼in. **$92**

#1179 **Tea Set,** Nippon, artist sgn. w/ green "M" wreath marks. **$149**

#1180 **Nut Bowl,** Noritake w/ moriage dec., chestnuts & green "M" wreath mark. **$34**

#1181 **Handled Basket** w/ coralene dec., minor loss to beading, U.S. Patent mark, dia. 5in. **$172**

#1182 **Covered Bowl,** Nippon w/ raised enamel scrolling, unmarked, lg. 6in. **$34**

#1182A **Covered Mustards,** Nippon, one w/ moriage dec., loss to lid. **$80**

#1183 **Nut Bowls,** Nippon & Noritake, ca.1910 & 1920, one w/ emb. basket design. **$92**

#1184 **Celery Set,** 5 pcs., ca.1925 w/ green tree crest mark, together w/ a Noritake vase, ht. 6in. **$115**

LOT 1376

LOT 1377

LOT 1378

A-IA Mar. 2003

Jackson's International Auctioneers

#1376 **Haviland Chocolate Set,** 13 piece in "Albany" patt. **$287**

#1377 **Haviland Tea Set,** 3pc. in "Albany" patt. **$126**

#1378 **Haviland China,** 7pc. set individual coffee service. **$115**

A-NH Aug. 2003   Northeast Auctions
Pennsylvania Chalkware w/ Polychrome Dec.

First Row
#432 **Seated Cat,** ht. 6¼in. **$900**
#433 **Pineapple & Pear** in form of a bank, hts. 9½in. & 3¾in. **$600**
#434 **Recumbent Ewe & Lamb,** ht. 6 in, wd. 8¾in. **$450**
#435 **Seated Squirrel Eating a Nut,** ht. 7in. **$200**
#436 **Figures of Two Birds,** ht. 4½in. & 6½in. **$600**
#437 **Painted Fruit-Filled Urn,** ht. 10¾in. **$200**

Second Row
#438 **Rabbits,** one crouched & one seated, hts. 4¼in. & 5¼in. **$1,900**
#439 **Seated Poodle,** ht. 6⅛in. **$300**
#440 **Seated Squirrels,** ea. eating a nut, ht. 6⅛in. & 5in. **$450**
#441 **Lovebirds,** two prs., ht. 6in. & 5¼in. **$350**
#442 **Figures of Two Dogs,** hts. 5½in. & 3in. **$200**

POTTERY / PORCELAIN

A-IA Mar. 2003

Jackson's International Auctioneers

RS Prussia, RS Germany & Others

#1185 Bowl, late 19th C. in satin finish, mold 128 w/ red roses, red RSP mark, dia. 10in. **$258**

#1186 Bowl, late 19th C. w/ various colored blossoms, red RSP mark, dia. 10in. **$488**

#1187 Bowl, late 19th C. w/ red florals & green accents, red RSP mark, dia. 10in. **$488**

#1188 Bowl w/ red & yellow blossoms & gilt highlights, red RSP mark, dia. 10in. **$575**

#1189 Bowl w/ red poppies on blue ground, red RSP mark, dia. 10in. **$172**

#1190 Cake Plate w/ pierced handles & waterlily dec., red RSP mark, dia. 11in. n/s

#1191 Shaving Mug, late 19th C. w/ floral dec. & red RSP mark, ht. 3½in. **$115**

#1192 Bowl, late 19th C. w/ floral dec., & red RSP mark, dia. 10in. **$86**

#1193 Cracker Jar, w/ autumn dec., mkd., ht. 7in. **$1,035**

#1194 Covered Egg Box, late 19th C. w/ rose band dec. & RSP red mark, lg. 4¾in. **$115**

#1195 Bowl w/ multi-colored florals, unmarked, dia. 10in. **$345**

#1196 Bowl, late 19th C. w/ cranberry dec. & red RSP mark, dia. 9¼in. **$172**

#1197 Tea Set w/ floral dec. professional repair to tea pot cover, unmarked, lg. 8in. **$201**

#1198 Celery, late 19th C. w/ hanging basket dec. & red RSP mark, lg. 9in. **$207**

#1199 Sugar & Creamer, late 19th C. w/ floral spray dec. & blue panels, unmarked, ht. 5in. **$103**

#1200 Cake Plate, late 19th C. w/ multi-floral dec. & RSP red mark, dia. 10in. **$431**

#1201 Vase w/ poppies & snowball dec., RSP mark, ht. 6in. **$264**

#1202 Cider Pitcher w/ RSP red mark, prof. repr., ht. 9in. **$172**

#1203 Tray, late 19th C. & dec. w/ red roses, RSP red mark, lg. 11½in. **$195**

#1204 Sugar & Creamer, late 19th C. w/ prof. repair to lip, RSP red mark, lg. 6in. **$57**

#1205 R.S. Poland Card Receiver w/ handle & RS Poland red mark, lg. 6in. **$57**

#1206 Cake Plate w/ pink roses & gilt foliage, dia. 11in. **$460**

#1207 Covered Mustard w/ floral dec. & RSP red mark & repairs, ht. 3in. **$69**

#1208 Berry Set, five pcs., w/rose dec. under satin finish, one bowl repr., RSP red mark. **$316**

#1209 Cake Plate w/ floral dec., unmkd., dia. 11in. **$143**

#1210 Card Receiver w/ red & yellow roses, green RSG mark, lg. 7in. **$34**

#1211 Muffineer, R.S. Germany w/ gold RSG steeple mark, ht. 4in. **$69**

#1212 Sugar & Creamer, late 19th C. w/ steeple scene, minor repr., red RSP mark, lg. 5in. **$230**

#1213 Sugar & Creamer w/ cottage scene, minor repr., red RSP mark, lg. 5½in. **$230**

#1214 Syrup & Underplate w/ ivy dec., lid repr., together w/ a **matching creamer,** red RSP mark, ht. 5in. **$34**

#1215 Bowl, German, early 20th C. w/ Prov. Saxe E.S. mark, lg. 5¾in. **$34**

#1216 Nappy, early 20th C. w/ stage coach scene, German E.S. mark, lg. 8in. **$69**

#1217 Covered Powder Box, R.S. Germany w/ blue mark, lg. 4in. **$34**

#1218 Sugar & Creamer, mkd. R.S. Poland w/ fitted silver plate caddy, lg. 8in. **$57**

A-PA Oct. 2002

Pook & Pook, Inc.

Third Row

#89 Plate w/ blue spatter rim & pineapple center, dia. 8in. **$7,475**

#90 Creamer w/ red & green spatter, ht. 3¾in. **$633**

#91 Teapot w/ red, green & blue horizontal spatter, ht. 6½in. **$518**

#92 Sugar Bowl w/ blue, green, red & yellow spatter, lid not orig., ht. 6in. **$6,325**

#93 Plate w/ green & purple spatter, dia. 7½in. **$431**

Fourth Row

#94 Leeds Candlesticks w/ brown & tan leaf dec. & female figures, ht. 10½in. **$4,025**

#95 Mocha Pitcher w/ crosshatch & band dec., reprs., ht. 9½in. **$1,610**

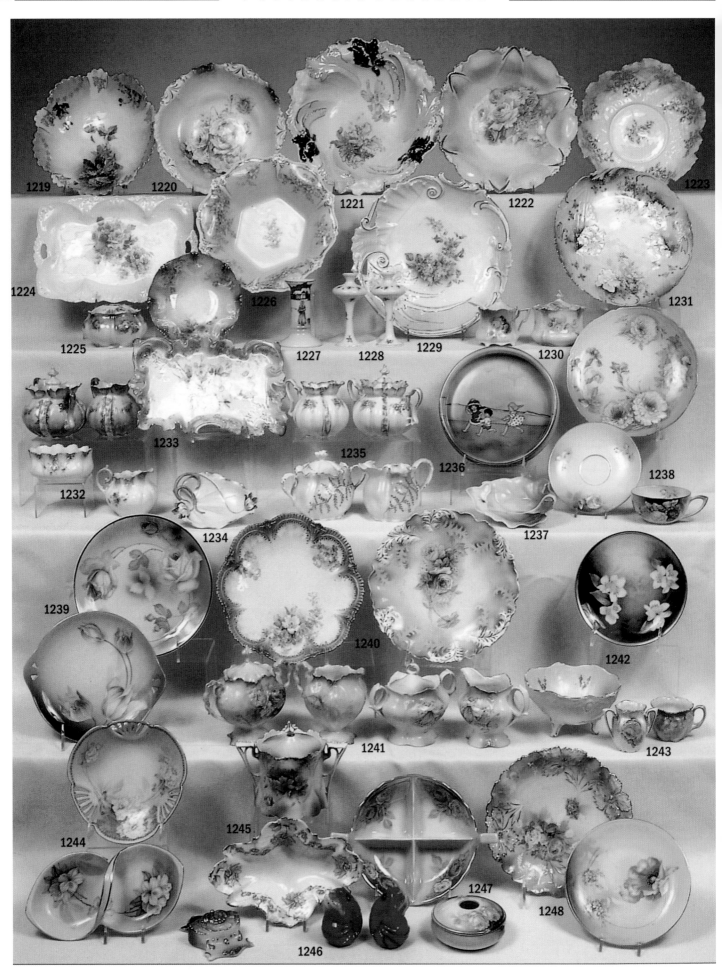

1219
1220
1221
1222
1223
1224
1225
1226
1227
1228
1229
1230
1231
1232
1233
1234
1235
1236
1237
1238
1239
1240
1241
1242
1243
1244
1245
1246
1247
1248

Jackson's International Auctioneers

#1219 Bowl, R.S. Prussia, late 19th C. w/ red mark, prof. repr., dia. 10in. **$92**

#1220 Bowl, R.S. Prussia, w/ red mark & minor flake, dia. 10in. **$92**

#1221 Bowl, Hutschenreuter, 20th C. w/ floral dec., sgn. "E. Dennie" w/ backstamp, dia. 12in. **$144**

#1222 Bowl, R.S. Prussia, 20th C. w/ red mark prof. repr., dia. 10½in. **$80**

#1223 Bowl, German, unmkd., w/ gilt dec., dia. 10in. **$46**

#1224 Dresser Tray, late 19th C. w/ red mark, lg. 11¾in. **$69**

#1225 Hair Receiver w/ repr. & **Bowl** w/ minor hairline, both w/ RSP red mark, dia. 6½in. **$34**

#1226 Bowl, unmkd., possibly R.S. Prussia, dia. 10in. **$138**

#1227 Candlestick, Royal Bayreuth w/blue mark, ht. 4¼in. **$69**

#1228 Flower Vases, mkd. w/ E.S. Germany, ht. 4½in. **$80**

#1229 Cake Plate, German, late 19th C., unmkd., dia. 11in. **$57**

#1230 Covered Sugar & Mustard, late 19th C., R.S. Germany. **$80**

#1231 Cake Plate, German, unmkd., dia.10in. **$69**

#1232 Sugar & Creamer, German, unmkd. **$115**

#1233 Dresser Tray, German, unmkd., lg. 11in. **$80**

#1234 Card Receiver, German, unmkd., lg. 5½in. **$57**

#1235 Sugar & Creamer, German, unmkd. **$115**

#1236 Child's Plate, Royal Bayreuth, dec. w/ children, blue mark, dia. 7½in. **$172**

#1237 Card Receiver, R.S. Germany, blue mark, lg. 5½in. **$34**

#1238 Plate, mkd. "Bavaria", dia. 8¼in. **$23**

#1239 Plates, German, pair, one w/ pierced handles, mkd. "R.S. Germany". **$34**

#1240 Plates, pair, ea. w/ R.S. Prussia red mark, dia. 8½in. **$138**

#1241 Sugar & Creamer, unmkd, & damaged; second set mkd. R.S. Prussia. **$69**

#1242 Footed Bowl & Plate, ea. mkd. R.S. Prussia, red mark. **$46**

#1243 Sugar Bowls, mkd. R.S. Prussia, both w/ some repr. **$17**

#1244 Pierced Bowl & Handled Basket, each w/ blue R.S. Germany mark. **$103**

#1245 Sauce Bowl & Covered Sugar w/ reprs., German, unmkd. **$34**

#1246 Lobster Salt & Pepper Shakers w/ wall match holder, mkd. "BT Germany". **$69**

#1247 Hair Receiver & Nappy, each mkd. "R.S. Germany". **$57**

#1248 Plates, one mkd. R.S. Prussia and one mkd. R.S. Germany, dia. 7½in. **$69**

Northeast Auctions

Staffordshire – Dark Blue

#464 Plates, "Bank Of The United States, Philadelphia," & 2 "Fair Mount Near Philadelphia," & 2 dark blue Staffordshire plates by Joseph Stubbs, dia. 10⅛in. **$650**

#465 Plates, 2 "Nahant Hotel Near Boston" by Joseph Stubbs, dia. 8¾in. & 8¼in. **$550**

#466 Plate, "Hoboken In New Jersey," by Joseph Stubbs, dia. 7¼in. **$400**

Northeast Auctions

Staffordshire

#467 Platter, "New York From Heights Near Brooklyn", medium-blue, by W.G. Wall, Esq., lg. 16⅛in. **$2,700**

#468 Platter, "Mendenhall Ferry," by Joseph Stubbs, medium-blue, lg. 6¼in. **$1,900**

POTTERY / PORCELAIN

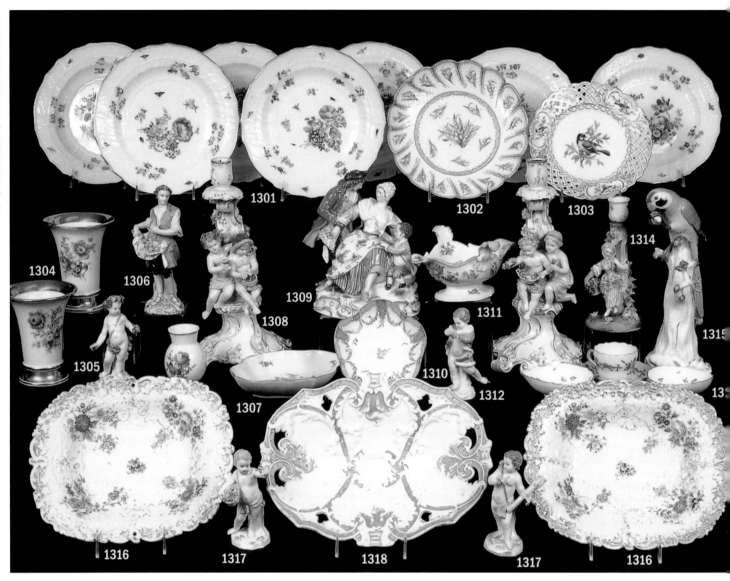

A-IA Mar. 2003

Jackson's International Auctioneers

#1301 Seven Meissen Cabinet Plates, 20th C., ea. w/ various painted flower bouquets w/ insects, blue underglaze crossed sword marks, one minor flake, dia. 9½in. **$488**

#1302 Meissen Cabinet Plate, late 19th C., decorated w/ lilies-of-the-valley on scalloped & lattice mold blank, blue underglaze mark, dia. 9in. **$103**

#1303 Meissen Cabinet Plate, 19th C., w/ painted bird dec. on reticulated rim, blue underglaze crossed swords, prof. repr., dia. 8in. **$69**

#1304 Meissen Vases, pr., 19th/20th C., w/ painted flower bouquets, blue underglaze crossed swords, ht. 5½in. **$201**

#1305 Meissen Porcelain Figure, 19th/20th C., of the infant Bacchus, minor loss & repr., blue underglaze crossed swords & imp. numbers, ht. 5in. **$287**

#1306 Sitzendorfer Porcelain Figure, 19th/20th C., of a flower seller, blue underglaze crossed lines, ht. 7½in. **$115**

#1307 Meissen Table Articles, pr., 20th C., w/ copper green flower dec. consisting of 7½in. oval bowl & 3½in. vase, blue underglaze crossed swords mark. **$115**

#1308 Meissen Figural Candlesticks, late 19th C., w/ infant figures resting on a base w/ applied florals, blue underglaze crossed swords marks, some prof. reprs. & losses to ea., ht. 12½in. **$1,725**

#1309 Meissen Porcelain Figure, 19th/20th C., of a couple w/ young child, some prof. repairs, blue underglaze crossed swords & incised marks, ht. 9in. **$1,092**

#1310 Meissen Cabinet Bowl, 19th C., 4-lobed form w/ floral swags, blue underglaze crossed swords w/ cancellation lines ground out, dia. 5½in. **$80**

#1311 Meissen Porcelain Sauce Boat, w/ scrolled handles & painted flowers, blue underglaze crossed swords, flake & tight hairline. lg. 8in. **$46**

#1312 Meissen Porcelain Figure, 19th/20th C., of a young boy skating, blue underglaze crossed swords & incised marks, ht. 5in. **$345**

#1313 Meissen Three-Piece Group, 20th C. consisting of a red dragon cup & saucer & a pair of handled sauces w/ flowers & insects, blue underglaze crossed swords, lg. 4½in. **$149**

#1314 Continental Porcelain Figural Candlestick, 19th C., of a young woman w/ flowers & grapes, blue underglaze crossed swords & star, some early repr. & losses, ht. 8in. **$258**

#1315 Meissen Porcelain Figure, 19th C., of a colorful parrot on tree trunk, some losses & reprs., blue underglaze crossed swords mark, ht. 11½in. **$402**

#1316 Meissen Porcelain Bowls, pr., 19th C. w/ hand painted flowers & gilt heightened relief dec., blue underglaze crossed swords. lg. 11½in. **$373**

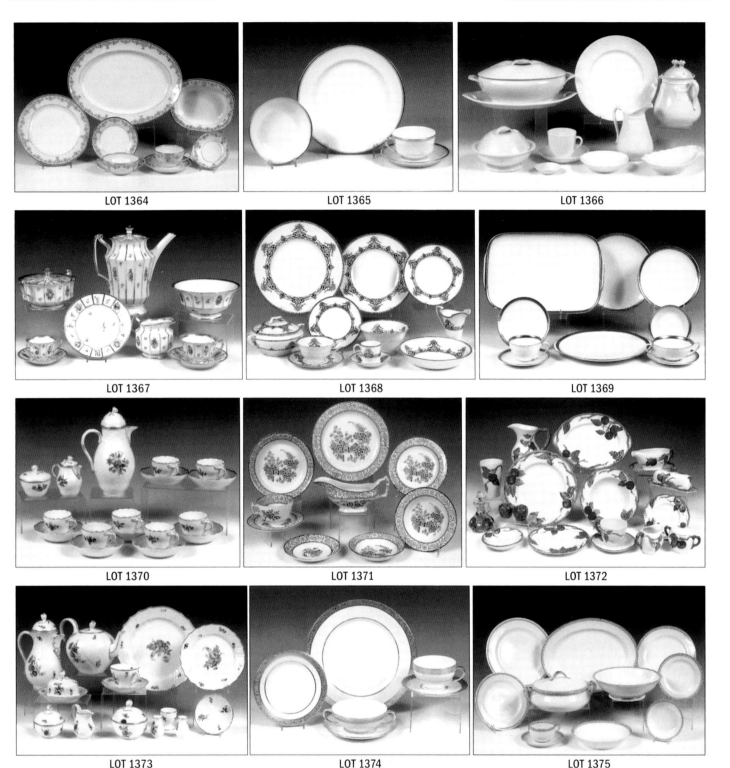

LOT 1364

LOT 1365

LOT 1366

LOT 1367

LOT 1368

LOT 1369

LOT 1370

LOT 1371

LOT 1372

LOT 1373

LOT 1374

LOT 1375

A-IA Mar. 2003

Jackson's International Auctioneers

#1364 Haviland China, 72pc. set, 12 4pc. place settings plus 10 cups, 5 bouillon soups & underplates & 4 serving extras. **$450**

#1365 Haviland China Dessert Set, 4pc. place settings for 8 plus extras, 36 pcs. total. **$115**

#1366 Haviland "H & Co" Dinner Service, all white, ten 5pc. place settings plus extras & 11 serving pcs., approx. 104 pcs.. **$316**

#1367 Royal Copenhagen Dinnerware, 36pc. set, in a floral pattern, demitasse cups & saucers, coffee pot, dessert plates, coffee cup & saucer. **$833**

#1368 Royal Worcester, 92pc. set, in "Doncaster" patt., twelve 5pc. place settings plus extras. **$402**

#1369 Hutschenreuther Porcelain, 81pc. set in "Carolin Magnus" patt., 13 serving pcs., 6 6pc. place settings plus extras. **$316**

#1370 Demitasse Set, 15 pcs., blue crossed sword marks. **$460**

#1371 Blue & White China, 73pc. set,

Woods Ware in "Wincanton" patt., 6 serving pcs., some minor losses. **$143**

#1372 Franciscan Pottery, 64pc. Set in "Apple" patt., 12 5pc. place settings plus 4 serving pcs. **$373**

#1373 Hutschenreuther Porcelain, 44pc. set in "Dresden" patt., 6 6pc. place settings. **$575**

#1374 Hutschenreuther Porcelain, 36pc. set in "Favorite" patt., 5 4pc.place settings plus extras. **$287**

#1375 Haviland China, 96pc. set in "Albany" pattern, 12 8pc. place settings & serving pieces. **$661**

POTTERY / PORCELAIN

A-IA June 2003

Jackson's International Auctioneers

Flow Blue
Items # 948-967 by W. H. Grindley &
Co. in the "Melbourne" Pattern, ca.1900
#948 **Chop Plate**, w/ backstamp, lg.
14in. **$92**
#949 **Meat Platter**, mkd., lg. 16½in. **$103**
#950 **Meat Platter**, w/ backstamp, lg.
16½in. **$103**
#951 **Chop Plate**, w/ backstamp, lg.
13½in. **$92**
#952 **Soup Plate**, w/ backstamp, dia.
10in. **$34**
#953 **Butter Pats**, set of 9, 8 w/ gilt
highlights, mkd., dia. 3¼in. **$373**
#954 **Soup Plates**, set of 6,
w/backstamps, dia. 9½in. **$201**
#955 **Plates**, set of 12 w/ backstamps,
dia. 9½in. **$483**
#956 **Plates**, set of 7 w/backstamps, 3
w/ chips, dia. 10in. **$143**
#957 **Plates**, set of 4 w/ backstamps, dia.
9in. **$138**
#958 **Plates**, set of 5 w/ backstamps, dia.
8in., together w/ a **Bowl**, dia. 10in.
$115
#959 **Gravy Boats**, pr. w/ gilt & backstamps,
lg. 8½in. **$126**
#960 **Covered Butter Dish** w/ orig. insert
& backstamp, dia. 8in. **$172**

#961 **Gravy Boat & Underplate** w/
backstamp, lg. 9in. **$103**
#962 **Covered Vegetable Dish** w/
backstamp & minor crow's foot, lg. 13in.
$138
#963 **Coffee Cup & Saucer** & 2 additional
saucers w/ gilt, one chipped. **$46**
#964 **Oval Bowls** w/ backstamps, lgs.
11in. & 10in. **$115**
#965 **Gravy Boat** w/ gilt & backstamp.
lg. 8½in. **$57**
#966 **Plates**, set of 6 w/ backstamps, dia.
6¾in. **$92**
#967 **Saucers**, set of 8 w/ backstamps,
dia. 6in. **$57**
#968 **Plates**, by Royal Copenhagen
"Versailles" patt., early 20th C., w/ gilt &
mkd. RC & Bauscher Bros. NY, dia.
6¼in. **$115**
#969 **Soup Plate**, Wedgwood "Chapoo",
ca.1850 w/ backstamp. **$92**
#970 **Continental Cream Jug**, ca.1865,
dec. w/ copper lustre, ht. 5½in. **$115**
#971 **Continental Milk Pitcher**, ca.1865,
w/ copper lustre, ht. 7½in. **$195**
#972 **Covered Vegetable** by Johnson
Bros., "Jewel" patt., ca.1900, lg. 12½in.
$69
#973 **Wash Pitcher** by W. Adams,
"Columbia" patt., ca.1875, w/ minor
flake, ht. 11½in. **$172**

#974 **Gravy Boat & Underplate**, Eng.,
unmkd., lg. 9in. **$69**
#975 **Tray**, by Grindley, lg. 12in. **$80**
#976 **Jug**, mid-19th C., w/ copper lustre
& yellow polychrome, ht. 6¼in. **$287**
#977 **Covered Vegetable** by Grindley &
Co. "Marechal Niel", ca.1896, lg.
12in. **$115**
#978 **Chop Plate**, Eng., late 19th C., lg.
12½in. **$115**
#979 **Covered Butter Dish**, A.J. Wilkinson
"Yeddo" patt. w/ gilt, no insert, dia. 8in.
$92
#980 **Plates**, Burgess & Leigh "Non Pareil",
7 6¾in. & 5 6in. saucers. **$138**
#981 **Covered Vegetable**, Doulton & Co.,
"Persian Spray" patt. damage to lid, lg.
13in. **$34**
#982 **Covered Sauce**, W.H. Grindley
Co., "Portman" patt. w/ hairline, lg. 9in.
$57
#983 **Bone Dishes**, Burgess & Leigh "Non
Pareil" patt., set of 12, lg. 6¾in. **$149**
#984 **Covered Sugar, Cream & Milk Jugs**,
"Ladas" patt., ht. 5½in. **$126**
#985 **Pitcher**, Ford & Sons "Tyne" patt., &
Covered Sauce "Avon" patt. **$149**
#986 **Sauce Ladles**, group of 4, ca.1900,
lg. 6½in. **$149**

A-IA June 2003   Jackson's
International Auctioneers

#831 **Bisque Figural Group**,
German, 19th C., dec. w/
gilt accents w/ printed
anchor mark, minor reprs.,
ht. 26in. **$1,955**

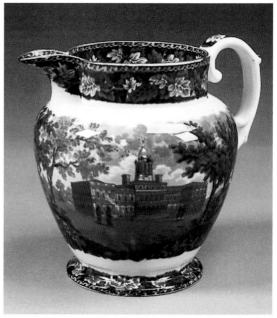

A-NH Nov. 2002   Northeast Auctions

#473 **Staffordshire Pitcher**, "City Hall/Hospital,
New York," dark blue, by Ralph Stevenson, ht.
7in. **$1,100**

The Shaker movement in America began in 1774 when Mother Ann Lee, an untutored English textile worker, arrived in this country with a small group of ardent followers. By the time of the Civil War membership had increased to around 8,000 brothers and sisters living in eighteen communities from Maine to Ohio. Shakers believed in celibacy and lived in communities that were largely self supporting. They were very traditional, believing in simplicity and conservatism which were heightened by religious strictures against any type of unnecessary decoration. Deliberately withdrawing from the world around them, members of this religious communal sect have left us a heritage of simplicity and beauty in their furniture, as well as every other Shaker craft. Their lifestyle is wholly without parallel in American history.

Shaker furniture is a major creative force in our decorative arts heritage because it is the only truly original American style of furniture. Harmony and quiet simplicity came naturally to the Shaker craftsman. His ambition was to produce works of the highest quality with the best materials to be found. Most Shaker pieces have simple, geometric lines and ingenious features such as complex drawer arrangements. Oftentimes, surfaces were left unpainted or covered with a thin coat of stain.

Since the "discovery" of Shaker designs during the 1920s, a number of American museums and collectors have amassed distinguished collections of the sect's furniture and artifacts. The word "Shaker," as in every other Shaker craft, is now being very appreciated at its true value and has become a magic term to collectors these days. Recent auctions have attracted serious collectors, as well as museum representatives, and their frenzied bidding has literally driven prices upward until many new heights have been realized in recent years.

A-NY June 2003 Willis Henry Auctions, Inc.

#23 **Oval Sewing Carrier,** pine & maple w/ orig. red crackled finish, fixed hoop handle & silk interior w/ needlecase & strawberry emery, ht. 6¼in. **$900**

A-NY June 2003 Willis Henry Auctions, Inc.

#8 **Bisque Doll** w/ sleep eyes, open mouth & four teeth, brown wig is part of popular ware bonnet, dressed w/ gray cloak "Duchess, A5/OM," ht. 13½in. **$1,100**

A-NY June 2003   Willis Henry Auctions, Inc.

#74 **Rolling Pin,** birch w/ orig. finish, Canterbury, NH, handles in shape of Canterbury chair finials, lg. 34½in. **$800**

A-NY June 2003   Willis Henry Auctions, Inc.

#28 **Two Sieves,** one maple w/ woven dark & light horsehair & steel tacks; the other oak w/ screen & copper tacks, ht. 1¾, dia. 4¼in.; ht. 5½, dia. 8¾in. **$550**

A-NY June 2003　　Willis Henry Auctions, Inc.

#112 Shaker Advertisement for "The Shaker Tamar Laxative", ht. 11, wd. 9in. **$1,050**

A-NY June 2003

Willis Henry Auctions, Inc.

#234 Applesauce Pail, pine w/ steel bands, turned lid w/ inset knob, canted sides & swing latch for lid, ht 9, dia. 8in. **$600**

A-NY June 2003　　Willis Henry Auctions, Inc.

#180 Stove, cast iron w/ attached iron tool holder at rear, Mt. Lebanon, ht. 27, lg. 33½in. **$2,250**

A-NY June 2003

Willis Henry Auctions, Inc.

#5 Rocking Chair, maple w/ orig. dark walnut stained finish, Mt. Lebanon, NY, w/ orig. red & green taped seat, ca.1880, #7. **$1,000**

A-NY June 2003

Willis Henry Auctions, Inc.

#100U Rocking Chair, maple, old refinish w/ green stripe tape seat, Mt. Lebanon, NY, #7, overall ht. 42in. **$1,300**

A-NY June 2003

Willis Henry Auctions, Inc.

#120 Pine Cupboard w/ traces of orig. yellow stained finish, two shelf interior, three in bottom, spring loaded steel door closures & cherry knobs, ht. 75, wd. 24¾, dp.13½in. **$4,000**

A-NY June 2003   Willis Henry Auctions, Inc.

#98 **Oval Box,** pine & maple w/ orig. blue painted finish, four fingers, copper tacks & iron points, small repair at base end, ht. 4¾, lg. 11¼in. **$3,000**

A-NY June 2003

Willis Henry Auctions, Inc.

#1 **Oval Box,** pine & maple w/ orig. chrome yellow finish w/ stained red interior, ht. 2¾, lg. 6½in. **$37,000**

A-NY June 2003

Willis Henry Auctions, Inc.

#97 **Oval Box,** pine & maple w/ orig. gold/yellow painted finish, four fingers, copper tacks & points, pencil signed inside lid, dated 1853, early repair split at base end, ht. 4¾, lg. 11¼in. **$3,000**

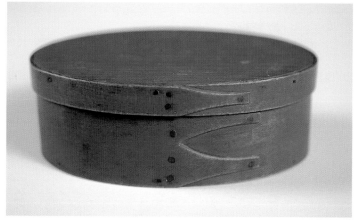

A-NY June 2003   Willis Henry Auctions, Inc.

#64 **Oval Box,** maple & pine w/ orig. chrome yellow finish, four fingers, copper tacks, Canterbury, NH, ca.1840, ht. 3¼, lg. 8in. **$30,000**

A-NY June 2003   Willis Henry Auctions, Inc.

#89 **Oval Box,** pine & maple w/ orig. red painted finish, three fingers, copper tacks & points, ht. 1⅝, lg. 4½ in. **$5,000**

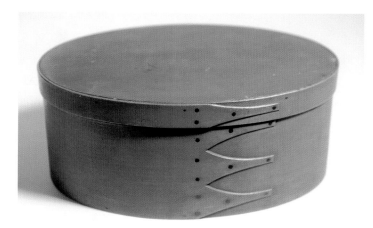

A-NY June 2003   Willis Henry Auctions, Inc.

#96 **Oval Box,** pine & maple w/ orig. red painted finish, four fingers, copper tacks & points, ht. 3½, lg. 8¾in. **$15,000**

A-NY June 2003   Willis Henry Auctions, Inc.

#31 **Oval Box,** maple & pine w/ orig. red stained finish, ca.1840-50, ht. 4¼, wd. 7, lg. 10⅛in. **$20,000**

A-NY June 2003   Willis Henry Auctions, Inc.

#100S Pegboards, four, pine w/ maple pegs, orig. red finish, Hancock, MA, ca.1830, lg. 58½, 59, 53 & 20in. **$950**

A-NY June 2003

Willis Henry Auctions, Inc.

#15 Spinning Wheel, maple, birch & oak, wool wheel stamped "FW" (Freegift Wells), Watervliet, NY, ca.1830. **$700**

A-NY June 2003

Willis Henry Auctions, Inc.

#100F Pouring Bowl, maple w/ carved pouring spouts on either end, sm. repair to lip, ht. 6½, lg. 25½, wd. 17in. **$750**

A-NY June 2003   Willis Henry Auctions, Inc.

#35 Sister's Sewing Desk, butternut w/ pine secondary, varnish finish, dov. drawers, orig. locks & key & orig. knobs, ht. 41½, wd. 31½in. **$16,000**

A-NY June 2003

Willis Henry Auctions, Inc.

#100 Blanket Chest, pine w/ orig. red painted finish & dov. drawers & base, maple knobs, Watervliet, NY, ca.1840, ht. 42½, wd. 37, dp. 17¾in. **$8,000**

A-NY June 2003

Willis Henry Auctions, Inc.

#60 Sister's Sewing Stand, tiger maple, maple & pine secondary w/ traces of orig. red painted finish, two dov. drawers w/ orig. brass pulls & snake legs, Enfield, CT, ca.1840, ht. 24, wd. 20½, dp. 18in. **$10,500**

SHAKER

A-NY June 2003   Willis Henry Auctions, Inc.
#185 Cupboard Over Drawers, pine w/ traces of orig. yellow & red painted finish, orig. cherry knobs on canted sq. foot, hinges repl., ca. 1840, ht. 75, wd. 42, dp. 17in. **$5,000**

A-NY June 2003   Willis Henry Auctions, Inc.
#290 Herb Chest, poplar & butternut w/ orig. reddish/brown painted finish, ca. 1850, ht. 26¾, wd. 27, dp. 12¾in. **$3,000**

A-NY June 2003   Willis Henry Auctions, Inc.
#141 Desk Box, butternut w/ tiger maple, dov. & diamond-shaped ivory escutcheon, simple int., ca. 1860, ht. 7, wd. 12½, dp. 10½in. **$900**

A-NY June 2003   Willis Henry Auctions, Inc.
#105 Work Table, pine w/ breadboard top, cherry skirt & birch legs, red painted finish w/ pegged construction, ca. 1830-40, ht. 26, lg. 42, dp. 24in. **$4,000**

A-NH July 2003   Northeast Auctions
#40 Mount Lebanon Revolving Chair w/ spider legs, ht. 25½in. **$5,000**

#41 Stand Table, Harvard Shaker Community, ca. 1840, ht. 26¾in. **$1,200**

A-NH July 2003   Northeast Auctions

#177 Trestle Base Dining Table, tiger maple & walnut, ht. 24½, top 32¾ x 59½in. **$2,400**

A-NH July 2003   Northeast Auctions

#48 Blanket Chest w/ hinged lid, applied breadboard molding above case w/ 3 fielded panels on the front & side, ht. 26½, top 19 x 40½in. **$6,500**

A-NY June 2003   Willis Henry Auctions, Inc.

#160 Dry Sink, pine w/ traces of orig. red painted finish, dov. enclosed gallery & bootjack ends, feet restored, ca.1840, ht. 31, lg. 34¼, dp. 15¼in. **$4,000**

A-NY June 2003

         Willis Henry Auctions, Inc.

#71 Basket, black on brown ash, twilled quadrifoil form, "emblematic of the Shaker vision of a radiant heavenly sphere", ca.1870-1900. **$55,000**

A-NH July 2003   Northeast Auctions

#176 Lowback Dining Chairs, assembled set. **$4,750**

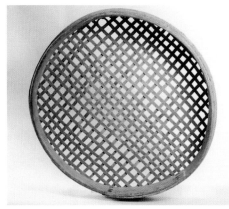

A-NY June 2003   Willis Henry Auctions, Inc.

#286 Bean Sieve, woven ash, oak rim & copper rivets, New Lebanon, NY, ca.1840-50, dia. 19in. **$200**

A-NH July 2003   Northeast Auctions

#38 Tiger Maple Slat-Back Side Chair w/ tilters. **$3,600**

#39 Work Table w/ scrubbed top & red painted base & one side drawer, ht. 30in., top 37¾ x 22in. **$2,000**

A-NY June 2003   Willis Henry Auctions, Inc.

#52 Baskets, three, black ash w/ carved maple hoop handles, one w/ tag around handle "Basket made by Shakers", ht. 11¼, 13¾ & 9in. **$1,100**

A-NH July 2003

Northeast Auctions

#60 Tall Chest of Drawers, Alfred, ME Shaker, stained pine, dov. const., ht. 61, wd. 40, dp. 20in. **$7,500**

A-NH July 2003

Northeast Auctions

#190 Chest of Drawers, Mount Lebanon, pine w/ ochre & red combed decor. on each drawer & Bennington-type knobs, ht. 73, wd. 42, dp. 24in. **$12,000**

A-NY June 2003   Willis Henry Auctions, Inc.

#79 Basket, "tub" form, black ash splint w/ delicate carved handle, New Lebanon, NY, ca.1860, ht. 1¾, lg. 7¾, wd. 6¼in. **$6,000**

A-NY June 2003   Willis Henry Auctions, Inc.

#252 Sewing Basket, finely woven black ash w/ double wrapped rim, gray silklined w/ tomato pincushion, attached inner basket, one handle repl. & one inner basket missing, ca.1850, ht 11, wd. 10½in. **$1,100**

A-NH July 2003   Northeast Auctions

#50 Grain Shovel, Pitchfork, Rug Whip & Rake, ht. of last 71in. **$850**

#51 Folding Wall-Hanging Drying Rack, Mount Lebanon, ht. 29¼, wd. 34¼, dp. 5in. **$400**

#52 Collapsible Winnower, diamond-form w/ remnants of S. Clough Meredith, NH label, closed 35 x 12in. **$300**

#53 Oval Covered Box w/ raised pierced handles, staved const. w/ interlace straps & remnants of red, top 22½ x 28in. **$1,500**

#54 Farm Bench w/ red stain on slightly raked cylindrical legs, ht. 19¾in. **$550**

#55 Staved Water Bucket w/ metal bands & diamond-form backplates for swing handle, ht. 10, dia. 12in. **$250**

#56 Sewing Cabinet in old red w/ two stacks of twelve drawers, ht. 34¾, wd. 16¾in. **$5,600**

#57 Quilt/Towel Rack w/ trestle legs, mahoganized, ht. 37, lg. 30in. **$350**

#58 Tailoring Stools, assembled pair covered w/ plaid fabric, one w/ red paint, lg. 18in. **$100**

#59 Storage Box w/ swing handle, ht. 7½ without handle, dia. 14¾in. **$200**

STONEWARE

Stoneware is another type of country pottery that has swung into prominence. Its production in America got underway around the mid-1700s and, because of its popularity, it was mass produced until the late 1800s.

Stoneware is a weighty, durable, dense pottery made from clay mixed with flint or sand, or made from very siliceous clay that vitrifies when heated to form a nonporous base. The common household vessels were glazed inside and/or outside to prevent porosity and resist chemical action. Most of the ware produced is salt-glazed. To produce this type of glaze, common table salt was heated and then thrown into the ware-filled kiln when firing was at the maximum temperature. The intense heat caused the salt to vaporize instantly, covering the objects with a clear, thin glaze; hence the term "salt-glaze". Frequently, the salt particles hit the vessels before being transformed into vapor, creating a pitted or pebbly surface on the stoneware.

When not salt-glazed, stoneware was coated with a slipglaze, often referred to as brown "Albany" slip, which consisted of a mixture of clay mixed with water. When applied as a finish, the mixture would fuse into a natural smooth glaze at certain firing temperatures.

The earliest stoneware was plain and unadorned but, by the turn of the 19th century, potters were using splashes of cobalt blue to decorate the gray and tan jugs and crocks. Gradually, their first squiggles evolved into the highly sophisticated freehand figures of the mid-1850s and '60s, then to the usage of stenciled patterns as interest declined.

Interest in stoneware today is not in its beautiful forms or colors, but in its decoration, the maker's name, location, and in rare instances a date, painted or incised into the clay. But, as a general rule, the more fanciful cobalt blue decorated vessels continue to increase in value, forcing the serious collector to be more discriminating.

A-NY Sept. 2003   Waasdorp's American Pottery Auction

#187 **Pitcher**, ½gal., unsigned, ca.1860 w/ overall double flower blue dec., w/ tight hairline running along bottom, ht. 8in. **$962**
#188 **Pitcher**, 1pint, unsigned w/ blue dec., & tight hairline from base, prof. rest., ca.1850, ht. 6½in. **$770**
#189 **Batter Pail**, 1gal., mkd. Cowden & Wilcox, Harrisburg, dec. front & back w/ blue plume, minor surface chip above name, ca.1870, ht. 8in. **$2,530**

A-NY Sept. 2003   Waasdorp's American Pottery Auction

#64 **Butter Churn**, 5gal., mkd. White & Son, Utica, NY w/ their signature, paddle tail bird design, some staining, ca.1865, ht. 17½in. **$13,200**
#149 **Jug**, 3gal., mkd. J. & E. Norton, Bennington, VT, w/ blue dec. & filled lamp hole at base in back, ca.1855, ht. 15½in. **$2,420**
#157 **Butter Churn**, 4gal., advertising churn, Bennington, VT, dec. w/ large floral blue design, ca.1865, ht. 16½in. **$2,200**

A-NY Sept. 2003
Waasdorp's American Pottery Auction

#105 **Crock**, 3gal., by Brady & Ryan, Ellenville, NY, ca.1885, dec. w/ two blue masted sailing ships, ht. 10in. **$10,725**
#66 **Crock**, 2gal., mkd. N.A. White & Son, Utica, NY, dec. w/ a blue heron & foliage, ca.1870, ht. 9in. **$7,700**
#89 **Crock**, 3gal., mkd. Pottery Works Little Wst 12 St., NY, ca.1870, "The Wedding Proposal" with image of a period gentleman & woman, ht. 10in. **$10,450**

A-MA Nov. 2002   **Skinner, Inc.**

Salt Glazed Stoneware With Cobalt Blue Decoration

First Row

#551 Crock, White & Son, Utica, NY, ca.1840-53, 1gal., minor base chips, ht. 6¾in. **$832**

#552 Jar, attrib. to the Cortland Factory, ca.1870, ½gal., ht. 7⅜in. **$411**

#553 Jar, Howe & Clark, Athens, NY, ca.1805-13, earliest known Athens mark, minor rim chip, ht. 8⅞in. **$9,400**

#554 Crock, Am., ca.1870, ht. 7⅝in. **$323**

#555 Jar, Cortland Factory, ca.1870,

½gal., minor interior rim chip, ht. 7⅜in. **$441**

#556 Crock, Wm. A. McQuoid & Co., NY City, ca.1863-70, 1½gal., minor chips to one handle, ht. 8¼in. **$1,058**

Second Row

#557 Jar, ca.1857-82, 1gal., impressed "Binghamton N.Y.,", ht. 7in. **$1,998**

#558 Jar, Nathan Clark Jr., Athens, NY, ca.1843-92, 2gal., ht. 9in. **$588**

#559 Cake Crock, Am. 19th C., 1gal., dec. w/ floral border, ht. 5¼in. **$441**

#560 Preserve Jar, "Commeraws Stoneware", NY City, ca.1790, minor old rim chips, ht. 9⅝in. **$2,233**

Third Row

#561 Preserve Jar, "A.P. Donaghho, Fredericktown, PA", ht. 9½in. n/s

#562 Crock, John Burger, Rochester, NY, ca.1860, 2gal., Albany glazed interior, ht. 8¾in. **$1,058**

#563 Pitcher, attrib. to McQuoid & Co., NYC, ca.1870, ht. 10¾in. **$940**

#564 Crock, William Roberts, Binghamton, NY, ca.1870, 3gal., hairline near base, ht. 9in. **$764**

#565 Jug, Lyons Pottery, Lyons, NY, ca.1855, 3gal., minor base chip, ht. 16½in. **$881**

A-NY Sept. 2003   **Waasdorp's American Pottery Auction**

#141 Syrup Jug, 2gal., mkd. Fort Edward Pottery Co., ca.1860 w/ blue dec., & prof. rest., ht. 14in. **$1,320**

#142 Cake Crock, 2gal., mkd. Bullard & Scott, Cambridgeport, MA, ca.1870 w/ cobalt blue squat bird, ht. 7¾in. **$632**

#143 Jug, 2gal., mkd. Hastun Ottman & Co., Fort Edward, NY w/ stylized floral dec., ht. 14in. **$154**

A-NY Sept. 2003   **Waasdorp's American Pottery Auction**

#135 Pitcher, approx. 1gal., mkd. Burger & Lang, Rochester, NY, ca.1870 w/ blue dec., & minor chip at base on back, ht. 9½in. **$1,375**

#136 Preserve Jar, 1gal., mkd. F. Stetzenmeyer & Co., Rochester, NY, w/ thick blue ribbed flower dec., w/ horizontal crack in bottom, ht. 9½in. **$715**

#137 Pitcher, 1½gal., mkd. F. Stetzenmeyer & G. Goetzman, Rochester, NY, w/ blue sunflower dec. & short hairline from rim to handle, ca.1857, ht. 11in. **$1,265**

A-NY Sept. 2003   Waasdorp's American Pottery Auction

#108 Crock, 6gal., dec. w/ chicken pecking corn, potter's mark not legible, surface chip on rim, ca.1870, ht. 13in. **$687**

#109 Jug, 4gal. by D. Weston Ellenville, NY w/ blue dec., restoration, ht. 10in. **$440**

#110 Jar, 4gal. by Riedinger & Claire, w/ blue dec. of singing bird, ca.1870, ht. 14½in. **$2,310**

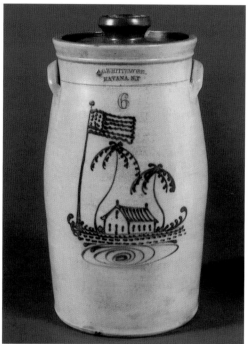

A-NH Aug. 2003

Northeast Auctions

#121 Churn, 6gal. w/ blue Am. flag, fort & palm trees, mkd. A.O. Whitemore, Havana, ca.1862-63, lid not orig., ht. 18½in. **$21,000**

A-NH Aug. 2003

Northeast Auctions

#122 Churn, 6gal. w/ imp. mark "T. Harrington/Lyons," ca.1851-1874 w/ blue dec., ht. 19¾in. **$35,000**

A-NH Aug. 2003

Northeast Auctions

#131 Jug, 5gal., mkd. Ft. Edward, NY Stoneware, w/ blue chirping bird on branch, ca.1861-91, ht. 18¼in. **$2,250**

A-NH Aug. 2003

Northeast Auctions

#133 Crock, mkd. Lyons, NY Stoneware, w/ blue double flower dec., ht. 12in. **$1,000**

A-MA Nov. 2002   **Skinner, Inc.**

#639 Bed Steps, cherry & pine, N. Eng., ca.1820-30, old surface, imper., ht. 21in., dp. 20¼in., wd. 18in. **$1,528**

First Row

#640 Redware Jar, Nathaniel Rochester, NY, 19th C., wear, ht. 7¼in. **$2,703**

#641 Stoneware Jug, Charlestown, MA, early 19th C., mkd. "Charlestown", minor wear, ht. 10in. **$382**

Second Row

#642 Stoneware Jars, glazed, two, John

Bell, Waynesboro, PA, ca.1875 w/ mottled brown & tan glossy glaze, minor rim nicks, ht. 6⅝in. & 6⅞in. **$705**

#643 Redware Jugs, two, eastern US, early 19th C. w/ mottled yellow, brown & light olive green, minor chips & glaze wear, ht. 9¼in. & 7⅛in. **$1,645**

Third Row

#644 Redware Pitcher & Jug, eastern US, early 19th C. w/ brown & green mottled dec., chips, ht. 8⅜in. & 6⅜in. **$1,528**

#645 Redware Handled Jar & Jug, eastern US, early 19th C. w/ mottled yellow, brown & olive green dec., chips, ht 7½ in & 6⅝in. **$2,233**

Fourth Row

#646 Redware Pitcher, eastern US, early 19th C., redware pitcher & jug w/ brown splotch dec. & a brown glazed stoneware pitcher, chips, ht. 6in., 5⅞in. & 5⅝in. **$1,116**

TEXTILES

The early settlers brought to these shores the best handworked patterns and techniques of their native lands. Women were accomplished with the needle and their creations were a matter of pride, as well as necessity. They literally threaded themselves into the patchwork of a new American life-style as they settled into their new environment. Every handcrafted, surviving example is an expression of their talent, and textiles are among the more diverse of American collectibles.

It has become increasingly difficult to find an early colorful quilt or woven coverlet these days. Coverlets remain among one of the more expensive of American textiles. The quilt collector focuses on the quality and vintage of the needlework, the diverse forms and condition. Within the past thirty years, prices for fine quilts and coverlets have escalated dramatically… yet good buys remain for the resourceful collector.

Many collectors have turned to other forms of bed covers such as the embroidered blanket, bedspreads of the white variety, stenciled spreads and all forms of embroidery including show towels made by the Pennsylvania Germans.

Colorful hooked and braided rugs command much attention these days, and fetch very substantial prices … especially those with original designs.

Samplers and needlework pictures became popular during the 18th and 19th centuries. More of these works of art have survived than any other type of fancy American needlework. The most intricately stitched American samplers and needlework, including elaborate mourning pictures, are extremely pricey. Many less elaborate pieces are still available … and, like other fine American textiles, very good investments.

A-MA Nov. 2002 Skinner, Inc.
#230 Jacquard Coverlet, NY probably by Harry Tyler (1801-1858), Jefferson County, ca.1838, cotton & wool double-weave, woven lettering, minor toning, 90in. x 79in. **$2,585**

A-NH Aug. 2003 Northeast Auctions
#346 Silk Needlework Memorial, wrought by Tryphena Richardson at Day's Academy, Wrentham, MA, est. ca.1808 for young women, sight size 14½in. x 17½in. **$22,000**

A-MA Nov. 2002 Skinner, Inc.
#458 Needlework Sampler, N. Eng., "Wrought by Sarah Goodridge, age 13 yrs., date 1804 or 1805, silk threads on linen ground w/ house flanked by pine trees, alphabet & verse, sight size 18⅞in. x 19in. **$3,173**

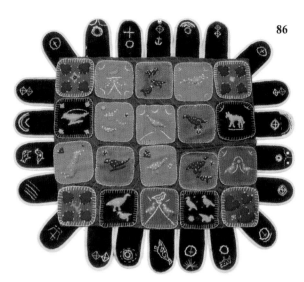

A-PA Oct. 2003   Conestoga Auction Company, Inc.

#86 Folk Art Penny Rug/Table Mat w/ animals & hearts, all done in shades of red, green, pink or white on tan, gray or black ground, each having a stitched design, ht. 24in., wd. 27in. **$2,500**

A-MA Aug. 2003   Skinner, Inc.

#489 Crazy Quilt, silk & velvet, Am., w/ stitched "1885" date, embellished w/ variety of embroidery stitches, painted motifs, black satin border, sq. 64in. x 64in. **$529**

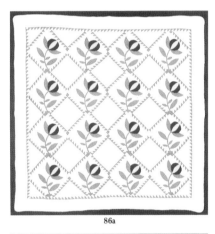

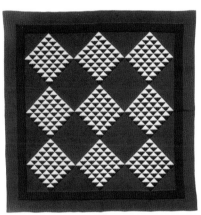

86a   86b

A-MA Nov. 2002   Skinner, Inc.

#516 Memorial Picture, silk needlework, N. Eng., early 19th C., depicting a young woman in mourning leaning against an urn-topped monument, sky done in watercolor in an oval, light staining, framed, 17¼in. x 15½in. **$2,233**

86d   86 E

A-PA Feb. 2003   Pook & Pook, Inc.

#86a Pieced Quilt, PA, w/ red & green tulips & intricate quilting. **$920**
#86b Pieced Quilt, early 20th C., w/ wine & yellow diamond & block patt. **$748**
#86d Ohio Appliqué Quilt w/ calico flowers & leaves. **$1,380**
#86e Jacquard Coverlet, PA, w/ floral design & tulip border. **$288**
#86c Pieced Quilt, PA, red & white w/ blocks of sawtooth bordered fans & half circles. **$1,093**

A-NH Aug. 2003   Northeast Auctions
#347 Silk Needlework Memorial, painted by Eliza Whittemore, age 13, w/ painted trees & distant landscape, ca.1815, sight size 20in. x 16½in. **$11,000**

A-PA Oct. 2002   Pook & Pook, Inc.
#59 Sampler, silk on linen needlework, wrought by Matilda Jane Dunlap at Miss Duston's School, w/ house flanked by cornucopia, tree, trailing vine, flowers & verse, 17in. x 16in. **$2,300**

A-PA Oct. 2002
Conestoga Auction
Company, Inc.

#572 Crazy Patchwork Friendship Quilt dated 1846 & 1880 w/ numerous elaborate needlework & scalloped edge, 62in. x 63in. **$522**

A-MA Nov. 2002   Skinner, Inc.
#524 Hooked Rug, wool & cotton, Am., 19th C., depicting love birds, mounted on wood frame, minor repr., 23¾in. x 36in. **$1,528**

A-NE Nov. 2002   Northeast Auctions
#520 Sailor-Made Sewing Stand, whalebone & mahogany, fitted w/ two stacks of drawers & heart inlay dec., turned bone supports & ball feet below two swiveling circle spoon holders, star-form inlay, ht. 9in. **$4,000**

A-NH Aug. 2003   Northeast Auctions
#1035 Appliquéd Quilt, "Urn of Flowers" patt., PA, dated 1850, 88in. x 80in. **$27,000**

A-PA Nov. 2002

Pook & Pook, Inc.

#404 **Coverlet,** jacquard, red & white by J. Cunningham, NY, dated 1840, w/ eagle border, soldier on horseback in corner & inscribed "Washington". **$1,265**

A-PA Nov. 2002

Pook & Pook, Inc.

#405 **Coverlet,** jacquard, blue & white, by Harry Tyler, NY, dated 1836 w/ monkey & tree border, lion corners, human & dog figures. **$610**

A-MA June 2003   **Skinner, Inc.**

#331 **Quilt,** pieced & appliquéd cotton, Am., 19th C., composed of forty-two eight point stars in deep red, blue & yellow printed floral patt. w/ off white backing, toning, stains, edge wear, 96in. x 104in. **$999**

#332 **Overshot Coverlet,** woven wool, Am., early 19th C., woven in a plaid patt. w/ center seam in predominantly navy blue, rust, olive green, mustard & off white accent colors, repairs, 88in. x 94in. **$206**

#333 **Patchwork Quilt,** pieced cotton, Am., 19th C., in navy blue, tan, & white, minor stains. n/s

#334 **Appliquéd & Pieced Quilt,** cotton, Tulip patt., Am. 19th C., red & green printed calico w/ tulip & flower motif, diamond & crescent shaped quilting, subtle toning, 84in. x 86in. **$2,115**

#335 **Jacquard Coverlet,** double-weave wool & cotton, Am., one-piece, minor wear stains, approx. 86in. x 78in. exc. fringe. **$499**

#336 **Coverlet,** three-color double-weave jacquard, Am., mid-to-late 19th C., w/ central floral & foliate medallion enclosed in oak leaf & acorn, diamond & foliate borders, red, blue & green w/ fringed edges, 75in. x 82in. **$529**

#337 **Pieced Quilt,** Harvest Sun patt., Am., 19th C., composed of nine eight-point stars enclosed in a swag & tassel border of red, yellow & green calico printed fabric on red ground, red & white calico print backing, green binding w/ feather & chevron patt. stitches, stains & wear, sq. 103in. x 103in. **$2,585**

A-PA Feb. 2003   Pook & Pook, Inc.
#75 Pictorial Hooked Rug, Am., 19th C., w/ spread winged eagle perched atop American flag & shield, 36½in. x 49in. **$2,875**

A-PA Feb. 2003   Pook & Pook, Inc.
#86f Crewel Embroidered Coverlet, N. Eng., ca.1800, twill woven w/ homespun wool & thistle vine motif, 77in. x 69in. **$5,750**

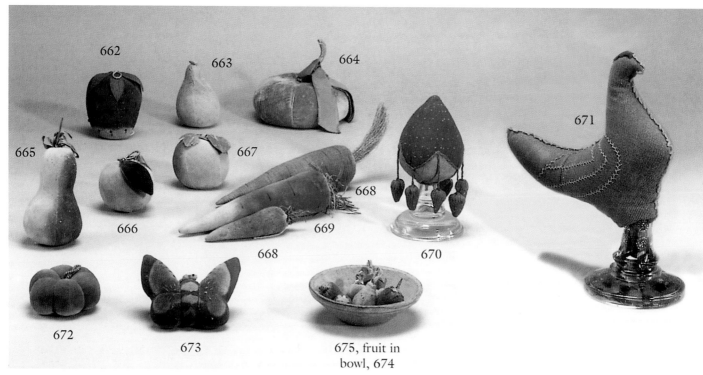

675, fruit in bowl, 674

A-MA Nov. 2002   Skinner, Inc.
Pincushions

#662 Strawberry, Am., early 19th C. w/ felt leaves & black glass straight pin "seeds", ht. 5in. **$823**

#663 Pear, Am., early 19th C., wear, ht. 4¼in. **$118**

#664 Squash, Am., early 19th C. w/ grosgrain ribbon & preserved gourd stem, ht. 6¼in., dia. 7in. **$235**

#665 Pear, Am., early 19th C., ht. 7⅛in. **$705**

#666 Apple, Am., early 19th C. w/ applied satin ribbon & velvet leaf, ht.

3½in. **$176**

#667 Apple, Am., early 19th C., ht. 3⅛in. **$705**

#668 Two Carrots, Am., early 19th C., straw tops & painted details, lg. 6½in. & 14in. **$264**

#669 Carrot, Am., early 19th C., lg. 10in. **$881**

#670 Strawberry, Am., 19th C., large stuffed form of pieced wool fabric, supported on colorless glass base, wear, ht. 8¼in. **$441**

#671 Rooster, Am., 19th C., stuffed woven wool form in light brown w/ tan

cotton & red wool yarn embroidered features on colorless glass stand, interior painted red & gold, ht. 14¼in. **$441**

#672 Tomato, Am., 19th C., ht. 1¾in., dia. 3⅝in. **$558**

#673 Butterfly, Am., early 19th C., wd. 5⅛in., lg. 4⅜in. **$588**

#674 Seven Mini., Am., early 19th C., incl. acorn, two strawberries, pear, carrot, apple, gourd, w/ painted detail, lg. 1¼in. to 3¼in. **$705**

#675 Painted Turned Pine Bowl, ht. 1¾in., dia. 5⅝in. **$499**

Early, interesting old toys – especially the hand-carved examples – are truly vivid expressions of the American craftsman's art of imagination. They are continuously in demand, and prices increase sharply each year. Those worthy of consideration as a "folk art" are very pricey, even though some are crudely whittled; others show fine craftsmanship and detailing. Among the most interesting of the early toys are the carved wooden dolls, squeak toys, wood and metal jumping figures, wood and chalk animals, whistles, miniatures, and the ever-popular "Sunday" toys when boisterous play was banned. The carved "Noah's Arks" were especially designed for this purpose. They oftentimes contained as many as fifty minutely carved and decorated animals, in addition to human figures.

The American toy industry was brought into being during the first decades of the nineteenth century. William S. Tower of South Hingham, MA, a carpenter by profession, has often been called the founder of the toy industry in America. In spite of the availability and wide usage of wood during this period, an increasing number of tin and iron toys were made. Many of the mass-produced toys were made during the 1870s, including the popular cast iron mechanical banks.

Because of the scarcity of earlier toys, today there is a rapidly growing band of enthusiasts buying up toys, almost regardless of the era – sometimes the items haven't been around as long as those doing the prospecting! But, whether it is indicative of a universal yearning for the good old days, or simply a case of monkey-see, monkey-do, the rush goes on.

A-PA May 2003

Noel Barrett Antiques & Auctions Ltd.

Schoenhuts

#213 **Clown** w/ chair & pedestal, all orig. clothing & leather ears, ht. 8in. **$247**

#214 **Clowns,** two in "Sunburst" suits, clothes soiled but orig., ht. 8 in. **$495**

#215 **Earless Clowns,** scarce, w/ all orig. clothing & traces of "foot print" on chests, ht. 8in. **$440**

A-PA May 2003   Noel Barrett Antiques & Auctions Ltd.

Schoenhuts

#221 **Barney Google & Sparkplug** w/ cloth dress, jointed wood, ex. cond., ht. 8in. **$942**

A-PA May 2003   Noel Barrett Antiques & Auctions Ltd.

Schoenhuts

#216 **Bactrian Camel** w/ glass eyes, orig. ears & tail, ht. 7in. **$797**

#217 **Giraffe** w/ glass eyes, orig. tail & ears, ht. 11in. **$467**

#218 **Ostrich** w/ painted eyes & darkened paint on one side of head, ht. 10in. **$245**

TOYS

A-PA May 2003   Noel Barrett Antiques & Auctions Ltd.

#223 Schoenhut Humpty Dumpty Circus Bandwagon, elaborately carved w/ minor repairs made to match moth damaged jackets, overall lg. 42in. $26,400

A-PA May 2003

Noel Barrett Antiques & Auctions Ltd.

#224 Schoenhut Trinity Chimes, paper on wood musical toy w/ eight chimes, missing two buttons & scroll top, ht. 17in. $165

A-PA Feb. 2003   Glass Works Auctions

#459 Tin Toy Horse Drawn Trolley, tin w/ orig. paint., some loss, lg. 6¼in. $425

A-PA May 2003

Noel Barrett Antiques & Auctions Ltd.

#225 Schoenhut Teddy Roosevelt in safari suit, some paint flaking on top & back of head, ht. 9in. $3,080

A-PA May 2003

Noel Barrett Antiques & Auctions Ltd.

#239 Kenton Globe Toy Stove, nickel plated cast iron w/ Kenton brand accessories, water reservoir lid has small break, ht. 19, wd. 23in. $1,980

A-PA May 2003   Noel Barrett Antiques & Auctions Ltd.

#236 Miniature Kitchen, German w/ blue delft style wall paper, painted wood furniture, miniature crockery, dishes, spice jars & kitchen tools, ht. 14, wd. 25, dp. 16in. $2,200

A-PA May 2003   Noel Barrett Antiques & Auctions Ltd.

#226 Schoenhut Mary & Her Lamb w/ desk, all orig. clothing exc. hat, some chipping on Mary's head toward back, ht. 7½in. $1,430

A-PA May 2003

Noel Barrett Antiques & Auctions Ltd.

#363 **Steiff Mickey Mouse Doll,** largest of Steiff Mickeys known, complete w/ ear tag & button, all orig. ht. 18in. **$13,750**

A-PA May 2003

Noel Barrett Antiques & Auctions Ltd.

#364 **Steiff Mickey Mouse Doll** w/ chest & ear tag, strong rubber stamping on foot, sewing repair to neck, pants faded, missing tail, ht. 12in. **$4,720**

A-PA Feb. 2003   Glass Works Auctions

#461 **Lil Abner's Band "The Dog Patch",** wind-up tin toy ©1945 by United Features Syndicate, Inc., all orig. & working. **$450**

A-PA Feb. 2003   Glass Works Auctions

#460 **Tin Wind-up Airplane** w/ orig. cast metal pilot & orig. paint, ws. 12in., lg. 16½in. **$425**

A-PA Feb. 2003   Glass Works Auctions

#462 **Double Decker Bus,** wind-up tin boy, litho on tin, working, ht. 3¾, lg. 9in. **$700**

A-PA May 2003   Noel Barrett Antiques & Auctions Ltd.

#601 **Carette 2 Gauge Live Stead 4-4-0 Engine & Tender,** cast iron & tinplate English profile engine with "L.N.W.R." tender, rest., lg. 23in. **$3,850**

A-PA Feb. 2003   Glass Works Auctions

#463 **Toonerville Trolley,** ©1922 by Fontaine Fox, litho on tin wind-up w/ orig. mechanism, working & animated conductor in front, ht. 6⅝, lg. 5in. **$625**

TOYS

A-ME June 2003   James D. Julia, Inc.

#163 **Paddy & The Pig** wind-up toy, Lehmann, ©1903, German, hand painted & cloth dressed, ht. 6in. **$900**

A-ME June 2003   James D. Julia, Inc.

#164 **KADI Toy,** Lehmann, German, w/ wind-up friction action, mkd. "Kanton, Peking, Shang Hai, etc." ht. 7in. **$480**

A-ME June 2003   James D. Julia, Inc.

#169 **Naughty Boy,** German, ©1903, animated toy, working, ht. 5in. **$862**

A-ME June 2003   James D. Julia, Inc.

#165 **Wind-up Tap Tap Toy** by Lehmann, German, hand painted, ht. 5½in. **$460**

A-ME June 2003   James D. Julia, Inc.

#166 **Wind-up Tut Tut,** Lehmann, German, w/ orig. working squeak bellows, ht. 7in. **$840**

A-ME June 2003

James D. Julia, Inc.

#173 **Marx Donald Duck Duet,** ©1946, tin Disney wind-up, jointed figure of Goofy dances as Donald beats drum, ht. 10½ in. **$420**

A-ME June 2003   James D. Julia, Inc.

#170 **Distler Toonerville Trolley,** German, ©1922, w/ animated character at controls, working, ht. 7in. **$345**

A-ME June 2003   James D. Julia, Inc.

#167 **French Victorian Woman Pulling Cart,** France, friction w/ tarnished surface, working toy, ht. 4in. **$143**

A-ME June 2003   James D. Julia, Inc.

#168 **New Century Cycle,** Lehmann, German, wind-up w/ spinning umbrella, blue gilt on tin ref., working, ht. 5in. **$420**

A-ME June 2003   James D. Julia, Inc.

#171 **Strauss Jazz Bo Jim,** USA, w/ jointed black man dances atop roof of cabin while playing banjo, working, ht. 10 in. **$420**

A-PA May 2003Noel Barrett Antiques & Auctions Ltd.
#602 Live Steam 3.5 Gauge GNR Loco & Tender, w/ English profile engine & tender, overall lg. 28in. $3,300

A-PA May 2003

Noel Barrett Antiques & Auctions Ltd.

#603 Bing Gauge 2 Live Steam 4-2-2 Engine & Tender, hand enameled tin English profile engine w/ brass plate "7094", w/ a "GNR" 6 wheel tender, overall lg. 22in. $5,170

A-PA May 2003   Noel Barrett Antiques & Auctions Ltd.
#604 Large European Train, painted tin w/ cast metal wheels, strong clockwork mechanism, monogram on each coach "E&J", glass windows throughout, overall lg. 94in. $2,970

A-PA May 2003   Noel Barrett Antiques & Auctions Ltd.
#606 Schoenner Clockwork 0-4-0 Engine & Tender w/ robust reversible clockwork mechanism, prof. rest. $715

A-PA May 2003   Noel Barrett Antiques & Auctions Ltd.
#605 Schoenner I Gauge Live Steam 4-4-0 Engine & Tender, hand enameled tin American outline engine, rest. w/ some new parts incl. headlight. $2,832

A-PA May 2003   Noel Barrett Antiques & Auctions Ltd.
#787 Lionel 402 Passsenger Set, incl. a #402 engine, baggage car (missing four wheels) & passenger coach, mkd. New York Central Lines, lg. 17in. $550

A-PA May 2003   Noel Barrett Antiques & Auctions Ltd.
#786 Dorfan "Alligator Engine" Freight Set, pulled by the #3930 4-4-4 electric engine, incl. box car (rest.), tank car (oxidation in spots on top), caboose (rest. roof & engine), lg. 13in. **$1,650**

786

A-PA May 2003   Noel Barrett Antiques & Auctions Ltd.
#790 Lionel Freight Set w/ 318 engine, gondola, flat car, tank car, reefer, cattle car, crane car & caboose, engine has new wheels. **$430**

A-PA May 2003   Noel Barrett Antiques & Auctions Ltd.
#823 Ladder Wagon, Pratt & Letchworth, painted cast iron w/ orig. figures, paint loss on horses, lg. 23in. **$1,320**

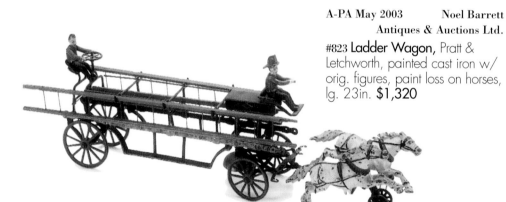

A-PA May 2003
Noel Barrett Antiques & Auctions Ltd.
#1108 Brio 440 Volvo Roadster, enameled tin, clockwork & rubber tires, made in Sweden, lg. 10in. **$357**

A-PA May 2003   Noel Barrett Antiques & Auctions Ltd.
#1110 TN VW Cabriolet, embossed litho. tin w/ battery illuminated motor compartment, lg. 9¾in. **$236**

A-PA May 2003   Noel Barrett Antiques & Auctions Ltd.
#1109 Ichiko Volvo 1600, embossed litho. tin, mismatched hub caps, lg. 11¼in. **$275**

A-PA May 2003
Noel Barrett Antiques & Auctions Ltd.
#1112 Bandai Jaguar 3.4, embossed litho. tin, crack in windscreen frame, lg. 8¼in. **$177**

Noel Barrett Antiques & Auctions Ltd.

#1111 **Bandai Opel Taxi** w/ luggage, embossed litho. tin, battery powered, lg. 7in. $319

Noel Barrett Antiques & Auctions Ltd.

#1116 **Hadson Jet Racer** w/ orig. box, litho. tin, friction drive w/ siren & fire, unplayed with condition, 11¼in. $1,375

Noel Barrett Antiques & Auctions Ltd.

#1113 **VW Karmann Ghia,** embossed litho. tin, missing tail light, friction not working, lg. 9¼ in. $189

Noel Barrett Antiques & Auctions Ltd.

#1068 **Rossignol Dump Truck,** litho. tin, clockwork, a pick-up truck w/ two side mounts, wear to tires, lg. 15¼in. $1,045

Noel Barrett Antiques & Auctions Ltd.

#1339 **Cor-Cor Chrysler Airflow,** pressed steel wind-up w/ battery operated headlights (missing), w/ European auto dealer's tag on bottom, lg. 17in. $1,155

Noel Barrett Antiques & Auctions Ltd.

#1352 **Caterpillar on Treads,** Arcade, cast iron w/ nickel plated driver, prof. rest., lg. 8in. $495

#1353 **International Tractor,** Arcade, cast iron w/ rubber treads, new driver, lg. 7¼in. $440

#1354 **Caterpillar Tractor on Chains,** Arcade, cast iron, lg. 6¼in. $660

A-PA May 2003   Noel Barrett Antiques & Auctions Ltd.

#1580 **Murray Navy Patrol Pedal Plane,** painted pressed steel w/ orig. decals, lg. 47in. **$880**

A-PA May 2003   Noel Barrett Antiques & Auctions Ltd.

#1581 **Good Humor Trike Cycle,** painted pressed steel w/ all orig. decals, lg. 36in. **$1,430**

A-PA May 2003   Noel Barrett Antiques & Auctions Ltd.

#1582 **American National Shark Nose Graham,** painted pressed steel w/ rear mounted spare tire, prof. rest., lg. 53in. **$1,475**

A-PA May 2003   Noel Barrett Antiques & Auctions Ltd.

#1583 **Steelcraft Buick Pedal Car,** painted press steel, prof. rest. lg. 45in. **$1,416**

A-PA May 2003   Noel Barrett Antiques & Auctions Ltd.

#1584 **Garton Race Car #60,** painted pressed steel, all orig., weak paint, lg. 46in. **$495**

A-PA May 2003   Noel Barrett Antiques & Auctions Ltd.

#1585 **American National Pedal Car,** painted pressed steel w/ orig. spoke wheels, overpainted, lg. 46in. **$1,375**

A-PA May 2003

Noel Barrett Antiques & Auctions Ltd.

#1456 **Gama Pan American Clipper,** litho. tin, friction drive, ws. 20, lg. 15in. **$192**

A-PA May 2003 Noel Barrett Antiques & Auctions Ltd.

#1459 **Marklin Tri-Motor,** constructor series, w/ clockwork mechanism & operating air flaps, one tire missing, ws. 22 in. **$1,210**

#1457 **Marx TWA Biwing,** litho. tin clockwork, missing celluloid props, ws. 19, lg. 14in. **$220**

A-PA May 2003

Noel Barrett Antiques & Auctions Ltd.

#1539 **Air Mail Truck,** Buddy "L" Jr., retains orig. rear gate chains, w/ overall wear, lg. 22in. **$3,740**

A-PA May 2003

Noel Barrett Antiques & Auctions Ltd.

#1540 **Ice Truck,** Buddy "L" Jr., painted pressed steel w/ orig. canvas cover & pull cord, paint loss overall wear, lg. 26in. **$1,650**

A-PA May 2003

Noel Barrett Antiques & Auctions Ltd.

#1548 **Bulldog Garage Wrecker,** pressed steel fantasy comp., truck w/ Mack front & spoke wheels w/ Steelcraft front cab, lg. 27in. **$825**

A-PA May 2003

Noel Barrett Antiques & Auctions Ltd.

#1543 **Tank Truck,** Buddy "L", prof. rest., lg. 32in. **$1,062**

A-PA May 2003

Noel Barrett Antiques & Auctions Ltd.

#1545 **Custom Red Baby Truck,** Buddy "L", prof. rest. & customized headlights & bumper, lg. 26in. **$605**

A-PA May 2003

Noel Barrett Antiques & Auctions Ltd.

#1559 **Kelmet White Dump Truck** w/ slip on rubber tires, wear, lg. 25in. **$825**

A-PA May 2003   Noel Barrett Antiques & Auctions Ltd.
#1562 **Kingsbury Aerial Fire Truck,** steel, motor driven version, some repaint & repl. ladders, lg. 35in. $1,265

A-PA May 2003   Noel Barrett Antiques & Auctions Ltd.
#1564 **Sturditoy Coal Truck,** steel dumping version, prof. rest., lg. 24in. $1,180

A-PA May 2003   Noel Barrett Antiques & Auctions Ltd.
#1566 **Sonny Parcel Post Delivery Truck,** steel w/ screen version, prof. rest., lg. 26in. **$550**

A-IA Oct. 2002

Jackson's International Auctioneers, Inc.

#185 **Buddy-L Aerial Truck** w/ ladders that extend to 50in., surface rust, in working condition. **$517**

#186 **Buddy-L Hydraulic Dump Truck** w/ lights & rubber tires, rust & some overpaint, lg. 26in. **$345**

#187 **Teddy Bear** w/ long brown & reddish mohair, fur paws, jointed, missing one ear, ht. 12in. **$17**

#188 **Japanese Race Car,** Jet Y-53, some fading, sparkler not working w/ "Leaf Trademark Y", lg. 12in. **$149**

#189 **Marx Mounted Magnetic Crane** w/ wood wheels & 85% orig. paint, lg. 16in. **$103**

#190 **Horse on Platform,** cloth covered molded body w/ four cast iron spoked wheels, tail missing, lg. 20in. **$172**

#191 **Cast Iron Rabbit** w/ fine fur patt., ht. 12in. **$316**

#192 **Door Stop,** cast iron Boston bull terrier. **$86**

#193 **Cast Iron Ham Boiler,** salesman's sample, mkd. H.B. 84, ht. 4in. **$11**

#194 **Liberty Bell Trade Simulator,** lock missing, ht. 9in. **$201**

#195 **Teddy Bear,** disc jointed w/ shoe button eyes, football body, repl. pads, losses, ht. 24in. **$373**

#196 **Cast Iron Door Stop,** black & white pointer, ht. 8in. **$230**

#197 **Effanbee "Baby Dainty" Dolls,** ca.1912-1922, w/ orig. clothing, pair. **$172**

#198 **Farmall Tractor,** #350, ¹⁄₁₆ scale, w/ box. **$46**

#199 **Schoenhut Dolls,** Maggie & Jiggs w/ comp. heads, orig. clothing. **$690**

#200 **Hy-Speed Coaster Wagon,** metal, paint fading & surface rust, lg. 18in. **$11**

#201 **Arcade Cast Iron Truck** w/ 80% orig. paint & decal, lg. 7in. **$316**

#202 **Marx Horse Drawn Delivery Van,** adv. Toylands Farm Products, clock works, missing front axle & wheels. **$69**

#203 **China Head Doll** w/ cloth body & old clothing, losses to shoulder & feet. **$69**

#204 **China Head Doll** w/ black curly hair, wooden arms & legs & several sets of clothing. **$373**

#205 **Bisque Doll Head** on kid body, mkd. A&M. **$115**

#206 **Hubley Cast Iron Ladder Truck,** ca.1930, all orig. **$316**

#207 **Ford Gumball Machine** w/ chrome base, ht. 12in. **$57**

#208 **Hubley Racers,** pr., one cast kiddie toy aluminum w/ rubber tires, lg. 6¼in., one cast iron boat tail w/ iron tires, mkd. JM 201. **$316**

#209 **Hubley Cast Iron Ladder Truck,** orig., lg. 8in. **$172**

#210 **Wooden Model Boat By "Rumalu,"** key wind, mounted for display, lg. 26in. **$57**

#211 **Cast Iron Doorstop,** covered wagon pulled by oxen, lg. 19in. **$143**

#212 **Arcade Allis Chalmers Tractor** w/ repl. wooden wheels, some loss to front of frame, orig. decal. **$80**

#213 **Cast Iron Items** incl. a doll-house size kettle, tea kettle & bill holder in shape of duck's head. **$34**

#214 **Cast Iron "Cowboy" Cap Pistol** by Stevens w/ orig. leather holster, ca.1930. **$80**

TOYS

177

178

179

180

181

182

183

184

A-IA Oct. 2002

Jackson's International Auctioneers, Inc.

Pedal Cars

#177 **Murray Sergeant Police Car,** prof. rest., lg. 36in. **$316**

#178 **GTO-AMF 510,** convertible, license "389," prof. rest., lg. 36in. **$230**

#179 **Hook & Ladder Pumper Car,** 519, prof. rest., plastic ladders, lg. 46in. **$230**

#180 **Murray Fire Truck,** all orig. w/ wooden ladders, some paint fading, lg. incl. ladders 43in. **$258**

#181 **Murray Speedway 500 Pace Car,** professional rest., lg. 35 in. **$287**

#182 **Garton Tin Lizzie,** tan & brown, fine prof. rest., lg. 40in. **$517**

#183 **Playland Earth Mover,** w/ dump, all orig. some minor rust, scrapes & scratches, lg. 47in. **$201**

#184 **Bat-Cycle X-15,** stick steering, prof. rest. w/ safety belt. **$316**

A-MA Nov. 2002   Skinner, Inc.

#688 Stick Barometer, rosewood marked "Woodruff's Pat. June 5, 1860 Charles Wilder Peterboro N.H.," orig. finish, ht. 39in. $3,290

#689 Woolwork Picture, three masted ship, probably Eng. 19th C., silk & linen thread details w/ wool padding, 19⅛in. x 23¾in., framed. $588

#690 Chest, three drawer, mini. pine, carved, Am., early 19th C. w/ painted dec., wear & losses, ht 9½in., wd. 9¼in. $264

#691 Box, covered pine, paint dec., Am.,

early 19th C. w/ wire hinges, mustard-colored paint w/ dark brown dec., wear, ht. 5⅞in., wd. 16¼in., dp. 8⅜in. $588

#692 Federal Birch Stand, w/ red paint, N. Eng., ca.1800 w/ drawer, repl. brass pulls, old surface, imper., ht. 27¼in., wd. 18½in., dp 16¾in. $2,115

#693 Federal Chest of Drawers, cherry, N. Eng., ca.1810, cockbeaded case, orig. brasses, old red stained surface, imper., ht. 34¼in., wd. 40¾in., dp. 19¼in. $940

#694 Federal Maple Stand, w/ red paint,

N. Eng., ca.1800, top w/ ovolo corners, orig. surface, minor imper., ht. 25½in., wd. 18½in., dp. 17½in. $1,645

#695 Wool Hooked Rug, floral design, Am., 19th C., worked in shades of red, blue, green, tan & brown, minor wear, 32¼in. x 24in. $470

#696 Stick Barometer, mah., marked "Charles Wilder N.H. Woodruff's Pat. June 5, 1860", refinished, ht. 38½in. $1,175

#697 Chamber Pitcher & Basin, creamware, Eng., 19th C. w/ handpainted floral dec., ht. 10in. $499

A-MA Nov. 2002   Skinner, Inc.

#482 Wooden Song Bird Trade Sign, by Elmer Crowell, Am. 19th C., cut-out panel painted mustard yellow w/ red wings & black highlights, wear, 40in. x 14in., ht. 73in. **$1,500**

#483 Cast Iron Butcher's Trade Sign, 19th C., w/ figure of a steer above three molded tools of the trade, traces of metallic paint, wear, ht. 19¾in., lg. 24⅛in. **$646**

#484 Rooster Weather Vane, pine w/ polychrome dec., Am., 3rd qtr. 19th C. w/ gray-white painted body, cockscomb & wattles w/ red paint & tail w/ black painted stripes, mounted on stand, wear, ht. 26½in. **$2,115**

#485 Wooden Eagle Figure, carved & painted, Am., 19th C., eagle & post carved from one piece of wood, weathered surface, age cracks, ht. 45½in. **$2,115**

#486 Rooster Weather Vane, zinc & copper, attrib. to J. Howard, Bridgewater, MA, 19th C., flattened full-bodied vane w/ red painted comb, wattle & feet, red painted emb. copper tail, wear, ht. 30¼in. **$16,450**

#487 Wooden Barn Owl, carved & painted, John Hyatt, Pekin, Ill, 20th C. w/ black paint & glass eyes, mounted on stand, wear & minor losses, ht. 15½in. **$2,938**

#488 Wooden Doll's Rocking Bench, carved & painted, Am., 19th C., grain painted w/ gilt stenciled floral dec., minor wear, ht. 11in., wd. 14in., dp. 11in. **$823**

#489 Maple Candlestand, NH, ca.1835 w/ orig. surface, imper., ht 26¼in. **$940**

#490 Wooden Wall Box, carved & painted, Am., 19th C. w/ light red wash finish, wear, ht. 9⅜in., wd. 14¼in. **$499**

#491 Tavern Table, pine, Lancaster County, PA, ca.1810, orig. red paint on base, vestiges on top, imper., ht. 28½in., dia. 25½in. x 20in. **$1,293**

#492 Dower Chest, PA, late 18th C. w/ till, old red ground paint w/ heart shapes outlined in yellow paint enclosing black grained dec., some rest., ht. 24in., wd. 51¾in., **$940**

#493 Children's Chairs, pine, two, Am., 19th C. w/ painted dec., one painted brown w/ mustard line dec., other olive green w/ yellow & black, wear, ht 14¼in. & 15½in. **$1,175**

#494 Child's Sled, wood & iron, Paris, ME, late 19th C., top painted red w/ handpainted blue, pink, yellow & green daisies, curved oak runners reinforced w/ iron straps, wear, ht 12⅛in., wd. 9⅞in., lg. 29⅜in. **$470**

#495 Child's Ladder-back Chair, pine, Am., 19th C., rush seat, old dark green & black paint, wear, ht. 15¼in. **$441**

A-ME June 2003

James D. Julia, Inc.

#666 Phonograph, Edison Diamond Disc Lab. Model, mah. upright, Chippendale style case for 76 records, incl. 6 records, plays but needs cleaning & grill cloth has tear in fabric, ht. 52in. **$402**

A-ME June 2003   James D. Julia, Inc.

#513 Regina Single Comb Music Box, carved oak case w/ five discs, two celluloid instruction tags, mechanically rest., crank not orig. **$1,725**

A-ME June 2003   James D. Julia, Inc.

#669 Hurdy Gurdy by Muzzio Organ Works, ca.1920s, plays 31 violin & flute pipes in front & bottom, all orig. except straps & wooden bottom frame. **$4,600**

A-NH Aug. 2002   Northeast Auctions

Oversized Stone Fruit

#358 Walnut, in form of box, hollow, lg. 5½in. **$900**

#359 MacIntosh Apple w/ stem in red & yellow colors, dia. 7in. **$1,600**

#360 Peach Halves, each painted w/ incised pit, ht. 4in. **$1,100**

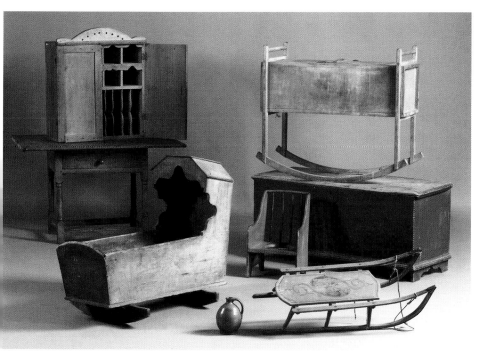

A-NH Nov. 2002   Northeast Auctions

#194 Hanging Cupboard w/ orig. blue paint, probably New Hampshire, ht. 29½in., wd. 25in., dp. 10½in. **$1,800**

#195 Tavern Table, William & Mary w/ breadboard top above drawer, ht. 26in., top 30in. x 43in. **$1,100**

#196 Hooded Cradle, child's w/ shaped crest & sides, ht. 31in., lg. 42in. **$400**

#197 Glazed Redware Jug, NH, ht. 7½in. **$400**

#198 Rocking Butter Churn, N. Eng., w/ blue painted surface, ht. 31¼in. **$1,000**

#199 Blanket Chest w/ old red painted surface, w/ cotter pin hinges & interior till, ht. 21½in., top 18in. by 48in. **$400**

#200 Potty Chair, child's w/ blue paint, ht. 18¾in. **$500**

#201 Sled, painted blue w/ black & gilt dec., lg. 31½in. **$350**

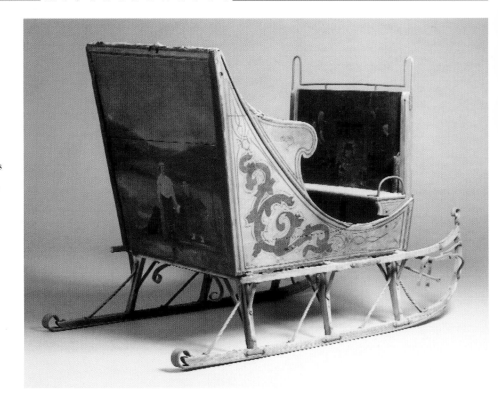

A-NH Nov. 2002   **Northeast Auctions**

#499 Sleigh, MA, dec. w/ genre scenes, back depicting farmers & their dog, underside of seat w/ inscription, "Jan. 27, 1810 / John L. Davis / Salisbury, Mass.", ht. 54in., lg. 76in. **$6,000**

Opposite:

A-MA Nov. 2002   **Skinner, Inc.**

#826 Trade Sign, bootmaker's double-sided, Cortland, NY 19th C. w/ gilt lettering "C. BRANDENSTEIN, MAKER," on a black sand textured ground, gilt borders & boot motifs on a red ground, signed "Hackett," minor wear, 18¼in. x 61¼in. **$8,225**

#827 Pail, grain painted, Am., 19th C., carved wooden handle w/ iron wire bail, stave & iron hoop const., "Willis" inscribed on side, paint wear, staves loose, ht. 9in., dia. 7¾in. **$294**

#828 Box, grain painted pine, Am., 19th C., w/ hinged lid & dov. const., applied carved molding. n/s

#829 Box, Stenciled Grain Painted Am., 19th C., w/ hinged lid, stenciled gilt dec., front w/ the initials "EJD," wear, ht. 5⅛in., lg. 11⅞in., dp. 5⅞in. **$235**

#830 Document Box, painted pine, Am., 19th C., hinged lid, dov. const. w/ applied molding on lid & base, minor wear, ht. 6⅜in., lg. 13½in., dp. 8⅛in. **$558**

#831 Ditty Box, painted wood w/ painted surface, Am., 19th C. w/ lapped band const., cover w/ yellow painted compass star, ht. 3⅛in., dia. 7¾in. **$1,058**

#832 Ditty Box, wood carved & painted, Am., 19th C. w/ lapped band const., cover w/ relief carved red painted five-point star, wear, ht. 3⅝in., dia. 7⅜in. **$1,528**

#833 Shaker Box, oval w/ gray paint, NY or N. Eng., probably mid 19th C., pine lid & bottom, maple side, copper tacks, wear, loss on lid edge, ht. 4¾in., dia. 11⅞in. **$646**

#834 Storage Box, oval maple, Am., late 19th C., lapped const. on cover & box, w/ dark gray paint in some of the recesses, crack & scratches, ht. 4⅝in., dia. 16¼in. **$2,233**

#835 Wooden Portrait Bust, carved & painted, Am., 19th C., wear, ht. 19¼in. **$3,173**

#836 Wall Box, pine, Am., 19th C., pierced & carved back & sides, yellow painted linear dec., wear, 13⅜in., wd. 11in., dp. 7in. **$1,175**

#837 Trade Sign, bootmaker's double-sided, wood, Am., 19th C., red lettering "H. MARTINDALE," minor wear, ht. 37¾in. n/s

#838 Six Board Chest, painted poplar probably PA, late 18th C., molded hinged top, dov. const. box on ogee bracket feet, old surface, imper. & repairs, ht. 20in., wd. 38½in., dp. 16in. **$1,998**

#839 Cupboard, pine w/ red paint, possibly N. Eng. ca.1830-50, cockbeaded corners, old surface, minor imper., ht. 40in., wd. 26⅛in., dp. 13in. **$2,938**

#840 Chest Over Drawer, pine, paint dec. N. Eng., 18th C., hinged top, thumb-molded drawer, old red painted surface, repl. wooden pulls, minor imper., ht. 28½in., wd. 41¾in., dp. 18½in. **$881**

#841 Shaker Wooden Bucket w/ green paint, 19th C. w/ turned wooden handle, wire bail, tongue-and-groove staved const., white painted interior, wear, ht. 7¼in., dia. 10½in. **$499**

#842 Six-Board Chest, pine, N. Eng., early 19th C., the hinged top w/ lidded till above case w/ quarter-fan inlays, orig. surface, minor imper., ht. 23in., wd. 43½in., dp. 17½in. **$2,938**

#843 Architectural Finials, wood, pair, Am., mid 19th C., painted white, weathered surface, one w/ crack, ht. 17in. **$823**

#844 Federal Candlestand, N. Eng., ca.1800, orig. blue paint, losses & repairs, ht. 24in., dia. 15¾in. **$1,058**

#845 Fire Bucket, leather, painted, Am., 1826, "James Fuller. Newton. 1826," ochre rim & handle, wear, repr. on handle, ht. 15⅝in. **$1,175**

#846 Fire Bucket, leather, painted, Am., early 19th C., yellow lettering "Sam Kingsbury No 1 1836," repainted over indistinct lettering dated 1814, loss on handle, paint wear, crack to base, ht. 13½in. **$1,528**

#695 Wool Hooked Rug w/ floral design, Am., 19th C., in shades of red, blue, green, tan & brown, minor wear, 32¼in x 50in. **$470**

A-ME June 2003   James D. Julia, Inc.

#620 Victor Monarch Phonograph, type "M", w/ carved walnut box & orig. Nipper plaque, "His Master's Voice", horn dia. 8in., nickel trim pitted & arm has shallow dents. **$1,092**

A-ME June 2003

    James D. Julia, Inc.

#529 Criterion Double Comb Music Box, mah. w/ three discs, picture in lid repl., mechanically rest., 11⅝in. **$977**

A-ME June 2003

    James D. Julia, Inc.

#530 Regina Double Comb Music Box, oak, paper inside lid orig., two orig. celluloid tags on inside, mechanically rest. w/ orig. crank, six steel discs, some are new, 15¼in. **$2,127**

A-ME June 2003

    James D. Julia, Inc.

#531 Regina Double Comb Music Box, oak w/ two orig. celluloid tags on inside, mechanically rest. w/ orig. crank, average condition, six steel discs 15½in., some new. **$2,415**

A-NH Nov. 2002   Northeast Auctions

#209 Tavern Table, N. Eng., maple & pine w/ oval top & box stretcher, ht. 25in., top 21in. x 27in. **$900**
#210 Corner Cupboard, Federal, maple, in two parts, shaped bracket feet, ht. 86in., wd. 47in. **$4,750**
#211 Etagère, N. Eng., figured maple & birch, w/ three drawers over three shelves, ht. 53in., top 12in. x 40in. **$4,500**
#212 Andirons, brass & iron knife-blade w/ urn finials & penny feet, ht. 20½in. **$700**
#213 Tavern Table, birch & pine w/ remnants of red wash w/ breadboard ends & flat box stretcher, ht. 27in., top 29in. x 43½in. **$1,300**
#214 Q.A. Tiger Maple Stand, N. Eng., w/ sq. top & slipper feet, ht. 25in., top

16½in. x 17in. **$1,400**
#215 Bowback Windsor Chairs, pr. w/ H stretcher. **$1,00o**
#216 Chippendale Tea Table, mah. w/ tilt-top & ball & claw feet, ht. 27½in., dia. 29½in. **$2,500**
#217 Hearth Equipment w/ iron candlestand on tripod base, incl. pair of gooseneck andirons, pot hanging rail supported by pair of arched legs, lg. 53½in; bulbous cast iron pot w/ swing handle & iron hanging hook, **$500**
#218 Candleholder on Stand, adjustable two-light, ht. 37in. **$200**
#219 Highchair, faux-rosewood w/ painted & stencil dec. w/ rod back, shaped seat, bamboo legs & footrest, ht. 33½in. **$500**

A-NH Nov. 2002   Northeast Auctions
First Row

#324 **Rockingham Coachman Bottle,** Bennington, 1849 w/ circular mark, ht. 10½in. **$400**

#325 **Lanterns** w/ glass globes, pr., tin w/ knob dec., ht. 13in. n/s

#326 **Staffordshire Cats,** black & gray, ht. 12in. **$450**

#327 **Fire Bucket,** leather, MA, dec. w/ Am. eagle w/ ribbon "Hamilton Fire Club" & "Williams" below, ht. 12½in. **$700**

#328 **Whale Oil Lamps,** pr, . Star & Punty patt. w/ flaring pedestal & hexagonal bases, ht. 13in.**$450**

#329 **Flint Enamel Milk Pitcher,** Bennington w/ molded dec., ht. 9¼in. n/s

Second Row

#330 **Sandwich Glass Fluid Lamps,** one w/ red cut overlay, other clear w/ stylized leaves & quatrefoils, on gilt dec., milk glass base, 12¾in. & 13½in. **$850**

#331 **Creamware Pitcher,** Eng. w/ black transfer dec. w/ "Captain Hull of the Constitution" w/ "Major Genl. Brown Niagara", ht. 5¾in. **$300**

#332 **Toby Pitcher,** Bennington, Benjamin Franklin, w/ a grapevine handle, ht. 6½in. **$200**

#333 **Toby Pitchers,** Bennington, first applied w/ boot handle; second w/ grapevine handle, hts. 5¾in. & 6½in. **$300**

#334 **Pearlware Pitcher** w/ crested eagle & E Pluribus Unum banner below 15 stars, reverse w/ sailing vessel & an amorous couple beneath spout, ht. 7½in. **$450**

#335 **Sandwich Fluid Lamp** w/ double cut pink overlay on black pressed glass base, ht. 12¼in. **$1,000**

#336 **Sandwich Fluid Lamp** w/ amber flashed font w/ sawtooth base on sq. marble base, ht. 10¾in. **$150**

Third Row

#337 **Wine or Spirits Bottle,** early Continental, olive-amber, ht. 8½in. **$3,750**

#338 **Redware Cow Creamer** w/ brown glaze, together w/ a Bennington flint-enamel creamer & another, all w/ covers, lengths 9⅛in. & 6¾in. **$200**

#339 **Sandwich Fluid Lamp,** cranberry cut to white on standard cut to match stepped marble base, ht. 13¼in. **$700**

#340 **Sandwich Overlay Fluid Lamp,** cranberry & white on standard cut to match stepped marble base, ht. 13¼in. **$700**

#341 **Rectangular Salt,** Am., Blue Diamond patt., lg. 3in. **$200**

#342 **Sandwich Cut Overlay Red Fluid Lamp** on milk glass, sq. base, ht. 9½in. **$250**

#343 **Book Flask,** flint enamel together w/ yellow-glazed Toby pitcher w/ Woodbridge, N.J. imp. factory cipher, hts. 5½in. & 4½in. **$200**

#344 **Toby Snuff Jar,** Bennington, olive-green flint enamel w/ 1849 circle mark, ht. 4¼in. **$200**

#345 **Jackfield Pottery Teapot & Creamer** & redware covered jug attrib. to Wedgwood & Burton, ht. 5in. **$50**

MISCELLANEOUS

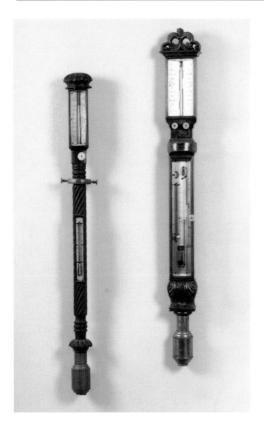

A-NH Aug. 2003   Northeast Auctions
#1012 **Gimbaled Ship's Barometer,** Eng. w/ circular scalloped finial above two registers on rope-twist body, w/ turned scalloped base & brass cup, ht. 37½in. **$4,250**
#1013 **Ship's Stick Barometer,** Eng. by J. Bruce, Liverpool w/ foliate finial above two registers & acanthus leaf base w/ brass cup, ht. 39½in. **$13,000**

A-ME June 2003   James D. Julia, Inc.
#532 **Regina Double Comb Music Box,** mah. w/ six 15½in. discs, part of left rear case is missing, minor dings & scratches, mechanically rest., crank not orig. **$2,012**

A-ME June 2003   James D. Julia, Inc.
#617 **Regina Double Comb Music Box,** oak case for 15½in. discs, all 27 steel discs are orig. **$3,105**

A-ME June 2003   James D. Julia, Inc.
#618 **Regina Single Comb Coin-Op. Music Box** for 15½in. discs, mechanically rest. w/ orig. crank, 6 discs not all orig. **$2,530**

A-ME June 2003   James D. Julia, Inc.
#613 **Polyphon Music Box,** w/ bells, walnut case w/ floral inlay, paper not orig. single comb box w/ 12 bells & 9 discs, mechanically rest., repl. crank. **$6,037**

A-ME June 2003   James D. Julia, Inc.
#614 **Imperial Symphoniom Double Comb Music Box** w/ six orig. 15⅝in. steel discs, orig. celluloid tags, orig. crank & mechanically rest. **$1,955**

A-ME June 2003   James D. Julia, Inc.
#615 **Regina Single Comb Disc Music Box,** mah. case w/ six orig. discs, mechanically rest. **$1,782**

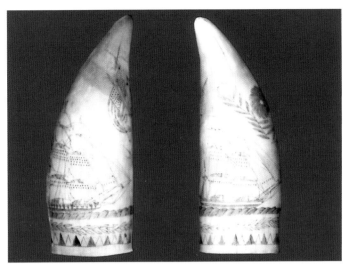

A-NH Aug. 2003   Northeast Auctions

#100 Scrimshaw Whale's Tooth, front & back w/ crossed Am. flags & military trophies embellished in red & blue, centering two ships, one w/ Am. flag, one w/ red flowerhead, both bordered w/ rope twist, laurel leaves & sawtooth in red & blue, lg. 6in. **$2,800**

A-ME June 2003   James D. Julia, Inc.

#516 Calliola, custom built, Wurlitzer type player w/ vacuum & blower units w/ 26 multi-tune rolls, in addition, a freestanding coin-op. box in shape of a mini. band wagon, needs repr. **$7,475**

A-NH Aug. 2003   Northeast Auctions

Cast Iron Fire Marks
#424 United Fireman's Insurance Co. of PA, w/ image of fire pump, lg. 11in. **$200**
#425 Fireman's Assoc. of PA w/ image of fire hose, ht. 11½in. **$400**
#426 Home Insurance Co. of New Haven, CT, w/ fireman, lg. 8½in. **$200**

A-NH Aug. 2003   Northeast Auctions

#101 Eagle Plaque w/ spread wings, carved gilt & polychrome dec., perched on two crossed & furled Am. flags, lg. 36in. **$1,900**

A-NH Aug. 2003 Northeast Auctions

#403 Drum, RI, dec. w/ eagle & serpent, "101" monogram in dec. tacks & yellow & red "JA" monogram over stars & eagle, purportedly belonged to Job Arnold who is listed in the IGI, born 1774, ht. 21in., dia. 25½in. **$4,500**

A-NH Aug. 2003 Northeast Auctions

#404 Civil War Drum of the 79th Regiment, Hastings, NY, dec. w/ eagle & shield w/ stars & stripes, medallion w/ inscription & "Excelsior" within red bands joined by ropes, ht. 13½in. **$500**

A-PA Sept. 2003

Pook & Pook Inc.

#80 Globes, celestial & terrestrial, pair, 19th C., by T. Harris & Son Opticians, London & C. Smith & Son, London, ht. 36in., dia. 18in. **$10,350**

#81 Telescope, brass table top, English, mid 19th C., ht. 19in. **$920**

A-PA Nov. 2002   Pook & Pook Inc.

#501 Pewter Cupboard, PA, walnut, 2 parts w/ open shelves & scalloped sides, rattail hinges & ogee bracket feet, rest., ht. 82in., wd. 73in. **$6,325**

First Row

#502 Puzzle Jug, English sgraffito w/ incised birds, ht. 6½in. **$1,200**

#503 Puzzle Jug, English, date 1870 w/ trailing slip dec., ht. 7½in. **$288**

#505 Bentwood Bride's Box w/ polychrome dec., ca.1820 w/ overall orange floral leaf dec., ht. 4in., wd. 11in. **$1,035**

#506 Chalkware Figure of Lamb, 19th C., on a green plinth, ht. 7in. lg. 8½in. **$345**

#507 Redware Flower Pot w/ undertray, glazed, mkd. "John W. Bell", repr. **$460**

#509 Slide Lid Boxes, two continental w/ dec., together w/ similarly dec. trinket box (second row). **$863**

Second Row

#510 Trinket Box by John L. Lehn, Am. 1792-1898, painted & stencil dec. w/ strawberry borders & pots of flowers on brown ground, ht. 7in., wd. 10¼in. **$863**

#511 Sgraffito Plate, earthenware w/ spread wing eagle & "Liberty" banner, by John J. Medinger, chips, dia. 9¼in., est. $500-800. n/s

#512 Redware Plates, pair mkd. "W. Smith Womelsdorf" w/ yellow & black trailing slip dec., losses, dia. 8¼in. **$805**

#513 Sgraffito Pie Plate w/ distelfink & tulip tree w/ ochre, green & brown glaze, by John J. Medinger, dia. 8¾in. **$2,185**

#514 Redware Plate w/ yellow criss cross slip dec., dia. 8¾in. **$518**

#519 Redware Plates, three matching w/ trailing yellow slip dec., dia. 7½in. **$1,035**

Third Row

#520 Vase, earthenware w/ two-handles, green & orange mottled glazing, inscribed "This vase was made by Jacob Medinger Feb. 15, 1931, at Limerick Pottery", ht. 11in., repr., est. $1,000-1,200. n/s

#521 Decorated Box, PA, ca.1900, attrib. to "Black" Sammy Stolzfoos (1876-1963) w/ yellow & red dec., ht. 4¼in., lg. 14in. **$230**

#529 Sgraffito Redware Dish w/ dec. & dated "Anno 1773" w/ leaping stag within floral & scroll dec., dia. 12½in. **$6,038**

#530 Document Box, tole w/ dome lid, PA, mid-19th C., ht. 7½in., wd. 10in. **$300**

#532 Flower Pot, orange & yellow glazed redware w/ undertray, mkd. "W. Smith

Womelsdorf" together w/ another example. **$489**

#535 Valentine, cut-out paper water color, in form of a heart w/ distelfinks & tulips, sgn. "D.Y.E." (David Y. Ellinger), retains the orig.Ellinger dec. frame, 7in. x 8in. **$1,610**

#536 Slide Lid Box, continental, early 19th C., dec. w/ horses & trees, together w/ a smaller example. **$1,093**

Floor

#537 Indian Basket, Maine, late 19th C. w/ red & blue potato stamp dec., losses, ht. 12in., wd. 19in. **$748**

#539 Stoneware Crock, WV, two-gal., mkd. "Palatine Pottery Co., Palatine, W. VA", w/ leaping horse (hairline), ht. 13in. **$201**

#540 Sewer Tile Figures of prowling lions, pair, Ohio, w/ mottled green/brown glazing, ht. 5in., lg. 13in. **$259**

#540a Box, N. Eng., dec. brasswood w/ overall yellow pinstripes & ochre grained dec., ht. 6in., wd. 17½in. **$201**

#540b Redware Dish w/ dec. by George Hubener, PA, dated 1792, dia. 14in. sold together w/ a copy of the same plate by Greg Shooner. **$1,265**

#540 Folk Art Carving of an elk standing atop a carved plinth w/ clock face & two panels, from Ohio Elks Lodge. **$86**

A-MA Aug. 2003

Robert C. Eldred Co., Inc.

#981 **Sailor's Valentine**, Am., framed, center painting depicts two cupids floating in a pink sky holding a ribbon mkd. "Love" surrounded by intricate shellwork in a floral patt., sgn., octagonal frame, 15in. **$20,700**

#982 **Framed Sailor's Valentine**, Am. w/ central circular painting depicting a mermaid & sailor at the shore holding hands, surrounded by intricate shellwork, sgn. & dated '83, oil on masonite, octagonal frame, 15in. **$21,850**

A-MA Nov. 2002 **Skinner, Inc.**

#496 Step-back Cupboard, N. Eng. w/ unpainted shelves on a cut-out base, orig. red surface, imper., ht. 79½in., wd. 39½in. **$3,525**

First Row
#497 Redware Plate w/ yellow slip dec., dia. 9¾in. **$705**
#498 Redware ABC Plate w/ yellow slip dec., N. Eng., wear & rim chips, dia. 10¼in. **$2,233**
#499 Redware Plate w/ yellow slip dec., wear & rim chips, dia. 8in. **$411**

Second Row
#500 Redware Plate w/yellow slip dec., PA, minor wear & chips, dia.

10⅜in. **$940**
#501 Redware Pie Plate w/ slip dec., PA, ca.1790, wear & rim chips, dia. 9⅞in. **$1,763**
#502 Redware Plate w/ yellow slip dec., eastern US, early 19th C., wear & rim chips, dia. 11⅛in. **$823**

Third Row
#503 Redware Plate w/ yellow slip dec., wear & rim chips, dia. 11⅛in. **$382**
#504 Tin Coffeepot, punch dec. hinged domed lid w/ brass finial, punch-work design, ht. 11¾in. n/s
#505 Redware Plate w/ yellow slip dec., early 19th C., wear, dia. 11½in. **$441**

Fourth Row
#506 Coffeepot, tin & stoneware, Bondine Pottery Co., Zanesville, OH, ca.1880, Albany slip glazed int., ht. 8in. n/s
#507 Redware Loaf Dish, yellow slip dec., wear & chips, 10¾in. x 11¼in. **$881**
#508 Stoneware Pitcher, blue & green sponge dec., PA, 19th C., ht. 6¾in. **$294**
#509 Yellow Covered Butter Crock & Pitcher, Am., ca.1880 , the crock w/ red & white linear slip dec., pitcher, not shown w/ blue stripe dec., crock ht. 4⅜in., pitcher ht. 8¼in. **$265**

A-NH Aug. 2003   Northeast Auctions

#824 **Tobacconist's** figure of a squaw in striding position holding cigars in one hand, overall ht. w/ box 55½in. **$12,000**

A-PA May 2003   Pook & Pook Inc.

#140 **Pewter Cupboard**, N. Eng., ca.1780 w/ four shelves above a base w/ single door, H-hinges & retains brown painted surface, ht. 78in., wd. 50½in. **$5,980**

#141 **Stoneware Butter Churn**, NY, 3-gal., mkd. "J. Hart Ogdensburg w/ cobalt floral dec., ht. 14in. **$345**

#142 **Stoneware Crock**, 19th C., 5-gal., w/ stylized cobalt foliage & #5, ht. 11¾in. **$230**

#143 **Stoneware Jug**, 19th C., 2-gal., w/ cobalt dec. of a speckle-breasted bird on branch, ht. 14in. **$863**

A-PA May 2003   Pook & Pook Inc.

#254 **Corner Cupboard**, PA, ca.1800, walnut, two-piece, resting on ogee bracket feet w/ spurs, ht. 84½in., wd. 46in. **$5,175**

#255 **Portrait of Girl**, seated in forest & holding a bouquet of flowers, oil on canvas, 34in. x 25½in. **$2,070**

#256 **Ladderback Armchair**, PA, five-slat, ca.1700, w/ rush seat, retains an old red stained surface. **$1,495**

MISCELLANEOUS

Opposite

A-PA Sept. 2003   Pook & Pook Inc.

First Row

#316 **Shaker Trinket Box,** late 19th C., w/ three fingers & old red wash surface, ht. 2in., lg. 6in. **$863**

#316a **Shaker Trinket Box,** late 19th C., w/ four finger const., ht. 4in., lg. 10¼in. **$863**

#317 **Chain Whimsey,** Am., carved & painted, 19th C., w/ figure of a caged man, retains old black painted surface, lg. 25in. **$518**

#318 **Slide Lid Box,** PA, painted Bucher-type w/ floral dec. & salmon bands, ht. 3½in., lg. 6¾in. **$1,265**

#319 **Watch Safe,** carved pine, 19th C., w/ seated woman reading a book, ht. 8in. **$690**

Second Row

#320 **Treen Inkwell,** Chester Co., CT, late 19th C., w/ gilded acorn dec., mkd. "S. Stilliman & Co.", ht. 2¾in., dia. 4¼in. **$403**

#321 **Pencil Box** w/ carved swivel lid w/ tulip, vine & pinwheel dec., & the name "Johanes Schmit", lg. 9½in. **$690**

#322 **Tortoise Shell Comb,** Jamaican, 19th C., in form of an Indian chief, lg. 6½in. **$230**

#323 **Burl Bowl,** N. Eng., w/ two handles, 19th C., ht. 6¼in., dia. 13½in. **$6,325**

A-MA June 2003   Skinner, Inc.

#300 **Needlework Sampler,** "Susanna Stanley Born October 24th–23,", probably PA, worked in silk on linen ground, thread losses, toning, staining, 15¾in. x 22in. **$2,233**

#301 **Portrait,** attrib. to Chester Harding, Boston & Northampton, MA, 1792-1866, ca.1840, unsigned, oil on canvas, molded giltwood frame, unlined, retouch to background, 29½in. x 24¼in. **$1,880**

#302 **Chippendale Tall Chest,** possibly N. Eng., last half 18th C., six thumbmolded drawers, bracket feet, repl. brasses, refinished, imper. & rest., ht. 57¾in., wd. 36in. **$8,225**

#303 **Federal Bureau,** tiger maple, N. Eng., ca.1810-20, four cockbeaded drawers on ring-turned tapering birch legs, cut-out skirt, old brass pulls, ht. 42in., wd. 39in. **$2,468**

#304 **One-Drawer Stand,** Federal tiger maple, N. Eng., ca.1800, ovolo corners above single scratchbeaded drawer, straight beaded skirt, ht. 26in. wd. 20⅞in. **$2,233**

A-PA Feb. 2003   Pook & Pook Inc.

#425 **Fat Lamp,** mini. wrought iron, w/ three legged trivet, ca.1880, ht. 4½in. **$863**

#426 **Rush Light,** wrought iron, Eng., ca.1700, floral engraved thumb piece, walnut base, ht. 8¼in. **$920**

#427 **Rooster,** 19th C., black, amber & red beads, ht. 12in. **$1,265**

#428 **Trinket Box,** dated 1794, polychrome dec. on ivory ground, 1¾in. x 7¾in. **$2,300**

#429 **Epaulet,** cut from funeral uniform of George Washington's pallbearers, brass buttons, silk pants on silk background, loss to paper face, 16in. x 17¼in. **$1,840**

#430 **Hearth Cranes,** pair, mini. wrought

iron, 18th C., 3½in. x 9in. **$173**

#431 **Pie Crimper,** carved whale bone, 19th C., unicorn form w/ mermaid tail, lg. 7¼in. **$1,380**

#432 **Wax Jack,** wrought iron, Eng., ca.1725 w/ engraved nippers & handle, ht. 4¼in. **$1,380**

#433 **Squeak Toy,** caged canary, late 19th C., ht. 7½in. **$518**

A-NH Aug. 2003   **Northeast Auctions**
#151 **Quilt,** pieced & appliquéd w/ floral pattern, worked w/ green calico diamond grid w/ flower stems in red & green print, 82in. x 100in. **$300**
#152 **Birdcage Windsor Side Chairs** painted green w/ bamboo turnings, each w/ mustard highlights. **$3,250**

#153 **Shield Form Plaque** w/ crescent moon & II, Am., fraternal, 8in. x 17½in. **$600**
#154 **Blanket Chest,** N. Eng., blue paint w/ boot-jack ends, ht. 22in., lg. 40in. **$750**
#155 **Armchair,** Sheraton thumb back w/ painted & stenciled dec. & gilt highlights. **$600**

#156 **Dome Top Trunk,** green painted w/ stylized bird & flower dec. **$600**
#157 **Hooked Rug,** room-size w/ wide black & brown border, camel field & scrolled leaf motifs in autumn colors, 6 ft. x 9 ft. **$600**

A-MA Nov. 2002   **Skinner, Inc.**
#426 **Shoe-Forms,** five, England, Continental & Am., incl. three wood, two w/ pincushion tops, painted, one stone & one porcelain w/ repr., ht. 1⅛in. to 9½in. **$1,410**
#427 **Shoe-Forms,** all carved wood, three painted incl. three w/ pincushion tops & one snuff box, ht. 2in. to 4½in. **$1,880**
#428 **Shoe-Form Articles,** incl. four carved wood w/ pincushion tops, one covered in leather, and two leather riding boots, ht. 2¼in. to 5⅝in. **$705**

A-NH Aug. 2003   Northeast Auctions
#609 Banister-Back Side Chairs, similar, N. Eng. w/ rush seat & Spanish front feet, one w/ lacy stenciling. **$3,750**
#610 Tavern Table, N. Eng., Wm. &

Mary, red painted w/ breadboard top w/ scrubbed surface & vase turned legs joined by stretchers, ht. 23½in., top 26in. x 47in. **$14,000**
#611 Redware Storage Jars w/ splash dec.,

two, N. Eng., hts. 6in. & 9½in. **$800**
#612 Redware Dish w/ squiggle dec. in mustard, dia. 10in. **$600**
#613 Candlesticks, pewter, baluster form, similar but not matching, tallest 7½in. **$1,700**

A-NH Aug. 2003   Northeast Auctions
#101 Even Arm Settle, oak, Arts & Crafts, lg. 78in. **$4,000**
#102 Bridge Lamp w/ favrile glass shade, mkd. L.C.T. & "Tiffany Studios,

NY, ht. 54¾in. **$7,000**
#103 Rookwood Pottery Vase w/ wax matte, 1922 w/ artist's initials, mounted as a lamp, ht. of vase 14½in. **$2,200**
#104 Desk Lamp, bronze "Zodiac", mkd.

"Tiffany Studios/NY", ht. 15¾in. **$2,200**
#105 Dining Table by Gustav Stickley w/ circular top above a flared pedestal & shaped feet, ht. 25in., dia. 59½in. **$3,500**

A-NH Aug. 2003   Northeast Auctions

#701 Stepback Cupboard w/ early blue paint, ht. 72in., wd. 36½in. **$3,500**

#702 Canton Covered Ginger Jars, pr., ht. 8in. **$300**

#703 Delft Deep-Dishes w/ blue floral motifs & mustard edge, pr., dia. 9in. **$600**

#704 Staffordshire "Fruit & Flowers," incl. teapot, sugar bowl & cover, unknown maker, together w/ a sugar box & cover,

Opposite:

A-MA Aug. 2003   Skinner, Inc.

#24 Stable Sign, wooden, painted, 19th C. w/ gilt lettering, losses, ht. 6½in., lg. 30in. **$353**

#25 Wall Pocket, wood, 19th C., w/ two drawers painted red, blue & white, ht. 7½in., wd. 8 3/8in. **$147**

#25A Wooden Bucket, miniature w/ red paint, 19th C., w/ stave & brass hoop const., ht. 4⅛in. **$206**

#26 Tinware, Am., 3 items incl. a round tea canister w/ fruit dec.; a dec. gooseneck coffeepot & a rectangular box w/ hinged lid embellished w/ yellow & red flowers, fruit & swags. **$1,880**

#27 Checkerboard, inlaid wood, alternating light & dark wood squares & ebony pegged frame, wear & age

creamer pitcher, two teabowls & saucers (7) by various makers. **$800**

#705 Staffordshire Pitcher by Clews, "Basket of Flowers & Vase" patt., ht. 8in. **$1,000**

#706 Chimney Cupboard, N. Eng. w/ blue paint, ht. 80in., wd. 49in. **$1,750**

#707 Lantern, N. Eng., half-round tin & glass, ht. 15in. **$400**

#708 Cupboard, N. Eng. w/ blue paint,

crack, 18½in. x 24in. **$264**

#28 Portrait of Boy with Dog, unsgn., oil on canvas, unframed, ht. 42in., wd. 20¼in. **$2,115**

#29 Shelf, painted to resemble marble in tones of amber, brown, green & beige, ht. 10in., wd. 42in. **$4,406**

#30 Coffee Mill, cast iron, mkd. "Enterprise Mfg. Co., Phil., USA," late 19th C., wear & drilled for electric fixture, ht. 24½in. **$499**

#31 Checkerboard, wood, painted red & black w/ gilt borders, minor wear, 11⅝in. sq. **$235**

#32 Double-Sided Game Board, wood, 19th C., w/ applied black painted frame w/ a checkerboard in black on red ground on one side, the reverse w/ a mill game in yellow on a red ground,

ht. 27in. **$900**

#709 Hat Box in floral basket patt. on blue ground, lined w/ Concord, NH news print, label inscribed "Warranted, nailed, bandboxes, made by Hannah Davis, Jaffrey, NH.", ht. 10½in., lg. 15in. **$1,100**

#710 Blanket Chest, N. Eng., w/ blue paint & bootjack ends, ht. 26in., wd. 49in. **$3,000**

wear, 12½in. x 13¾in. **$646**

#33 Chest of Drawers, grain painted, ca.1825, simulated tiger maple, opalescent & clear pulls, ht. 62in., wd. 45in. **$1,880**

#34 Bride's Box, wood w/ polychrome painted dec. w/ laced lapped panel const., painted red & black w/ yellow highlights, wear, ht. 9⅝in., dia. 14in. **$470**

#36 Windsor Chairs (partial) w/ orig. yellow paint dec., set of 7, N. Eng., ca.1830, imper. **$3,408**

#37 Dressing Table, w/ yellow paint dec., ht. 32in. **$1,175**

#38 Coffee Mill, mkd. "Enterprise Mfg. Co.", cast iron w/ red & black dec., & gilt highlights. **$1,175**

#39 Candlestand, Federal, maple w/painted green base, ht. 29in. **$3,819**

MISCELLANEOUS

#681 Blanket Chest, N. Eng., Wm. & Mary w/ hinged top opening to a well over two long drawers, ht. 39½in., wd. 37¾in. **$5,750**

#682 Rockingham-Glazed Plates, 5, dia. 9⅝in. to 10⅞in. **$2,500**

#683 Blanket Chest, N. Eng., in red paint, w/ lift top, rat tail hinges, opening to a compartment lined w/ New Hampshire newsprint dated 1829, over two long drawers, ht. 43in., top 17½in. x 40in. **$3,400**

#686 Rockingham-Glazed Plates, 5, dia. 8¾in. to 11⅛in. **$300**

#687 Rockingham-Glazed Pie Plates, molded beneath the base w/ a conforming border of hearts, together w/ a slope-sided bowl, both unmarked, dia. 11⅜in. & 9¾in. **$200**

#686 Hooked Runner, beige ground w/ geometric motifs in red, black, green, orange & pumpkin within rose diamond border, 22in. x 118in. **$1,500**

#94 Q.A. Looking Glass, walnut, Eng., 18th C., w/two-part bevel-edged glass, minor imper., ht. 43in., wd. 15¼in. **$1,763**

#95 Rococo Mirror, walnut & gilt gesso, N. Europe, late 18th C., old finish, minor imper., ht. 29in., wd. 12½in. **$881**

#96 Courting Mirror, eglomisé & wood, probably N. Europe, 18th C., black painted frame w/reverse-painted floral crest. n/s

#97 Q.A. Side Chair, MA, 1740-60 w/old black & brown grained surface, a re-upholstered seat & Spanish feet, surface abrasions, ht. 41in. **$1,116**

#98 Weather Vane, molded copper, Am., probably 18th C., composed of two pieces of sheet copper riveted together w/ molded wings & corrugated tail, dark patina, iron shaft & metal stand, ht. 22¼in., lg. 26in. **$5,875**

#99 Chair Table, red painted cherry & pine, N. Eng., last half 18th C., top tilts on horizontal supports, minor imper., ht. 28½in., dia. 42½in. **$4,994**

#100 Gate-Leg Table, Wm. & Mary, tiger maple & maple, MA, mid-18th C., w/drawer, imper. & repr., ht. 27¾in., wd. 48in., lg. 56½in. **$3,878**

#101 Stoneware Jug w/cobalt blue dec., by Nichols & Boynton, Burlington, VT, ca.1856, 4 gal., repr., chips & hairlines, ht. 18in. **$940**

#102 Tap Table, maple & pine, N. Eng., early 18th C., old refinish, minor imper., ht. 25½in., wd. 24½in., dp. 19½in. **$9,988**

#307 Dinner Service, assembled Imari-dec. ironstone comprising of 37 pcs., some marked "Mason's Patent." $3,750
#308 Welsh Dresser, George III, oak, in two parts, ht. 77in., wd. 70in., dp. 18¼in. $7,000

MISCELLANEOUS

A-PA Feb. 2003   Pook & Pook Inc.

#150 Corner Cupboard, PA, cherry, ca.1810 w/ molded cornice, bracket feet, ht. 89in., wd. 40½in. **$9,775**
#151 Mug, Rose Medallion, mid 19th C., ht. 4in. **$403**
#152 Bowl & Footed Tray, Rose Medallion, scalloped edge, 19th C., dia. 10in., lg. 12in. **$1,093**
#153 Tea Set, partial, Rose Medallion, 19th C.,incl. teapot, covered sugar & creamer, three cups & seven saucers. **$173**
#154 Brush Box, Rose Medallion, 19th C., Mandarin patt., ht. 2¾in., lg. 7in. **$748**
#155 Famille Rose porcelain, sixteen pieces, 19th C., incl. 10 plates, dia. 8in., bowl, dia. 10in., and 5 plates, dia. 9½in. **$1,150**

A-MA Nov. 2002   Skinner, Inc.

#602 Paneled Pine Cupboard, Mid Atlantic States, ca.1830-50 w/ old mustard-colored paint, minor surface imper., ht. 77¼in., wd. 41⅜in., dp. 18¾in. **$4,770**
#603 Redware Handled Jar w/ cover, Am., early 19th C. w/ brown sponge dec., wear, chips on cover edge, ht. 8in. **n/s**
#604 Salt Glazed Stoneware Jar w/ cobalt blue dec., attrib. to Thomas Commeraw, NY, minor chips, hairlines, ht. 11⅜in. **$2,233**

A-OH Oct. 2003   Garth's Arts & Antiques

#72 **Flax Wheel,** sm. w/ a single flyer, ht. 34in. **$373**

A-OH Oct. 2003   Garth's Arts & Antiques

#39 **Sheraton Secretary,** two-piece, attrib. to CT, refinished cherry w/ pine & poplar secondary woods, minor rest., ht. 78¾in. **$3,450**
#40 **Staffordshire Bowls,** two w/ red & green floral dec. **$115**
#41 **Flint Glass Compote** w/ flared rim, dia. 12½in. **$690**
#42 **Brass Andirons** w/ repr. to feet, ht. 20½in., together w/ shovel & tongs (not shown) w/ brass handles & ball finials, 19th C., lg. 27in., 28½in. **$316**

A-OH Oct. 2003   Garth's Arts & Antiques

#146 **Corner Cupboard,** two-piece, cherry w/ old refinish, pine secondary wood, ht. 85¾in., wd. 40¾in. **$4,025**
#147 **Tea Set,** 11 pieces, soft paste "Primrose" patt., stains & some damage. **$431**

MISCELLANEOUS

#551 Pieced Quilt w/ alternating green & white calico triangles, some staining, 80in. x 90in. **$517**

#552 Highchair, early ladderback, refinished maple & hickory w/ cornhusk seat, ht. 35½in. **$180**

#553 Pie Safe, walnut w/ poplar secondary wood, punched tin front w/ fan & star dec. & two dov. drawers, ht. 54½in., wd. 42in. **$575**

#554 Stick Spatter Plates, four w/ crazing & edge wear. **$230**

#555 Tape Loom, ash or oak w/ orig. dark surface & arrow shaped finial drilled for hanging, ht. 22¾in., wd. 9¼in. n/s

#556 Stoneware Crocks, two w/ cobalt blue dec., larger w/ double handles & glued cracks in base, ht. 15in., two gal. ovoid crock dec. w/ stenciled designs on either side, wear & hairline, ht. 10in. **$402**

#535 Country Corner Cupboard, one-piece w/ old glass panes, repl. brass pulls, ht. 86in. wd. 53½in. **$2,300**

#536 Andirons, brass w/ matching log rests, seamed const., ht. 14½in. **$115**

CARPET BALLS

#1 Children's, four w/ multiple cobalt stripes; red & orange plaid, burgundy & black plaid, red & green circles, minor wear from use, dia. 1⅝in. **$690**

#2 Women's, eight w/ red & green spatter; lilac circles; stripes & red circles, dia. 2¼in. **$1,437**

#3 Men's, four, light & dark green plaid & blue & yellow plaid, wear, dia. 2¾in. **$661**

#4 Men's, extra large, light blue & green stripes; brown plaid, yellow & light blue plaid, lilac & mottled salmon, wear, dia. 3⅛in. **$833**

A-OH Aug. 2003   Garth's Arts & Antiques

#277 Fireside Bench, country pine w/ old refinish, mortise & peg const. & w/shoe feet, rest. to back & rear foot trimmed, ht. 59½in., wd. 56in. **$690**

#278 Coverlet, OH, blue & natural, sgn. "D. Kell, Jackson Co., Ohio" in corner blocks, light staining, 81in. x 86in. **$1,897**

#279 Stoneware Churn, mkd. "B.S. Mfg. Co., Ltd., Bradford, 4", w/ cobalt dec., drilled for lamp, rim chip, ht. 16½in. **$345**

#280 Carving, wooden horse & rider, dark red & black finish, ht. 16in. **$115**

A-OH Oct. 2003   Garth's Arts & Antiques

#137 Empire Sideboard, attrib. to Anthony Quervelle, Philadelphia (1835-1849), refinished mah. & mah. flame veneer w/ pine secondary wood, marble top center section w/ mirror, veneer rest., ht. 59in., wd. 67in. **$3,162**

#138 Platter, Pitcher & Handleless Cup & Saucer, Adam's Rose patt., dec. w/ red roses, all w/ stains. **$258**

A-SC Dec. 2002   Charlton Hall Galleries, Inc.

#672 Bronze Hat & Umbrella Stand w/ bear & cub in tree, ht. 69in., wd. 29in. **$1,300**

672

A-MA June 2003   **Skinner, Inc.**

#112 Chippendale Mirror, mah. & gilt gesso, probably Eng., late 18th C., old refinish, minor imper., ht. 44in., wd. 19½in. **$3,055**

#113 Mirror, walnut & gilt gesso, European, late 18th C., shaped gilt gesso bracket, ht. 34in., wd. 13in. **$1,410**

#114 Chippendale Side Chairs, pair, mah., probably MA, 1760-80, serpentine crests, pierced splats set into molded shoes, molded shaped slip seats, refinished, repr., ht. 38¾in. **$1,293**

#115 Chippendale Slant-lid Desk, mah., probably MA, ca.1780, thumbmolded lid, cockbeaded case, front carved claw & ball feet, rear ogee bracket feet, brasses appear to be orig., refinished, imper. & repr., ht. 44½in., wd. 40in., **$3,290**

#116 Bidjar Rug, Northwest Persia, 2nd qtr. 20th C., overall Herati design in midnight & ice blue, rose, ivory, orange & blue-green on terra-cotta red field, 5ft.2in.x 7ft. **$1,116**

#118 Rococo Mirror, walnut & gilt gesso, European, ca.1750, molded gilt incised liner on shaped bracket w/ central tied ribbon & flanking vines, ht. 41in., wd. 15in. **$1,645**

A-MA June 2003   Skinner, Inc.

#164 Mirror, gilt & painted, N. Eng., ca.1825, split-baluster frame, applied brass rosettes, imper., ht. 31in., wd. 15½in. **$441**

#165 Mirror, gilt gesso & painted, Federal, probably Am., 1820-25, molded cornice w/ applied balls, punchwork panel, black painted liner framing glass, minor imper., ht. 24in., wd. 13½in. **$558**

#166 Mirror, Federal giltwood eglomisé, probably MA, ca.1815, molded cornice above fishermen scene, mirror flanked by pilasters w/ rope twist detail, minor imper., ht. 29½in. **$529**

#167 Pillar & Scroll Clock, Federal mah., Silas Hoadley, Plymouth CT, ca.1825, wooden polychrome & gilt dial, Arabic numerals centering an eagle & shield w/ 30-hour wooden weight-driven movement, imper., ht 31½in. **$2,468**

#168 Sideboard, mah. carved & veneer, probably MA, ca.1825, repl. brass pulls, old refinish, imper., ht. 47½in., wd. 53½in., dp 20½in. **$1,175**

#169 Pitcher, porcelain w/ gilt "United States" inscription, L. Straus & Sons, NY, late 19th C., green printed maker's mark on base, minor gilt wear, ht. 9½in. **$1,293**

#170 Pillar & Scroll Clock, Federal mah.,

Wadsworths, Lounsbury & Turners, Litchfield, CT, polychrome & gilt wooden dial, floral spandrels & 30-hour wooden weight-driven movement, refinished, rest., ht. 31in. **$3,408**

#171 Banquet Table, Federal mah. carved & veneer, probably N. Eng., ca.1825, two parts, top w/ rounded corners & hinged leaves on cockbeaded skirt joining base & ringturned spiral-carved legs, refinished, ht. 29in., dp 46½in., wd. 87in. **$3,408**

#172 Side Chairs, set of four, carved mah. veneer, probably NY, ca.1815-25, curved front rails, upholstered slip seat, old refinish, repr., ht. 30½in. **$2,585**

MISCELLANEOUS

A-MA June 2003   Skinner, Inc.

#284 Canteen, wood, paint dec., Am., 19th C., initialed "TRC", sunburst dec. in red & mustard on black ground, wear, ht. 6in., dia. 5¾in. **$1,645**

#285 Box w/ Drawer, Am., black w/ paint, 19th C., dov. const., lower drawer lined w/ red, green & blue scrolled foliate wallpaper, wear, ht. 5⅛in., wd. 7¼in. **$940**

#286 Box, oval covered w/ black paint, Am., 19th C., lapped finger const., imp. "Levi Beal", minor wear, ht. 1⅝in., dia. 4⅛in. **$1,175**

#287 Wooden Items, three , Am., 19th C., green-painted oval tub w/ stave & lapped band const., ht. 9in., diam. 17¾in.; an oval covered pine box w/ carved lapped finger const. & heart

motif, ht. 2¾in., diam. 7in.; & a salmon-painted candlebox w/ sliding lid, wear, ht. 3⅝in., lg. 14¼in. **$1,528**

#288 Limner's Work Chest, painted, N. Eng., late 18th C., case w/ 16 thumb-molded sm. drawers, bottom w/ similar long drawers, incised "W", "T" and "1781", painted top overhangs poly-chrome drawer, w/ green sides, orig. round brass pulls & surface, surface imper., ht. 37¾in., wd. 32in. **$7,050**

#289 Portrait, attrib. to Aaron Dean Fletcher, VT & NY, 1817-1902, early 19th C., unsigned, oil on panel, orig. surface, 24in. x 19¾in. **$4,994**

#290 Settee, Windsor, painted, N. Eng., early 19th C., bamboo-turned, tapering & incised spindles, plank seat, old gray-green paint, minor surface imper., ht.

36in. **$4,348**

#291 Carved Head of Boy, pine, old dark natural patina, no stand, imper., ht. 10¼in., wd. 7in., dp. 8in. **$1,880**

#292 Game Board, two-sided w/ polychrome painted wood, Am., 19th C., applied molding, checkers & Parcheesi boards, wear, 16in. x 16⅜in. **$3,055**

#293 Drum, painted, "Manufactured by M.W. Stevens, Pittsfield, Mass. 1845", lacking drumheads, other losses, ht. 8½in., dia. 11½in. **$235**

#294 Wool Hooked Rug, floral, Am., 19th C., clipped wool fabric strips hooked to burlap backing, shades of rose, red, tan, brown & blue, wear, minor edge losses, 37½in. x 59½in. **$588**

A-MA June 2003   Skinner, Inc.

#310 Horse Weather Vane, molded copper, Am., 19th C., flattened full-body w/ zinc ears, verdigris & gilt surface, mounted on hollow copper rod, no stand, wear, dents, ht. 17½in., lg. 33¼in. **$2,820**

#311 Banner Weather Vane, sheet iron, ca.1841, cut-out letters & numerals "OIS 1841", mounted on iron rod, traces of black paint, no stand, weathered surface, bullet hole, ht. 19½in., lg. 14¼in. **$823**

#312 Banner Weather Vane, probably J.W. Fiske, NY, late 19th C., cut-out scroll design sheet copper banner & cruciform tail, old gilt surface on black metal stand, repr., dents, minor loss, ht. 16½in., lg. 48¼in. **$4,113**

#313 Eagle Weather Vane, molded copper & zinc, Am., 19th C., figure w/ raised outstretched wings mounted on a sphere w/ traces of gilding on a verdigris surface, incl. black metal stand, weathered surface, several minute holes,

ht. 11½in. **$3,995**

#314 Horse Weather Vane, gilt copper "Patchen", attrib. to Harris & Co., Boston, ca.1868-82, molded sheet copper w/ zinc ears, old gilt surface w/ traces of verdigris, mounted on black painted copper rod, incl. black metal stand, repaired bullet holes, minor dents, ht. 20in., lg. 32in. **$3,055**

#315 Arrow Weather Vane, copper, Am., late 19th C., sphere finial on an arrow w/ corrugated sheet copper tail, verdigris patina, incl. black metal stand, ht. 14in., lg. 30¼in. **$1,175**

#316 Pickerel Weather Vane, painted carved wood & copper, Am., late 19th C. to early 20th C., fish w/ applied corrugated sheet copper fins, white painted surface, mounted on a metal rod & oak stand, weathered surface, ht. 9⅛in., lg. 16⅜in. **$1,880**

#317 Chest Over Drawers, pine, paint dec., N. Eng., late 18th C., molded lipped top above deep well & single thumbmolded drawer on cut-out bracket

feet, orig. blue-gray grain painted surface, minor imper., ht. 36¾in., wd. 44¾in. **$3,055**

#318 Windsor Sack-Back Chair, painted, N. Eng., ca.1790-1800, bowed crest, shaped arms, shaped seat on bamboo-turned & swelled splayed legs, old dark brown repaint w/ yellow striping over earlier red, minor imper., ht. 38¾in. **$1,998**

#319 Wool Hooked Rug, floral, Am., 19th C., wear, repr., stains, 30in. x 54in. n/s

#320 Plant Stand, painted, probably N. Eng., late 19th to early 20th C., molded tripod cabriole leg base, orig. blue-green paint, minor surface imper., ht. 51in., wd. 20in. **$940**

#321 Chest Over Drawers, red painted cherry, CT, mid-18th C., molded lift top on case w/ two thumbmolded false drawers, three working drawers on base, orig. brasses & red painted surface, minor rest. & imper., ht. 47½in., wd. 47¼in. **$8,225**

A-IA July 2003   Jackson's International Auctioneers

#614 Post Card w/ image of Uncle Sam titled "Fantasy Zeppelin" w/ approx. 100 unusual cards. **$201**

A-OH Aug. 2003   Garth's Arts & Antiques

#154 Corner Cupboard, two-piece, cherry w/ old dark finish, poplar & pine secondary woods, sm. section of waist molding missing, ht. 78½in., wd. 78½in. **$3,737**

#156 Stoneware Crock w/ cobalt blue bird dec., 3 gal., ht. 12in. **$575**

#157 Stoneware Churn w/ cobalt dec., mkd. "E. Norton & Co., Bennington, VT 6", ht. 19in. **$345**

#155 Rush Light Candlestand, yew wood & walnut w/ turned column & iron rush light holder & candle socket counter balance at top, 18th C., ht. 44in. **$1,150**

A-IA July 2003   Jackson's International
Auctioneers

#823 **Trade Card** w/ image of Uncle
Sam, for Hamilton & Mathews, one
corner slightly rounded & creased, 3in.
x 5⅛in. **$690**

A-PA Nov. 2002   Pook & Pook Inc.

#436 **Girandole Mirror,** Federal, Am. or English, ca.1800, crest w/ spread winged
serpent on rock plinth. **$4,025**
#437 **Slant Lid Desk,** Chippendale, Virginia, ca.1780, walnut w/ fitted int., ht. 44in.,
wd. 41½in. **$9,775**
#438 **Tall Case Clock,** Chippendale, Philadelphia, mah., ca.1780 w/ 8-day brass
works, sgn. "James Heron Newtown Ards", ht. 93in. **$9,475**

A-SC June 2003   Carlton Hall Galleries, Inc.

#425 **Majolica Jardinière on Stand,** late 19th early 20th C., chips on rim of pedestal, 2
pcs., ht. 36in., dia. 13¼in. **$850**